Phoenix Rising

*A Playbook for Building a
Mid-Major College Basketball Program*

Aaron A. Mitchell

M&B Global Solutions Inc.
Green Bay, Wisconsin (USA)

Phoenix Rising

A Playbook for Building a
Mid-Major College Basketball Program

Front cover photo: Tony Bennett, John Martinez, Jeremy Ludvigson, Dean Rondorf, and Ben Johnson celebrate as the clock hits zero, confirming the first trip to the NCAA tournament for the UWGB basketball program in 1991. (*University of Wisconsin-Green Bay Archives*)

Back cover photo: Dick Bennett brought an intensity to the University of Wisconsin-Green Bay men's basketball program throughout his tenure. (*University of Wisconsin-Green Bay Archives*)

ISBN: 978-1-942731-39-9

Published by M&B Global Solutions Inc.
Green Bay, Wisconsin (USA)

University of Wisconsin-Green Bay men's basketball coach Dick Bennett (left) with the author's parents, Pete and Betsy Mitchell, in 1991. (Mitchell family collection)

Dedication

To my loving family, past, present, and future

Contents

Foreword

Gene Keady

Purdue University Basketball Coach
1980 - 2005

Gene Keady was a five-time national coach of the year during his tenure with Purdue. (Purdue University Archives)

You have very little to gain and potentially a lot to lose as a power conference basketball program when you schedule a lesser-known, mid-major school for a nonconference game. That was the case in 1991 when we invited Dick Bennett's University of Wisconsin-Green Bay squad to Purdue for a game at Mackey Arena.

My assistant, Bruce Weber, was making out the schedule for that season and asked, "What about these guys? Are they any good?" I knew about the UWGB program and told him, "Yeah, they're pretty good."

Little did I know just how good. They played us on our court and beat our butts, 69-53. Dick's son, Tony, led UWGB with 20 points that night.

Tony was a special kid, I

could see that. I had the good fortune of coaching him earlier that year with the USA Pan American Games team that included the likes of Grant Hill and Christian Laettner. I really enjoyed being around him. Not only was he a talented ballplayer without question, but he was also very smart and cared for the team. He really understood people and knew how to connect with others.

One memory in particular stands out. Our squad of college all-stars got beat in the semifinals by an experienced Puerto Rican team that included several players who were already in the NBA. True to form, Tony came over to my condo that night and surprised the heck out of me. He wanted to know if *I* was okay. He was looking after *me*. It was an eye-opener for me to see that type of maturity and empathy in a twenty-two-year-old kid, and it's something I've remembered ever since. That year, coaching for and against them, was my initiation to the Bennett family.

I coached basketball for half a century at nearly every level, a path with similarities to Dick's career. I know how difficult it is to do what he was trying to do at UW-Green Bay: build a program from the ground up, gain respect, and get bigger schools like Purdue to just give you a chance.

I respected and appreciated the way Dick approached the game. His teams weren't flashy and didn't do anything unexpected, but you could count on them to be disciplined and fundamentally sound. More importantly, we shared the belief that good basketball is about more than just talent, and the true measurement of a coach's impact and success goes beyond a win-loss ledger.

In basketball, as in life, character is everything.

I had great parents who taught me that, and it's always been part of my coaching philosophy. I tried to recruit kids who had character, wanted a college degree, and were willing to be taught. It's a mindset that Dick demonstrated throughout his coaching career, and now Tony has carried on while winning a national championship at Virginia. We need more coaches like them.

Introduction

March of 1979 marked the birth of Division I men's college basketball in the modern era. The NCAA tournament, an open-style playoff designed to crown the champion of college of basketball, was freshly renovated with a new seeding system and increased field. Boasting a once-in-a-generation superstar lineup, 1979's iteration of the Big Dance captivated the public for three weeks, culminating in one of, if not *the*, greatest championship game matchups in tournament history.

The show began with three traditional powers – UCLA, North Carolina, and Notre Dame – all snagging No. 1 seeds. But it was the fourth top seed, a mid-major previously unknown to the national media, that stole the nation's heart. On the back of a mop-headed senior superstar, Larry Bird, Indiana State skated through the regular season undefeated, easily winning their Missouri Valley Conference Tournament and propelling the team to the top rank in all of college basketball. Nineteen other conference champions and seventeen at-large qualifiers rounded out the field of forty.

The tournament's opening weekend provided the drama we've come to expect from March Madness, serving up two huge second-round upsets. A ninth-seeded Penn team defeated top seed North Carolina, while tenth-seeded St. John's beat the Tar Heels' ACC brethren, Duke, on a day that became known as "Black Sunday." Catering to those who love an underdog story, both Penn and St. John's won again in the Sweet Sixteen, setting up an Elite Eight matchup of upstarts for a chance to get to the Final Four.

In a back-and-forth affair, the Ivy League squad from Penn narrowly edged the Big East's St. John's, 64-62, to secure the school's first and only Final Four appearance. Joining Penn in the semifinals were independent powerhouse DePaul from Chicago and Jud Heathcote's Michigan State Spartans of the Big Ten, the latter of which had plenty of Hollywood appeal courtesy of their sophomore point guard sensation Magic Johnson. Those three schools, along with the sole remaining No. 1 seed, Indiana State, traveled to Salt Lake City for the tournament's final weekend.

The hype surrounding the Final Four was enormous as people prepared to witness Bird and Magic on the sport's biggest stage. Both future National Collegiate Basketball and Naismith Memorial Basketball Hall of Famers proved worthy in their semifinal matchups, with Magic logging a triple-double as the Spartans easily disposed of Penn, and Bird securing a Herculean 35-point, 16-rebound, and nine-assist effort as the Sycamores moved past DePaul.

With Bird/Magic round one officially scheduled, the stage was set for the highest-rated college basketball telecast of all time – a Homer-esque epic of contrasting styles, stars, and teams.

The game itself was solid, though not flawless. An off night from Bird (just 7-for-21 in field goal attempts) and a strong performance by Magic helped Michigan State take a nine-point lead into the half. The Spartans extended the lead to 50-34 early in the second half and ultimately ended the Sycamores' perfect season, 75-64. Magic Johnson was named the tournament's Most Outstanding Player, and college basketball as we know it today was born.

Riding the success of the 1979 NCAA tournament and the sudden growth of television options, coverage of college basketball quickly expanded with CBS and ESPN beginning a partnership to share coverage of the majority of tournament games just three years later. The tournament itself, powered by an increase in interest and revenue, underwent multiple expansions in a very short stretch. The field expanded to forty-eight teams in 1980, fifty-three teams in 1983, and sixty-four teams in 1985.

With more teams and expanding visibility, the 1980s and 1990s became college basketball's golden era. It was no wonder that as the exposure and money increased, major conference programs were able to exert their influence and tighten their grip on the tournament. Major conferences grabbed most of the "at-large" bids available for the NCAA tournament, as well as the once-great, but now relegated, National Invitational Tournament (NIT).

Unlike their football brethren, the open style of the NCAA tournament ensured an opportunity for the less-blessed schools – the mid-majors and low majors – to earn the right to experience the spotlight, and a glimmer of hope for creating an everlasting imprint.

This is the story of one of those mid-major teams.

UWGB's first men's basketball team finished 16-8 in the 1969-70 season. Back row: assistant coach Chuck Aslakson, Marc Schmidt (34), Terry Schott (42), Jim Hafeman (32), Bud Mosso (14), Dave Haglund (10), head coach Dave Buss; Front row: Bob De-Vos (22), Bob Popp (44), Ray Willis (52), Dennis Woelffer (54), Bruce Johnson (30), Wayne Wilson (20). (University of Wisconsin-Green Bay Archives)

Chapter 1

Birth of the Phoenix
(1969-1985)

To set the stage for what unfolded in Green Bay in the late 1980s and early 1990s, it's imperative to start with an understanding of the region, its people, and Wisconsin's rich sports history.

Midwestern and decidedly blue-collar, the vast majority of Wisconsin's population resides in the southeastern quadrant of the state, an area that includes the state's seven largest cities and represents the heart of its athletic scene. Sports have always been a lifeblood of Wisconsin, and in the late 1970s and early 1980s, this world was a relatively even mix of professional and collegiate interests.

NFL football was, is, and perhaps always will be king in Wisconsin, where the majority of the state (and parts of Michigan's Upper Peninsula) passionately support the league's oldest franchise. Though located in

Green Bay, the Packers are undoubtedly a state-wide property, in part because the team regularly played some home games each year in Milwaukee from 1934-1994.

Under authoritarian head coach Vince Lombardi, the Packers enjoyed one of the greatest dynasties in professional football history during the 1960s, but by the late '70s and early '80s, the franchise was in disarray. The team hit an all-time low in 1987, when *Sports Illustrated* wrote a piece entitled "Troubled Times in Title Town," ultimately suggested the city sell the franchise in light of a myriad of issues.

The college product enjoyed similar state-wide admiration, but has always played second-fiddle to the Packers. For decades, Marquette University, the state's largest private school located in Milwaukee, offered a club that provided some Saturday entertainment. But by 1960, the Catholic school had folded its football program, leaving the University of Wisconsin's Badgers as the only remaining Division I team around.

Wisconsin, the state's premier public university and a member of one of the NCAA's seminal major conferences (the Big Ten), also enjoyed a period of success in the late 1950s and early 1960s. The Badgers played in three Rose Bowls in a ten-year period between 1953 and 1963, including the "Game of the Century" – a 1963 battle that saw No. 2 Wisconsin, behind quarterback and Green Bay Preble High School graduate Ron Vander Kelen, mount a furious fourth-quarter comeback and nearly take down No. 1 USC, only to fall 42-37. Twenty-five years later, that same high school would produce a basketball star named Tony Bennett.

By 1964, the Badgers had taken a turn for the worse and were nearly unwatchable throughout the 1970s. The program would not play in another bowl game until 1981, and continued to struggle throughout the 1980s until hiring Notre Dame's defensive coordinator, Barry Alvarez, to lead the program in 1990.

With football on the downswing during the 1970s and early 1980s across the state, and a dearth of ice hockey options, sports fans were left with baseball in the summer months and basketball in the winter to fill the void. Ironically, in spite of ideal geography, no hockey team had taken hold of any serious statewide attention. The Wisconsin Badgers hockey team has come closest, ranking as one of the most successful collegiate hockey programs of all time. Though serious pushes were made to get an NHL franchise into Wisconsin (most notably in 1989-90), those efforts were ultimately unsuccessful.

Professional basketball enjoyed a brief stint as king during the early 1970s. Legends Lew Alcindor and Oscar Robertson helped the Milwaukee Bucks win an NBA title in 1971 and play for a second in 1974. But by the late 1970s, the Bucks were rebuilding and collegiate basketball had risen to the top, thanks to the sustained success of the Marquette Warriors.

Technically, the state of Wisconsin was home to two Division I men's basketball teams during the 1970s, but you could be forgiven for overlooking the Big Ten club. The Wisconsin Badgers were dreadful and smack in the middle of suffering through an atrocious forty-two-year, post-season drought. In contrast to the Badgers, the Marquette Warriors enjoyed a decade at the top of the NCAA basketball heap.

After a 5-21 season in 1964, Marquette hired legendary coach Al McGuire, and within three years, McGuire had the program straightened out. In 1966-67, the Warriors made it all the way to the NIT championship game, which started a string of eleven consecutive post-season trips. McGuire's success culminated in 1977, when Marquette defeated North Carolina to claim the school's first and only NCAA championship.

McGuire retired after that season with an amazing 78.7% winning percentage, and both an NCAA (1977) and NIT championship (1970). To the school's delight, his replacement, Hank Raymonds, picked up right where McGuire had left it and kept the post-season string alive.

It is against this backdrop that our protagonist, the University of Wisconsin-Green Bay Phoenix men's basketball program, entered Wisconsin's sports scene.

Through the Ranks

As a state, Wisconsin has routinely demonstrated its commitment to education by devoting significant resources to developing one of the nation's largest public university systems. The Wisconsin State Senate created the University of Wisconsin System, as it's known today, in 1971. It eventually grew to include thirteen full universities and thirteen additional branch campuses for freshman and sophomores. The University of Wisconsin-Green Bay (UWGB) was one of the full universities that merged into the University of Wisconsin System.

Founded in 1968 in a single building that now serves as an elementary school near Green Bay East High School, UWGB moved to its current 200-acre campus on the northeast edge of town in fall of 1969. The picturesque, rural campus sits just beyond the bustle of town, overlooking Lake Michigan's bay of Green Bay and serving equally as a nature preserve and hiker's haven. The school was never financially wealthy, but from its inception has provided intercollegiate athletic opportunities for its student body.

To that end, UWGB fielded its first men's basketball team just one year after the school's opening for the 1969-70 season. As a newcomer to college athletics, the school opted to join the National Association of Intercollegiate Athletics (NAIA), an alternative to the NCAA tailored toward small colleges and universities. Nevertheless, the school's administration defined the ultimate goal during the team's first press conference – to become a major college program as soon as possible.

The team's initial nickname was the Bay Badgers, and the program tried to model itself after the UW-Madison campus, donning cardinal and white uniforms. Its schedule that first season was comprised primarily of small-school competition, nearly all in Wisconsin, Minnesota, or Michigan. Under the leadership of Coach Dave Buss, the Phoenix won its first game against the now-defunct Milton College in southern Wisconsin and finished its first season with a winning record of 16-8.

"Our first year proved we could compete with schools within our own state and gave us a talking point in our recruiting," noted Buss.

By 1970, UWGB was ready to create its own image, separate from UW-Madison. The UWGB student newspaper conducted a mascot challenge, and on September 30, 1970, the school's new and lasting nickname,

UWGB's first attempt at the Phoenix mascot (left) was simple by modern standards, while the team's cheerleaders played to a sparse crowd at the Brown County Arena in the early years of the program. (University of Wisconsin-Green Bay Archives)

the Phoenix, was born, narrowly edging out the second-place finisher, the Tomatoes.

That year, the Phoenix showed improvement, posting a 23-5 record, qualifying for the NAIA tournament, and earning the program's first post-season victory, a 75-74 first-round win over Dominican. The victory itself was the stuff of legend as UWGB trailed by one with one second to play. Standing under the opponent's hoop, UWGB's Bud Mocco "arched a perfect pass to Ray Willis, standing on the other foul line, who caught the ball and shot it in the same motion and made it," recalled Buss.

UWGB would play two more NAIA seasons, advancing in the association's postseason both years before jumping to NCAA's Division II. Division II didn't seem much different than the NAIA for the Phoenix. In 1973-74, Buss's club compiled a 20-8 record and again made the postseason, a remarkable feat in the team's first year at the Division II level. Two more Division II tournament appearances in the next three seasons reaffirmed that this program was continuing to rise.

By the 1976-77 season, UWGB had built the experience and talent necessary to take another step forward, doing so largely with locally grown players. Powered by the emergence of Green Bay Southwest sharpshooter Tom Anderson and Pulaski big man Ron Ripley – two family names that would play prominent roles on future UWGB teams – the Phoenix rolled up a 25-2 regular-season record that included the school's biggest win to date, a 57-50 stunner over Division I national power DePaul, which had advanced to the Sweet Sixteen in the Division I NCAA tournament the previous season. Nevertheless, hopes for bringing home a title ended prematurely with a rare early-tournament loss to North Dakota.

Undeterred, and with the return of Anderson and Ripley, the Phoenix proceeded to post the school's best season in 1977-78, racking up thirty wins including four in the NCAA Division II tournament. Those accomplishments earned the team the right to play in the title game against Cheyney State, coached by future Temple coach John Chaney. Buss's Phoenix lost by seven points, but with a runner-up finish at the Division II level, talk of a Phoenix rise to Division I began in earnest.

UWGB lost Anderson to graduation, but Ripley's return in 1978-79 helped propel UWGB back to the Division II championship game. In a twist of fate, the Phoenix's match-up with North Alabama took place exactly nine days before the iconic Bird versus Magic showdown.

UWGB again fell short of its ultimate goal in losing the title game, but now those conversations about moving to Division I were increasing in volume and gaining momentum each day.

Pushed forward by the dream of opportunity, visibility, and legitimacy, UWGB Athletic Director Bruce Grimes launched a preliminary investigation into the potential move to Division I. By August of 1979, the study committee had concluded it was feasible. However, the program would need to overcome a few hurdles to make this move a reality.

First, Grimes estimated it would cost approximately $3 million for a ten-year Division I program, a sum that would need to be raised through private funding. On top of that, pursuant to NCAA rules, Division I opponents would have to make up at least 85% of the team's schedule, a significant requirement for a team with few Division I contacts. And then there were the real questions concerning conference affiliation and the impossibility of proceeding long-term without one.

The entire Green Bay community was engaged in the debate for much of the fall of 1979. This is what happens in small towns. School officials

UWGB's 1977-78 team finished runner-up in the NCAA Division II tournament. Back row: athletic trainer Bud Jorgensen, head coach Dave Buss, Tom Anderson (40), Dave Getman (42), Sam Stuessy (34), Jim Zill (54), Ron Ripley (50), Charlie Lorenzi (44), Rory Lindgren (22), assistant coach Chuck Aslakson. Front row: Dave Hanson (10), Jed Grams (14), Jerry Blackwell (12), Mike Hanrahan (20), Bryan Boettcher (52), manager Dan Timm. (University of Wisconsin-Green Bay Archives)

met with community business leaders, the athletic department met with donors and backers, and every media outlet in town printed and re-printed pros and cons of a potential move to Division I.

Taking the Plunge

On November 23, 1979, Chancellor Edward Weidner announced the school's intention to move to Division I beginning with the 1981-82 season. Weidner, the former chairman of the political science department at Michigan State, drew on the Spartans' experience transitioning into the Big Ten in the late 1940s and early 1950s.

"When (Michigan State) went to the Big Ten, John Hannah (Michigan State president at the time) made a real university out of a cow college," Weidner stated, "That gave me great orientation into what we were talking about here."

Of all folks involved, none were happier than Dave Buss. Buss had grown into a local legend and excitedly agreed to stay on as head coach of the Phoenix through the first season of the transition. Yet even Buss acknowledged that this move would be considerably more challenging than the program's previous transitions.

"We're not going into the Big Ten or the Pac-10 or the ACC. It's a little different ballgame," noted Buss, "You enter at a low Division I level. We can compete at a low Division I, moving to middle Division I."

Prominent coaches were highly skeptical of the move. Digger Phelps, head coach at Notre Dame, suggested the program would be better off staying a premier Division II team, while DePaul's Ray Meyer warned that it would take at least five years for UWGB to even establish itself. Both coaches agreed that scheduling would be extremely challenging, with Meyer prophetically mentioning a potential paradox. "If you're not good at the start, you won't win. And if you're good, many teams won't play you."

The long-term concern of conference affiliation loomed very large. A conference affiliation would provide assurances in scheduling, home games, and travel, as well as the potential to play for an NCAA tournament berth. Without one, any chances of long-term success were essentially nil.

Complicating the matter, previously independent schools had scooped up available conference openings, all seeking the right to earn an automatic bid to the Big Dance. Where sixty-eight schools claimed Division I independence in 1979, only twenty-one remained independent just a year later.

Undeterred, UWGB scoured the conference landscapes throughout 1980 and 1981, ultimately seeking entrance into the Midwestern City Conference, a newly formed group of teams that included Loyola, Evansville, Xavier, Butler, Oral Roberts, and Oklahoma City. But that conference ultimately rejected UWGB's request, and no other conference appeared to present a viable option for the school.

Dangerously, while the basketball team had secured the necessary financials and enjoyed yet another trip to the NCAA Division II Final Four in the 1980-81 season, university officials resigned themselves to the reality that UWGB would play at least their first Division I season as an independent.

Tom Anderson (40) dribbles past DePaul's Curtis Watkins during the Phoenix's 67-60 loss in 1976. UWGB upset DePaul in the rematch in 1977 in Green Bay. (University of Wisconsin-Green Bay Archives)

Division I Independence

UWGB cobbled together its 1981-82 schedule from the coaching staff's limited connections to meet the NCAA's 85% Division I opponent requirement. Like the sixteen other programs that had made the jump to Division I since the 1979 Tournament, UWGB had to take whatever it could get.

Even with Grimes and Buss spending the better part of eighteen months arranging what they could, most of UWGB's schedule was made up of low major programs and home-and-away, two-game sets against other comparable Division I independents like UNC-Wilmington, Arkansas State, Illinois-Chicago, Valparaiso, and Northern Iowa. The two shining

Dave Buss compiled a 271-102 record during his time as UW-Green Bay's first men's basketball coach. (University of Wisconsin-Green Bay Archives)

scheduling successes were a pair of Big Ten matchups, including a road game at Michigan State and an entry into the Wisconsin Invitation Tournament, which ultimately led to a game against Wisconsin.

While the Badgers disposed of the Phoenix by a dozen, the Spartans nearly lived to regret their generosity as UWGB forced overtime and came within one point of pulling off a major upset. Coach Jud Heathcote ripped his team's effort, but Kevin Smith, the Spartans' all-Big Ten guard, was more gracious, saying, "They've got some good big guys and they played us tough all night – they surprised us."

"What we had to learn early in this first year in Division I was just where we fit in," recalled Buss. "Our players had to develop the mental frame of mind that they *belonged* in this division."

The team experienced some major successes, including a seven-game winning streak in January 1982, and ultimately finished above .500. It was a testament to Buss's legacy that he remains the only coach in college basketball history to lead the same school to winning records in their first seasons in the NAIA, NCAA Division II, and NCAA Division I.

But for all his excellence on the sidelines, Buss was creating friction away from the hardwood, particularly with Associate Chancellor Don Harden. Buss had dismissed two popular seniors from the squad with just three games left and had been outspoken about his disdain for the Mid-Continent – a league that UWGB was seriously considering for conference affiliation.

This conflict came to a head on April 5, 1982, when the Green Bay media reported that Buss would not be back as the Phoenix coach. With the situation spiraling, UWGB called a press conference four days later, where Chancellor Weidner confirmed the news that Buss had been dismissed. Buss was understandably bitter, particularly at Harden. Jabbing at Harden's lack of athletic department or coaching experience, Buss raved to the papers, "Don wants a coach that's a puppet. I feel if he wants to coach, he has to go out on the floor."

In a sign of the times and financial position of the school, the lingering story after Buss's firing was not how the team would respond, but instead how UWGB was going to find a way to continue to use Buss. With the program suffering a $50,000 loss in its first Division I season and still owing Buss $30,000 per year for two more contracted seasons, the school was pressed to make every penny count. The university toggled through ridiculous proposals, including Buss working on "UWGB history projects" or joining the women's basketball program as an assistant coach under the very capable Carol Hammerle, all while the former coach interviewed elsewhere. It took him four months, but Buss eventually landed an assistant coaching job with UNLV under legendary coach Jerry Tarkanian in September 1982.

It was a bittersweet end. Buss was the first and only coach the Phoenix had ever known. He was successful at every level and finished his career in Green Bay with a 271-102 record, a .727 winning percentage. He'd led the Phoenix to twelve winning seasons in thirteen years, including nine postseason appearances. Buss was named Division II Coach of the Year in 1979 and had successfully transitioned the team not once, but twice – first from start-up to NCAA Division II power, and then to a winning Division I program.

In the end, poor financials, a bleak conference outlook, and negative public opinion led to Buss's inevitable sacking. But while saying goodbye to Buss may have been tough for some fans, it certainly helped UWGB's chances to band together with other low- and mid-level independents.

The Lien Years

In a surprising move, UWGB administration announced Buss's replacement at the same press conference they announced his departure, introducing assistant coach Dick Lien (pronounced "lean") as the program's new head coach.

Lien's first foray with the Green Bay media foreshadowed his tenure with the program. Upon being introduced, Lien took the podium and, just a few moments into discussing his philosophies, passed out. He appeared to recover momentarily, only to pass out a second time, after which he was rushed to the St. Vincent Hospital by a rescue squad. It was an inauspicious start to a dreadful tenure.

However, with Buss out of the picture, the single most positive and impactful event of the Lien era took place almost immediately upon his promotion.

The Association of Mid-Continent Universities (AMCU) was born in June of 1982 at the O'Hare Hilton in Chicago and would be the conference home to UWGB. After a series of meetings, the Phoenix agreed to start the conference with seven other schools: Cleveland State, Eastern Illinois, University of Illinois-Chicago (UIC), Northern Iowa, Southwest Missouri State, Valparaiso, and Western Illinois.

Cleveland State, preparing to enter its tenth season in Division I, was a driving force in the league's formation, having spent years experiencing the hardships of independent basketball. Beyond the Vikings and Valparaiso, the rest were new to the NCAA's top tier and eager to obtain some assurances of viability. The league's formation gave UWGB the stability it needed.

Although in theory the Phoenix could now play for a bid to the NCAA tournament, never let it be said that the NCAA made it easy for low or mid-level schools to get access to their crown jewel. A rule passed just the year before required all new conferences to wait five years before granting the conference champion an automatic bid into the tournament. For the AMCU, this meant it may have to wait until the 1987-88 season to get a team into the Big Dance.

In 1982, that five-year wait may have seemed interminable, but by 1985, the state of basketball at UWGB was so dismal that there were legitimate doubts the program could remain in Division I. Three seasons of Dick Lien basketball had produced results even the most cynical of prognosticators would have had a hard time dreaming up.

UWGB finished dead last in the AMCU in the 1982-83 and 1984-85 seasons, while scrounging up a sixth-place finish in the intermediate season. The Phoenix failed to muster double-digit wins in *any* of those three years, compiling a mere eight conference wins in *total*. Worse yet, in Lien's last season, UWGB managed only two wins against Division I opponents and four wins overall.

It would be unfair to credit all four of those wins to Lien, for the woeful coach actually resigned in mid-February, a few days before the team scooped up their fourth win of the year. Upon his departure, Lien cited two conditions he failed to meet for success in Green Bay: winning and earning fan support. But while Lien acknowledged his shortcomings, he was flippant in finding excuses that contributed to his demise, including a lack of financial commitment from the school, a lack of community involvement or local business support, poor fans, and a dearth of good players.

Though "better coaching" was conspicuously absent from Lien's list, his rant framed the very question this book ultimately seeks to resolve:

What does it truly take to succeed as a mid-major in Division I men's basketball?

Chapter 2

A Coach with a Plan
(1985-1988)

History will tell you that regardless of sport, there is perhaps no greater factor in the sustained success of a team than its head coach. This individual, much like the president of a corporation, determines the team's strategy, controls personnel, sets expectations, manages the program's opportunities, and affects the team's chemistry.

Nowhere is this more evident than in college basketball, where player turnover forces programs to adapt to new personnel every few years. To complicate the matter, coaches at mid-major programs are particularly challenged as they must achieve greatness with typically inferior resources.

Coaching philosophies, like their creators, come in all shapes and sizes: Nolan Richardson and his frantic, fast-paced offenses at Tulsa were a precursor to his 40 Minutes of Hell at Arkansas; Paul Westhead's goal of a shot within six or seven seconds at Loyola Marymount; Pete Carril and the iconic Princeton Offense; Gene Bartow, once John Wooden's successor, and his clean-cut style at Alabama-Birmingham; Mark Few's simple and deliberate style at Gonzaga; Gregg Marshall's passionate and animated energy, and Brad Stevens's stoic reverence all have found great success in different and unique ways.

And while experience has shown that vastly different styles can lead to strikingly similar successes, one commonality remains: no mid-major basketball team has ever achieved lasting greatness without excellent coaching.

The Hire

Speculation about Lien's successor began immediately, and within twenty-four hours, an extensive and impressive list of potential candidates had formed.

A number of in-state names were immediately thrown out as possible replacements, including qualified coaches like Rees Johnson from UW-Parkside near Kenosha, Mike Heideman from St. Norbert College in nearby De Pere, and a successful local high school coach in Keith Wall from Green Bay Preble. On top of those local names, famous coaches in bordering states, including Michigan State assistant coach Tom Izzo and Minnesota assistant coach Phil "Flip" Saunders, were also quick to express interest.

It became clear early in the search that Lien's criticism of UWGB's financial commitment had some merit and could hinder the school's ability to hire a replacement. UWGB's recruiting budget, a paltry $10,000 per year, was less than half as much as most of its contemporaries. Even worse, Lien's $25,800 yearly salary made him merely the tenth-highest-paid coach in the University of Wisconsin System, ranking behind eight *non-Division I* coaches.

One of those in-state coaches earning significantly more than Lien emerged as the front-runner for the job: UW-Stevens Point's Dick Bennett.

Bennett had made a name for himself throughout Wisconsin with his staunch fundamentals and aggressive "push" defensive principles. With twenty years of coaching experience at both the high school and college levels, Bennett had connections, and respect, everywhere. In his most recent stint at UW-Stevens Point, Bennett had accumulated 174 wins and led the Pointers to a runner-up finish in the NAIA in 1984.

Dick Bennett's official portrait upon being hired by UWGB in 1985. (University of Wisconsin-Green Bay Archives)

Even with more than seventy coaches expressing interest in the position, UWGB's administration moved deftly through the interviewing and evaluation process. Bennett was on the short list of four finalists within two weeks of the season's end, along with Bradley assistant Tony Barone, Pittsburgh assistant Jay Eck, and former Iowa assistant Jim Rosborough.

Don Harden met with the Pointer's coach on Thursday, March 28, 1985, and convinced Bennett that the challenges he would face – those that Lien had pointed out – could be overcome. Harden set realistic expectations and made no mention of winning championships. The immediate goal was to make the Division I program competitive.

"He made it clear to me that we basically had a few years, perhaps three, to become competitive. If that were to happen, everything would – the city, would fall in love with the program and so on," Bennett recalls, "But if it did not happen, we likely would have to go back to the Division (II) status, because that's the way it had to work. We just needed to make some legitimate progress, and I felt like we could do that. I thought that we could get good kids who would be competitive."

The timing also seemed perfect as Bennett's star guard at Stevens Point, Terry Porter, was graduating. (Porter would go on to a seventeen-year NBA career and the Portland Trail Blazers retired his number 30.) That left Bennett with the option of rebuilding in Stevens Point or starting from scratch elsewhere. Less than twenty-four hours after their meeting, Harden offered Bennett the position and he accepted on the spot.

A day later, UWGB held a press conference and announced Bennett as its new head coach. The university had upped the salary, giving him a three-year contract at $42,000 per year, and had assured the coach this was not a win-at-all-costs situation.

"They made it clear, 'You do this the way *you* want to do it. We don't have any expectations. We are going to be as patient as can be. You will not feel any pressure from us,' " Bennett says.

On His Own Terms

It's entirely unfair to summarize a person's life by their three greatest loves, but if ever such an exception could be made, it was with Dick Bennett. Like the legendary Vince Lombardi before him, Bennett had an extremely focused set of priorities, dedicating his full mind and body to his family, his faith, and basketball (in some order).

"You knew from the moment you met him that his entire life was basketball, and his family, church, God, his faith," says Scott LeMoine, a UWGB player from 1988-92. "He was a very faithful man, obviously. But there really wasn't much else to his life. He lived, breathed and died basketball, like that was his whole life. And his family bought in."

Bennett was raised in Pittsburgh in a strict household where religion was embedded in his DNA. "I went to Catholic school in grade school," he says, "I had a notion in me that the Lord was in charge of my life, and if I just would yield – I guess I had that notion that I would yield and somehow, even bad decisions would turn out well."

That faith led Bennett on a winding coaching path in Wisconsin, starting as an assistant jack-of-all-trades at West Bend High School in the 1960s before landing his first head coaching job at tiny Mineral Point High School.

"I didn't do a particularly good job there," he notes, "I was full of ideas, but not full of a lot of substance. I had a decent team – we were about .500, and it should have been better."

Bennett coached at Mineral Point for two years before agreeing to take the head job at equally small Marion High School. And though he spent just one season at Marion, the experience helped Bennett hone in on one of his true passions – the idea of building a basketball program on his own terms.

Bennett took that mindset with him when he agreed to coach New London High School, more determined than ever to build a program from the ground up and do things his way.

"I chose a job that was really down, and that was New London. I had this mentality that I wanted to be able to do it my own way," he says, "I didn't want to step in to where there was a ton of tradition and people would say, 'Well, this is the way we always do it.' "

The Bulldogs struggled mightily in Bennett's first season.

"Everybody was wondering, 'What are they doing?' " remembers Bennett. "I worked night and day with the young kids. I actually brought the freshmen in on the weekend and worked with them. By the third year, those freshmen I worked with were juniors ... and we went to the sectional finals again."

Bennett, with his wife Anne's support, next took the head job at Eau Claire Memorial and enjoyed four more successful years, finishing his career with back-to-back trips to the WIAA State Tournament and an appearance in the 1976 Class A state championship game. It was at that point Bennett turned his attention to the college game.

"Stevens Point opened up," he explains. "Bob Krueger had stepped aside and his assistant took it on an interim basis. I was one of five finalists and I was offered the job."

Bennett used his nine seasons at Stevens Point to build and hone his defensive scheme, known as the "push" defense, all while turning the Pointers into a national powerhouse at the NAIA level. Through it all, Bennett remained true to his upbringing, faithful and humbled by his experiences.

"All of the starting jobs I had were really hard in that first year. But somehow, at a point when it seemed like it wouldn't turn, it turned," he says. "I never doubted that it was not my own strength that made me act and think and feel that way after difficult seasons and games and circumstances. And so, with every season – I think with every change, my faith grew, because I was thankful."

Dick Bennett's Philosophy

So what did Bennett bring with him to Green Bay?

Like many great coaches, he was a confident, driven competitor who carried his own unique approach to the game of basketball. Core to Bennett's strategy was a fundamental principle – he wanted to eliminate the potential for "losing" by eradicating mistakes. It was something the blue-collar, Packers-centric town had witnessed succeed before.

Bennett described his philosophy this way:

"When (people) talk about playing not to lose, that is a different mentality – one that I *don't* believe in. That means playing hesitantly and being afraid to do stuff.

"But *eliminating losing* ... When I went to Green Bay, I sold it kind of as a Lombardi idea, because I had watched and went through that era watching everything ... he just eliminated mistakes. (The Packers) weren't over-penalized, they had a simple program based on execution, and it was easy to sell that idea in a place like Green Bay. We're just going to eliminate losing.

"In the end, what you find is more teams lose than are beaten – meaning, you get to the end of the game and guys take some of the dumbest shots. Instead of being sound, they'll go for steals or blocked shots. They'll commit silly fouls trying to reach around. And that's where games are lost.

"If you can just eliminate that kind of mentality... you're going to be in the game and opponents are going to lose. And my teams ... they don't beat themselves. That's essentially what it is."

Bennett's coaching history gave him ample time to study the habits of winners and losers, and through that analysis, he discovered that losing programs almost always fell victim to the same, repeating errors.

"You could almost predict that you'd see a lot of turnovers; you'd see them consistently be outrebounded; you'd see them shoot a poor percentage," Bennett summarizes. All, as Bennett recognized, could be controlled by coaching disciplined players, irrespective of talent.

"You can keep people off the glass, you can take care of the basketball, you can shoot good shots, you can always get back defensively. That's one thing you have control over – getting five people back to set your defense. You can do that with hard work."

And so, the bedrock of Bennett's methodology was cemented in an unwavering obsession with defense. There have been dedicated defensive coaches before and since, but Bennett's passion ran as deep as any coach's in history.

"(The plan) was simple. It was to build a program around a solid defensive system. You can always be competitive defensively, without question. We were patient, we took care of the basketball. But we built everything around our defense."

Ben Johnson, a Phoenix star from 1988-92, summarized his coach, stating, "His programs have always been about defense. Solid, strong, intense, man-to-man defense."

Bennett had no place for those who didn't accept his defensive dedication.

"Rule number one: you don't play defense, you don't play," LeMoine recalls. "Our defense was so team-oriented that you had to buy in and you had to trust your guys on the team to be there for you with what we were trying to accomplish."

If played to perfection, Bennett's systems had almost no flaws.

"There are no holes in Coach Bennett's defensive scheme. It's complete," says Chris Westlake (1993-95), "Whether Coach was playing the push defense or playing the pack defense, it was complete. It followed it all the way through to the rebound with how the rotations went."

Almost as an after-thought to his dogged man-to-man defense, Bennett implemented the same motion offense with the Phoenix as he had with the Pointers before them. Bennett was more flexible on the offensive side, willing to modify his principles to fit the skills of his roster.

"Philosophy-wise, we were pretty much a man-to-man defensive team and a motion offensive team," explains defensive standout Gary Grzesk (1992-96). "But depending on the year, he would kind of change our screening system to fit everyone's strengths and weaknesses."

The advantage of his all-out dedication to one side of the ball? Bennett's teams kept scores low, possessions at a premium, and gave themselves a chance at the end of games.

"You could roll out the balls and play a certain way and beat a certain number of teams if you had more talent than them, but I think the system lent itself to beating the best teams in the country," adds Grzesk. "We had a unique enough system that would allow us to overachieve and beat some teams that maybe had more individual talent than what we did."

"There are stories and stories and storybooks and chapters about teams that are less talented winning, and Coach has probably authored those books ten times over," observes sharpshooter Mike Karisny (1986-90). "He's done it better than almost anybody I've ever seen in the history of basketball."

Dick Bennett's son, Tony, a future NCAA national champion coach himself at Virginia, was one of his father's most successful disciples.

"You have to have, in my opinion, a system that is tried and true," notes Tony Bennett, "because unless you're doing stuff differently, you're not going to be able to out-recruit a lot of the high majors with a talent base. So you're going to have to find sneaky-good players, and you're going to have to have a way in which you play and do things that will give you a chance."

Changing the Culture

Dick Bennett brought a unique style to Green Bay, but despite the vote of confidence from the administration, he was behind the eight ball in the spring of 1985. He needed to address three primary issues immediately: his staff, his players, and his community. Not surprisingly, Bennett had a plan to handle all three.

First, Bennett needed to quickly assemble his staff – a task that, thanks to UWGB's strained budget, only required two hires. Bennett leaned heavily on known commodities, filling his top assistant coach position with Rod Popp, one of his assistants from UW-Stevens Point, and his second assistant with another UW-Stevens Point member in Steve Swan. Swan's position at UWGB would, in many ways, resemble the role he had at UW-Stevens Point – a bit of a utility man, serving in some capacity as marketing director, sports information director, scheduler, and recruiter, along with his duties as assistant coach.

Next, Bennett needed to assemble a group of players with whom he could be competitive. His review of the existing talent left something to be desired.

"I have not seen a guy (on the current roster) who can score even a consistent twelve points a game," he said at the time. "I am hopeful that each player goes home this summer and addresses his shooting. That is the single most important problem we have to work on."

In short order, and armed with a slew of scholarships, Bennett added six freshmen and a junior-college transfer to the 1985-86 roster.

"It was a bit late for me to bring in a lot of recruits, but we brought in a bunch of freshmen who were good kids, and then we knew we could add to that," Bennett says.

By October, three of his season-opening starters were newcomers to the program.

Finally, Bennett needed to address the neglected fan base in Green Bay. Though the program played at the Brown County Veterans Memorial Arena, a facility capable of holding more than 5,000 fans, the Phoenix hadn't come close to filling it in recent memory. Attendance during Lien's three seasons had been atrocious, with the team drawing over 2,500 fans only five times, topping out at 3,312 fans in 1983 for a game against Division III UW-Oshkosh.

Exuding confidence, Bennett addressed the topic head-on in his introductory press conference: "I think as people become aware of what we're trying to do, the crowds will grow in ever-increasing numbers."

But Bennett was savvy enough to recognize he could not rely on his team's play alone. He had to make a dedicated effort himself to marketing his program. Bennett had a plan for making the Phoenix appealing to the greater Green Bay area, committing to a door-to-door style campaign to sell his team.

"I felt that the key was to somehow marry the university to the city. I mean, it could not just be that school out there – we had to appeal to the community and the area," he explains. "I remember getting a list of all of the service clubs in the greater Green Bay area and visiting every single one of them in the first two years – it was something like seventy-five or so – to sell what we were trying to do, what we needed to do."

Armed with a proven coaching philosophy, a competent staff, the best players he could manage on short notice, and a commitment to increase community engagement, Bennett set off to satisfy Harden's request of making the team competitive at the Division I level.

Players You Can Lose With

Despite the new energy and positive changes, the Dick Bennett version of the Phoenix failed to improve the outcomes seen during the Lien years, at least in the beginning. In Bennett's first year, the 1985-86 squad managed to increase its win total to five, but had just three wins against Division I opponents (all in the AMCU), and tied for the worst record in the league.

And yet, there were signs of improvement in precisely the areas Bennett had identified. Turnovers were down, free throw percentage was up, and the defense was successful in limiting possessions, reducing shot opportunities by more than eight attempts per game and ultimately dropping scoring by more than three points per game.

Rod Popp left the Phoenix after that first season to become head coach at Viterbo College in La Crosse, leaving Bennett with one vacancy to fill. Thankfully, Green Bay had the perfect replacement coaching just down the street – St. Norbert College head coach Mike Heideman.

Heideman had known Bennett for years, back to their days coaching against each other at the high school level, and joined Bennett at a few open gym sessions early in the summer of 1986. It was at one of these sessions that Heideman made his pitch.

"One day he just sat next to me and said, 'You know, I'd really like to help you. I'd really like to help you get this thing going,'" Bennett remembers. "And that was all he had to do, was say that, and I hired him."

As Bennett prepared for his second season, he focused on finding and

Dick Bennett addresses his team during a 67-63 loss to the University of Miami on December 9, 1985. (University of Wisconsin-Green Bay Archives)

cultivating young talent with high character, seeking to change the culture from the bottom up.

"A lot of the guys that carried over to my first year (1986-87) really had to fight through what I'd call the mentality of accepting losing," notes Karisny, an incoming freshman. "It was easier to accept. When we got there, there were a group of guys that came in and I think we weren't used to losing. We all were among the better teams in the state of Wisconsin or wherever we would come from."

Karisny was an example of what his coach was looking for – players of high confidence who he could not simply win with, but also lose with.

Tony Bennett notes how that trait was a focal point for his father throughout all of his coaching life.

"(His) famous line that he shared at his Washington State introductory press conference (in 2003) was, 'In order for me to build a program here, I've got to recruit players and a staff that I can lose with first before I win.' He said, 'Because I know we're going to get beat, it's going to be hard.' And he said, 'I've got to know that I've got guys that I can lose with first, because eventually we're going to grow and glean that wisdom that comes from adversity and apply it, and we'll be successful *if* we have those kind of guys.' "

Backing Away from the Edge

Even as the team's persona was evolving, the 1986-87 Phoenix limped to a 1-5 start, punctuated by an embarrassing loss at Iowa State.

"They had a coach named Johnny Orr, and a guy named Jeff Grayer played," recalls Karisny of the future Milwaukee Bucks first-round draft pick. "He went up and he dunked on me, and he hung over the rim and looked down on me. And I said, 'I didn't see this at St. Mary's (High School), right?' And they just kicked our ass."

The energy surrounding the program, coupled with the sustained frustration of losing and a coach hell-bent on perfection, created a combustible environment. It was a moment in time when everything Bennett was building was on the verge of collapse.

That was when the Big Ten's Northwestern Wildcats came to Green Bay, and the Phoenix delivered a Christmas miracle.

That young Phoenix team of high school winners cobbled together a staggeringly competent performance that hadn't been seen in Green Bay since the Dave Buss era. With an invigorated home crowd, Bennett's Fighting Phoenix kick-started the basketball revolution in Wisconsin.

UWGB raced to an 11-0 start, then a 31-19 halftime lead which garnered a standing ovation from the crowd. Bennett's club weathered Northwestern's second-half comeback efforts and ultimately sealed the deal with a 61-49 victory – the program's first win over a Big Ten opponent. It was a victory that had seemingly appeared out of thin air and given life to a failing team.

Bennett acknowledged the impact the game had on the fans, and the fans, in turn, had on the game.

"The crowd played a very significant role," he said in post-game comments. "This is the first time it's happened since I've been here. We gave them something to cheer about, and they didn't stop cheering."

It also left a lasting impact on Bennett, who, years later, still considered it the program's turning point.

"It was literally a turnaround overnight. To this day, I can't explain it."

"I remember it like it was yesterday, the fans rushed the court," Karisny said three decades later. "I hardly played at all, but I remember being interviewed like I was some rock star. It was a great feeling and ... it was a turning point for our program. It was time to establish Green Bay as a program to be dealt with."

A week later, UWGB traveled to Miami (Florida) and had the audacity to pull of its second win in Division I against a major conference school, beating future Bucks player Tito Horford and the Hurricanes by seventeen points. A switch had been flipped, and though a talent gap remained, the Phoenix had figured something out.

"We began to re-set ourselves and began to not be able to roll over," Karisny states. "Pretty soon, teams that maybe were beating us by ten, we were like in the game with them."

Bennett's vision had found roots.

The season's crescendo reached a peak in February 1987 when UWGB welcomed conference top dog Cleveland State to town for a game that gave the Phoenix legitimate conference credibility. The Vikings had been the darling of the 1986 NCAA tournament, pulling off two major upsets on their way to a Sweet Sixteen berth, and the 1986-87 squad was nearly as strong.

"They had a guy named Mouse McFadden, who was their best player. And we played them in Green Bay and we beat them in overtime," recalls Karisny, who hit a key free throw near the end of the game.

"I remember making a free throw in overtime to kind of seal the win, and looking over and just giving (my dad and family) one of the biggest fist-pumps and having the whole section stand up."

With a third signature win under its belt, the Phoenix finished Bennett's second season with a respectable 15-14 record, including a solid 8-6 conference record, good for fourth behind Southwest Missouri State, Cleveland State, and UIC. UWGB also collected its first AMCU tournament victory against Northern Iowa, and nearly pulled off a second against Southwest Missouri State before falling 61-59 in the semifinals.

"The teammates that were there, I think they were like doing handstands because they felt such a difference between the 5-23 year before," notes Karisny. "We needed that (Cleveland State) win as a team, and it validated our position in terms of our rebuilding of the program. You get those wins like Cleveland State, Northwestern, those are the points in time, those checkpoints that you need to have that are going to reinforce what we've been working so hard to get."

Fruits of Labor

Bennett continued to work hard at honing his craft during his third offseason.

"I can't tell you how many camps I worked in the summer. I would be gone constantly," he says. "We needed the money, because I wasn't making any money, (but) those were tremendous times and you'd share an idea and pick up an idea – that sort of thing."

Bennett's hard work was showing returns. His team had rounded the corner, and even with a challenging mid-major schedule, was able to demonstrate consistency, game-in and game-out.

In perhaps the most memorable game of the season, UWGB headed to Mount Pleasant, Michigan, for a date at Rose Arena with Central Michigan. Led by their all-conference guard and future Phoenix Suns star, Dan Majerle, the Chippewas were fresh off a 22-8 season that saw them sweep through the MAC Tournament and earn the right to play UCLA in the first round of the 1987 NCAA tournament.

The arena "had the high school gym feel – it was tight, not a big arena; it was more of a gym with four walls," explains Karisny.

But home had been good to Central Michigan, who hadn't lost a game there the entire prior season. The Chippewa fans maintained a unique tradition in the late 1980s: "When they made their first basket, they threw toilet paper on the floor and the student section actually picked guys out at the end of the bench and pelted them," recalls freshman Dean Vander Plas. "I was obviously one of those kids that they decided to drill."

Despite the hostility, UWGB escaped with a four-point victory that was the signature victory of its 8-1 start to the season.

"These are teams that maybe the average college fan didn't know, but we knew how good they were and they went on to do very well in the NCAA tournament as well," Bennett says. "Maybe we didn't know it at the time, but that was the time where our program was being established."

With Vander Plas in the starting line-up, the team managed an im-

UWGB's Frank Nardi hurdles a Southwest Missouri State player to grab a loose ball during a 77-65 loss on February 6, 1988. (University of Wisconsin-Green Bay Archives)

pressive run, finishing 18-9 overall. More importantly, the team was highly competitive in the conference. With a 9-5 AMCU record, the Phoenix found itself third in the year-end standings – the team's highest finish in five seasons of Division I basketball.

"We had a very good team," Karisny says. "We had Richard Sims, Frank Nardi. These are fantastic players, but for whatever reason, we all didn't quite buy-in. I think some of that might have been the little bit of the hangover effect from getting beat up the previous years."

"The first groups that we brought in were just really good people, and then it took us a little bit of time to establish," notes Bennett.

The bar had been raised, and with a home-grown squad of athletes, Bennett's own expectations were sky-high for 1988-89.

AMCU on the Rise

UWGB wasn't the only AMCU school with a coach that was shining. During the same three-year stretch, Cleveland State's Kevin Mackey and Southwest Missouri State's Charlie Spoonhour were busy helping the conference, and all mid-majors, take one giant leap forward.

Mackey had been hired by Cleveland State from Boston College in 1983, and immediately rebuilt the floundering Vikings. Mackey implemented a high-octane offensive system that had his players running the floor and hoisting shots at seemingly every opportunity. His scheme, known as the "Run 'n' Stun," helped Cleveland State win twenty-one games in Mackey's second season, and a school-record twenty-seven games in his third.

That record-breaking 1985-86 season featured two all-conference seniors and star freshman, Ken "Mouse" McFadden. The Vikings waltzed to the conference regular-season title with a 13-1 record, and then double-dipped with a conference tournament championship, overcoming an MVP performance by future NBA star Kevin Duckworth to squeak past Eastern Illinois, 70-66, in the final.

"They just didn't even let you breathe. They just smothered everything you did," Bennett recalls.

Even without an automatic bid (the league had to wait until 1987-88 to get that), the Vikings received the league's first NCAA tournament bid as a 14 seed. Their prize was the opportunity of a lifetime – a matchup with Bobby Knight's Indiana Hoosiers in the first round.

Cleveland State's full-court pressure defense caused fits for the General and his militia. Though the game was close, the Vikings led most of the way and pulled off the greatest upset in school (and, at least at the time, conference) history. The feat was all the more impressive when considering Knight brought largely the same Indiana squad all the way to the 1987 NCAA Championship the following year.

The Viking cruise continued when they took care of St. Joseph's in the second round, making Cleveland State the first 14 seed to ever advance to the Sweet Sixteen. The national media was abuzz with talk about Cleveland State and the AMCU, including college basketball character Dick Vitale, labeling it "strawberry shortcake time" for the conference. The Vikings nearly sunk David Robinson and Navy in the Sweet Sixteen, and if not for a questionable jump-ball call at the end, the Vikings may have played for a chance to go to the Final Four.

In contrast to Kevin Mackey's "Run 'n' Stun," Charlie Spoonhour's Southwest Missouri State Bears played a style much closer to UWGB. Spoonhour demanded discipline and preached tough, man-to-man, half-court defense and patience on offense. "Spoon" had a propensity to stalk the sidelines, stomp his feet, and manifest intensity.

"Any team that Southwest Missouri put on the floor was the best team that we ever played, because they played so well on both ends," praises Bennett. "And they had Charlie Spoonhour, who was just one of the best I've ever gone against."

While Cleveland State was making a run for the ages in the NCAA, the 1985-86 Bears were busy making a similar run in the nation's other post-season tournament, the NIT. The Bears began by beating Pittsburgh in the first round – the school's first Division I post-season win in their first attempt – and followed that up with a signature fourteen-point victory against Rick Majerus's Marquette squad in the second round.

Hysterically, both Pittsburgh and Marquette had little tape on the Bears – only a worthless "game film" sent to them courtesy of Cleveland State's Mackey. The film was a 27-point Bears loss early in the season that hardly reflected the team they were by the end of the year.

"I had said the greatest thing that could happen would be if Cleveland State sent that film to our NIT opponents," Spoonhour remembers. "We played so bad in that game ... there's no way anyone could tell anything about what we do."

Like Cleveland State in the NCAA tournament, Southwest Missouri State also lost its third post-season game by one point. However, the AMCU's two premier teams had captured the national media's attention and earned the conference some badly needed national attention.

Equally importantly for many of its members, the post-season tournaments brought some cash flow to help their strapped athletic budgets. For UWGB, this was critical. The conference split of the earnings gave UWGB a little over $30,000, much needed income to expand its recruiting efforts.

Both of those squads returned strong in 1986-87, with Cleveland State racking up twenty-five wins, and Southwest Missouri State taking the conference crown with a 28-6 record. This time, it was Southwest Missouri State, with the top scoring defense in the entire country, taking home an at-large NCAA tournament bid and a No. 13 seed. And like the Vikings the year before, the Bears shocked the college basketball world with a first-round upset over No. 4 seed Clemson. Spoonhour's staunch defense limited future Chicago Bulls center Horace Grant, the ACC Player of the Year, to just 16 points, including two points in the second half.

Unfortunately for the Bears, they ran into college basketball royalty in All-American Danny Manning and the Kansas Jayhawks. It took every bit of a monumental 42-point performance by Manning for the Jayhawks to claw their way back from an early Bears advantage, and ultimately pull out a four-point win, 67-63.

Meanwhile, Cleveland State's twenty-five wins were good enough to get an NIT berth. The Vikings also capitalized, winning their first game against Mack McCarthy's Tennessee-Chattanooga by simply running their opponent out of the gym. And like the Bears, Cleveland State's post-season hopes ended in the second round with a two-point home loss to Illinois State.

Nevertheless, as they had the year prior, both programs had gained the conference much-needed national attention, particularly in the NCAA tournament, where the AMCU was the only conference in the country to have two double-digit seeded entrants pull first-round upsets in back-to-back seasons.

Small-time Troubles

In the NCAA, and particularly as a mid-major nobody, the penalties for moral and ethical failures can be catastrophic. Cleveland State found that out the hard way in 1987-88. It started with an NCAA report issued in December 1987 that Kevin Mackey had violated NCAA recruiting rules four years earlier by improperly providing benefits to three foreign recruits (including future NBA star Manute Bol), and further, that athletic officials at Cleveland State had provided false and misleading information during the investigation.

Bol, for his part, stated that while he may have received a plane ticket paid for by Cleveland State, he received nothing else of note. But it was of little consequence that neither Bol nor either of the other two recruits ever suited up for the Vikings. The NCAA slapped the program with a two-year ban on playing in its tournament and a one-year ban from live television appearances.

UWGB's Roger Ripley puts up a shot against Southwest Missouri State as Dean Vander Plas (34) looks on during a 77-65 loss on February 6, 1988. (University of Wisconsin-Green Bay Archives)

Cleveland State's issues were not over. Four months later, it was reported that one of Cleveland State's stars on the 1985-86 Sweet Sixteen team had played as a convicted felon and received free legal counsel that may have violated NCAA rules.

The inquisitions into Mackey's program didn't sit well with many who felt the NCAA was engaged in selective enforcement, a practice with roots going back as far as at least the early 1970s, when the NCAA ran a questionable inquisition into Jerry Tarkanian's Long Beach State program. While ignoring rumors of recruiting improprieties at the country's premier program just down the street, the NCAA opened an investigation that would've put Woodward and Bernstein to shame.

An expose in *Sports Illustrated* on June 10, 1974, laid out the entire vendetta-driven exercise, showing the excessive lengths the NCAA was going through to try and bury a program that had little to hide. The NCAA sent investigators to campus on a regular basis to harass players for hours, then proceeded to broaden the search by talking to family members, friends, high school coaches, teachers, boosters, and even conducting handwriting analysis. The NCAA team asked questions about the program in at least nine different states.

Tarkanian put the NCAA squarely in his crosshairs, writing an opinion piece in a local paper chastising the NCAA for only seeking to punish small schools while avoiding larger infractions by its money-makers. Undeterred, and in spite of thousands of man hours, the NCAA's final report offered little to justify the effort, concluding that Long Beach State would be put on probation for at least three years.

Fifteen years later, when hearing of the penalties levied on Mackey's program in 1987, Tarkanian again took aim, famously saying, "The NCAA is so mad at Kentucky, it's going to give Cleveland State two more years of probation."

Concerns over inequitable treatment aside, the midseason probation announcement against Cleveland State threw the AMCU for a loop. That 1987-88 season would be the conference's first getting an automatic bid into the NCAA tournament, but with Cleveland State as a championship contender and recent history as a guide, the conference realized it could be in a bind.

A year earlier, the Metro Conference had been in a similar situation and suffered a terrible fate. Memphis State – one of the Metro's best – had been put on probation and was banned from NCAA tournament play. Nevertheless, the Metro had allowed the Tigers to play in the conference tournament, believing the NCAA would take the Metro's second-best team if Memphis won it all. The NCAA had no such intention, and when the Tigers did just that, the NCAA left the Metro Conference out in the cold.

The AMCU, with no tournament on the books, was in worse shape, simply hoping that the Vikings would fail to capture the regular-season crown. Thankfully, Spoonhour's Bears won the conference by a single game, capturing the AMCU's first automatic bid. For a second straight year, the Bears received a 13 seed, but this time dropped a four-point, first-round game to UNLV.

Meanwhile, the down-and-out Vikings had put together a quality 22-8 season. Though banned from NCAA tournament play, they faced no such restrictions on playing in the NIT, where they beat Illinois State in the first round before losing to Ohio State in the second round. It marked the third straight year that Cleveland State had succeeded in winning at least one postseason game.

With both teams returning top talent, including the 1987-88 AMCU Player of the Year in Cleveland State's McFadden, the AMCU firmly established itself as one of the top mid-major conferences in the country.

Dick Bennett's Core Principles
Exposure like that generated during the late 1980s runs by Cleveland State and Southwest Missouri State offered a huge opportunity to the

AMCU member institutions in the form of visibility. With that visibility came recognition and the ability to market, sell, and promote.

Bennett was also aware of the trappings that had set back the Cleveland State program. Mirroring his lessons to his players, Bennett committed to avoiding self-inflicted errors in recruiting. To that end, he established a set of core principles, or pillars: humility, passion, unity, servanthood, thankfulness.

His words hit a chord with many of his players, including Vander Plas: "I think as you humble yourself, you get hungry – I think that's what Coach always taught is that, 'Stay humble, stay hungry.' "

Bennett's son, Tony, lived those principles from an early age and carried them with him in his later years of college coaching.

"My father, when he established those, we call them pillars, but are the principles of his program. No one has them all down, but the five pillars, five principles of humility, passion, unity, servanthood, thankfulness. I think when you start recruiting to those pillars, and those things are important, and those things are real, well, those are universal. That means you're going to fit into the community, the town, the city whatever ... no one has them all, no one's perfect, certainly there are mistakes. But I think that's real."

"They really didn't have anything to do with x's and o's. It was more how you carry yourself as a person and as a teammate," comments Grzesk. "I think all of those guys that were on (my) team, and probably the teams before and the couple teams after, all played with a servant's mentality that were willing to sacrifice for the betterment of the team."

Chapter 3

Recruiting the Right Players
(1988-1989)

Saying the deck is stacked against mid-major programs when it comes to recruiting mistakenly suggests they even have a chance to compete for top talent against the power conferences. Nothing could be farther from the truth. McDonald's All-Americans don't go to mid-majors. Seven-footers with an ounce of skill don't go to mid-majors.

The reasons are obvious. Power conference schools have more money, better facilities, deeper alumni foundations, more diverse educational offerings, and in successful programs, a history of grooming players for the professional game. You can't blame a player for taking a rosier path when offered.

Coaches at the mid-major level must excel at finding the right talent to meet their specific needs. They don't have the luxury of picking and choosing from the best players available and setting them loose to play their own game. Rather, mid-majors must recruit lesser-known players who don't quite reach the level of power conference talent. And those players must have skill sets that mesh well with the system they run. On top of that, they must do so with smaller coaching staffs, fewer recruiting resources, and more limited funding, making that deep dive for talent even more challenging.

Recruiting 101

Dick Bennett used his core principles to guide his recruiting, placing considerable weight on a player's moral character in addition to physical attributes and skill set. Unlike many of his counterparts willing to take a chance on a player with questionable morals in view of their potential, Bennett was steadfast in refusing to compromise on that point.

"We really looked for character ... the one (dimension) we'd never shortchange was the mental, the character side," notes Bennett, "We would take character with either of the other dimensions – the physical or the skill side. But we would *never* take the physical or the skill if the character was not there. That was just an iron clad, unwritten rule that I had always followed.

As Tony Bennett recalls, this rule stuck with his father for life.

"When I took over for him at Washington State, his words to me were, 'Whatever you do, you may be able to do it a little quicker if you don't do it this way, but do not take a short cut on character.' "

With character as his North Star and defense as his map, Dick Bennett enjoyed an advantage over many other mid-major coaches – he wasn't looking for the same players they were. He wanted high-character people from winning programs that fit unique roles in his defensive system.

"Coach Bennett didn't have a great reputation as a recruiter, but he knew what would win for him. I mean, he had tough, hard-nosed kids," notes Gary Grzesk. "He knew the type of player that he wanted to recruit and coach, and he knew the type of player he would have success with."

"He always recruits players to *his* system," agrees Ben Johnson. "He has never ever deviated from it, and if he were coaching today, he still would have guys that fit into his system."

"The guys that Coach recruited, he recruited to mesh well with what he was doing," adds Logan Vander Velden (1990-94).

"He was very good at recruiting guys that fit *his* system. Not always the best basketball players," says Scott LeMoine. "It's not always about letting one person shine. You kind of have to do it as a team."

"You can't have four guys who think they're the best player on the team, and that they're going to get all the shots, and that they're going to be the star," explains Eric LeDuc (1989-93). "(It's important) that people acknowledge the fact that, hey, I'm going to play a role. Maybe that means that I'm not going to score the most points, but it also means maybe we're going to win more games than maybe the raw data, the analytics would show."

There was another secret to Bennett's recruiting philosophy – his dedication to the Wisconsin athlete. As a coach with ties to all corners of the state, Bennett was certain he could recruit blue-collar players right in his own backyard. And doing so would allow him to accomplish a few objectives simultaneously. For starters, he could obtain talent without wasting limited resources.

"I had always respected the high schools in the state, and so I felt like we could get enough good players in our state who weren't being recruited by Wisconsin or Marquette, and that is essentially what we did," Bennett says. "Those kids were not recruited by other Division I schools, but they were great kids and they had plenty of skill, and they were willing to do anything we asked them to do, and so it was a perfect population for us to recruit."

In addition to maximizing his limited resources, Bennett knew that recruiting locally brought with it a built-in fan base following their high school stars.

"I wanted as many Fox Valley, Milwaukee – state kids who our fans could identify with," he explains. "I thought that was really important, as opposed to trying to recruit nationally."

"You had a lot of Wisconsin people. You had a lot of people that had good careers in high school and had, I'm not going to say followings, but

Mike Karisny, who played his high school basketball half an hour away, was a key early recruit for Dick Bennett. He's shown here in a 1989 game against Western Illinois. (University of Wisconsin-Green Bay Archives)

people followed them," points out LeDuc, a native of Burlington, Wisconsin. "People knew who they were. They played in state tournaments, they made all-state teams."

Mike Karisny, who played his prep ball thirty minutes away in Menasha, Wisconsin, agrees. "Our roster was littered with people who had at least fan bases that would come from Pulaski and from Franklin and from Menasha and Appleton to see their local guys play," Karisny says. "I don't want to overstate this, but that definitely had a feeling of importance and it was a part of why the revolution occurred. That was kind of special to have that many from northeast Wisconsin."

Finally, whether it was a product of similar backgrounds or the uniqueness of Wisconsin, recruiting players locally gave the team built-in commonalities that helped promote team chemistry.

"You had a lot of guys that had kind of similar basketball backgrounds, so it was easy to fit in," LeDuc says. "The teams that were successful, whether it was because people were from a common background or you could very quickly get them to buy into a sense of community once they were on the team."

Even those who joined the Phoenix family from south of the state border quickly fit in.

"Being an Illinois guy, Wisconsin's just – people don't always understand – Wisconsin's way of life is just different, it's cool," comments LeMoine. "It's relaxed; it's everybody knows each other; it's something that I really liked and appreciated."

All of this helped Bennett narrow his recruiting list, and once he zeroed in, his own recruiting style came into the equation. For one thing, it meant appealing to the players' families.

"Coach Bennett really recruited my parents," remembers Dean Vander Plas, a native of Oostburg, Wisconsin. "My mom and dad really liked what Coach was about and thought that I would become a better man if I went and played for him. So they were all in, too, when Coach said, 'Hey, let's do this.'"

Bennett also had his stable of selling points.

"We weren't within the city, so we sold them on, 'You will really become close. This is a family.' Of course, we sold them on the academics – you always do that – we always had them meet people who loved our program, but were excellent educators. We always took them to the arena. We said, 'Here's where you'll practice (the on-campus Phoenix Sports Center), but now you're going to play downtown in the arena.' They liked that, of course."

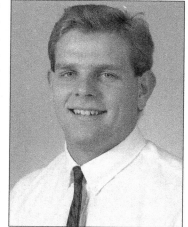

Dean Vander Plas played his prep ball at Oostburg High School, about an hour from Green Bay. (University of Wisconsin-Green Bay Archives)

Cold winters? Lack of night life? Other challenges of Green Bay?

"I tried not to deal with the negatives," Bennett says. "I tried to sell everything about our program as a positive. If somebody said the way we played was a negative, I made sure when I was done with that kid, he saw it as a positive. When they'd say, 'Look, they don't even play on campus,' I would sell the notion, 'Yeah, but we play down by Lambeau Field.'"

Bennett was unafraid to leverage his existing group of high-character players to help his efforts.

"Every year the new recruits came in, we were a huge part of showing them around and getting to know them, and kind of passing things on," LeMoine says. "That was just kind of what you did. It was just like, 'Yeah, come on in.'"

The result?

"We got guys that were a whole lot better than people realized," beams a proud Bennett. "We could find those hidden gems that others would maybe say, 'Well, maybe this guy's not a highlight tape – he doesn't dunk or he doesn't fly up and down.' But we saw soundness and the ability to handle the basketball."

The 1988-89 Team – Three Years in the Making

By 1988-89, Bennett's fourth full season at UWGB, he finally had the opportunity to coach a roster nearly entirely composed of players he had recruited. By design, most of his returning talent was Wisconsin kids.

The exception were the seniors who were freshmen on the 1985-86 team that went 5-23 in Bennett's first season. Three of the four – big man Pat Taphorn, and forwards Adrian Bolding and Bernie Tompa – were from Illinois, while guard Marquise Hines was from Whitefish Bay, Wisconsin.

Junior Roger Ripley, a 6-9 center from nearby Pulaski and the younger brother of Ron Ripley, a UWGB legend from Dave Buss's best teams, was also a freshman during Bennett's first year. But because of a season-ending injury four games into the 1986-87 season, Ripley was able to obtain a medical redshirt and was only entering his junior year of eligibility in 1988-89.

Joining Ripley in the junior class were two players Bennett had recruited during his second season. Dan Oberbrunner, a 6-4 forward from Franklin (Wisconsin) High School, had largely been relegated to the bench his first two seasons with the Phoenix. Meanwhile, Karisny, a 6-2 guard from St. Mary Central High School in Menasha, had impressed with his ability to score, making over 44% of his shots from beyond the three-point line.

A career with the Phoenix almost never was for Karisny. He had played poorly in a high school all-star game as a senior, prompting Bennett to pass. But in a tale told many times during the Bennett era, fate intervened and gave Karisny a second chance.

For Karisny, that fate was in the form of a chance meeting with Tony Bennett later that summer.

"(Tony) said, 'If you want to, come up and play pickup ball. We're going to play at GB, and we've got a couple guys coming in like Terry Porter," Karisny recalls. "So I came up and we played some pick-up. Coach Bennett, (after the pick-up game) walked out and he said, 'I made a big mistake, I need to offer you a scholarship.' "

The 1988-89 team also had two sophomores on the roster from drastically different backgrounds. Vander Plas was a guy who looked more likely to put on pads and a helmet than lace up his basketball shoes. The 6-4 forward had been getting looks from Big Ten teams to play football.

"Football is what I'm built to do, and probably what my better sport was," Vander Plas says, adding that his real passion was basketball. "I've always just loved the game. And so when Coach said, 'You mind if we pay for your college education and you come here and play the game of basketball?' I thought, 'That's a pretty good deal!' "

Vander Plas would go on to make basketball a major part of his life, coaching the Ripon High School boys for twenty-one years. His youngest child, Bennett (Ben), was a four-year player and helped lead underdog Ohio University to an NCAA tournament upset over Tony Bennett's Virginia squad in 2021.

UWGB's second sophomore, Chris Yates, was one of Bennett's rare out-of-state finds, and perhaps the best athlete Bennett had landed to-date. A 6-3 guard from Berrien Springs, Michigan, Yates had loads of athletic ability and scoring potential, but also had poor grades and a low ACT score. Bennett stayed faithful while Yates raised his grades and test scores, and once eligible, Yates signed with the Phoenix.

Bennett's first three recruiting classes built on each other and he had continued to adjust his sights higher. For his fourth recruiting class, Bennett sought a blockbuster class to stamp his mark on the program.

One Big Recruiting Class

Bennett had a plan from the first day he took over at UWGB – build toward a large, high-quality recruiting class that he could mold into a cohesive, defensive juggernaut over the next four to five years. His vision required hitting a home run in recruiting at least once.

"Every place I went, I've always recruited one large blue-chip class," notes Bennett. "You can't do it your first year, because you get the job usually in April. It's too late, so you get good people to fill in. But then the second year or the third year, you begin working on this group of sophomores or juniors in high school, and you bring them in. And that's what I did at Green Bay."

As he had the previous two years, Bennett tasked his two assistant coaches, Mike Heideman and Steve Swan, with finding talented high school players flying under the radar – those with good ability, but modest junior seasons. His goal? Lock the best high school talent he could find by fall of 1987, using the early signing period to secure his target high school seniors.

By the beginning of that 1987 summer, the Phoenix staff had identified four high-quality targets.

Without question, the least-surprising and most-talented recruit of the class was Dick's son, Tony. A lightning-quick, sharp-shooting lefty point guard at Green Bay Preble High School, Tony appeared to have unlimited shooting range. During his junior season in 1986-87, he averaged 21 points per game and was named second team all-state by the UPI.

Keith Wall, his high school coach, had an old-school style that mirrored that of Tony's father. In fact, Wall had highly respected the elder Bennett for years.

"(Coach Wall) was one of my favorites, and still is," Tony recalls fondly. "He would never let me dribble between my legs when I played for him. And he always made me jump off of two feet. We used to get in these wars, and I mean I knew him ever since I was a little kid. Sometimes I'd do it on purpose just to make him mad, but it was always good."

Tony Bennett was the most polished basketball player UWGB had ever recruited, and between his junior and senior year, he began to become the most well-known. Tony's status reached new heights when he was invited to play in the nationally recognized B/C All-Stars Basketball Camp in Rensselaer, Indiana, for five days in June of 1987. The all-star exhibition masquerading as a "camp" brought in the nation's top high school talent, along with plenty of big-time coaches with scholarships to offer. With guys like Bobby Knight (Indiana), Gene Keady (Purdue), and Lou Henson (Illinois) hanging out in the stands, it was clear this was no casual week of fundamentals development – this was the big-time.

While future NBA star Shawn Kemp, introduced to the camp as "the best player in America," took home top honors in the slam dunk competition, Tony found a way to carve a niche, taking second place out of around 200 contestants in the three-point shooting competition.

For Dick, recruiting Tony was inevitable. He checked all the boxes.

"He was pretty highly recruited," remembers Ben Johnson, Tony's childhood friend from growing up in Stevens Point. "But then, a lot of people didn't even really recruit him because they just figured, 'Hey, he's going to go play for his dad.' "

"It was very strange, very unique," Tony says. "Deep down inside, I knew I wanted to probably play for my father and play for Green Bay, but I wanted to see, how high can I get recruited? I wanted to at least take a visit and check this out. And so that was always kind of rumbling around."

Johnson was also a high-character, known commodity. The rock-solid, 6-2 guard from Stevens Point had a long history with the Bennetts that started when his family moved from Minnesota to Wisconsin in 1981.

"I was in seventh grade and met Tony the first day of school," Johnson says. "Tony, me, and a bunch of other childhood friends, we all loved basketball and our relationship grew from there."

Johnson was a regular at Dick Bennett's summer camps, and the coach developed an affinity for his tenacity, heart, and work ethic. It was at one of those camps, when Johnson was just thirteen years old, that the coach made a permanent impression on his future recruit.

"He pulled me aside and said, 'Ben, if you're really willing to work hard, you can be something,' " Johnson recalls. "I'll never forget that. That was kind of the first time he had spoken to me on just kind of a different level to other players. So I think from that moment on – I'm like twelve or thirteen years old – and I'm like, yeah, I was going to go play for that guy no matter where he was."

As with Tony, the smart money was on Johnson signing with Green Bay.

Next on Dick Bennett's wish list was Dean Rondorf, a lanky 6-7 forward from West Bend East High School in southeast Wisconsin who Steve Swan had found at a big man's camp in Western Michigan. Rondorf, a guard when he started playing in high school, grew six inches between his freshman and sophomore seasons. With the skill set and late growth, projections were that he could be a scoring threat down the road. But the competition for his talents was heated.

"Going into my senior year, I started getting recruited by a bunch of different programs," notes Rondorf. "Evansville University, Western Illinois, Eastern Illinois – so it was exciting."

Fourth on Bennett's wish list was LeMoine, a true big man from Rockford, Illinois, and a natural fit for Bennett's defense. LeMoine was a team-oriented, 6-9 rim-protector who, once he got stronger, could be a solid contributor for the team.

As a junior, LeMoine set his high school team's record for blocked shots in a season at 104, all while averaging 10.3 ppg and seven rebounds per game. His stock took off during the summer of 1987 as he made the camp circuit. It began with LeMoine's stellar performance at the Blue Chips Camp in Shepherdsville, Kentucky, where he was named to the all-tournament team.

"I played Shawn Kemp one game, held him to like four points, and that was a huge game for me," recalls LeMoine. "I think that's one of the places where I got a lot of attention was after that game."

Indeed, that stop alone generated interest from a number of programs including Wichita State, Bradley, Davidson, UT-San Antonia, Air Force, and Navy.

Heideman found LeMoine at the start, but once Bennett saw him play, the coach was hooked.

"Where we got sold on him was at the (Blue Chips) big-man's camp against Kemp," Bennett says. "Of all the kids (Kemp) went against, LeMoine played him the smartest. He frustrated him a little with his smarts."

Flawless Execution

In lieu of home visits, Bennett invited all four of his targets and their parents to a joint campus visit in the fall of 1987.

"We put all the parents and kids together, and they hit it off wonderfully," Bennett says. "I treated (Tony's) mother just like another parent. She seemed to enjoy it."

Unconventional as it was, the weekend was a slam dunk.

"They brought us in on a Friday evening, and we sat on campus and had a dinner with our families," Rondorf explains. "My mom and dad were there, and of course Dick and Mrs. Bennett – Anne – and then Ben's parents and Scott's parents, and so it was kind of neat. We did a bunch of things as a family on Saturday, and then again, our parents did some things. That was one of the main factors for me is that they really just got our whole families involved."

LeMoine agrees. "I don't even know if that would work nowadays or not, but that family atmosphere, that was so cool, and having all of us together."

Convinced of their character and fit, Bennett offered all four scholarships during the early signing period of 1987. It was an objective he viewed as critical to his recruiting success, stating, "I don't feel we could recruit these guys in the spring. It was so critical that we beat people to the punch."

LeMoine was the first to declare his intention to join UWGB.

"Green Bay was my first and only visit," he says. "After that weekend, I called every coach back and said, 'I'm done. I got it. I know where I'm going.'"

Johnson and Rondorf quickly followed LeMoine's lead.

Then, with Tony's decision still looming, UWGB's recruiting efforts took an unexpectedly fortuitous turn. A fifth target, Larry Hill from De La Salle High School in Chicago, had surprisingly emerged around the same time as a realistic candidate.

Measuring in at 6-7, Hill had broad shoulders and exceptionally long arms, with unparalleled leaping ability. As a junior and backing up all-state forward and Northern Illinois recruit Brian Banks, Hill averaged a meager five points and four boards per game. Still, he was ranked as one of Chicago's top twenty players going into his senior year.

While he had been getting attention from high-quality mid-major programs like Northern Iowa and Northern Illinois, UWGB had emerged as a front-runner. Offering Hill a scholarship was a no-brainer for Bennett, and on October 28, 1987, Hill became the fourth recruit to commit to UWGB. As Rondorf discovered in an all-star game in Dubuque, Hill's talent was apparent.

"Once I saw him play, I was like, 'Man, this is great. This is going to be fun.'"

With a perfect four-for-four start to the recruiting season, Dick put the pressure on Tony to commit as only a father can.

"My dad kind of said, 'Listen, you know, four other guys have committed, you've been on your visit, you know about this.'" Tony recalls. "He's like, 'You've got until the weekend, and if you don't decide you're coming, then I'm going to pull the scholarship off the table. And you know, if it's there, it's there. And if it's not, it's not and you can go from there.' I was so mad that he said that to me. And it was that night he told me that I

scored like 46 or 44 in that game, and after every basket, I would just glare at my dad like, 'Go ahead, you pull that off!'"

The family showdown ran its course, and by the end of the weekend, Tony's inevitable commitment followed, giving Dick Bennett a clean sweep in recruiting.

"He was the last one to sign and come in, but he was involved heavily in the recruitment of each of those kids," notes Dick. "I think he was just teasing me, I don't really know, but he was very involved in the recruitment."

"Obviously, everybody knew Tony was going," LeMoine says. "He was trying to be like, 'Oh, I'm still looking at other schools.' We're like, 'No, you're going to go play with your dad, it's okay.'"

"I wanted to help Green

Dick Bennett poses in his office wearing a Green Bay Preble High School basketball sweater during the time his son, Tony, starred for the Hornets. (University of Wisconsin-Green Bay Archives)

Bay become a great team and play and win a conference tournament, and get to the NCAA tournament and try and advance, and I wanted to have a chance to try to see if I could play after in the NBA," Tony says. "I thought this was my best opportunity."

Paternal pressure aside, Tony was happy to have placed his future in his father's hands.

"Playing for my father, I knew he thought I had something in me that could touch greatness as a player and I knew I could trust him. And I knew he was not going to hold back – he was going to push me and challenge me."

Dick Bennett had established his first blue-chip class – a group of players that would help build a culture of success at Green Bay.

Tony Bennett's freshman photo in 1988. (University of Wisconsin-Green Bay Archives)

"We kind of had this hot-shot recruiting class for Green Bay," comments Johnson. "Tony was Mr. Basketball in Wisconsin and we had a huge recruiting class our freshman year."

Addressing the media after Tony's commitment, Dick Bennett beamed at his program's good fortune.

"This is just terrific. Talk about a turnaround in terms of recruiting. We had hoped for the majority, but to hit on all five ... We had a huge list of possibilities, but chose the five best for us."

Not to be lost in the shuffle, UWGB added a final piece to the recruiting class in the spring of 1988. The staff had been monitoring Chicago native Tony Ciaravino, a two-sport star (baseball and basketball) and teammate of Hill's at De La Salle. On the basketball court, Ciaravino was considered a tough-nosed, gritty guard, and received attention from other mid-major schools including UTEP and UC-Irvine. On the diamond, Ciaravino was receiving attention from Illinois State and was considered a potential MLB draft prospect. However, it was Green Bay where Ciaravino felt most at home, and he signed with Bennett in the spring of 1988.

It would be Bennett's finest class ever, and the coach was hardly able to contain his enthusiasm: "I just have a very good feeling about those kids. Before they're done at this institution, I think they're going to do something amazing."

NIT or Bust

Bennett was itching to test his talented roster, and it started in the 1988 offseason, where he pushed his players to their limits.

"We didn't get to go home in the summer, Vander Plas says. "We stayed up there and worked out. They didn't have the limitations on how much you could be in the gym that they do now. I'll say that was probably the biggest adjustment."

Once summer turned to fall, Bennett could hardly contain himself. He broke his own philosophy of staying focused on what's in front of you. Instead, for the first and only time in his UWGB career, the coach opted to put the goal of making a postseason on the table. Uncharacteristically, he even went so far as to give his players practice shorts that had "NIT" printed on them.

"That was our goal," recalls LeMoine. "Coach had it put on our shorts. We were going to make that NIT tournament, at least. That was the minimum."

"That was the only year that I was there that we talked about a postseason tournament," adds Vander Plas. "We weren't going to settle for anything but the NIT. But we were so young."

Gone were the top three scorers from the 1987-88 team that had gone 18-9. The trio of Richard Sims, Frank Nardi, and Michael Connors had accounted for 53% of the team's total points, but more importantly, had been mentors and leaders for the young players.

"I remember watching Richard Sims, Frank Nardi, Roger Ripley, Karisny," Tony Bennett says. "You could feel them getting better and better. And I was like, 'Okay, this is great.' "

"Richard (Sims) was probably the best basketball player I had ever played with," comments Vander Plas. "His athleticism, you know, he was just smooth. He was kind. He didn't have to be, because you're all competing for playing time and stuff like that, but he was very kind."

Replacing the void were the six freshman, five of whom Bennett opted to keep on the active roster. Only the still-maturing Rondorf was set to redshirt.

Searching for the Formula

The 1988-89 Fighting Phoenix had the look of something new. Fresh faces brimming with confidence complemented the familiar cast members who had demonstrated ascending potential. It was the start of a new era, a basketball revolution, in Green Bay.

And yet, as the season unfolded, the unusual mix of old and new also generated diverging outlooks and experiences. Bennett's message of servanthood existed, but it had not yet taken full hold of the team. And it showed when the issue of playing time arose.

"We were having to balance out a lot of players who felt they were good enough, and unfortunately, you can only play five," Karisny says. "We had ten, twelve guys who probably legitimately felt they should be playing."

To the disappointment of its growing fan base, this odd confluence of unaligned goals and expectations plagued the Phoenix. Manifesting itself in the form of ever-changing lineups and substitutions, Bennett appeared frustrated early in the season as the team looked to develop an identity.

In spite of a 3-0 start including two dominating victories, Bennett used three different lineups. He shuffled seniors Bolding, Tompa and Taphorn, junior Ripley, and freshman Johnson at the forward positions, while juniors Oberbrunner and Karisny each had a shot as starting guards. The only constant through three games was his son, Tony.

Part of Bennett's uneasiness was related to the inferior competition the

Phoenix had faced. Northern Illinois represented the only Division I school of the bunch, and while the Huskies would quickly improve in the coming years, the 1988-89 squad was sub-par and would finish 11-17.

That all changed in game four, which marked the start of grueling seven-game stretch where the Phoenix would face three teams that would make the NCAA tournament in 1989. Bennett knew this nonconference run would ultimately prove whether this team could live up to their NIT hype.

It began on December 5, 1988, at Evansville against one of those three future tournament teams. The Purple Aces, an NIT team in 1988, were a strong Midwestern Collegiate Conference team that routinely drew 10,000-plus fans for its home games.

Bennett gave his athletic freshman Larry Hill a start at forward, but he was overmatched and unable to control the glass. Evansville outrebounded UWGB 40-21, and though Tony Bennett poured in 26 points on 10-of-16 shooting, it was not enough. The Phoenix dropped to 3-1 with a 68-60 loss.

Five days later, the Phoenix slipped again, this time in painful fashion at home against Central Michigan. Superstar Dan Majerle had moved on to the NBA, but his brother, Jeff, helped the Chippewas mount a monstrous 20-point comeback at the Brown County Arena. Majerle helped Central Michigan finally take the lead for the first time on his jumper with twenty-five seconds left. A Tony Bennett turnover on the next possession ended UWGB's night, as Central Michigan secured the win after trailing for more than thirty-nine minutes.

It was a devastating loss for the Phoenix, but not unappreciated by the Chippewas. Their head coach, Charles Coles, noted in his post-game remarks: "You don't come back on Bennett. Bennett's a legend. When you come back on Green Bay, you cherish it."

Five games in, Bennett had used five different starting lineups and started eleven different players. The only consistent thread was one of the blue-chippers from his big class, Tony Bennett, who was leading the team averaging 18.6 ppg.

Like it or not, the Evansville and Central Michigan games had brought focus to the Phoenix's unflattering persona – they were an immature roster, dotted with talent but lacking the understanding of how to win. Bennett needed to regain his team's focus and return to the fundamentals that had made him successful throughout his career. How did he do it?

"Coach took our (NIT) shorts away, and we went back to basics," remembers Vander Plas. "That was it for talking about the postseason. Coach just went back to, 'Let's get better every day.' "

Peak and Valley

A two-week hiatus for finals helped the Phoenix forget its previous two losses, and the team responded by easily disposing of a weak Detroit Mercy team right before Christmas, bringing the team's record to 4-2.

Bennett's sixth starting lineup in as many games – with freshmen Tony Bennett and Johnson teaming up with senior forwards Bolding, Tompa, and Taphorn – had finally quenched the coach's thirst for success. Bennett

Athletic power forward Roger Ripley, a graduate of Pulaski High School a short drive from the Brown County Arena, dunks during the Phoenix's 86-61 victory over Ferris State on December 3, 1988. (University of Wisconsin-Green Bay Archives)

repeated a lineup for the first time when his team took the court against its toughest competition to date – a 6-2 Colorado State team coached by the legendary Boyd Grant. The Rams, led by senior forward Pat Durham, featured a 2-3 zone defense and were the favorites to win the Western Athletic Conference.

The game's importance was not lost on the Phoenix's fans, who showed up in droves with more than 5,600 packing the Brown County Veteran's Memorial Arena. They would not be disappointed.

In a battle of two of the best defensive teams in the country, UWGB took an early lead, and to the raucous crowd's delight, never relinquished it. Neither team shot the ball well (UWGB shot just 38%), but Tony Bennett played exceptionally well, scoring 23 points on 9-of-14 shooting and adding six assists. Grant was complimentary of Tony after the game: "He's a first-class player, there isn't any doubt. If the guy was 6-3, they'd already be trying to draft him in the NBA."

Meanwhile, the big men for the Phoenix excelled on the glass, grabbing seventeen offensive rebounds and limiting the Rams to their lowest scoring output since 1985. The combination resulted in a convincing 58-43 Phoenix win.

It wasn't quite a blockbuster, but certainly a measuring-stick victory against a top-quality mid-major. And yet, the Rocky Mountain high was short-lived. Two days later, UWGB traveled to Idaho to play in Boise State's Albertsons Holiday Classic before the New Year. Though little known nationally, the tournament was a big deal to the players.

UWGB easily disposed of Stephen F. Austin in the tournament's opener behind one of the best games of Adrian Bolding's career. The senior went 4-of-6 from the field and 5-of-5 from the line to finish with 14 points, setting up the Phoenix against the hosts in the championship.

The Broncos were the reigning Big Sky Champions and carried the talents of Wilson Foster and future NBA guard Chris Childs. But more important than the roster, the Broncos simply did not lose at the BSU Pavilion, having amassed a staggering 29-3 record over the previous two and a half seasons.

Like a pesky virus that keeps coming back, the inexperience of the Phoenix reared its ugly head yet again. UWGB did stay close to one of the premier mid-major programs most of the way, but in a story that would be repeated often during that 1988-89 season, the Phoenix simply lacked the maturity to finish.

Bennett's squad battled all the way back from a double-digit halftime deficit, only to come up just short, losing 68-66. Though Tony Bennett was named to the All-Tournament Team, the loss ended the Phoenix's three-game winning streak and dropped its record to 6-3.

The Ultimate Offense vs. the Ultimate Defense

"It was the wildest game ever. As a player, as a fan, it probably had everything you'd want, but it was craziness."

That's how Ben Johnson described UWGB's New Year's bash at Loyola Marymount on January 2, 1989.

The Lions, with their unique philosophy and transcendental talent, were squarely in the midst of one of the great runs in college basketball history. Loyola Marymount's coach, Paul Westhead, previously coached an L.A. Lakers team that included Kareem Abdul-Jabbar and rookie Magic Johnson. Westhead's Lakers won the NBA title in 1980 and all seemed well in the world. That is, until Westhead and Magic butted heads the following season. By 1981-82, Lakers management had canned Westhead in favor of Pat Reilly.

Westhead took over the Loyola Marymount program in 1985-86 and immediately implemented a run-and-gun style of play that, in spite of its relative simplicity, was something the college basketball world had never seen. In principle, Westhead believed in being the best conditioned team in the country, hoping to run his opponents out of the gym. His teams sprinted the floor at every opportunity and sought quick shots, scoring in bunches while tiring out nearly everyone they faced.

In Westhead's second year, he successfully convinced two USC freshmen, Bo Kimble and Hank Gathers, to transfer to Loyola Marymount. Together, Westhead, Kimble, and Gathers formed a core that would transform the Lions and transfix the college basketball world for the next three seasons.

Loyola Marymount had spent the last month of the previous 1987-88 season ranked in the top 25, thanks to a massive twenty-three-game winning streak that ended with a second-round NCAA tournament loss to Dean Smith's North Carolina Tar Heels. By 1988-89, Gathers and Kimble were both NBA top prospects, and to no one's surprise, the Lions led the NCAA in scoring in 1987-88 (110 ppg), 1988-89 (112 ppg), and 1989-90 (122.4), the last of which still stands as the NCAA record. Gathers led the country in scoring in the 1988-89 season, averaging 32.7 ppg, while Kimble would one-up him the following year with 35.3 ppg. Gathers, in particular, seemed like a nightmare with legs.

"Hank was super-athletic and he was nasty, like he was a talker," comments Vander Plas, who was pegged with guarding Gathers much of the game. "He just had a knack for playing above everybody else. And he knew exactly when that ball was going to go up. Boxing him out was a nightmare."

Everything about these Loyola Marymount teams ran counter to Bennett's philosophy, and Bennett knew as much when he scheduled the game.

"Coach Bennett always did stuff like that to try and test his system, so he knew it would be a track meet," explains Johnson. "At that point in time, we didn't play the Pack (defense) – we were playing that pressure, Stevens Point on-line, up-line defense."

Nevertheless, both coaches were defensive in their pre-game comments.

"To have a relentless, non-stop running game you, as a coach, must give up some of your control. Therein lies why coaches are fearful of it," poked Westhead. "As a group, we feel it is our job to be under control. We must control everything from what they eat in the pre-game meal to what out-of-bounds play to call, to whether you can play with your shirt in or out. We leave nothing to chance."

While Westhead indirectly jabbed, Bennett was uncharacteristically direct.

"We try to give players enough freedom and style where they can play. But moving up and down the court with one or no passes is not the way the game was designed to be played," Bennett noted. "It might be fun to watch and play, but I don't know if it's optimum. A lot of people think passing, off-the-ball movement, and team defense are part of the game."

Bennett had reason to be optimistic. The two clubs had met the year before in Green Bay, and though the Phoenix had been defeated 70-67, UWGB had succeeded in slowing down Westhead's offense, holding the Lions to their second-lowest scoring output that season. Bennett knew the formula to keep his team in the game.

"Their whole defense was predicated on pressure, trying to get you to go fast and take a quick shot," Bennett noted. "We broke their pressure, but we did not fall into the trap of just taking it down and scoring immediately. If it was really an easy layup or something, we took it, but then we would set up and rotate the ball."

Playing the top prospects in the nation on their home court in California was the team's first Hollywood experience, and the players relished the big-city lights.

"We go out and play the big bad Loyola Marymount, and I'll never forget, in warmup lines, they played the song, *I Love LA*," recalls Tony. "It was just one of those moments. We're like, 'Look at us. We're college kids, we're out in LA, and they're playing this song and here we are playing!' It was the coolest thing."

Once the game started, it appeared the Lions' frenetic pace would overpower the Phoenix.

"They had all sorts of driving lines and dunks and things like that, and we couldn't get back enough," Johnson says. "They're hitting threes in transition, and of course Coach is going crazy."

To those familiar with the Phoenix's style, the first twenty minutes almost seemed to be in fast-forward. Down 53-40 at the half, Bennett laid into his team.

"All you can hear down the hall is (Bennett shouting to his staff), 'These guys refuse to lose the weight. They refuse to get in shape! If I've told them once, I've told them a million times, they refuse to lose the weight!' And all of the sudden we look up, and two of the players are crying," Johnson says. "He's screaming this from down the hallway. He's not even in the same room as the guys. Coach Bennett had a magical way of getting his points across."

For some, these tactics could've been detrimental, but Bennett knew the make-up of his squad. His players responded and, as directed, began controlling the pace with their deliberate, half-court game. The slower style also invited more physicality, which led to high emotions.

"The second half, it's a bloodbath, there's bodies everywhere," states Johnson. "We're getting screwed by the officials like we knew we would."

But the strategy was paying off and UWGB fought all the way back, taking a one-point lead at 67-66 with under nine minutes to play in the game. From there, the game would remain tight.

Gathers lived up to his billing and scored 33 points on 14-of-18 shooting despite Vander Plas's best efforts. But UWGB's fab freshman, Tony Bennett, delivered a career performance. The younger Bennett connected on 16 of 20 field goals, including 7 of 8 on three-point attempts, and finished with a career-high 41 points to go with five assists.

"They let you get a lot of pretty good rhythm threes. They just want you to fire it up," Tony recalls. "It was probably one of the easier 40-point games you'd score."

Gathers and Tony Bennett duked it out, but as the final minutes ticked away, the officials decided the game's outcome. First, with the Phoenix down by two and less than a minute to play, the officials whistled the UWGB star for his fifth foul – his second call in less than two minutes.

"They had their own referees from their league, and they called two ridiculous fouls on Tony and fouled him out of the game," remembers Dick Bennett.

"The ref fouled him out," comments LeMoine. "We just straight up got hosed on the foul they called on Tony to get him out of the game."

And yet, a Vander Plas layup with less than ten seconds left tied the game 83-83. But on what would become the last Lions' possession of the game, Enoch Simmons drove the lane and the officials again blew the whistle against Green Bay, tacking senior Marquis Hines with a foul and giving Loyola Marymount two free throws with just two seconds remaining.

"It was the most delayed whistle I've ever seen in my life," says LeMoine. "You talk about a team that was America's Cinderella, they did not want anyone to beat them. They were loving the whole up-and-down."

Simmons hit the free throws and the Lions won the game. Karisny summed up the sour taste: "We went there and got beat on a phantom call."

If the players were mad, it was nothing when compared to Dick Bennett. The head coach quite literally lost it at the end of the game.

"I was so upset at that time that I chased the officials off the floor," he admits.

As the officials scrambled out the door, the elder Bennett tossed a chair in their direction, prompting his players to jump in.

"Coach Bennett takes off after the refs," Johnson describes. "Tony and I look at each other and we're like, 'Let's go get him,' and we chase Dick down!"

"My dad, he was so mad, and you know his fiery Italian side got into him. He chased down the officials and he was barking at them as they were running into the locker room," says Tony. "In the handshake line, one of those players, I think it was (Jeff) Fryer, was like, 'Hey man,' he goes, 'you're a really good player, but your dad is nuts!' "

"I think there was a picture in the paper the next day. Somebody holding onto him, like yelling at the official. I think Vander Plas was holding him," recalls LeMoine. "Yeah, he was a little hot."

Slightly more composed after the game, Bennett tried to explain his frustration. "I'm not proud of my actions tonight, but you have to understand we came off a similar situation in the game against Boise State. I wish officials would take their jobs as seriously as the players do. I would like the kids on the floor to be able to decide the outcome of the game."

But like his halftime tirade, the coach's emotions rubbed off on the team.

"That's where you see again Coach Bennett's passion for winning and fighting for his kids and fighting for his team," Johnson says. "It was good stuff. He never disappointed that way. You knew he was fighting for you."

The win helped right the ship for Loyola Marymount, and the Lions went on to win the PCAA conference tournament and earn the right to play in the NCAA tournament for the second straight year. The following year (1989-90), Loyola Marymount would have the school's most memorable season ever, spending more than half the year in the top 25. Tragedy would strike late in the year, however, when Gathers passed away after collapsing on the court from an irregular heartbeat during the conference tournament. It was the second time he had collapsed that season. Kimble and the rest of team carried forward to make a magical run to the Elite Eight in the NCAA tournament.

For the Phoenix, the game served as a moral victory, if not an actual one. UWGB had succeeded in dictating tempo in the second half and held the talented Lions in check.

"That was half of what they were used to scoring, and we had them," Vander Plas states. "We just couldn't quite close the deal on the road."

"They wanted to just get the ball out of the net and go, but we always got back and made them set up," explains Dick Bennett. "We didn't run and gun, and we didn't let them do the same."

The game also spotlighted Tony Bennett. An Italian league scout approached Dick Bennett afterwards and inquired about Tony's willingness to play professionally overseas. Tony was of special interest given his family's Italian heritage, which may have allowed the team to use him without utilizing a valuable foreign player roster spot.

"It was a good amount of money. I think it was a hundred thousand, which at that time seemed like a lot," Dick Bennett says. "It was not really a hard decision, either for him or me. He was going to stay in college."

"I remember someone came up (to my dad) and said, 'I think your son has a chance to maybe play professionally after.' I remember that got back to me," Tony says. "I didn't pay too much (attention). I felt like, hey, you know we hadn't played anybody big time yet. But I was like, 'I think I can hang.'"

It wouldn't be the last time a professional team gave Tony Bennett a hard press.

AMCU Nightmare

The Phoenix shook off the loss three days later, securing a 33-point win against Chicago State on January 5, 1989, and improving to 7-4 entering conference play. It had been a bumpy ride, but the Phoenix maintained the dream of making a postseason if it could maneuver through its conference schedule.

Dick Bennett publicly praised his team's cohesiveness, though he was still searching for a steady lineup. Outside of Tony Bennett, who was second in the conference in scoring with 21.8 ppg, only Karisny was averaging more than 10 points per game. The coach's hope was riding on the team's inherent depth – a whopping ten players on the team were averaging more than ten minutes per game, including three of his freshmen – Tony Bennett, Johnson, and Hill.

Entering the conference schedule, experts predicted UWGB to finish in the top four of the AMCU. Sitting at the top was Northern Iowa, which turned some heads with an 8-3 non-conference record. Next, and more expected, was Southwest Missouri State, which had racked up a 7-5 non-conference record and had the coaching, experience, and horses to get to its third straight NCAA tournament.

Rounding out the top four conference contenders was an entirely unheralded entry: Bob Hallberg's UIC Flames, who had rebounded from a dreadful 8-20 season in 1987-88 to finish the 1988-89 nonconference at 7-5, with quality wins over Butler, Loyola, Illinois State, and Creighton.

Outside of the top four, only Cleveland State seemed capable of seriously challenging any of the con-

Ben Johnson (23) puts in a layup during UWGB's 66-65 loss to Illinois-Chicago on January 21, 1989. (University of Wisconsin-Green Bay Archives)

ference's top teams, even though injuries and transfers had decimated the Vikings. The remaining schools – Western Illinois, Eastern Illinois, and Valparaiso – all were destined for the bottom half of the conference.

Asked and Answered

Two questions loomed large as UWGB entered conference play. First, could this team learn how to finish games? And second, was this group ready to challenge the conference elites, like Southwest Missouri State and Northern Iowa?

The unfortunate answer to the first question came much too quickly. UWGB started the conference slate with a three-game losing streak that included a two-point overtime home defeat against Cleveland State and a one-point home loss to UIC. Both games saw the Phoenix hold significant leads, only to give them away down the stretch. Sandwiched between those two was a gut-punch 63-49 loss at lowly Valparaiso – a Crusaders team that would finish the year with just ten wins.

Worse yet, after a gimme win against UW-Parkside (an NAIA school), the Phoenix lost a mid-January, nonconference contest to Wright State in broken-record fashion. The Raiders, an independent school entering its second year of Division I, overcame a halftime deficit to down Bennett's club, 77-72.

Of the four losses, Cleveland State may have been the hardest, at least for Tony Bennett.

"I remember my dad just wearing me out, kind of saying, 'You don't belong at this level. You know those are real players, you're more of a Division III player, you can't handle it,' " Tony says. "He knew what fired me up. He's like, 'You can't play; you can't play.' So that was just marked in my mind that week in practice."

The only positive from the stretch was the growth of UWGB's sole sophomore, Vander Plas. Against UIC, Vander Plas had made the Flames look foolish with a quick first step and surprising mobility, netting 14 points and nine rebounds.

As January 1989 wound down, UWGB had lost six of eight games, with four of those losses by two points or less. Worse yet, at 7-7, any dreams of getting an NIT bid were long gone. The first question – whether this team could figure out how to win close games – had been answered with a resounding no.

The answer to the second question – whether or not UWGB was ready to compete with the conference elites – was, well, fuzzier.

UWGB had its first shot on January 30, 1989, when the Northern Iowa Panthers, sporting an impressive 13-4 record including a 3-1 conference mark, came to Green Bay. The Panthers had a big advantage over UWGB inside thanks to Jason Reese, who had put up 30 or more points four times already, and his productive cohort in 6-9 Steve Phyfe, who was averaging just over 13 ppg.

From the tip, both Reese and Phyfe were unequivocally on fire, with neither missing a shot *the entire game.* Reese's 20 points and Phyfe's 14 led the way for the Panthers, and left the Phoenix defenders helpless to stop them.

But even with their two best players firing on all cylinders, Northern Iowa could not put away UWGB. And for the first time since the Loyola Marymount game, the Phoenix played with a sense of urgency. The fiery Italian side of Dick Bennett again reared its head and earned him not one, but two technical fouls in the first half. And like it had before, Bennett's over-the-top intensity served to spark the team emotionally.

"When he got those two technicals, it really picked us up," remarks Tony.

Bennett's technicals altered the way the officials called the game. In the first half, Northern Iowa was in the bonus less than ten minutes in. But in the second half, the Panthers never attempted a free throw while themselves being whistled for twelve fouls.

It also kick-started Bennett's players, with the team getting contributions from unusual places. Karisny and Oberbrunner combined to contribute 25 points, and Hill chipped in a season-high eight points. Perhaps the best performance came from Johnson, who played with reckless abandon and won seemingly every loose ball.

"I don't know how many defensive plays he made down the stretch, but he had his hands virtually on everything," remarked Dick Bennett after the game.

The Panthers' Phyfe agreed. "(Johnson) sees a loose ball or we get the ball in our hands, and he's on it. He'd come over to help out. He was all over the court. That's the best defense we've played against in the league so far."

For once, the Phoenix didn't crumble. With the scored tied and less than three minutes to play, multiple players rose to the occasion. Tony Bennett worked the clock on two possessions, scoring four points; Tompa drew an offensive foul on Reese; Vander Plas had a critical rebound, and the team held Northern Iowa scoreless to secure a 70-64 win.

Whether a product of genius or pure luck, Dick Bennett's tirade had sparked his team's biggest win in nearly two months. It was like a B-12 shot in the arm.

"This was probably the most critical game of the season, because if we didn't get this one, it would have been difficult to establish anything in the conference," notes Karisny. "It told everyone we can win close games, that there's nothing different about playing the first thirty-five minutes and the last five minutes."

The Phoenix followed up its big win with a resounding home victory over Western Illinois two days later, improving its record to 10-8. But the celebration was short-lived, as the team traveled to Springfield, Missouri, on February 4, 1989, for a battle with conference royalty, the Southwest Missouri State Bears.

The Bears played at Hammons Student Center, one of those hostile mid-major environments with stands packed with noisy locals who were brutal on opponents and provided a tangible lift to the home squad. The Bears hadn't lost a conference game at home since 1986, and 9,051 fans didn't seem keen on seeing that streak broken against UWGB.

"The students would sit right behind our bench," Karisny says. "I don't know of any other place where they sit right behind your bench. And you talk about those cheers, I mean there were so many swear words and cuss words – it was literally, I would say, intimidating to play there. That was the toughest place I ever had to play, and we played at some big places."

It didn't help that Southwest Missouri State had the Phoenix's number. Entering the game, Bennett's Phoenix teams were 0-10 against Charlie Spoonhour's Bears, and UWGB as a program was a dismal 2-14 all-time.

"Southwest Missouri was easily the best team in the league. They had Charlie Spoonhour, who was always one of my very favorite coaches," Dick Bennett recalls. "He had really good, tough players. Mentally and physically just a notch above anything we saw in our league. And then he had always one or two great finesse players – you know, really good shooters."

A freshman cast and confidence from a win over Northern Iowa were simply not enough to match Spoonhour's talented club on its home turf. Behind a 20-6 scoring run in the middle of the first half, Southwest Missouri State built 28-16 lead and UWGB never got closer than seven points the rest of the way. The 64-48 loss was a devastating blow, and a stone-cold reminder that UWGB was at least a step, if not a few, below the Bears and the conference's elite.

"Spoon and Coach (Bennett) were very, very similar," comments Vander Plas. "The style of play that we both played was in-your-grill defense. We tried to cut floors in half, make you play on half the floor, really never let the ball reverse. Well, they did the same thing we were doing, and

honestly, they had better athletes. We just couldn't figure them out."

Karisny agreed with the talent sentiment, and added, "They *expected* to win. And at Green Bay, a part of the turnaround is we didn't. We probably *thought* we could win, but I think as a team, we didn't *expect* to win like they did. And that meant the difference in a few of those games."

Sitting on a 2-3 conference record and 10-9 overall, UWGB had firmly settled into the middle of the conference pack. The early results were mixed on whether UWGB was ready to compete with the conference elites, but with eight games left to play and no hope of an NIT bid, opportunities remained to settle the question.

Signs of Life

Along with rematches against the Bears and Panthers at the end of February, UWGB had six other regular-season games against the rest of the pack. True to

Tony Bennett puts up a shot during UWGB's loss to Southwest Missouri State on February 20, 1989. (University of Wisconsin-Green Bay Archives)

its immaturity and inconsistency, the Phoenix went 3-3 in those games. There were, however reasons for optimism.

First, Vander Plas continued to impress, particularly in the team's second victory over UIC. Hallberg's club, acutely aware of how Vander Plas had beaten them a month earlier, switched their mode of attack.

"They played a 1-3-1 zone, and we went at it with a 2-1-2, and it meant

I was going to get to catch the ball in the middle and generally got to make some plays there," explains Vander Plas. "I think had six or so assists, almost all throwing lobs to Roger Ripley for dunks."

Ripley finished with a career-high 19 points, while Vander Plas added to his passing game with his own career-high 20 points.

And second, Tony Bennett continued to flash his world-class talent. Nowhere was this more evident than in the team's loss to Cleveland State on February 11, 1989. The game represented only a minor variation on the season's theme of blown leads and close losses, with the Phoenix giving away a 12-point lead with twelve minutes to play.

But it became a special night for the team's freshman phenom, who had not forgotten the tongue-lashing he'd gotten from his father after the teams' earlier matchup.

"Cleveland State had (NBA star) Alvin Robertson's brother, Kenny, who was leading the country in steals," Dick Bennett explains. "I remember saying, 'He's going to lock up this young freshman.'"

Only he didn't. With Tony's godparents in town as witnesses, the younger Bennett put together a magical performance that remains the highest scoring output in school history.

"You try every game, but I really wanted to play well in that game," Tony states. "It just got going, and I was like, 'Hmm, these guys can't guard me today.' I could feel it, I could bag my shots, I could get by them off the dribble, and you just could kind of – you just got it going."

Tony turned in a ridiculous first half, scoring 23 points by nearly every way known, all while fighting through a shin injury. Tony's leg flared up during the halftime break, and Dick Bennett threatened to keep his son on the bench if the injury worsened. So Tony, ever the competitor, never subbed out. Playing the entire second half, Tony added 21 points to his total to finish with 44 points.

Tony hadn't forgotten his father's chastisement from earlier in the year.

"There was always a lot of this, 'Alright, you still think I'm a Division III player pops?' And no disrespect to Division III players, but it was just kind of like that," recalls Tony. "But we ended up losing the game, so it was kind of all for naught."

Reality Bites

The answer to the second question – whether or not UWGB was ready to compete with the conference elites – remained elusive. Amazingly, UWGB found itself in third place in the conference on February 20 as the largest crowd ever to fill the Brown County Arena for a Division I basketball game came to see if *this* would be the game that UWGB finally could beat Southwest Missouri State.

Unfortunately, the song remained the same. The Phoenix dropped its fourteenth straight game to the Bears, 62-52, in a contest the players felt was decided by the officiating. Second-half calls had put the Bears in the bonus just nine minutes in, sent UWGB's Roger Ripley to the bench for a ten-minute stretch, and knocked Tony Bennett out of the game with two minutes to play.

Dick Bennett was so upset that he refused to talk publicly after the game. But perhaps the most frustrated person was Tony, who, quite out of character, voiced his frustrations.

"It's a double standard," he said. "I thought they had a double standard tonight. I think about 6,000 people would probably agree with that."

A loss in the next game to Western Illinois dropped UWGB to 13-12, putting the Phoenix in fourth place ahead of their final game against a conference elite.

In the team's fourth signature conference game of the year, UWGB managed to storm into the UNI-Dome in Cedar Falls, Iowa – a place Northern Iowa had been 14-0 on the season – and again pull out a squeaker, 68-65. Tony Bennett led the way with 23 points, setting a UWGB Division I record for single-season scoring, while Johnson added a career-high 13 points.

The win gave UWGB a clean sweep against the Panthers, cancelling out its 0-2 effort against Southwest Missouri State. The Phoenix's inconsistency permeated its output for the year as it finished the season 14-13, including a disappointing 6-8 conference record that netted the fourth seed in the conference tournament.

The Last Crusade

In 1988-89, the AMCU opted to hold its conference tournament at the venue of the highest-seeded team, which just so happened to be the same venue it had chosen for all four previous incarnations – Springfield, Missouri. Southwest Missouri State, who finished the season with a 19-9 record, 10-2 in the conference, was the conference favorite to return to the NCAA, but nipping at their heels was Northern Iowa, who had compiled a close 18-9 overall record.

Prior to the tournament, the conference announced Tony Bennett as a second-team all-AMCU player and AMCU Newcomer of the Year. This came as no surprise – Tony had averaged 19.1 ppg (the only Phoenix player in double-figures), and finished in the top ten in six statistical categories.

As the fourth seed, UWGB's first-round opponent would be the fifth-seeded Valparaiso Crusaders, a team that had never won a conference tournament game. Valparaiso lived and died by the long ball, having attempted more than twice as many three-pointers (577) than the next closest AMCU team (236). That strategy had paid off with season splits against Northern Iowa, Southwest Missouri State, and UWGB, as well as a non-conference win over No. 19 Notre Dame.

For the Phoenix, its entire season, along with the hopes and dreams of its four seniors (Bolding, Tompa, Taphorn, and Hines), rested on their performance. There's an old adage that you play like you practice, and if the regular season was the warm-up, then nothing could have been truer for UWGB. The game against Valparaiso followed the same course the Phoenix had charted nearly a dozen times.

It began with Bennett's ever-changing lineup. While eleven players were averaging at least ten minutes per game, none other than Tony were playing more than 23 mpg. Bennett again shuffled the deck, this time dealing Ripley a ninth start of the year and putting Vander Plas on the bench for most of the game.

"Coach Bennett took me out of the starting lineup because he wanted to win the tip against Valpo, put Roger in there," remembered Vander Plas. "It irritated the heck out of me because I thought I earned the playing time. I was still a bit selfish. I think maybe Coach was breaking me a little bit."

Without Vander Plas on the floor, Valparaiso took an early lead, but UWGB fought back with stout defensive pressure and forced a number of turnovers. In typical fashion for the 1988-89 program, UWGB found itself with a comfortable 48-38 lead with under eight minutes to play, and dreams in the semifinals danced in their heads.

But, as it had many times throughout the regular season, UWGB gave it all away. The added size Ripley provided proved ineffective as the Crusaders owned the glass down the stretch and outrebounded UWGB by fifteen for the game. Riding a 13-3 run, Valparaiso tied the game at 51-51 and with less than 45 seconds left and got the ball with a chance to win. On the Crusaders' final possession, guard Todd Smith released a jumper over Tony Bennett with just seconds remaining. The shot was way short, but the Crusaders' Scott Anselm tipped the ball into the basket as time expired, giving Valparaiso its first conference tournament win ever, 53-51.

Valparaiso would lose in the semifinals to Southwest Missouri State, which went on to win the AMCU conference tournament and earn its third straight NCAA tournament bid. There would be no magical run this time, as Spoonhour's club, a 14 seed, bowed out in the first round to eventual runner-up Seton Hall, 60-51.

Alpha and Omega

Painful in the moment, the Phoenix's loss was a merciful end to a frustrating season. Bennett felt his team had succumbed to precisely the mentality he had coached away from.

"We got really tentative," he says. "We were so afraid of losing that we lost."

"We weren't mature enough yet," Vander Plas admits. "We couldn't quite finish the deal defensively. Record-wise, it was the worst year we had when I was at Green Bay. We were in games and just couldn't quite pull them off."

"We should've been better, but our talent was heavily laden in our freshman class," notes Karisny. "It would be unfair to expect your freshmen to do a lot, with the exception of Tony, who carried us for a lot of games."

"Tony was pretty advanced, and I felt like if we could augment his particular skills, it would help us," adds Dick Bennett. "It meant that we had to get the guys to accept a role in getting him open and giving him more of a green light. "It gave us some wins, but we still weren't good enough to beat the good teams that year."

For the four seniors, it was a brutal finish to a long career. They had grown with their coach and helped the program climb from conference doormat to mid-level conference contender. They were the builders that had worked through the hardest years of the basketball revolution to cement the foundation for the future. And it had rubbed off on Bennett's blue-chip class.

"Great teammates, guys I'll never forget," Tony says. "Marquis Hines was a point guard. This was going to be his time. And then here I come in, you know the coach's son, this freshman. And man, he just loved me like a brother. I think that's got to be one of the best and coolest acts of a quality person."

"We respected all those guys," states Scott LeMoine. "I learned very quickly that I had a lot of work to do to get to their level. Those guys were quiet, but they just played their butts off all the time. They always accepted us. They always made us feel part of the group."

With Dick Bennett's first big class getting a year under their belts, the future was bright. But all of that was contingent on Tony Bennett. Unbeknownst to the team, Dick and Tony engaged in a serious offseason discussion about whether UWGB was the right fit for Tony.

"My dad and I sat down and said, 'Is this working? Can I – is this really working? Is this too much, me playing here?' " Tony recalls. "He said, 'You know, Charlie (Spoonhour) would take you.' I have such respect for him and he was a heck of a coach and built the program, and they were sort of the gold standard for us at the time."

To the lasting benefit of his teammates, school, and city, Tony decided to stay.

Chapter 4

Buy-In and Role Acceptance
(1989-1990 - Part 1)

Overcoming the seemingly impossible to achieving the improbable – that's greatness. In the terms of mid-major college basketball, where individual talent may appear to be the seemingly impossible barrier, greatness hinges on funny mathematics.

A cohesive collection of individuals – all willing to sacrifice personal potential to achieve a common goal and dedicate themselves to the abstract "greater good" – under the right parameters, have the opportunity to generate a whole which is greater than the sum of the parts.

The principle is not innate. It requires a coach who can credibly communicate a vision for success and inspire cooperation, as well as a group of accepting, unselfish players who are open to receive the message and commit to united success, irrespective of personal accolades. Minus either of those, greatness will be forever elusive.

Servanthood

Dick Bennett's 1989-90 roster had been all his – players hand-picked by him and his staff, partially for their skills and athleticism, but also intentionally for their high resiliency, intrinsic drive, and strong moral character.

Bennett loved players with those internal strengths, because these were precisely the individuals who would be most receptive to his concept of "servanthood," one of his program's core traits. The ability to sacrifice and put one's self second to the greater good was paramount directly correlated with the drive, resiliency, and moral character Bennett had ensured his roster represented.

"You have to have kids that will lay it on the line," he says. "You can't have these guys that come in and just want to jack the ball every time they touch it or they're concerned about their scoring statistics. It lends itself well to the grinders – the kids that'll just go on the floor for the ball or do anything you ask them to do."

Judging from his players' reactions, Bennett's strategy was successful.

"Coach always talked about the synergy of the program, and just that the whole was bigger than the sum of the parts," comments Ben Johnson. "That's who we were, and that's who we tried to be. That's who he sold us on who we needed to be. At the end of the day, it was about the group, it was about the team, it was about the basketball chemistry, and those are things that Coach Bennett instilled in us."

Mike Karisny agrees. "He was able to make his team greater than the sum of its parts. The best coaches do that, and clearly he did that for most of his career."

"Coach Bennett got everyone to *believe* more than anything, adds Scott LeMoine. "We aren't the tallest; we aren't the most athletic; we aren't the quickest, whatever. But this is who we are. And if you just stay true to that, good things will happen. That part was just cool, to see everybody, 'Hey, this is my role, and I'm going to be the best I can be at that role, whether it's screening, rebounding, or defense.' "

With accountability came pride as well.

"There were a number of us on the team that hated losing more than we liked winning," states Dean Vander Plas, "and I just think it was miserable losing in that sophomore year."

Diamonds in the Rough

Bennett returned a sound cast of players with tremendous experience from the 1988-89 season, but he knew the importance of another solid recruiting class.

"We feel we need two solid recruiting years back-to-back," Bennett explained at the time. "We think that will be the key to putting us over the top."

He wouldn't know it at the time, but his small class of 1989-90 would exceed his wildest dreams.

The first recruit Bennett locked up was, in brief, one of the best signings in school history. John Martinez, a deceptively crafty 6-foot point guard from Milwaukee whose passing game and court vision outshone his more-than-capable scoring ability, had been largely overlooked by the state's premier programs. As a high school junior, Martinez had averaged 15 points per game, finished first team all-state, and led his Milwaukee Marquette squad to the WISAA (private schools) state championship.

He was a quiet leader and came from a winning pedigree, but UWGB nearly missed out.

"Rudy Keeling was the assistant coach at Marquette, so I kind of knew him from there," Martinez recalls. "When he got the head coaching job (at Maine), I went out there to visit and got an offer from them."

But once Bennett saw Martinez play, he couldn't contain his excitement and offered him a scholarship. Sensing a fit with Bennett and relishing an opportunity to play close to home, Martinez signed with UWGB in April 1988.

"It happened fairly quickly, but it happened late," Martinez says. "Thankfully, it did happen, because looking back, I think it was the perfect fit for everyone involved."

On signing day, Bennett beamed: "I threw all my energy into signing him. Martinez was my choice all along. He comes from an excellent system and he's an excellent defensive ball player."

His backcourt teammate, ascending sophomore Tony Bennett, saw Martinez's potential as well: "I remember we tried like heck (to recruit him) when I saw John Martinez play. And I think that was a key, when John and I became the backcourt."

Dick Bennett's message of servanthood resonated loud and clear with Martinez.

"We just knew as a team, and this is a credit to Coach Bennett and the coaching staff, they gave us the (blueprint) of what we needed to compete, and if we all bought in, that's you're best chance to succeed. And that's what we did."

Bennett was less conventional with his three remaining scholarships. After inviting six players for a campus visit, Bennett and his assistants, Mike Heideman and Steve Swan, made scholarship offers during the early signing period to the top five on a first-come, first-served basis. The first three to accept would be in.

Logan Vander Velden, a 6-9, 180-pound string bean from the small town of Valders, Wisconsin, was the first to sign in November 1988. Vander Velden had averaged 22 ppg and 10 rpg as a junior, earning honorable mention all-state honors. Having previously played AAU ball with Tony Bennett, Ben Johnson, and Dean Rondorf, Vander Velden knew the Phoenix and those relationships likely helped him spurn his other offers from Maine, UC-Santa Barbara, and Eastern Illinois to stay in-state.

"As soon as I took my visit, I think it was two days later I called them and I said I was coming," recalls Vander Velden. "I was pretty much a homebody going through high school and family was important to me, and obviously playing for Coach was a big factor."

Bennett was high on Vander Velden's potential.

"The more I saw him, the more I liked him," Bennett commented at the time. "He's got excellent quickness. He's the kind of guy we have to get in here. Logan is the kind who's going to get better, and by the time he's a junior or senior, probably is going to stand out."

Bennett's other hit was a rare out-of-state signing. Jeremy Ludvigson, a mullet-sporting 6-7 forward from Edgewood, Iowa, was considered a better-than-average shooter with a good post game.

Playing style did little to influence Ludvigson. Rather, three factors convinced him to attend UWGB.

"I didn't get recruited heavily Division I," Ludvigson recalls, "so the fact that (UWGB was) Division I, I loved the coaching staff, and Green Bay was not too far away from home."

Bennett praised Ludvigson upon his signing.

"Jeremy is not as physically talented, but he may be a bit more complete. He can dribble, pass, shoot, and rebound. He's steady. Jeremy is going to be a solid player throughout most of his career, if not spectacular."

Martinez, Ludvigson, and Vander Velden were all capable basketball players, but more importantly, each were willing to sacrifice.

"You're going to have to land guys that believe in your system, and then have to teach them how to play the game," notes Martinez. "If you don't buy in, then you're just going to have a very average team, below average, and there's not going to be any success there."

Vander Velden and Ludvigson redshirted, leaving Martinez to join red-shirt Dean Rondorf as the team's only two active freshmen for 1989-90.

"It was an easy transition for me, or an easier transition for me because Coach Bennett's coaching style was very similar to my high school coach," Martinez says. "Very demanding defensively, hard-nosed basketball, earn-everything-that-you-get type of thing."

Redshirting Vander Velden had been the plan from day one.

"We were able to be really upfront and say, 'We feel you need to gain some strength,' " remembers Bennett. " 'Don't worry about us trying to stick you down inside. We are going to try to use that great gift you have for shooting the basketball as a perimeter player, and you need to become stronger and continue to develop defensively,' which he did."

Similarly, Ludvigson was a scrawny 190 pounds with plenty of room to grow.

"I don't remember that there was much of a discussion beyond, 'Hey, we're thinking we're going to do this, does it make sense?' " Ludvigson says. "And I'm like, 'For sure! Give me another year. You're going to give me a five-year scholarship? Like okay!' "

Ready for a Winner

By 1989, the city of Green Bay was desperate to support a winning pro-gram, any winning program. UWGB even investigated adding men's hock-ey to its athletic program. And while the idea was enticing, in the end, it was difficult to reconcile the financial commitment.

Thankfully, the region was treated to a bit of Majik in the fall of 1989, the likes of which Green Bay Packers fans had not seen since Vince Lom-bardi left town. The Packers provided a temporary return to glory, pro-pelled by a young, blond renegade quarterback. Three years before the Brett Favre era began, it was Don Majkowski who quarterbacked the Pack-ers. As the leader of the "Cardiac Pack," a team that had ten of its sixteen games decided by four points or less, Majkowski finished the year second in the NFL's MVP voting, rekindling claims that "The Pack is Back."

While the city buzzed with the ups and downs of its signature fran-chise, the Phoenix went to work preparing for the 1989-90 season. Ben-nett's squad featured five upperclassmen, including three seniors who all had started at least a dozen games in their first three years.

Fifth-year senior Roger Ripley was one of the best athletes on the team and the likely starter at center.

"Roger was a big dude – super strong," describes Ludvigson. "One time (in practice), he pump faked and I jumped, and as I was coming down he went back up and just flattened me on the floor. Coach Bennett says, 'Get Jake or whatever his name is from Iowa off the floor.' I'm like, 'Wow, no love.' "

Senior Mike Karisny, the second-leading scorer on the 1988-89 team, was one of the team's top deep threats.

UWGB's 1989-90 roster featured an influx of young talent for Dick Bennett. Back row: Dean Rondorf (22), Larry Hill (24), Logan Vander Velden (32), Roger Ripley (52), Scott LeMoine (45), Jeremy Ludvigson (44), Chris Yates (13), Dean Vander Plas (33). Front row: Tony Ciaravino (21), Ben Johnson (23), Dan Oberbrunner (30), Mike Karisny (3), John Martinez (20), Tony Bennett (25). (University of Wisconsin-Green Bay Archives)

"He hustles so much, and offensively he has improved his ball handling tremendously," noted Bennett before the season. "It's going to take some excellent play to unseat him."

Dan Oberbrunner rounded out the senior class. As a junior, Oberbrunner started sixteen games and finally found his groove as a regular contributor. Still, his coach pushed hard noting, "Dan will have to give us more this year to play on as regular a basis as he did last year."

The junior class featured two players headed in opposite directions. Vander Plas, a sure-fire starter and foundational member of the club, came into the year with extra motivation from his unexpected benching in the AMCU tournament: "That's what I kept going back to all off-season," he says. "When there was a run that I had to do that I wasn't particularly fond of doing, I'd think about that."

Meanwhile, Chris Yates's future was murkier. On the floor, Yates had been a disappointment and lacked the consistent play that Bennett demanded from his players. Off the court, Yates had failed to live up to Bennett's high character requirements.

Yates had been arrested during the offseason for allegedly slapping his girlfriend. Two months later, rumors began circulating that Yates would be leaving UWGB, and he had left informal workouts during the summer to attend to a personal matter in Michigan. But by October, Yates was back saying the right things and had reaffirmed his commitment to UWGB.

And then there was Bennett's big sophomore class.

Johnson was a sure starter for his defense alone, but had also improved his shooting and ball-handling skills. He had caught up to the speed of the game.

"That (freshman year) was the first time I'd ever not started," Johnson says. "My pride was wounded, I was damaged, I was hurt, and obviously that lit a fire under me. They always say the year you improve the most is between your freshman and sophomore year in college, and no doubt about that. I came back a way different player, again because of what you learned you're *not*."

Johnson was also quickly stepping into the role of a vocal team leader.

"My personality on the court is very full on, it's very voluptuous, but I had to learn to dial it back (as a freshman) because we had some other seniors that were good guys," he says. "Those guys actually taught me how to be a leader, and how to be a captain, and how to talk to guys differently."

Athletic freak Larry Hill had also improved. Hill's 6-9 frame, coupled with his massive wingspan, gave him the opportunity to be an X-factor for the Phoenix.

"His length, his ability to shoot the 15- to 18-foot jump shot, to get to the basket, and athletically, he was as good as anybody on our team," notes Dean Rondorf. "Larry was 6-9 and long, and he had a presence in there."

Meanwhile, big man Scott LeMoine had gotten stronger and was likely to split some time at the center position, primarily for his defensive prowess. And spunky Tony Ciaravino remained a practice bulldog, helping Tony Bennett prepare each week.

Olympic Dreams

And as for Tony?

"Everybody just kind of knew their role and they accepted that role, and knew Tony was the guy, but we were going to support him," comments LeMoine. "You have to have that one stud player. If you don't have that, you're in trouble."

Tony pushed himself hard and got plenty of support from his teammates, including best friend Ben Johnson. The two maintained a sibling-like rivalry and competitiveness that drove both to improve.

"I don't think a day went by that we didn't try to literally kill each other playing one-on-one. Hours on end," recalls Johnson. "Neither one of us wanted to ever lose, and neither one of us gave an inch or a quarter. You knew for that day, it's like 'Goll dang it, I better bring it. If I don't, I'm going to get blitzed.' "

Tony had spent part of his offseason training away from his teammates. As one of the top forty-eight players in the country 17-20 years old, he had been invited to play in a four-team U.S. Olympic Festival tournament in Colorado Springs. The festival took place in July 1989 and was a who's who of young collegiate talent with guys like Bobby Hurley (Duke), Kenny Anderson (Georgia Tech), Don MacLean (UCLA), Harold Minor (USC), Terry Dehere (Seton Hall), Lee Mayberry (Arkansas), and Todd Day (Arkansas) taking part.

"That was a huge moment for me, playing with some elite guys that ended up some legitimate NBA players," Tony says. "I had a good (freshman) year, and I thought, 'Boy, I think I can play.' I believed in myself. But then I went to that thing, and that was the so-called McDonald's All-Americans – guys that are potential lottery players."

Tony played on the North squad coached by Michigan State legend Jud Heathcote. Over the week, the two forged an unusual bond.

"He called me Scott the whole time, because he had coached Scott Skiles," Tony recalls. "He'd be like, 'Scotty, Scotty,' and I'd be like, 'Coach, it's Tony.' And after like two or three times, I just started responding to Scotty. Coach Jud was awesome, and that's kind of where I got to know him well."

The North team also included two Spartans (Mike Peplowski and Matt Steigenga), as well as future NBAers Anthony Peeler (Missouri), Byron Houston (Oklahoma State), Corey Williams (Oklahoma State), Jeff Webster (Oklahoma), and Antonio Harvey (Southern Illinois).

Tony held his own, averaging seven points, three assists, and two rebounds per game for his gold medal-winning team.

"That was huge because I left there and said, 'I don't have to take a backseat to any of those guys from a playing standpoint. I've seen who the so-called best are, and certainly respected how good they were, but it didn't faze me. It almost was like 'okay.'"

Heathcote was impressed.

"I think Tony can play at the Big Ten level. Guys down there were always asking me who was standing out, and I always mentioned Tony Bennett," Heathcote said after the festival. "In the last eight minutes, we could

John Martinez (left) and Tony Bennett gave the Phoenix a dynamic backcourt that was a strength of the team for the rest of their careers. (University of Wisconsin-Green Bay Archives)

Aaron A. Mitchell

Dean Vander Plas heads downcourt after making a steal against Austin Peay on December 7, 1989, much to the chagrin of the Austin Peay bench. (University of Wisconsin-Green Bay Archives)

play anybody we wanted. Usually, Tony was in there."

The unusual invitation had helped Tony fine-tune his game, and entering the fall, Dick Bennett noticed as much.

"He has quickened up his ball handling," Dick said. "He's really worked on his right side. He's tougher defensively. He's looked inside more with the ball, and he's done it on a daily basis."

All In

As practices began, the confluence of new talent and veterans that had experienced disappointment generated an atmosphere of pure dedication. Dick Bennett's vision was coming to fruition. At the forefront was a player-driven movement to fully commit to the program. The players gathered and set expectations on what the team's focus would be.

"We agreed to an honor code amongst college kids about what we were going to do as a team. Nobody was going to be deterred during the season," recalls Vander Plas. "We put the college life on pause to go through that season."

The result was a perceptible shift into a servant's mindset.

"I felt that was a breakthrough year for us, 1989-90," states Karisny. "Our whole was greater than the sum of our parts. We had chemistry, we had a brotherhood, we had unselfishness, we didn't care who scored."

"It was about winning, and everybody was kind of sharing that same mentality," adds Martinez.

There would be no "NIT" shorts or talks of post-seasons, but Bennett knew the team would be good.

"I thought it would be probably the best team, other than 1987-88,"

~ 60 ~

he says. "These were all the kids I had recruited, so I felt confident that we could get them to play both ends of the floor and that we would be a very competitive group."

An Unexpected Opportunity

As a freshman, the talented Martinez wasn't exactly sure how he would play with Tony Bennett.

"Tony was a year ahead of me. He was the coach's son, and he was definitely going to be playing," recalls Martinez. "Now, how am I going to be able to fit in with that?"

For better or worse, Martinez didn't need to answer that question to see the floor early on. Nearly a month before the team would play its first game, Tony developed an arthritic condition on his right foot.

While the foot was not broken, the injury had the potential to linger. The situation escalated a few weeks later when Tony developed hip tendinitis just ten days before the season opener. Recovery would take a few weeks, and Tony would miss the season's start. Martinez was the next man up.

"Up to that point, I had been primarily like second team," Martinez explains. "I was kind of thrown right into the fire. That was an interesting experience, because I was definitely not anticipating that happening."

Dick Bennett spun the situation into a positive for Martinez. "It's a blessing in disguise, because he's going to play against good people on the road and we'll find out."

The Land of Lincoln, Part 1

A fair mix of road games against major conference foes (Northwestern and Illinois) and quality mid-majors (Illinois State, Central Michigan, and Boise State) populated the Phoenix's nonconference schedule, coupled with winnable home games against lesser competition the likes of Austin Peay, Michigan Tech, and Chicago State.

It all started on the road at Illinois State. The Redbirds had enjoyed a string of postseason appearances in the mid-1980s, including three straight NCAA tournament bids from 1983-85, but had finished a disappointing 13-17 in 1988-89. Bob Bender, a former assistant at Duke, had been hired in the offseason to right the ship, and utilized a full-court pressure defense intended to suffocate opponents.

As nearly 10,000 people packed the newly built Redbird Arena, Bennett rolled out a starting lineup of Martinez and Karisny at guard, Hill and Yates at the forward positions, and Ripley at center.

The Illinois State defense succeeded in applying pressure to UWGB, forcing a number of turnovers. But it also gave up easy buckets when Martinez and the Phoenix could break the press, and UWGB took a 29-26 halftime lead. Bennett worked through his roster and found a balanced scoring attack, as eight players scored at least six points, and UWGB was able to build a six-point lead with under three minutes to play.

It was at that point the previous year's demons threatened to return. Thanks to terrible free throw shooting (UWGB was 2-6 with two front-end bonus misses), Illinois State tied the game at 59-59 and forced overtime. But this year's Phoenix were a year older and wiser.

Bennett surprised the Redbirds in OT by switching to a 1-3-1 zone, and the move paid off as the Phoenix grabbed a 69-63 lead with under two minutes to play. Illinois State nearly pulled off a second comeback, but UWGB forced a turnover in the final seconds to give the Phoenix a valuable opening-game win.

In the moment, it was hard to make heads or tails of the victory. The team had blown a lead in regulation and Martinez looked shaky, but UWGB did succeed in winning on the road against a team that would go on to make the NCAA tournament that season.

The good news was that Tony Bennett was recovering and would only miss one more game. The bad news was the next game was on the road against the Big Ten's Northwestern Wildcats. Worse, Hill was suffering from a sprained ankle. Dick Bennett made just one lineup change, starting Vander Plas and bringing Karisny in as the first guy off the bench.

In contrast to the packed house in Normal, Illinois, three days earlier, a meager 3,000 fans made the trek to Welsh-Ryan Arena to watch Chicago's Big Ten team. If Bennett had any dreams of an upset like the one that had served as a turning point in 1986, his hopes were shattered early in the first half when Northwestern went on a 40-20 sprint to claim a dominating 50-29 halftime lead. The game was never close after that, and UWGB left Chicago with its tail between its legs, losing 87-65.

The loss shook the confidence of the locker room and questioned the players' true commitment.

"This is the worst I've felt after a loss," noted Johnson. "I think that's the general feeling. I think we have to find out about the character of our team."

And yet, there were two positive signs. First, unlike the previous season, Bennett was quickly settling on a more structured rotation of players. Ripley, Vander Plas, Johnson, Tony Bennett, and Martinez were all expected starters, with Karisny filling a sixth-man role, and Hill and LeMoine likely to get playing time to spell the big men.

Second, Tony was ready to return. In a scheduling quirk, the Phoenix was able to play a mid-season exhibition against Athletes in Action, and Tony was terrific. He regularly beat two former professional guards in Lorenzo Romar and Rod Foster on his way to eighteen points and seven assists.

Tony's return would invariably mean less time for Martinez, but the experience he'd picked up in Tony's absence was invaluable.

"John was really good, but he was a guy who needed confidence," Dick Bennett comments. "So the fact that he was getting those minutes allowed him to show what he could do."

A Winning Streak

Tony Bennett returned to meaningful action on December 4, 1989, at Central Michigan. As it had the year before, UWGB jumped out early and held a double-digit lead in the second half. And just like as it had the year before, UWGB let the Chippewas come back. When Central Michigan took the lead, 55-54, with 2:30 left in the game, it looked like history was going to repeat itself.

But this Phoenix squad had a year more experience, and it showed. On the ensuing possession, Martinez found Tony alone on the left wing, where the younger Bennett buried a three-pointer to reclaim the lead for the Phoenix. One possession later, Tony had a nifty drive and dish to Ripley, helping the Phoenix seal the deal with a 65-57 victory.

The victory against Central Michigan validated the hope that sprang from the Illinois State win: that this team may have learned how to close out games. UWGB followed up its win over Central Michigan with four more wins in mid-December. It started with a 24-point blowout against Austin Peay at the Brown County Arena. Down three players to suspension, the Governors committed seventeen turnovers and were simply overmatched.

Two nights later, UWGB again came up big down the stretch in beating Missouri-Kansas City, a team in its first year of Division I basketball. Karisny was particularly strong, scoring 16 points, including a three-pointer in the final moments that gave the Phoenix a lead it wouldn't relinquish.

Four days later, UWGB blew out Division II foe Michigan Tech, high-

Tony Bennett drives past a Michigan Tech defender during the Phoenix's 67-57 victory on December 13, 1989. (University of Wisconsin-Green Bay Archives)

John Martinez looks to pass as redshirts Logan Vander Velden (left) and Jeremy Lud-vigson watch from the bench during UWGB's 60-39 victory over Chicago State on December 28, 1989. (University of Wisconsin-Green Bay Archives)

lighted by Hill's 4-for-4 performance in thirteen minutes of action. Hill was figuring things out, and followed his Michigan Tech performance with a 15-point outing on the road at Boise State. UWGB again dominated from the start, holding the rebuilding Broncos to a meager 15 points in the second half on less than 19% shooting from the field.

It was UWGB's fifth win in a row, and fourth in five games by double-figures. At 6-1 and with a week off before its next game, the players focused on getting through their finals and resting their early-season aches.

The Land of Lincoln, Part 2

Two days before Christmas, UWGB traveled to Champaign for *the* marquee matchup on the Phoenix schedule – a date with the No. 5 team in the country, the University of Illinois.

The "Flyin' Illini" had made the 1989 Final Four, and despite losing two first-round draft picks in Kenny Battle and Nick Anderson, looked stronger than ever in 1989-90. Fresh off a victory over No. 4 Missouri, the Illini had star power to spare, starting with superstar guards Kendall Gill and Steven Bardo, and forward Marcus Liberty. This was the highest-ranked team UWGB had ever faced. And to make matters worse, Illinois was almost unbeatable at home where it had won twenty-seven straight.

"Oh God, they were loaded," recalls Dick Bennett. "They had probably the best team in the country talent-wise. That was a nightmare."

Martinez had grown up watching the Illini and was star-struck by what he saw in Champaign.

"Before going to Green Bay, I was a big Illinois fan. I used to wear these guys' jerseys. Kendall Gill was sitting there right next to me. How ironic it was as a player to have the player's jersey and then playing against him."

These were the games that Bennett prayed for. A chance to put the

Phoenix name on the map, ascend from regional novelty into the national collegiate discussion. And perhaps to Illinois's surprise, the game was a bruising, physical matchup worthy of the Big Ten.

"That was before the blood rule. Ervin Small took my nose off in the first half and I was profusely bleeding everywhere," Vander Plas relates. "My jersey just kept soaking it up, and you took some Kleenex and stuffed it in your nose. In today's game, I think would have been out for at least a half to try to get that thing to stop, but there you just showed how big a man you were and kept playing."

Somehow, Bennett's plan to slow the game kept Illinois from exploiting the talent gap, at least for a while. With patient offense, interior baskets, and smothering half-court defense, UWGB stayed in the game. The Phoenix trailed by just six points at the break and were down 53-41 with 7:30 to go in the game.

But as the game wore on, UWGB's mistakes took their toll and Illinois's athleticism overwhelmed the Phoenix. Illinois went on an 18-6 run over the last 7:30, and with seventeen second-half points from its best player, Kendall Gill, the Illini closed out UWGB in a closer-than-the-final-score-looked 71-47 victory.

"It made you realize how fine a line we had in order to beat those teams," Tony Bennett says. "It kind of got our attention like, 'Man, you've got to be flawless, or close to it. You've got to play a certain way and be so good.' Like, 'Alright, this is how we're going to have to do it to beat these great ones.' "

"That was really the only game I've ever played in where I didn't think we were going to win," states Martinez.

Christmas found UWGB sitting pretty with a 6-2 record, with quality wins against Illinois State and Central Michigan. The two losses against the Big Ten, though anticipated, confirmed that the program was not yet ready to compete against major-conference foes.

Thankfully, the coaching staff had gifted the team a gimme, scheduling a home matchup against independent Chicago State on December 28. At 0-8, the Cougars were little match for the Phoenix, which rolled to a 60-39 victory. The game was notable because it was the first time that Bennett experimented with playing Vander Plas and Hill together.

"For us to be as good as we can be, Larry has to be a prominent person in the scheme," noted Bennett. "The combination of Dean and Larry offers us interchangeability. So if you were able to get a matchup where Dean can go down inside, you can pull Larry out or vice versa."

Vander Plas wasn't one to complain.

"Larry was good, he was *super* good. When we put Larry on the floor with me, we went to a top-bottom blocker situation. We had normally been side to side, but with Larry, we finally had a big who could move. It was a game-changer, because we added some length."

UWGB's final two games before the conference schedule were against teams that would become very familiar, as both were committed to joining the AMCU in 1990-91.

UWGB played the first, inconsistent independent Northern Illinois, on

Ben Johnson (left) scans the Northern Illinois defense as Dick Bennett (far left) looks on anxiously during UWGB's 60-56 victory on December 30, 1989. (University of Wisconsin-Green Bay Archives)

December 30, 1989. The Huskies, a stagnant program over the previous three years, were revitalized under first-year coach Jim Molinari. Behind the play of guard Donald Whiteside and forward Donnell Thomas, Northern Illinois had shocked Nebraska, a top-notch program in the Big Eight, as well as MAC powerhouse Toledo, but still came into the game with only a 4-4 record.

The game itself was a back-and-forth affair that would foreshadow the teams' future rivalry. Stout, man-to-man defense by both programs made their coaches proud.

For the fourth time that season, UWGB was tested in the final minutes. And for the fourth time, the Phoenix rose to the challenge. Bennett's crew put together defensive stop after defensive stop in the final moments, and when they needed it, hit their free throws to seal a 60-56 victory.

As 1989 came to a close, the Fighting Phoenix basked in a Division I school record 8-2 start to the season, its confidence and consistency growing.

Birth of the Pack Defense

January 10, 1990, was a red-letter day in college basketball history. UWGB played one of its worst games of the year that day against Akron, but in the process, changed its program forever.

The Zips had a recent history of success under Bob Huggins, who coached Akron to four consecutive twenty-plus win seasons from 1985-86 through 1988-89, including one NCAA tournament appearance and two NIT bids. Huggins left to take the Cincinnati role, and his replacement, Coleman Crawford, had performed admirably in his inaugural season, helping the Zips to a 6-1 record.

Like Northern Illinois, the Zips had agreed to join the AMCU in 1990-91 and would become a familiar foe. But by the end of the forty minutes, the Phoenix probably had hoped Akron would stay in the Ohio Valley Conference. Crawford's Zips thoroughly manhandled the Phoenix in all aspects, beating Bennett's club soundly, 66-52.

The game would be entirely forgotten in the annals of both schools were it not for a sport-altering decision that Bennett made afterwards.

Up to the Akron game, Bennett had been the mastermind behind the push defense, an attacking defensive strategy in which perimeter defenders played close, tight defense on all perimeter players without the ball, looking to force turnovers and pressure passing lanes.

"We started out with the push defense my freshman year," explains LeMoine. "We got teams onto one side and we didn't let the ball reverse and all that. Holy cow, that's tough defense to play, especially with the 45-second shot clock that we had."

The push defense was a particularly effective defense with quick, long, athletic guards and wings who could block passing lanes and create turnovers. Bennett had reaped huge rewards

Dick Bennett shouts instructions as Tony Ciaravino (left) and Scott LeMoine look on. (University of Wisconsin-Green Bay Archives)

with the defense during his tenure at UW-Stevens Point, with star talent like 6-foot-3 Terry Porter at guard. But at Green Bay, with the talent gap working in reverse and a pair of 6-foot guards, the push defense exposed the smaller and slower Phoenix.

As Martinez acknowledges, "If you're going to be playing two 6-foot guards at the same time, then there's a risk of other teams taking advantage of their height against you."

"For the first five years, four years at Green Bay, we were pushing the ball outside – we were really pushing it hard to the outside – which meant our help came from the baseline," notes Bennett. "Our big people had to rotate out on the baseline and our weak-side players had to really sink and fill in the lane. We were getting caught with our small people underneath a lot."

In a moment of brilliance and frustration following the Akron loss, Bennett dreamed up the "Pack" defense that would make him famous.

"That's when I decided I didn't want John (Martinez) or Tony (Bennett) to get caught underneath all the time. We started shading the ball back toward the middle so our help came from the top. We could keep our bigger people home, and we could keep our guards on the perimeter."

"He really made that change simply because the game started to change. The game became more about dribble penetration," notes Johnson, who was a defensive specialist. "The push, or the on-the-line up-the-line, worked better when he was at the D-3 level or the NAIA level at Stevens Point. Because why? Because he had better talent. (But at the Division I level), you give that guard the angle to dribble penetrate, now he's good enough, quick enough to make you pay. Your help rotation is late, and now your weak-side defensive rebounding coverage is late, and just it becomes a merry-go-round."

With a defense where defenders off the ball sagged off their match-ups to offer help, the Phoenix could clog the lane, eliminate easy interior baskets, and increase rebounding odds.

"When you are all-out selling out, full on denial, all that ball reversal and everything like that, I mean it was hard. Especially with a 45-second clock, it was crazy," notes LeMoine. "So instead of just full out, all deny on that reversal, you can reverse the ball if you want to go high and wide or whatever. We're going to let you do that so we weren't so overcommitted that we were getting beat off the dribble."

Tony Bennett was the embodiment of the word "intensity" during his playing career with the Phoenix. (University of Wisconsin-Green Bay Archives)

"You talk about a brilliant decision and how it's changed the game?" comments Tony Bennett. "That was significant because it allowed us a chance to play, to rebound."

"(Coach Bennett) comes up with the Pack, kind of to slow down that dribble penetration and a little more containment, especially when the ball's up top," adds Johnson. "Instead of forcing him to the baseline, the ball's going away toward the baseline, he influences the middle, so everyone has to change their stance. So now it becomes, philosophically and theoretically, the whole defense now shifts.

"Now, here was the beauty of everything he did. And I don't know – he's smart, but I don't know if he planned this – when you play the push, I mean it is balls to the wall. You deny penetration by the pass, deny swings, deny ball reversal, high intensity on the ball. And so (in 1989-90), you took all these guys that were playing kamikaze push defense, and now you put them in the Pack, but we still play with the same amount of intensity on the ball and in the gaps. It was masterful, it was a thing of beauty."

The move transcended the 1989-90 Phoenix, affecting defensive coaching for decades.

"I stayed that way through the rest of my years at Green Bay, and I stayed that way at Wisconsin, and then even out at Washington State, and Tony still teaches that way (at Virginia)," Dick Bennett states.

Indeed, in a curious twist of fate, thirty years after Bennett's famous creation, the 2019 National Championship game saw a battle of two teams playing the two defenses for which Bennett was most known. Tony Bennett, coach of that 2019 National Champion Virginia team, explains:

"Texas Tech played more of the old-school push. My dad had a huge influence on Texas Tech, and the assistant coach who runs that defense told me that. He said, 'I have studied your dad. What we do is a result of what he used to do at Stevens Point and the early years at Green Bay.'

"My dad, for two years didn't want a ton of college basketball. He watched us, but he loved – he always watched Texas Tech. He said, 'Now that team is tough.' He said, 'That's defense.' He'd always tell me that. 'Now they play *real* defense. You know you guys, you pretend, that's *real*.'

"I'll tell you a funny story – we beat Auburn (in the 2019 Final Four). He doesn't go to the game. And I remember I went into his room, his room was next to mine, and I said, 'Dad, we're playing for the championship.' I said, 'Now, I know how much you think of Texas Tech. That's there – they defend. I've told you –'

"It was almost like he was trying to like do what he did when I was a player, which was challenge me and warn me, which I knew. And I'll never forget, I was like, 'Are you kidding me? We're playing for the championship.' He said, 'You know, they play real defense. You're going to find out, son. You don't know, and I've *tried* to tell you over the years that you have to be –'

"And it was just like, 'What?!' (But) he might be right. That might be the way, because they were something."

Johnson, who remains close with the Bennetts, confirmed that the debate continues to torment Dick Bennett.

"To this day – to *this day* – hours before Virginia played in the National Championship, Dick and Tony were still talking about – when the ball is out in front, can you *pack*? When the ball goes to the side can you *push*? They're still debating that to this day. That's how serious this man is about the game and defense and always tweaking, always thinking, always is there a better way to do it. And that's the beauty of Coach Bennett."

Great Expectations

No one in the UWGB circle comprehended the expansive impact the pack defense would have when it was implemented. Most were focused on the Phoenix's 8-3 record and harbored hopes of earning a postseason bid. UWGB sported an impressive 4-0 record in games decided in the final minutes, a complete turnaround from the previous year.

"We weren't ready to win as freshmen or understood what it took to win, and just the little things that, you know, the discipline on defense, staying in your stance, staying alert, sprinting back every time, setting a good screen to get a shooter open," remembers Johnson. "But hopefully the teaching is right, and the teaching is good and in place, and you've got willing pupils, which obviously we were. Another year of experience, now you're readier to win."

Historical precedent dictated that UWGB would need to get to at least twenty wins and finish in the top three in the conference to have any hope of an NIT berth. So the target was set as UWGB began its conference season.

Chapter 5

Controlling Your Conference
(1989-1990 - Part 2)

The yearly goal of all college basketball programs, large and small, is to play in the postseason. A team's ability to achieve this is inextricably linked to its success against conference opponents. Stated simply, if you can't win in your conference, you won't get to the postseason.

In a minority of conferences, like the Ivy League and (formerly) the Big Ten, the regular-season champion is granted an automatic berth to the NCAA tournament, making every conference game essential.

For the rest, however, the winner of the conference tournament at the end of the season earns an automatic berth to the NCAA tournament. With at-large bids to the NCAA tournament a rarity for mid-majors, their only real shot at the Big Dance is to win their conference tournament.

Success in those conference tournaments is tied into seeding, and in some instances, game locations, which are based on the teams' regular-season conference record. Those same conference wins become invaluable when seeking entry to the sport's secondary tournament, the NIT, which rarely, if ever, grants a mid-major school a bid if they did not finish in the top three.

Postseason bids could be lost in the nonconference, but coming full circle, could only be won with conference success.

1990 Conference Outlook
Southwest Missouri State and Northern Iowa were again picked as league favorites entering the 1990 AMCU conference season. Northern Iowa had pulled the conference's biggest nonconference stunner when it defeated in-state bully, the Big Ten's Iowa Hawkeyes, in front of 22,700 fans in the UNI-Dome. Mounting a five-point comeback with less than three minutes to play, the Panthers earned a 77-74 victory, the team's first over Iowa in seventy-seven years.

Northern Iowa also had the advantage of being the hosts of the 1990 AMCU Tournament, an honor that had historically bestowed its recipient a significant advantage in reaching the Big Dance. In 1989-90, that selection was hardly scientific – both UWGB and Northern Iowa had submitted bids

Aaron A. Mitchell

The UWGB brain trust watches the action during the Phoenix's 60-56 victory over Northern Illinois on December 30, 1989. Assistant coaches Steve Swan (left) and Mike Heideman flank Dick Bennett, with athletic trainer Otis Chambers at right. (University of Wisconsin-Green Bay Archives)

to host the tournament, and the powers that be determined the fairest way to determine the winner was ... by coin flip. Northern Iowa won the toss.

UWGB and UIC were also considered contenders, picked to finished third and fourth in the conference. Like Northern Iowa, UIC had earned a big non-conference win when they knocked off a ranked Michigan State team at UIC Pavilion. It was the second UIC victory over the Spartans in the past four years, and the Flames followed it up with a second signature win, a one-point victory against the Big Eight's Iowa State Cyclones, also at UIC Pavilion.

Western Illinois, not expected to do much before the season, had also enjoyed a strong nonconference performance, making it a dark horse fifth team. After that, with Cleveland State still ineligible to compete for a conference championship, Eastern Illinois and Valparaiso were left battling at the bottom.

With its top-heavy depth, conference officials were cautiously optimistic that the AMCU, or "Mid-Continent" as it was increasingly being referred, could get as many as three postseason bids. To be one, UWGB needed to demonstrate consistency, beating up on the lower half of the conference while at least splitting with the top half.

Consistently Inconsistent

The Phoenix opened its conference schedule in mid-January 1990 with four games in nine days, including contests against both Southwest Missouri State and Northern Iowa. It was a gauntlet beginning to be sure, and proved much tougher than UWGB had hoped, with three of the games decided by two points or less.

The opener was a home game against Eastern Illinois – a team the Phoenix and over 5,400 Green Bay fans expected to beat. Clearly rebuilding, Eastern Illinois had lost six players from its 1988-89 team that averaged more than ten minutes per game, including the conference Player of the Year, Jay Taylor.

Four sophomores started for the Panthers, who gave the Phoenix everything it could handle. But as the Phoenix had done throughout the non-conference schedule, players stepped up and UWGB took control. This time, it was behind their cagey linebacker, Dean Vander Plas.

"That was one of those games that ... you just had a feeling like when (your team) needed something, the ball was just going to be in your hands," remembers Vander Plas. "Tony was so good at the free throw line that you knew at the end of a game that they *weren't* going to foul him, so you just better be ready."

Vander Plas was.

With the game tied at 52-52 and less than a minute to play, Vander Plas snagged a critical offensive rebound, was fouled, and hit two free throws to give UWGB the lead. Then, on the Panthers' ensuing possession, Vander Plas delivered on defense.

Inadvertently stuck guarding Eastern Illinois's point guard, Jeff Nelson, Vander Plas blanketed the ball handler.

"I just tried to keep him out of the lane, keep him away from the middle. With the clock running down, he decided he had to make something happen. The only thing he had was the baseline, so I just pushed him that way and put my hands straight up."

Nelson had no choice but to fire away.

"I tried to jump into him, get the foul, but he played great defense,"

Dean Vander Plan celebrates as Larry Hill looks on during UWGB's 58-56 victory over Eastern Illinois on January 13, 1990. (University of Wisconsin-Green Bay Archives)

noted Nelson afterwards. "I didn't have a shot at all."

Vander Plas snagged the loose ball with less than fifteen seconds left and nailed two more free throws to give UWGB had a four-point lead and seal the win. For the game, Vander Plas finished with 17 points and 12 rebounds.

The Herculean effort needed to secure a home victory against Eastern Illinois offered little momentum for the Phoenix going into its second conference game against Southwest Missouri State, even with it being a home game.

Like a broken record, UWGB dropped its fifteenth consecutive game against Charlie Spoonhour's club, 74-60. Tony Bennett (25 points and eight assists) and Larry Hill (14 points on 7-for-11 shooting) played well, but UWGB was outrebounded nearly two to one, and the Bears were in the bonus with more than ten minutes to go in both halves.

"We were tough, they were tougher. We were tough-minded, they were even more tough-minded," said Ben Johnson of the Bears. "Total credit to them."

Thankfully for the Phoenix, history also repeated itself five days later in a road test against Northern Iowa. It wouldn't be easy, but UWGB took care of business in the closing moments to secure the program's ninth consecutive win over the Panthers. Dan Oberbrunner provided a lift on the offensive end for the Phoenix, connecting on 6-of-8 shots for 15 points.

Meanwhile, the Phoenix shut down UNI's star center, Jason Reese, thanks to excellent fronting defense by Roger Ripley with backside help. The team forced Reese into seven critical turnovers that helped keep UWGB in the game.

"They defend the inside the best of any team I've played against," Reese

Dan Oberbrunner emerges from a scramble with the ball during UWGB's 86-76 victory over Cleveland State on February 5, 1990. (University of Wisconsin-Green Bay Archives)

UWGB athletic trainer Otis Chambers holds back an irate Dick Bennett during the Phoenix's victory over Cleveland State at the Brown County Arena. (University of Wisconsin-Green Bay Archives)

said afterwards. "It seems like there's three guys on me every time I touch the ball."

Two nights later, UWGB played a sneaky-good Western Illinois Leathernecks squad that had put together an impressive 11-5 record, including a surprising 3-0 conference tally with wins against contenders UIC and Northern Iowa. Western Illinois played an intense, man-to-man trapping defense, going full-court as often as possible.

UWGB got up early and led 27-14 at the half, and at one point held a 17-point lead. But the Leathernecks' defensive pressure helped chip away at the lead, cutting it to eight with just over ten minutes to play. Bennett tried a mass substitution, resting four of his starters, but the move backfired and in four minutes Western Illinois had taken a five-point lead. The Leathernecks held in the final minutes, downing UWGB 49-48.

It was a gut-punching loss, and the first slip-up the team had in a close game all season. At 2-2 after the first four conference games, the team had hardly inspired.

Putting it all Together

A favorable schedule and some high-quality play helped the Phoenix finally piece together two very impressive weeks of basketball in late January and early February. It started with a role reversal on the road at UIC on January 29, 1990, where it was UWGB that found itself down 15 points with ten minutes to play. The Phoenix put together a stunning 20-3 run that included a trio of three-pointers by Tony Bennett and Oberbrunner to take the lead, and a key Hill block on the final shot attempt sealed the victory for UWGB.

Tony had a quiet day, finishing with just 15 points, and his lack of scoring fired up his father.

"He makes me mad," Dick Bennett said. "He's got this idea that he shouldn't be scoring. He needs to stay aggressive to the basket. We cannot afford to not have him score."

Two days later, Tony appeased his father, pouring in 23 points against Cleveland State. But the game was most notable for what happened after Tony fouled out of the game. With 4:29 to play, Dick Bennett switched from his pack defense into a 1-3-1 zone to neutralize the Vikings' attack. The move paid off, and with 22 points from Vander Plas, the Phoenix prevailed, 91-83.

UWGB easily took care of business next in a home bout against conference punching bag Valparaiso. Bennett's club put together a complete 69-53 victory, winning its third straight and improving to 13-5 overall and 4-2 in the conference.

Two nights later, on February 5, 1990, the Phoenix again beat up on Cleveland State behind another big night from ... you guessed it, Vander Plas. The bruiser shot 7 for 11 from the field and finished with 19 points. But it was Tony's offensive explosion of 31 points on 12-for-16 shooting that stole the show and prompted Kevin Mackey to call him the best player in the league after the game.

The win over Cleveland State put Dick Bennett over the .500 career winning percentage mark for the first time in his Division I career. He would never again fall below that threshold.

UWGB got its fifth straight win on February 10, shooting a school-record 71% from the field in a blowout 86-64 win over Eastern Illinois. The Phoenix was particularly dangerous from beyond the arc, where Tony went 4-for-5, Karisny 3-for-5, and Oberbrunner 4-for-4 as part of a season-high 20 points. Meanwhile, Johnson held the Panthers' best player, Dave Olson, to just 12 points.

The win put UWGB at 15-5 overall, 5-2 in conference and squarely in second place. Nipping at its heals was Northern Iowa, which had rebounded from a rough 3-3 start, while Western Illinois, who had started the conference schedule 5-0, looked to be a team trending in the wrong direction.

Team	Conf.	Overall
Southwest Missouri State	6-1	16-5
UWGB	5-2	15-5
Northern Iowa	5-3	14-5
Western Illinois	5-3	14-8
UIC	3-5	11-9
Eastern Illinois	2-6	8-11
Valparaiso	0-6	2-16
Cleveland State	N/A	8-10

Larry Hill slams one down during UWGB's 64-50 triumph over Northern Iowa on February 17, 1990. (University of Wisconsin-Green Bay Archives)

Importantly, the two weeks of consistent basketball helped Bennett establish his rotation. Tony and Vander Plas were obvious stalwarts, with Oberbrunner, Ripley, Karisny, Johnson, and Hill all rounding out the top seven. Martinez had been hampered by an injury, but would be the eighth upon his return.

Just Bear-ly

The Western Illinois aberration in mid-January aside, UWGB was chalking up consistent wins against those conference foes it was supposed to beat, and their early season split against Southwest Missouri State and Northern Iowa was, at a minimum, acceptable. Their rematch against the Bears, however, was not encouraging.

Both clubs entered the game on February 12 riding five-game win streaks thanks to stellar defensive efforts. And while Bennett was eager to exorcise his demons, the Bears brought with them the conference's leading scorer (guard Darryl Reid) and leading rebounder (forward Lee Campbell). Oh, and the conference's top home court advantage.

"To me, (Springfield, Missouri) was the most similar (to Green Bay) as far as just a community that was behind their team, and just rowdy, and that team was so good. I mean Charlie Spoonhour had them going," says LeMoine.

"Spoon's Temple of Doom," remembers Tony Bennett. "That was such a great setting, and they were tenacious."

For thirty minutes of basketball, UWGB gave it everything it had, shooting 54% in the first half and keeping victory in sight. The Phoenix even took a six-point lead (23-17) at one point before leaving the floor up one at the half. With the game tied at 44-44 with just under nine minutes to play, it looked as though UWGB had finally given themselves an opportunity to beat the Bears.

But as they had the previous fifteen match-ups, the wheels fell off, albeit much closer to the finish line than in past iterations. The Phoenix managed just eight points in the final eight minutes, while the Bears' Reid put in nine points alone during the same period. In the end, UWGB dropped its sixteenth straight game to the Bears, 63-52, and sank into a three-way tie for second with Northern Iowa and Western Illinois.

The repeated struggles against Southwest Missouri State were painful to swallow, particularly as the Bears continued to beat UWGB at its own game.

"Coach Spoonhour (was an) incredible teacher, just like Coach Bennett," Johnson says. "Incredible system, incredible defensive-minded, great philosophy. And they had a touch more talent than we did. So therein lies the result. They were better at being us than we were at being us, because they were disciplined, they didn't beat themselves, they shared the ball. They played Bennett ball better than we did."

Sprint to the Finish

The loss to the Bears stung, but UWGB still had fifteen wins and was now entering the final quarter of their schedule, where it would play six games in thirteen days. Begrudgingly, Bennett had begun answering questions about this team's potential to get to the postseason.

"I think to receive any serious consideration, we'll probably have to win five of (the last six)," noted Bennett. "Twenty seems to be the cutoff point. People look at it, 'That team won twenty games. That's pretty good.' "

Karisny took it one step further. "If we get twenty and two in the tournament, then it has to be automatic." And so the march to twenty wins began in earnest.

Experiencing déjà vu, UWGB followed the Bears loss with a win over Northern Iowa. The Panthers entered with a conference-best 7-2 road record and the second-leading scorer in Jason Reese. But the Phoenix were 7-1 at home, and as both teams found out, still had Northern Iowa's number.

Behind a 17-1 second-half run that blew the game wide open, UWGB put the game away. Stifling defense from Ripley and Hill had Reese flustered.

"The way they play, I don't think we'll ever beat them," he said. "I can't see it. We don't match up. They have to be the best-coached defensive basketball team I've ever faced."

With the team's sixteenth win and a sweep of the Panthers, UWGB effectively secured second place in the conference with three conference games to play. The Phoenix made that placement official two nights later.

Against Western Illinois, a team in desperate need of a win, UWGB played an excellent first half and took a minimal lead to the locker room. At halftime, assistant coach Mike Heideman showed his expertise. First, he instructed the offense to clear out for Tony Bennett to work against senior guard Johnny Hawk, as the Leathernecks had refused to offer help on that matchup. He also directed the team to work curl cuts to get the basketball to the hoop for easy buckets. The offense immediately improved, and UWGB quickly built a 17-point lead, eventually sailing to a 77-61 victory and avenging the team's embarrassing loss earlier in the season.

The win did wonders for the Phoenix's postseason hopes, bringing its seventeen wins closer to the NIT's magic "20-win" number. It also improved their NCAA tournament potential. With the No. 2 seed, UWGB would not have to play Southwest Missouri State (the No. 1 seed) if at all, until the conference championship game.

Two days later, on February 21, 1990, UWGB played a nonconference revenge matchup against Akron, a future Mid-Continent Conference foe. The Phoenix hadn't forgotten their 14-point loss in early January. In one of the most dominant defensive performances of the Dick Bennett era, UWGB held Akron to just 13 points in the first half. The Phoenix continued the onslaught in the second half, routinely beating the Zips' trapping defense and shooting well over 80% for the half. The Phoenix had its eighteenth win, and getting to twenty wins now seemed more likely than not.

Riding a three-game win streak, UWGB's next game – its fourth in eight days – was February 24 against UIC at the Brown County Arena. UWGB was tops in the conference in team defense, but in this matchup, it was UIC's trapping pressure that frustrated the Phoenix and helped UIC overcome a 10-point deficit to force overtime.

Bennett utilized his 1-3-1 zone in the game's precarious moments, and that, along with his constant dedication to eliminating the opportunity to fail, helped UWGB take control in the extra period. Going 14 of 15 from the free throw line in the extra period, UWGB grabbed its nineteenth win of the season and fourth in a row. With at least three games to play and a near guarantee against conference bottom-feeder Valparaiso, the magic number of twenty wins seemed a virtual certainty.

The final regular-season home game came on February 26. As it had with Akron, UWGB played its second game of the season against nonconference opponent Missouri-Kansas City.

It was a senior night to remember at the Brown County Arena, as all three outgoing Phoenix veterans provided some scoring punch in a game that was hardly competitive. Ripley scored 10 points and added five assists and Karisny added 11 points. But it was one of UWGB's unsung heroes, Dan Oberbrunner, who stole the show. Oberbrunner connected on 5-of-7 three-pointers and led the team with 22 points as the Phoenix rolled to victory, 83-66.

It was a special way for the Phoenix to achieve the magic number of twenty wins, and a vocal 4,800 fans gave a standing ovation to the team's senior class.

"When we came in as freshman, it didn't seem like there was a lot of great games, great atmosphere in the Brown County," remembers Rondorf. "Well, then that turned around with Dan Oberbrunner and Mike Karisny and Roger Ripley as seniors."

"Quite frankly, I didn't expect (twenty wins) this year," noted Dick Bennett. "I wanted to be really competitive this year, and I felt the future was bright."

But Bennett remained skeptical of his team's chances of securing an NIT bid: "I think our chances are pretty good, but I don't know. My limited experience with it two years ago didn't reveal anything. Their standards vary."

Kevin Mackey, Cleveland State's head coach who was intimately familiar with the NIT, noted that a snub was still possible, stating, "Green Bay is good enough to play in the NIT, but I don't think they get the respect around the nation that they deserve because of name recognition."

Mackey's warning aside, UWGB began the process of requesting a home game, should they get selected by the NIT. One of the challenges that would recur in subsequent seasons was the Green Bay Home and Garden Show, planned annually for the second week of March in the arena. Nevertheless, athletic director Dan Spielman submitted a formal bid to host a game, including putting up the necessary monetary guarantee, specifying that the only date UWGB could possibly host was March 13.

For its part, the NIT acknowledged that UWGB was on its radar. John Powers, Executive Director for the NIT, was quoted saying, "I know they're ranked 70. The Mid-Continent is a good conference. We're aware of all the teams, at least we'd like to think we are."

UWGB tacked on a twenty-first victory to its resume for good measure in its regular-season finale at Valparaiso. It was an uncommon oddity that both UWGB and Valparaiso's conference seeds (No. 2 and No. 7) were secured before the match-up, meaning the teams would be meeting again in the conference tournament. Nevertheless, the win provided UWGB with another notch on its belt, and marked the team's sixth straight victory, putting the Phoenix at 21-6 overall and 9-3 in the conference.

The season's turning point?

The Akron loss that spawned Bennett's change to the pack defense.

"I had been wrestling in my mind, 'Do I want to continue to do what I'm doing defensively? Or do I want to go to a more conservative approach, protect the lane, not get our guards rotate so much down to the baseline and get caught underneath?'" Bennett noted. "I made the change after that Akron game because they hurt us. They kind of sliced us up a little bit."

Numbers don't lie, and through those final sixteen games following the Akron loss, UWGB's defense had become elite, holding eleven of its opponents to less than 50% shooting. Meanwhile, the Phoenix excelled at eliminating losing, committing the fewest turnovers in the conference and making over 77% of its free throws, good for second best in the nation.

And though Bennett had yet to get through Charlie Spoonhour's Bears, the Phoenix had dominated the rest of the conference, winning the games they should and regularly beating the other the top-tier teams like Northern Iowa and UIC.

The Next Step

The Mid-Continent Conference recognized the Phoenix's elevated play and named Dick Bennett its Coach of the Year. Tony Bennett easily made First Team All-Conference, but lost out to Southwest Missouri State's Lee Campbell for Player of the Year in a tight race. Vander Plas, the only other Phoenix player to average double figures scoring, took home Honorable Mention All-Conference.

The 1990 Mid-Continent Conference tournament took place in Cedar Falls, Iowa – home of the Northern Iowa Panthers. With Southwest Missouri State earning a bye, the second-seeded Phoenix were the conference's top team playing in the quarterfinals.

History was not on the Phoenix's side – the program had enjoyed only one conference tournament win since joining the conference in 1982. But earning at least one win in the conference tournament seemed all but a requirement of earning NIT consideration.

With Tony Bennett fighting a bruised shin, Dick Bennett made a decision early in the game to leave him on the bench unless absolutely necessary and gave Martinez the start. That decision lasted all of three minutes. UWGB found itself down 9-4, and with 17:03 left in the first half, Dick relented and put Tony into the game. Tony never came back out.

Valparaiso had switched up their approach since the two teams met four days earlier. Homer Drew's club spread the floor, isolated its ball handlers, and looked for drive-and-kick options for open three-pointers in playing to the Crusaders' strength. The move temporarily stunned the Phoenix, but after a few moments of adjustment, UWGB regrouped and regained the lead.

Though the Phoenix was unable to run away with the game, it was able to keep the Crusaders in check. Tony Bennett's 17 points and four assists led the way, but Vander Plas was also superb, adding 16 interior points en route to a 64-57 Phoenix victory.

Western Illinois, the No. 3 seed, easily disposed of Eastern Illinois in its quarterfinal match to become UWGB's semifinal opponent. And in an epic triple-overtime thriller that saw six UIC players foul out, the No. 4 seed and home team Northern Iowa Panthers defeated the Flames. It was Northern Iowa's first tournament win and earned it the right to play top-seeded Southwest Missouri State in the semifinals.

The Phoenix's quarterfinal win was monumental without question, and like longed-for good fortune that finally materializes, hard to really absorb. UWGB, having never won a semifinal game in the Mid-Continent, was on the precipice making the conference championship and one step from an automatic berth into the NCAA tournament. It seemed likely to earn an NIT bid regardless.

All of the speculation meant nothing when the teams took the floor. Western Illinois was a fast, physical team, and like the Phoenix, known for its defensive pressure. That intensity kept the score close in the first half, and the Leathernecks were up by four points with five minutes to play in the game.

Then, in a span of two minutes, the Phoenix put together a mini-run that began with a Vander Plas 12-foot jumper from the left, followed up by back-to-back swished jumpers by Tony Bennett. With 3:48 to play, UWGB had regained a 45-44 advantage.

Neither team scores over the next two-plus minutes as both defenses clamped down. Ben Johnson hit two free throws with 1:29 left, but Western Illinois added an easy layup on the ensuing possession, cutting the UWGB lead back to a point at 47-46. After a stop, Western Illinois had the final possession with 25 seconds left.

A chance to play in the conference championship and the postseason hung in the balance. Dick Bennett kept his team in a 1-3-1 zone defense, as he had for the final ten minutes. A Tim Chase three-point look clanked long for Western Illinois, Hill grabbed the rebound and was fouled with one second left. His two free throws sealed the victory, 49-46.

"We probably played thirty minutes of good defense, and survived the last ten with our zone," Bennett said after the game.

It would not be the last time he used the zone to confound the opposition, but not always with the same results.

UWGB had earned the biggest Division I win in school history. The victory gave the Phoenix a chance to play for an NCAA tournament bid in the conference championship. Equally valuable, that game would be broadcast on ESPN, marking UWGB's first-ever appearance on national television. Almost as an afterthought, an NIT bid seemed certain should the Phoenix (23-6) fall in the conference championship.

Recalls Tony Bennett: "When you're building a program, there are these little hurdles you clear. You get to this point, and then you get to the next step. And for us to get to an ESPN game, to get to the conference championship and have a chance to play in an NCAA tournament was unbelievable."

Prime Time

The good news kept coming when the Phoenix found out who it would be playing. There was no question the team was rooting hard for Northern Iowa in the second semifinal, having beaten the Panthers twice already in 1989-90, and ten straight going back to 1986. In contrast, Southwest Missouri State, UWGB's kryptonite, had beaten the Phoenix *sixteen* straight times.

Late in that affair, it looked like the Bears, who held a nine-point lead with less than two minutes to play, were a lock to advance. But Northern Iowa stormed back in the closing moments to tie the game, and with two seconds left, connected on a full-court pass to Jason Reese, who took one step to the right and dropped in an easy layup as the horn sounded to give the Panthers a miraculous 63-61 victory.

That set the stage for UWGB to play Northern Iowa in the UNI-Dome on March 7, 1990, with a trip to the NCAA tournament hanging in the balance. As the Phoenix prepared, Tony's shin injury remained a serious concern. Blood had pooled around his ankle, coloring the foot a nasty shade of "injured," and limiting his quickness.

"He's a step slow, perhaps two steps slow because of the injury," noted Dick Bennett before the game. "He's done a lot with quickness over the years, but he's just simply not able to slide or be explosive, so he's got to use his moxie."

But Tony's injury couldn't minimize the team's assuredness, particularly given the history.

"We had their number," recalls Karisny. "Just like Southwest Missouri had our number, we kind of had their number."

And yet, with an NCAA bid on the line in front of a house packed with Panthers fans and a national television crew there to broadcast every play, all bets were off. The Phoenix coaching staff understood the pressure and looked to lighten the players' spirits.

"We had to relax the kids, so as coaches, we put on a skit in the hotel. We did imitations of the players," remembers Dick Bennett. "They were just crying they were laughing so hard, and so we went into the game pretty relaxed and I remember singing to them ... *Whatever will be will be – Que Sera Sera,* ... Over the years, I did a lot of really goofy things that kids remember."

The football/basketball UNI-Dome was a sight in and of itself.

"It was kind of like half of a high school game," LeMoine says. "The end and one side had portable bleachers that were just packed, and then you had half of it like the stadium of the football thing. But those stands that were right around, those kids got crazy nuts, and that was pretty cool to play at."

ESPN sent Sean McDonough and Mike Rice to call the game, and the exposure, both personally for the players and for the program as a whole, was enticing.

"It was a chance to play on national TV. I just remember the environment was neat," Vander Plas says. "It was loud in there, and it was electric."

"I remember being so hyped up that friends and family could watch you play," Karisny says. "Back in 1990, (playing on TV) was a huge deal because you're not going to have a lot of your friends and family travel eight or ten hours to watch you play, and I remember we came out a little tight."

As nearly every recent entry in the UWGB vs. Northern Iowa saga, this game was destined to be a plodding, methodical affair. But unlike previous outings where UWGB had jumped out to early leads, on this night it was the Panthers who shot out of the gates, scoring on four of its first five possessions while the Phoenix went scoreless.

UWGB's players were pressing, and nerves looked like they had come into play. No place was that more evident than midway through the first half when Roger Ripley, receiving a beautiful pass from a penetrating Tony Bennett at the block, proceeded to not simply miss

Northern Iowa's Steve Phyfe (50) goes up for a basket as UWGB's Ben Johnson (23) establishes position during the Panthers' victory in the UNI-Dome, earning them a trip to the 1990 NCAA tournament. (Special Collections & University Archives, Rod Library, University of Northern Iowa)

– but to *air ball* – a slam dunk attempt.

The seniors weren't the only ones pressing. Tony, clearly limited in mobility, settled for open jumpers early, but was unable to find any rhythm and missed on three open attempts in the first ten minutes. With 11:20 left in the first half, UWGB had dug itself a 12-4 hole.

By the second media break, UWGB was acclimating and had at least stopped the bleeding. A jumper in the paint by Hill, followed by open three-pointers from Johnson and Karisny, and a wide-open layup by Oberbrunner over the next seven minutes gave the Phoenix some confidence. But during that same stretch, Northern Iowa had bettered the Phoenix's effort, increasing the lead first to nine points and then to eleven, taking a 29-18 lead into the half.

The Panthers' hounding defense compounded UWGB's offensive woes, forcing poor shots that resulted in a pathetic 34% first-half shooting performance, all while being outrebounded 14-9. Tony's first-half shooting in particular had been abysmal, going 0-for-5 with no points. It wasn't simply that he was unable to hit his open looks, but with his swollen ankle, he was too slow to get past his defender or draw much of a double team.

The second half would be one of steady runs for both teams, beginning with the first possession when Tony worked off a Vander Plas screen and knocked down an open three-pointer. His first points of the game cut the deficit to 29-21. Johnson came up with a steal and Hill scored on a put-back layup, cutting the margin to 29-23.

The streaky Dan Oberbrunner then caught fire. First, after a steal, Tony hit Oberbrunner for an easy fast-break layup. Two possessions later, Oberbrunner knocked down a three-pointer. On the next possession, Oberbrunner caught a pass at the top of the key and knocked down his second consecutive three-pointer, tying the game at 31-31.

Northern Iowa, through their junior forward Troy Muilenberg, answered the Phoenix torrent with a methodical 11-2 run over the next five minutes, reclaiming a 42-33 lead with 6:36 left in the game.

Just when it seemed Northern Iowa was ready to deliver a knock-out blow, UWGB mounted another comeback. Karisny free throws, a nifty left-handed bank shot by Vander Plas, and a quick baseline jumper by Ripley helped UWGB cut the lead, and after Tony Bennett delivered a sneaky pass to Hill for an easy layup, the deficit was two with 1:10 left.

With NCAA dreams very much in the balance, Northern Iowa walked the ball up the floor, intending to run down the clock, and UWGB buckled up for a critical defensive possession. The Panthers ran the shot clock under 10 seconds before Muilenberg, getting the ball on the left wing, dribbled baseline and bounced the ball off his foot out of bounds.

But in the confusion, one of the officials had whistled Oberbrunner for a blocking foul on Muilenberg's drive. It was a big call, and a questionable one at that – Oberbrunner had position and there was little contact.

Muilenberg connected on both of his freebies, putting the Panthers up four. Vander Plas turned the ball over on the next possession, and after some additional free throws, Northern Iowa had a 53-45 and the school's first NCAA tournament bid.

"They just got on a roll and we couldn't get it undone," recalls Vander Plas.

The NCAA dream was dead, at least for 1989-90.

"You work so hard all year for that one moment," Vander Plas noted after the game. "You're anticipating, then it's like the bottom drops out for a second.

"My whole career we never lost to them, except one time to go to the NCAA tournament," Karisny says. "I remember hanging up my uniform in the locker and crying and saying, 'I'm never' – I can almost like feel it yet, even thirty years later. It's a hard feeling."

Consolation Prize

At 23-7, UWGB remained hopeful that it would still receive a coveted NIT bid and have the chance to play in the program's first Division I postseason. Nothing was a guarantee, but the team gathered at Coach Bennett's home the day of the postseason selections in hopes they would receive the NIT's call. The Bennetts created a familial setting that reflected the program's and community's persona.

"We were living in this relatively small home," Dick explains. "We invited all the media to our home, and my wife had made hot fudge sundaes for them all."

"Mrs. Bennett always made the best hot fudge sundaes – the original fudge, you know, homemade fudge," adds Vander Plas.

The phone wouldn't stop ringing, but the team had to sit and wait.

"I kept getting calls at home from different people, and we'd get all excited, and I'd say, 'Oh, it's so-and-so. No, this isn't the call," Bennett remembers with a laugh. "Then finally the call came from Dan Spielman, our athletic director. He said, 'Yep, we're in. We have to go to Southern Illinois, who had won twenty-six games and gotten snubbed by the NCAA.' "

"The phone rang, and all of the sudden Coach came running down and said, 'We got practice!' " remembers Vander Plas.

"I remember getting that call – we didn't know (for sure) we were going to get into the NIT tournament," Tony Bennett says. "We were so fired up to get into the NIT. I just look back being thankful and hungry."

"We were good enough to play in the NCAA that year, but it was also a necessary step for the Green Bay program," nots Karisny. "The NIT, in retrospect, was probably the best thing that ever happened to the program. It sucked for me personally because it was my last year ... (but) it was a tonic that was needed to prepare us for the future years."

UWGB had drawn arguably the most difficult opponent and the top mid-major to make the NIT. The Southern Illinois Salukis had finished the season 26-7 and carried a huge chip on their shoulder, believing they had been slighted by the NCAA tournament selection committee. They had failed to seal an automatic bid, dropping three-point loss in the Missouri Valley Conference championship game to Illinois State, but still felt they were deserving of an at-large bid.

"You're like, 'Okay, we've got to go play the conference champ that lost in their conference tournament, that was ranked at points throughout that year, and we've got to go to their place,' " Vander Plas recalls.

"The people there were so upset, their staff was so upset because they didn't get that bid," notes Dick Bennett. "They had a press conference and the whole gist of it was about how upset they were that they didn't get into the NCAA, and would this affect them?"

"I remember their coach making some comments to the local newspaper that he felt it was a disgrace that they didn't make the NCAA," Karisny states. "And I loved that – it gave us, privately, a little fuel. We thought, 'Wait a second, we didn't get in either.' "

The advantage in being a mid-major team with an early conference championship game was that UWGB had more than a week of rest between the Northern Iowa game and the Southern Illinois game. The time off gave Tony's shin a little more time to heal.

In the meantime, WBAY – Green Bay's local CBS affiliate – rushed to secure the rights and gather the resources to televise the game in the Green Bay market. Sports anchor Bill Jartz would do play-by-play, with UWGB's own athletic director, Dan Spielman, joining for color commentary.

For the third straight outing, UWGB was playing the biggest game in school history, and on paper, it was the underdog. The Salukis had a higher computer ranking than every Phoenix opponent other than Illinois and Southwest Missouri State. On top of that, they were a nearly unbeatable 12-1 at home and had the experience of having played in the NIT a season before.

"They were so confident that they were already talking about going to New York and stuff like that in the NIT," remembers Karisny.

But once the game started, you never would have known any of that. UWGB rolled up an early lead and looked like it might blow the game open with a nine-point advantage midway through the first half.

"We were lathered up, like 'Let's go,' " recalls LeMoine. "We were on a high. We just kind of knew we were going to win."

However, when Johnson took a seat with foul trouble, it opened the door for the Salukis to fight all the way back and take a 36-30 lead into the half.

But coming out of the locker room, the Phoenix defense changed the narrative, shutting down Southern Illinois' running offense during a 19-4 run, building a 49-40 lead it would never relinquish.

In what proved to be one of the easier victories the team would see, UWGB won its first Division I postseason game 73-60, holding the Salukis to a season-low points on a season-worst 32.1% shooting percentage.

"We played a heck of a game, at their place. And you know, I just felt like it was never in doubt," remembers Vander Plas. "You just felt like, 'We own these guys.' So to get our first postseason win was pretty cool."

Not only had UWGB made the postseason, it had won a game and advanced. It was no small feat, as UWGB was one of only four (out of sixteen) road teams that were able to pull the first-round NIT upset. It was a great achievement for a program that, less than a decade earlier, had been playing Division II.

"That was, I think, a pivotal moment, where we went into Carbondale and just really took it to a team that probably deserved to be in the NCAA tournament in Southern Illinois," comments Tony Bennett.

Well-rested and showing no ill effects, Tony led all scorers going 9-for-16 from the field and finishing with 26 points. Rich Herrin, the Salukis' head coach, called Bennett "as good a guard as we've played all year long."

It was certainly a complete, full team effort.

"Tony had a good game, but so did Roger Ripley, so did Dean," notes Karisny. "Everybody stepped up to a degree. It wasn't luck that we beat them."

Along with Ripley and Vander Plas, Johnson played huge, scoring 14 points, grabbing seven boards, tallying four assists, all while hold the Salukis' star, Jerry Jones, to just 11 points. Meanwhile, Hill also came up aces, recording a double-double (12 points, 10 rebounds), as well as four blocks.

"It gave us that little taste," adds Dean Rondorf, "that we belonged."

Spirit in St. Louis

The victory over Southern Illinois set the stage for a second-round matchup at Saint Louis on March 20, 1990. Now, for the fourth consecutive game, UWGB was playing in the biggest matchup in school history. Saint Louis called the Kiel Auditorium, an arena built in the 1930s, home.

"It was like a theater sort of, downtown St. Louis, but it was energetic in that place," describes Vander Plas.

The Billikens, from the strong Midwestern Collegiate Conference, had lots of recent NIT experience. In 1988-89, Saint Louis had finished as a runner-up, recording wins over Southern Illinois, Wisconsin, New Mexico, and Michigan State before finally falling to St. John's. This 1989-90 version of the Billikens had a similar make-up, having finished the regular season with a solid 17-11 record.

The Billikens also had star power with their 6-foot-8 senior forward Anthony Bonner. Bonner was a high-flying, double-double freak who attacked the rim and projected as a first-round pick in the upcoming NBA draft. Bonner's 19.7 ppg and 13.6 rpg both led his team, and he finished his career as the school's all-time leading scorer.

"They were talking about Anthony Bonner as a lottery pick, and you're like, 'We get to play him,' " recalls Vander Plas. "He was good, he was super good."

Beyond Bonner, Saint Louis also had other dangerous weapons with guard Charles Newberry (12.8 ppg and 5.8 apg), forward Kevin Footes (14.0 ppg and 4.3 rpg), and 7-foot freshman Melvin Robinson.

The Phoenix's margin for error was slim. As it had five days earlier, UWGB raced out of the gate after the opening tip. Oberbrunner continued his hot streak, knocking down two three-pointers and scoring eight of the Phoenix's first ten points as the club built a 10-2 lead.

Saint Louis countered with a full-court trapping defense, and made its money on fast-break baskets. The lead vanished twice as fast as it had been built, and the Billikens tied the game 14-14 by the 10:00 mark of the first half. The see-saw affair would see mini-runs by both teams in the half, with UWGB taking a 29-26 lead to the locker room.

Defensively in the first half, the Phoenix were exceptional in the half-court, though it struggled on the boards and gave away too many second-chance baskets. Offensively, the Phoenix were able to get open looks by moving the basketball, and for the most part had success converting.

Rich Grawer, Saint Louis's coach, made two major halftime adjustments to neutralize some of the Phoenix's strength. First, Saint Louis, the superior team athletically, made the effort to work the ball inside, getting easy opportunities for the 7-footer Robinson. Second, Saint Louis switched defensively to a 2-3 zone to neutralize UWGB's hot shooting.

Both had an impact, but neither were determinative. Indeed, throughout the second half, both teams continued to trade baskets – a number of which were lob-dunks for the Billikens – and the lead, right down to the final electric minute.

Saint Louis held a 55-54 lead with 46 seconds left in the game. Coming out of a timeout, UWGB inbounded to Hill, who was quickly double-teamed. Bonner stripped Hill and was subsequently fouled. With fouls to give, it took two more hacks before Bonner actually went to the line.

Bonner, a 70% FT shooter, swished the first free throw but bricked the second, and Vander Plas grabbed the rebound. Down two with 25 seconds to play, UWGB had a chance to tie or take the lead in the NIT's second round.

Tony Bennett found Vander Plas at the top of the key. The big forward took two dribbles to the lane and shot an open 12-foot jumper with 18 seconds left. The ball clanked off the back iron, but bounced right back to him and he immediately went back up. For a moment, it looked like Vander Plas had the perfect play, but before the ball could descend, it was rejected by Saint Louis forward Don Braun. The Billikens gathered the ball, passed away from the Phoenix players seeking a foul, and got it back to Braun for a game-winning layup.

The Phoenix's second upset bid had come up just short, ending its season.

"I don't know how we didn't win that game," LeMoine says. "We should've had it."

"I got my shot blocked at the end," Vander Plas says. "I make that shot, we advance. They got to it and we didn't, so we got to go home."

Karisny was more forgiving.

"We could never put enough pressure on Saint Louis to feel like maybe they were in peril of losing the game. And unfortunately, we came out on the short end of that one. The NIT is all about matchups. If we'd have played that game in Green Bay, we'd have beat them because of the energy there."

Necessary Steps

The Saint Louis loss marked the end for seniors Dan Oberbrunner, Roger Ripley, and Mike Karisny. Oberbrunner, for his part, had done all he could to extend the run, turning in vital performances in critical games during the last half of the season.

"Dan was a heck of a player, just a competitor. Could shoot the lights out," notes Rondorf. "You kind of want to emulate some of those seniors who didn't really get a lot of time as freshman as sophomores, like Dan did, and worked his way into a having a successful career at Green Bay."

Ripley, an interior presence on both ends of the floor, would be hard to replace, both athletically and from a character perspective.

"The Roger Ripleys – those guys will do anything to help us be successful," recalls Dick Bennett fondly. "Those are the kind of guys we want."

"Roger was just that huge teddy bear, and just a fun-loving guy," states Rondorf. "Just a good person, like everyone in our locker room was."

Karisny, arguably the most colorful of the three, had managed to simultaneously bring both intensity and light-heartedness to the program.

"He was one of those guys who was real charismatic," adds Rondorf. "He'd shoot and hit threes, and get the shooters out and like holster them up and stuff like that. And it was all good and he got the crowd going, which was phenomenal."

"The seniors at the time, Mike Karisny, Dan Oberbrunner, Roger Ripley ... they were great mentors," says Logan Vander Velden. "There was never a point where there was much of a split or anything within the locker room."

Indeed, it was the relationships that would be hardest to replace.

"The greatest part of memories is not just the basketball time, it's the friendships and this group of guys that was amazing and so different," remembers Karisny. "That feeling of comradery and brotherhood – it carried forward through generations of Green Bay basketball. And I'll cherish that forever."

The seniors had not reached the mountaintop, but took pride in helping shape the basketball renaissance in Green Bay.

"That's when the program had re-set itself," states Karisny. "And I was kind of in the middle of that."

"It was kind of the signal that we had turned things around because we had a young team and thought we would be considerably better the following year," says Dick Bennett. "Just a real important stepping stone."

While the Phoenix raised the bar for its own program, it worked in tandem with Northern Iowa in raising the conference's social status as well. The Panthers, a 14 seed, pulled an upset in their first-round NCAA match-up, beating Missouri on a last-second tip-in for the school's first tournament win. They would fall two days later to Minnesota, but for the third time in five years, the Mid-Continent had won a tournament game.

Midwestern mid-majors as a whole were wildly successful in the 1990 Tournament. The University of Dayton, an MCC team, upset the 5 seed Illinois Fighting Illini – a dark horse Final Four contender – before falling in their second-round game. Xavier University, another MCC team, danced all the way to the Sweet Sixteen after upsetting the third-seeded Georgetown in the second round. And Ball State University, a 12 seed MAC school, matched Xavier, first beating 5 seed Oregon State by one point, and then knocking off the 4 seed Louisville Cardinals by two points before falling to the eventual NCAA champions UNLV by just two points. The Ball State game was UNLV's only NCAA win by less than ten points.

The winds of change were blowing.

Chapter 6

Bonding
(1990 USSR Trip)

Even with the right players buying into the right system, programs can fail to achieve success without striking a level of cohesiveness and chemistry. Beyond simply accepting their roles, teams achieve more when their players feel a sense of responsibility toward, and even care for, each other.

One way to build that chemistry is through shared adversity. This serves to ground expectations, create commonality, shape objectives, define roles, and cement bonds capable of surviving apart from the particular challenges overcome.

It's not unusual to find teams that have risen to great heights – college basketball or otherwise – first experienced and overcame challenges or setbacks. The best of those grew stronger as a result of the bonds created and learned to embracing their strengths. More importantly, they compensate for each other's weaknesses.

One Crazy Idea

Fate brought Dick Bennett and Soviet basketball coach Boris Kazebin together in August of 1989.

Kazebin had traveled to the US, interested in learning a defensive style of basketball he could take back and teach to his teams in the USSR. At a clinic in Milwaukee, he had found his guru in Dick Bennett.

"I saw his was my perspective on basketball," Kazebin said a year after meeting Bennett. "I was coach in this division, my team went from eleventh to first place on defense."

As the two coaches hit it off, the kernel of a unique idea took root in both men's minds.

"He spoke to me about organizing a trip to the Soviet Union the next summer (1990), and we talked about it at length," Bennett recalls. "I said I'm very interested because we have the opportunity to make a foreign trip, and we would have to line up some sponsorship and raise some money and so on. But it is definitely something I would like to do, because we have a fairly experienced team and it would do them a lot of good."

The NCAA allowed each team to take one trip overseas every four years.

By spring of 1990, the USSR trip had become an idea that Bennett couldn't let pass. With Kazebin's guiding hand, the Phoenix's tour was planned for June 9-27, 1990, and included three, three-game tournaments, the first in Kar'kov, the second in L'vov, and the final in Kiev. In exchange for coordinating the team's itinerary, Bennett agreed to host Kazebin later that year for a month in Green Bay, where he could shadow Bennett and learn from him on the job.

For all of the reasons Bennett found the USSR irresistible, his players found the idea ... crazy.

"I remember him saying that we originally were going to go to Aruba to play in a tournament. And we were all like, 'Yes!' " says Scott LeMoine. "And then he came in and he's like, 'You know, we have this once-in-a-lifetime – the Soviet Union popped up.' And we're like, 'What?! Wait a minute! Beach, sun, or the Soviet Union?' "

"Who in the hell takes a team to Russia for eighteen days at the end of the Cold War? I mean who does that?" adds Ben Johnson with a laugh. "You can go anywhere, you can go to the Bahamas, you can go to Italy, you can go to Australia. But Russia? Russia. With no food and no water – no drinkable water – you know they had the whole Chernobyl thing?"

If anything, his team's response only served as motivation for Bennett.

"I was told we were the first college team ever to make a trip inside the Soviet Union," notes Bennett. "Three weeks, which was probably a week too long, because they were really a third-world country at that time. But that's one of the all-time great experiences I've ever had."

Fulfilling his end of the bargain, Kazebin had taken the bull by the horns and managed nearly all of the logistics for the Phoenix.

"He was really the guy who promoted it from his end and said that he would get everything scheduled," Bennett says. He would take care of all transportation, housing, and meals in the various places we would go. All we had to do was to line up our transportation to Russia and then raise enough money."

Pepsi-Cola Bottling Company of Northeastern Wisconsin made a $20,000 donation to assist with the airfare costs, and Kazebin took care of the rest.

Once the details were set, Bennett set his own team's prep schedule. NCAA rules allowed teams utilizing their international trip to organize ten additional practice days beforehand, giving Bennett an additional month of coaching that summer.

"He used that strategically, to be around his team more and get all of his systems in and all of that," Johnson explains. "So basically we ended up spending the whole dang summer together. So there's no break, there's no fun."

NCAA rules also allowed graduated players from the 1989-90 team to travel. While Karinsy turned down the chance to go in favor of beginning his family real estate career, Oberbrunner and Ripley jumped at the chance.

"Coach being a competitor, Coach said, 'Listen, we're going to win. We're coming over here to prove that we are a good basketball team,' "

John Martinez (sitting on the bench in white) poses with some of his hosts during UWGB's trip to the Soviet Union in 1990. (University of Wisconsin-Green Bay Archives)

remembers Dean Rondorf. "And so Dan played a lot and Roger played a bunch."

Aside from Karisny, Chris Yates was the only other player on the NIT team not to make the trip. Yates, whose uncle had been killed in late May 1990, was left behind for undisclosed reasons.

Back in the USSR

The team flew into Moscow on June 7, 1990, and met Kazebin.

"He had an airplane – Russian plane – lined up and we boarded the Aero-flat," states Bennett.

The team quickly learned that flying in the USSR was not what they were accustomed to.

"We hopped on a military plane and you know, there's a table in the back, a couple of us are playing cards, goofing around, and all of the sudden the plane just starts to take a nosedive," remembers LeMoine. "We're like, 'What the heck?' All of the sudden it levels out and we find out that the pilots are letting people go up and take turns practicing flying the plane. And they're just having fun."

"Coach Swan was there, and all of the sudden the plane's doing some funny things, adds Rondorf. "We're like, 'What is going on?' And someone said, 'Well, Marie's flying the plane.' Coach Swan's face just got like dead serious, and he's like, 'We've got to get her out of there now!' And it was just so funny."

"Yeah, that lasted all of about a minute before Coach put an end to that," says Logan Vander Velden.

The Moscow flight was just one of many unique experiences associated with the team's air travel.

Aaron A. Mitchell

"The airports were like a runway with like a boxcar next to it," explains LeMoine. "I remember praying that we would land. It was some of the scariest flights I've ever been on in my life."

"Everybody used to applaud whenever we landed, just because we landed safe," adds Vander Velden.

"I'll never forget they unloaded our luggage ... they pulled maybe twenty feet away from the airplane and just started chucking stuff over the side," remembers LeMoine. "You had to figure out who had your bag and which way he was chucking."

On the ground, it was apparent that the Soviet Union circa 1990 was drastically different from the United States.

"It was a fascinating time to be in you know the Ukraine," notes Tony Bennett. "It was a world unlike anything we had seen."

It began with the basics.

"We had to carry all of our own stuff, you know, toilet paper, soap, everything you had. They had no refrigeration, so everything was warm. We ate a lot of cabbage and black bread," recalls Dick Bennett.

"I just remember getting gas was like a huge deal," says John Martinez. "There's huge lines down the block just to get gas. Having to deal with things like that on a daily basis just was eye opening."

"Bread lines and gas lines, and the food they prepared for us," Jeremy Ludvigson says of his memories. "The food they served us was awful, and it was the top of the line."

Johnson also recalls the players' experiments with the local cuisine: "We ate bread with this marmalade jam on it, and then we ate eggs and this meat that we swear was ... it was *not* meat. We thought it was probably cat – that was the running joke, it was cat."

Unlike some of his teammates, Vander Plas lucked out by finding someone who could competently cook something basic, but entirely edible.

"This little old lady that was cooking for us – she couldn't speak much English, but she knew how to say 'mashed potatoes.' She would say, 'Mashed potatoes, yeah? Mashed potatoes, yeah?' And we would say, 'YES!' because we were eating cabbage and some (long pause) tough 'steak,' we'll call it."

Even finding decent water was a challenge.

"We're drinking these eight-ounce bottles of – they called it 'minerale, minerale.' It's mineral water that tasted like dirt and sediment and rock, but it was the very best that they had to offer us," notes Johnson.

"There were a few things you weren't sure about – so we're drinking either carbonated water or Pepsi during timeouts just for hydration," says Tony Bennett. "You ever try to drink carbonated water or a Coke while you're trying to hydrate and play? So yeah, it was interesting."

And yet, the resources available were the top of the line in the USSR.

"Most nights, they would bring us Pepsi, which was a big deal because Pepsi had just started to be produced in the Soviet Union," explains Vander Plas.

In spite of the hardships, that level of generosity showed the quality of the Soviet people.

"My notion of the Soviet people was out of whack," remarks Dick Bennett. "They want the same things we want. They take great pride in their families and the kind of work they do."

"They cheered for their home team, but we never really felt like, 'Man, they're really against us.' They cheered great plays that we did," recalls Rondorf. "The people we encountered generally were happy that we were there."

Tour guide Boris Kazebin also ensured the UWGB traveling party was treated to the sights and culture of the Soviet Union.

"We saw the changing of the guard at the Lenin tomb the night before we flew out of Moscow; we went to a Russian rock concert; we toured all of the war gardens, and learned so much about Russian history," recollects Dick Bennett. "Boris had everything lined up. We had so many tours – we were touring even the days of games."

"I take pride when I see the Red Square and St. Basil's Cathedral and think, 'You know, I stood right there, and how beautiful it was,' " says Rondorf. "I don't get that experience unless I go to the University of Wisconsin-Green Bay."

(From left) Dan Oberbrunner, Scott LeMoine, Jeremy Ludvigson, and Logan Vander Velden take in the sights during UWGB's 1990 trip to the USSR. (University of Wisconsin-Green Bay Archives)

For some, like Vander Plas, one of the most impactful events was seeing the Nutcracker ballet.

"None of us had ever been to the ballet before, you know," Vander Plas notes. "That was the first ballet I'd ever been to, and I had to go all the way to the Ukraine to get to one. But it was definitely a bonding experience with my teammates."

You Can't Win Them All

When it came time to actually play the games, UWGB found itself in dilapidated facilities against inconsistent talent. The venues reflected the hardship within the communities housing them.

"Small, tiny little gyms, so obviously, just the locals came to show up," remembers LeMoine.

UWGB players receive gifts from the hosts during their trip to the Soviet Union in 1990. (University of Wisconsin-Green Bay Archives)

"Very downtrodden. Warped floors. You know, just real old buildings ... it was literally like playing in a barn," notes Dick Bennett. "We played in gyms that any grade school in (Green Bay) would put to shame."

The tournaments were loosely structured to provide an increasing level of difficulty in each game.

"Normally, the first game would be against a club team ... and they were okay, but not particularly good," states Dick Bennett. "The second and third games, we would play their pro-type teams. They were all men, I mean they were all older than us."

"Some of the teams were bad, like high school kids. Some of the teams were really good. You didn't really know what you were going to get," recalls LeMoine.

The games had a decidedly European flair. The Soviet teams had big players who preferred to be shooters rather than bang inside. This style played to the Phoenix's strengths, as its in-your-face defensive style frustrated softer Soviet teams.

"They're great one-on-one players. They're all skilled. All five players can shoot the basketball. But they don't understand the *team* concept yet," remarked Johnson during the trip.

And if the Phoenix had been concerned about their opponent? Well, Kazebin, thought he could fix that ... literally.

"He was always worried about whether we were pleased with everything, and he offered – if we needed to win a game, he said, 'I can arrange so you win,'" says Dick Bennett, laughing. "I said, 'This is a trip, an educational experience, and we just want to get some playing experience, but we don't have to win these games, we just want to grow as a team.'"

Rejecting Kazebin's offer, the tightening Phoenix team fairly won its first two tournaments, starting the trip 6-0. And after each tournament, the hosts would present gifts to the Phoenix players and coaches. These "awards" for winning the tournament were often Soviet trinkets and treasures, like fancy china, table settings, Russian hats, dishes, and history or art books.

UWGB's last tournament was in Kiev, and again, the Phoenix won its first two games. Its final opponent was Kiev Budivelnyk, a team that had won the Soviet Union Premier Basketball League in 1988-89. That team was a mix of Soviet legends, and "these young colts that were going to be their next Olympic team," as Bennett describes them.

While the matchup seemed like a great test for the Phoenix, factors outside of the Bennett's control – those that Kazebin's earlier proposition suggested – came into play.

"I'll never forget it, the last game, we're 8-0, and Boris said to me –he always called me 'Deeck.' He said, 'Deeck, you no win this game.' That's what he said. "I said, 'What do you mean we won't win the game?' I said, 'We're playing well, why can't we win?' He said, 'I cannot explain, but you no win.'"

Kazebin's meaning became clear as the game went along.

"The refs … there was no way!" remembers Johnson. "We lost on a last-second deal, but it was a home job the whole time."

"We were winning at halftime, and I'll never forget, three Russian diplomats just storming out of the stands going straight to the locker room. And you just heard screaming and yelling," explains LeMoine. "And then the second half, the refs just swallowed the whistles. They just basically looked at us like, 'Sorry dude, you're not winning this one.' And they just murdered us. They beat us, but it was like, there should've been an investigation. It was bad. They were not going to lose that last game."

Dick Bennett put the circumstances aside and was nothing but gracious in defeat.

"That might have been the finest-looking team I've ever coached against. They had two seven-footers who were built very much like Roger Ripley, only seven feet. They had a 6-10 small forward who was very quick and a great shooter. Their guards were 6-5 and 6-4."

The respect Bennett showed was reciprocated as well.

"When they presented the crystal vases to Kiev for the championship, they walked right over and presented it to each of our players. They gave our players the championship awards in recognition of how well we played and how well we had done on the trip."

Like they had after many games, the Soviet athletes came back to the Phoenix's hotel and formed friendships with the players.

"The last night after it was all said and done, we hung out with a couple of them," remembers LeMoine. "I didn't really realize that for those guys on the Russian basketball team, they were actually in the military, and their posting was the basketball team. It was a very eye-opening trip."

"One or two of them could speak really good English and they would interpret and we'd just, you know, get to know the guys we'd just played against," says Vander Plas. "The big thing was the bonding experience that we had."

While the players hung out, the coaches and administration were treat-

The Kiev Budivelnyk roster featured a pair of seven-foot post players who dwarfed the UWGB players. (University of Wisconsin-Green Bay Archives)

ed to large, jubilant dinners after each tournament.

"I hate to say it, but we drank more cognac and vodka than we probably should have," remembers Dick Bennett, "They'd have about twenty-five to thirty toasts per dinner. They toast everything ... It was just an incredible experience."

"There are some great stories of the coaching staff celebrating or having to go to these functions where they have to salute, and vodka and cognac flows freely," adds Tony Bennett. "We have some funny memories of seeing our coaches in ways we hadn't before."

Fortunate Sons

Two days after the game, the Phoenix players were on a plane headed for home, humbled by their experience and with a newfound appreciation for what they had waiting for them.

"I'll never forget when we landed, Ben (Johnson) coming off the bus and getting on his knees and kissing the ground," says Tony Bennett.

"All I can say is we are so fortunate to be Americans and to be able to live in this country," Johnson noted upon the return. Decades later, he elaborated. "To see people that live with far less than we do, that's the first take that I got from that trip. "Like, 'Woah, let's never complain about what we have.' We have hot water and we've got more food than we know what to do with, and let's not waste food anymore, and just little things like that."

Tony's comments mirrored his friend's.

"Some of the people stuck there don't have half the things we do. The people are great, but we're just fortunate."

"Things that we take for granted here is like the biggest thing in the world over there, at least at that time," Martinez says. "I've never forgotten that. It definitely makes you appreciate everything that you have here and what we have going on here."

It wasn't the first time Dick Bennett had delivered that message of humility – one of his core principles – to his team.

"I think it was my sophomore year, Coach Bennett, on Thanksgiving Day, took us to a homeless shelter and we helped feed the homeless," remembers LeMoine. "He was very big on making sure that you understood what you had and you appreciated it, and you didn't take advantage of it and you helped other people. Those kinds of lessons have always stuck with me."

Whether a part of Dick Bennett's genius or a fortunate side effect, the culture shock and hardship had served its purpose in bringing the team together.

"I think it brought us closer together as a team," states Martinez. "Experiencing something like that overseas together, our team camaraderie was definitely a lot better after that trip."

Vander Plas echoes that sentiment. "There's something to be said about brothers being together, and it just meant we had to spend another month together getting ready."

"It bonded us together," says Tony Bennett. "You're spending so much time beyond. Extra basketball practices and the games are good of course, but there's a cultural side of it, and just a relational side of it that's pretty unique. That was significant."

"The hotels were pretty average at best. The food was average at best. But yet, we experienced it together *as a team*. And that was the part that was so much fun," states Rondorf. "We joked and we laughed. Lot of bus rides, lot of flights."

Was it all a stroke of genius or just good fortune? To Johnson, it was unequivocal shrewdness:

"(Coach Bennett) drew a line in the sand and he said, 'It's Dick Bennett against the world. And I'm going to see ... will these guys band together?' So he was purposely meaner, tougher, harder on us than any time I can really remember during my time at Green Bay. Again, one of his greatest strengths is there's a method to his madness. 'You guys are going to band together and it's going to be me against you and I don't care if any of you like me or not, but you're going to learn to love each other. You're going to *love* each other and you're going to get through this together.' And by gosh, that's exactly what we did.

"Looking back on it now, I'm so glad that we went there. Talk about a once-in-a-lifetime opportunity, but it just, it was crazy," summarizes LeMoine.

"Amazing experience. But who in the hell takes a team to Russia at the end of the Cold War?" reiterates Johnson. "There's one constant in all of that madness, and it's (Coach Bennett). And again, therein lies his brilliance. Because he knew."

Time to Heal

The extra month of basketball helped fast-track the team's development.

"It was almost like another season, even though it was only a few weeks," notes Martinez. "It catapulted us as a team to where we needed to be."

Guys like rising sophomore Dean Rondorf saw huge personal progression. "It was big for me in my development. "I got more playing time than I ever had. So for me, it was a great experience."

Bennett was excited about the progress, stating at the time: "I think we found a few new players. A couple young kids ... There was a cohesiveness that developed among our top players."

While nearly everyone went forward, two players stood out to the coach: redshirt freshman Jeremy Ludvigson and rising sophomore John Martinez.

Bennett boldly proclaimed that he felt Ludvigson had made the greatest strides on the trip, and Ludvigson saw it the same way.

"It was kind of my come-out party," he says. "I started playing really well over there. That was really cool, because it's like, 'Okay, we're going over there to play. I'm a redshirt freshman, I'm going to play the next year.'"

As for Martinez, Bennett had high hopes even before the team left that his sophomore guard was closing the gap with Tony, stating, "his only

John Martinez accepts a crystal vase from the Kiev Budivelnyk coach following UWGB's final game in its 1990 trip to the USSR. (University of Wisconsin-Green Bay Archives)

weakness was challenging the ball defensively, and he's gotten much better at that. He's much closer to Tony now than at any point in time."

Three weeks of tournament action in the Soviet Union helped validate that proclamation.

"I thought John Martinez really came of age on that trip, because there was a game or two on that trip that Tony could not play. We held him out and John really took a leadership role, and, I think we won two one-point games in the process," recalls Dick Bennett.

Most importantly, when paired with Tony, Dick saw the magic: "I thought that was a special combination. It was excellent chemistry."

***

As a post-script, Dick Bennett made good on his promise to Boris Kazebin. That October, Kazebin came to the US and lived with Dick and his wife, Anne, shadowing the coach and absorbing all he could about Bennett's defensive style.

Kazebin also worked hard with Bennett in trying to recruit two of the Soviet players UWGB had played against to come to Green Bay. The Phoenix were very serious about both players and explored multiple avenues to get them admitted to the school and eligible to play. In the end, a number of obstacles, including disputes over their amateur status, precluded them from joining UWGB.

Tony Bennett, wearing a 00 jersey, looks to penetrate during one of UWGB's exhibition games in a small Soviet Union gym. (University of Wisconsin-Green Bay Archives)

And it wouldn't have been a Boris Kazebin encounter without the humorous flaunting of the rules.

"One day, he came home with a car, a used car. And I said, 'Boris, you don't even have a driver's license. How in heaven's name did you get a car?'" remembers Bennett. "And he looks at me and he says, 'Me Russian boy. No worries.' He was a guy – he was a wheeler-dealer. That's what he was. And I don't know how he got the car, but he had a car."

Chapter 7

Big-Time Opportunities
(1990-1991 - Part 1)

Mid-major programs must create public awareness to land recruits, generate revenue, and develop credibility in the minds of post-season tournament committees charged with handing out coveted at-large bids.

The challenge is that opportunities to create that visibility can be hard to come by. Unlike their major conference counterparts, mid-major participants do not have statewide fan bases, rarely play in front of massive college crowds, and generally do not have large corporate sponsors.

Postseason tournaments provide the best chance to achieve national attention. But for mid-majors who haven't reached those heights, the only hope is finding a high-profile, major conference opponent willing to schedule them in the nonconference schedule.

The catch, of course, is that there is little incentive for a major school to waste time with a good, but nationally unknown, mid-major school. Indeed, the better the mid-major program, the less likely it is to be scheduled.

A loss for the major can seem devastating, while a win may be difficult to come by and at the same time completely expected and valueless. It's simple math. If a win versus a quality unknown is viewed the same as a win versus a poor low-level school, who can fault the big boys for padding their nonconference schedules with weaker opponents before they have to face their own grueling conference schedules?

The best mid-major programs have taken advantage of these fleeting opportunities – almost always on the road – to force themselves into the national conversation.

So You're Saying There's a Chance

Scheduling for a mid-major during the late 1980s and early 1990s was a nightmare. Schools like UWGB needed wins on the schedule to tally an objectively impressive record, but also had to flash enough eye-popping quality wins to get the eye of a postseason committee. The problem was with the latter requirement – most major conference teams refused to play genuinely tough mid-major competition, fearing a loss would be difficult to justify to an uninformed public. When they did, it was on their terms, and at their house.

"We went on the road a lot, and we always had a schedule that was a little heavier away than home, which was hard but it helped us get ready for the conference," explains Dick Bennett.

The job of calling schools, making deals, and getting the games started with Bennett and AD Dan Spielman, but eventually shifted to Bennett's assistants. His goal was to load up his nonconference with challenges.

"I wanted to schedule tough, because I think that's where you learn. You have to stretch. You've got to get out of your comfort zone, and the only way to do that is to play people better than you."

Bennett's philosophy had evolved from the disappointments he'd witnessed in 1987-88. UWGB had tallied a solid 18-9 record, but with a weak nonconference schedule, it had missed out on the NIT.

The following year, the strength of schedule improved, largely due to strong mid-major competition like Detroit-Mercy, Colorado State, Boise State, and Loyola-Marymount. Those were the like-minded programs looking to challenge themselves.

A year later in 1989-90, UWGB had been able to book two Big Ten schools (Northwestern and Illinois), and quality mid-major opponents like Central Michigan, Austin Peay, Boise State, and Akron, all with a mind on the program's finances.

"We had to boost the budget, and the only way you can do that besides ticket sales – which were improving right along – you're going to have to take some guarantees. You know you're going to have to go on the road and play," Bennett says. "We were able to get some home-and-homes, but we still took guarantees. We scheduled as tough as we could. We had very few gimmes."

By 1990-91, the staff had set its most difficult nonconference schedule to date, a devilish slate designed to push Bennett's team to the limit, but also offer multiple opportunities for signature victories.

November 24, 1990	at Austin Peay St.
November 27, 1990	SAN FRANCISCO ST.
December 1, 1990	BOISE ST.
December 4, 1990	at Colorado
December 8, 1990	at Clemson
December 15, 1990	SIU-EDWARDSVILLE
December 21, 1990	at DePaul (Old Style Classic)
December 22, 1990	TBD (vs. Oklahoma St. or Southern Illinois)
December 29, 1990	CENTRAL MICHIGAN
January 2, 1991	NEBRASKA
January 21, 1991	at Chicago St.

While the Clemson game was a standalone one-game agreement, UWGB was able to secure a huge two-for-one arrangement with Colorado, playing on the road in 1990-91 and 1992-93, while getting a home game in 1991-92. It was one of the shining successes for UWGB in scheduling during this era.

The Phoenix was also invited to participate in DePaul's holiday tournament, being given the honor of playing DePaul in the first round and receiving a guaranteed game against either Oklahoma State or Southern Illinois a day later.

In addition, the schedule further included back-to-back home games against the typically strong Central Michigan Chippewas and Big Eight powerhouse Nebraska.

The Nebraska development had been particularly unique, with the teams originally agreeing on a one-game deal set to be played during the 1988-89 season. But just before the season started, Nebraska called and had to cancel the game, having inadvertently scheduled a game over the NCAA's 27-game limit. The Phoenix obliged, and to Nebraska's credit, they altered their deal, agreeing to play one game at UWGB (1990-91) and one game at Nebraska (1991-92).

"We had a chance to play against Nebraska, Colorado, Colorado State. Those were big-time for us," remembers Tony Bennett.

"Coach didn't do us any favors, because he knew in order to get a postseason bid, if you didn't win the (conference) tournament, you were going to have to play some folks," adds Dean Vander Plas. "So we played some folks my junior and senior year in the nonconference. Nebraska came to town, and we went and played at Colorado, we played at Clemson, played DePaul in their own tournament, played Boise. He decided to ramp stuff up and we had a little fun."

In-State In-Fighting

While UWGB had success in getting Big Eight schools on its schedule, it continued to strike out with in-state big brothers Wisconsin and Marquette.

"Neither Marquette nor Wisconsin would play us in those years. That always bothered me," notes Dick Bennett. "We knew they wouldn't come to the Brown County Arena, but they didn't even want to talk to us about games."

With Wisconsin, the situation became public in 1988 when Bennett wrote a letter to Wisconsin head coach Steve Yoder, requesting a game. Yoder never responded to Bennett's letter, but when asked about the matter, was quoted saying, "We've not talked about it, and I don't think we have anything to gain by that, I really don't. I don't think the University of Wisconsin has a thing to gain by playing Green Bay."

Yoder's obstinance became the Badgers' company line, and he repeated it nearly every time he was asked about it during his tenure.

Though Wisconsin hadn't played UWGB since 1981, Bennett's request was hardly unheard of. Indeed, nearly all Big Ten schools were willing to play mid-major teams within their state on a routine basis, and all other than Indiana and Purdue would play at least one in-state mid-major *each season* during the 1980s. No Big Ten school took as extreme a position as the Badgers under Yoder.

But Yoder's view was not new. The idea of a major conference program shunning rising in-state mid-majors has existed throughout college basketball history, even with programs that appear to be above reproach.

Legendary coach John Wooden and his UCLA teams, as well as cross-town rival USC, famously refused to schedule budding Long Beach State under Jerry Tarkanian in the early 1970s, believing the game offered no value.

In the 1970s and 1980s, the machine that was Kentucky shut down any notion of playing Denny Crum's budding Louisville teams. The two programs would go twenty-four years between games, even as the Cardinals rose to national prominence with their NCAA Championship in 1980. It wasn't until a forced meeting in the 1983 NCAA tournament that the programs played, with Crum's Cardinals prevailing.

Kentucky proved to be a serial offender, often refusing to play any mid-major state schools. As Western Kentucky was busy locking up five post-season bids in the 1980s, the Wildcats kept them off the calendar. The two schools met just one time in the 1980s, and as with Louisville, it took an NCAA tournament date to get it done. It wasn't until December 1990 that the two teams finally agreed to meet in a regular season game, three years after the Hilltoppers' last postseason bid.

The key difference between those notable examples and Wisconsin was that Yoder's club was terrible. Prolifically bad. During Yoder's six seasons with the Badgers, the program compiled a horrific 68-103 record and never finishing better than seventh in the Big Ten. The last thing Yoder wanted was to give a better in-state coach an opportunity to showcase his talent at the UW Fieldhouse.

None of that softened the blow to Dick Bennett when he heard Yoder's position.

"I think that's a very poor statement on his part. It shows an almost complete lack of respect for us. I'm very disappointed," Bennett said. "I don't think he gains anything by *not* playing us. They are not that good. I'm not saying we're better than Wisconsin, or that we'd beat them on any kind of consistent basis, but they are not that much better than we are."

The repeated scheduling denial stung the Phoenix players, most of whom were Wisconsin kids to begin with and dreamed of the chance to play against the teams they'd watched growing up.

"No one would play us. We were dying to play Wisconsin or Marquette, but couldn't get those games," remembers Tony Bennett.

"I wanted to play at Marquette and Wisconsin when I was there. I craved that," recalls Mike Karisny. "But they wouldn't play us. It was a different time then."

Even without the Badgers on the schedule, UWGB had plenty of prime-time chances for showcase performances.

Ripening Roster

The success of the 1989-90 UWGB team had obliterated any fears that the program would have to return to Division II.

"That (exposure) was critical," notes Bennett. "It seemed to endear us to the whole Green Bay area. Everybody seemed plugged in at that time to what we were doing when we made that NIT, and it really kind of guaranteed that our program was over the hump."

Expectations for the 1990-91 team had escalated, at least in the eyes of basketball junkies. By 1990, the AMCU had rebranded itself the Mid-Continent Conference, and publications like *Inside Sports Magazine* and *Street & Smith* saw UWGB as the favorite. Much of the hype centered on the team's star and preseason favorite to win Player of the Year, Tony Bennett.

The team's sole senior, Dean Vander Plas, also returned to help lead the offense.

"Dean was a real hard-headed guy, but smart, and used his physical abilities to his best," comments Dean Rondorf.

Alongside those two returning All-Conference players, the 1990-91 squad returned junior forward Ben Johnson, the team's defensive ace.

"He evolved into a guy that could score a little bit, but at first, it was just like lockdown defense," states Scott LeMoine.

Also back was junior center Larry Hill, the team's fourth-leading scorer and rim protector. Dick Bennett focused on Hill's potential in his preseason assessment.

"I think he's going to be a really fine player this year. As to whether he'll be an excellent player, I think it's within him, when he really desires it."

Bennett had no reservations when it came to sophomore John Martinez as the fifth starter. After the USSR trip, Martinez hit the weight room and added ten pounds to his frame, dispelling concerns that Bennett may have had about his durability.

Part of Bennett's dedication to Martinez may have been the due to the infatuation his wife, Anne, had with John's game.

"There were three players that she absolutely fell in love with," notes Bennett. "The first one was Terry Porter (at UW-Stevens Point). The second one was John Martinez, and of course, she loved the way Tony played. Those were the three that she earmarked."

"I think for me, it was a matter of making the coaches understand that we could play together, which is kind of a big deal," remembers Martinez. "I mean, you have two six-foot guards. You know, it's a little unusual."

By the fall of 1990, Bennett needed no further convincing, and neither did Tony.

"It takes so much pressure off me because he can handle the ball, and he's got to be one of the best passers I've ever seen," said Tony. "I was down as the Olympic Festival and I saw Kenny Anderson and some of those guys. John can pass the ball like those guys, he's got that knack."

The two were destined to become an extremely special backcourt, the likes of which few mid-major programs have ever fielded.

Bennett relied on the combination of improving redshirt freshmen Jeremy Ludvigson and Logan Vander Velden, along with junior Scott LeMoine to back up Hill and Vander Plas at the three big positions.

Each of the three brought distinctly different skill sets to the table, with Ludvigson providing the most polish, LeMoine the strongest defensive abilities, and Vander Velden the most raw talent combined with a good outside shooting touch. In Vander Velden's mind, the Soviet Union trip convinced him he still had a ways to go.

UWGB's 1990-91 roster included a mix of veteran and young players. Back row: Ben Johnson (23), Eric LeDuc (52), Jeremy Ludvigson (44), Larry Hill (24), Scott LeMoine (45), Logan Vander Velden (32), Dean Rondorf (30), Dean Vander Plas (33). Front row: Tony Bennett (25), Tory Smith (34), Tony Ciaravino (21), Mark Andres (31), John Martinez (20). (University of Wisconsin-Green Bay Archives)

"I was 6-9, 195 pounds," notes Vander Velden. "We were playing professional teams over there, and physically it was a struggle. I had all the skills, but the physical part of the game, I struggled with."

The end of the 1989-90 season brought questions about forward Dean Rondorf, who had come to a turning point in his career. Physically immature and not fully committed in his second season, Bennett had given him a frank assessment at year-end.

"He goes, 'Dean, I don't think this is the right fit for you.' And I just was kind of like, 'Wow.' It just kind of that punch in the gut," recalls Rondorf. "I just remember sitting there in kind of awe, but the first thing that popped in my mind is that, 'Coach, I can't fail, I can't let you down. I can't let myself down, I can't let my family down.' I don't know why he allowed me to stay with the program, but that's kind of where it changed, that's where it clicked."

For the first time in his three-year career in Green Bay, Rondorf was all in.

After those nine, the lineup was very thin, with no depth at all at guard beyond Bennett and Martinez. Personal issues continued to plague Chris Yates, and Bennett chose to redshirt him in hopes of returning for his senior year in 1991-92.

That left junior Tony Ciaravino as the only returning backup guard. It was a position Bennett set out to fill with at least two true freshman, if he could find them.

New Pieces

Dick Bennett's recruiting efforts for the 1990-91 season had been a mixed bag. With four scholarships available, Bennett again sought to sign high-potential players early in the fall of 1989. He saw immediate success in landing his first and top target, Torriano (Tory) Smith from Buena Vista High School in Saginaw, Michigan.

Smith was, Bennett's words, "easily physically the most gifted" player ever to find his way to Green Bay. But he came from a tough background.

"His mother was murdered in Buffalo, New York, when he was, I think, thirteen, and he lived with his grandmother," recalls Bennett. "When I did go over there to recruit him, he had to have people watch my car, he had to meet me at various places and walk me everywhere. He never left me alone because he lived in a very, very dangerous neighborhood."

Smith's skills were undeniable, but he had admissions challenges and needed to retake the ACT just to meet acceptance criteria. UWGB stuck with Smith through that process, and he rewarded the Phoenix by joining the club.

Bennett wasn't as fortunate with his other early recruiting efforts. Running out of time and options, he signed Mark Andres, a 6-1 guard from Rhinelander, Wisconsin, who had averaged 22 ppg as a senior. Andres and Smith would be active members as true freshmen on the 1990-91 team.

The final addition to the Phoenix roster was a rare transfer in May 1990. Sophomore Eric LeDuc, a 6-7 swingman from Burlington, Wisconsin, had been interested in UWGB when he was in high school, but the timing was not right for the Phoenix. The crew-cut LeDuc instead pursued a career at Army, destined to prove he could make it at West Point. A year later, the situations had changed for both sides.

"I was aware of Green Bay. Obviously they were kind of up and coming, and Dick Bennett was already a Wisconsin basketball icon from his Stevens Point days," says LeDuc. "When I decided I wanted to leave (West Point), that was the first place that I had my high school coach call ... I went into the Army on June 6th, and I left West Point the following year on June 7th. That following weekend, I came up to Green Bay."

LeDuc would have to sit out the 1990-91 season, but had three years of eligibility left and was destined to make a great complement to Ludvigson and Vander Velden.

Backcourt Blossoms

Unquestionably, the team would go as far as the synergy between Tony Bennett and John Martinez could take them.

"We always felt that they were the best," Dick Bennett says. It sounded like an exaggeration, but we had the stats to prove it. That was certainly one of the best guard combinations in the country."

If the first few weeks of the season were any barometer, the sky was the limit.

Martinez and Bennett dominated in UWGB's first exhibition game against Marathon Oil, scoring 37 of the team's 91 points in a 28-point rout. The second exhibition game against the Ukrainian national team saw them play just as well and generated a major compliment from Vladimir Gorbulin, the Ukranian coach. His team had played the Wisconsin Badgers earlier on the trip.

"Madison was a taller team, but the playmakers in Green Bay were better, 25 (Tony Bennett) and 20 (John Martinez)," he said.

The backcourt brilliance continued as the regular season opened. Austin Peay State, under new head coach Dave Loos, controlled the tempo for most of the game and held a 50-38 lead deep into the second half. But with a guard-driven 15-4 run, UWGB methodically took the game over and earned a 67-61 victory with Tony Bennett and Martinez combining for 31 points and 13 assists.

As November 1990 came to a close, the Phoenix earned a 32-point victory over Division II opponent San Francisco State. Tony and Martinez again stole the show, combining for 34 points and seven assists. The game was utterly forgettable, save for a moment of intensity that illustrated both the frustration opponents felt trying to contain the Phoenix backcourt and the strength of bonds that held Dick Bennett's team together.

It happened in the first half, when Tony Bennett was called for a charge on a layup attempt, colliding with San Francisco State's Ennerea Maxwell Jr. The two players were tied up, and a pushing match ensued. Dean Vander Plas was having none of it, rushing to the scene, removing Tony, and getting right in Maxwell Jr.'s face.

"They tried to get Tony, you know, just get him off his game. And I think my job was to make sure that they didn't," remembers Vander Plas. "That game, specifically, that guy was trying to go at Tony, and I just let him know in no uncertain terms that that wasn't going to be allowed, especially at the Brown County Arena."

"(Dean) would always take care of me," Tony says. " 'Hey, someone's giving you a problem, bring 'em my way, Tony, I've gotcha.' You'd hear guys just crunch as he'd hit backscreens and hammer them."

The Phoenix's first serious test came in the third game on December 1, 1990, against Boise State at the Brown County Arena. The Broncos, a team with postseason experience, were 3-0 on the year and meeting UWGB for the third consecutive year. The 1990-91 version had added eight new players and saw the growth of its young 6-9 center, Tanoka Beard, who had averaged 13.6 points per game and taken home Big Sky Freshman of the Year honors the previous year.

And yet, with Martinez and Tony Bennett playing 79 of 80 minutes, the Broncos were overmatched. Tony, in particular, was stellar, scoring 20 points on perfect 7-of-7 shooting, while the team also got some help from Larry Hill, who stepped up large with 13 points and seven rebounds. UWGB remained unbeaten at 3-0, handing the Broncos their first loss of the year, 67-59.

Knocking Down Boulders

UWGB was thrilled to have its first chance for a signature win against the Big Eight's Colorado Buffaloes. But the game almost never happened. A heavy snowstorm delayed the team's travel to Boulder, Colorado, and the

John Martinez drives through the Boise State defense as Dean Vander Plas provides interference during UWGB's 67-59 victory on December 1, 1990. (University of Wisconsin-Green Bay Archives)

Phoenix's plane touched down just hours before tip-off.

"I remember us not knowing if we were going to get out there," notes Vander Plas, "because it was snowing like the dickens."

"We did not get into Boulder until the afternoon of the game. We had no chance to practice there," adds Dick Bennett. "We checked into a hotel and took a nap, ate, and went to the game."

For some programs, the disrupted routine may have been too much, but not for Dick Bennett's club.

"I have to think that all of the hardships we experienced in travel over in the Soviet Union made that possible," he says. "It was not something we hadn't done before. And so it was not a big deal to the players at all, to go out there and play a good game."

The Buffaloes were 3-1, led by new head coach Joe Harrington. Harrington had taken his previous school, Long Beach State, to two NIT appearances and brought a running style to Colorado. His "press, run, score" motto meshed perfectly with the team's two best players, first-team All-Big Eight center Shaun Vandiver and senior guard Steve Wise. Neither would disappoint Harrington in this game.

Colorado's Shaun Vandiver (35) works for position against Tony Bennett (25) and Larry Hill during their game in Boulder on December 4, 1990. (University of Colorado Boulder Libraries)

In the battle of styles, UWGB's patient attack proved more successful in the first half, as the Phoenix was able to slow down the game. Confidence built as UWGB led 36-30 going into the half, despite just four points from Tony Bennett.

Harrington made adjustments to speed up the tempo at the break, and Colorado busted out of the gate, going on a 12-4 tear, capped by a Vandiver layup that put the Buffaloes up 42-40. That's when Harrington got in his own way.

On the ensuing possession, UWGB broke the press and Martinez, receiving the ball on the wing, drove the lane and was fouled by Vandiver. The call sent Harrington into a tizzy, and his tirade earned him a technical foul. Martinez calmly stepped to the line and knocked down four free throw attempts, and on the ensuing free possession, Hill hit a 10-foot jump shot to cap a critical six-point swing that gave UWGB a 46-42 lead.

UWGB's lead expanded to seven points as the game ticked under 10 minutes, but Colorado would not fold and regained the lead with just under four minutes to play. That's when junior Ben Johnson put his improved offensive game on display.

Johnson first knocked down a three pointer to give UWGB the lead, 73-71, and after Colorado tied the game, drained another to give the Phoenix a 76-73 advantage it would not relinquish. Martinez and Tony Bennett helped seal the game with critical free throws, and Hill blocked a Wise three-point attempt with 20 seconds left to stamp the major victory UWGB had been searching for.

The 83-78 victory marked UWGB's first win against a major conference opponent since the club beat Miami (Florida) on January 3, 1987. It was a victory no postseason committee could overlook.

"These are opportunities to prove that we belong, because you get those labels of being a mid-major," states Rondorf. "Going to Colorado, beating them there, on the road, was great."

"That was a big deal, and we went to their place and took care of them," comments Vander Plas. "I just remember the plane ride home was pretty happy."

The Buffaloes had given UWGB their best punch, with Vandiver scoring 20 points and Wise 29. The Phoenix had done the same, getting 36 points and 10 assists combined from its Martinez and Bennett backcourt. But the x-factor for UWGB had been Johnson and his clutch 17 points.

Faced with the unenviable task of explaining his team's loss, Harrington praised the Phoenix and educated the media.

"I'm sure a lot of people around the country won't be convinced Wisconsin-Green Bay is a good team, but they didn't win 24 games without a reason. We got beat by a good team."

Bad Breaks

UWGB rode in to Clemson, South Carolina, two weeks before Christmas with a 4-0 record and optimistic about its chances at getting a second win against a major conference opponent. While the Phoenix took the game very seriously, the Tigers' fans found the whole idea laughable.

"Their student section wasn't big, but when we came running down the tunnel, they started singing 'Oh Christmas Tree, Oh Christmas Tree' because our warmups were green and red," recalls Rondorf. "I just remember thinking, 'Oh my gosh, this is not good. They're making fun of us.'"

Clemson fans had every reason to feel confident. The Tigers were a Sweet Sixteen team the year before, and returned their first-team All-ACC center and bulging beast of a human, Dale Davis. (Davis was a lottery pick in the 1991 NBA Draft and played sixteen seasons in the league.)

"Dale Davis was by far the biggest man I've ever played against in my life," Rondorf says. "He literally could have picked me up almost by the back of my jersey and just kind of set me aside and said, 'I'm going to go get this rebound.' He was just so strong."

Thankfully for the Phoenix, the task of guarding this giant did not reside with Rondorf, but rather with emerging junior Larry Hill. Hill had adjusted well to his full-time starting role, and in addition to his improvement on the defensive end, was also flashing overall consistency, racking up 10.7 points and 5.2 rebounds per game.

"He didn't even know how good he could be. Here he was, 6-8, long, he was athletic, he was skilled," Dick Bennett says. "He was just really coming into his own."

The addition of Hill to the budding backcourt seemed nearly unstoppable. "When you have him *and* Tony, that's a game-changer," states Vander Plas.

Hill would be matched up on Davis, but Bennett knew he needed help and gave junior Scott LeMoine a start as well, thinking the additional defense and height could stymie Davis's game. The move paid early dividends for UWGB, with Hill quickly tallying three blocked shots and the Phoenix holding an early lead in front of 5,000 stunned Tigers fans at Clemson's Littlejohn Coliseum.

"We were kind of giving Larry a hard time going into that game – you know, just goofing around and what Dale Davis was going to be doing to him. But he stepped up to the plate," recalls Martinez.

And then, without warning, tragedy struck. With six minutes to play in the first half and the Phoenix up 22-21, Hill leapt and blocked a Ricky Davis runner. On his way down, Hill collided with Rondorf and landed awkwardly, injuring his wrist. Hill remained on the ground as a concerned coaching staff came off the bench to check him out, before he rose and walked slowly to the bench.

At the time, no one knew the severity of the injury, and the Phoenix weathered Hill's absence early, actually increasing its lead with some nifty shooting from Tony Bennett.

UWGB took a 34-27 lead to the locker room at half, but the joy was short-lived. Hill was out for the game, and LeMoine, one of the only Phoenix big men to really contain Dale Davis, picked up his fourth foul early in the second half.

UWGB was left with Vander Plas and Ludvigson to handle the monster, and neither were capable of containing him. "It was like, 'Let's go feed you to big old Dale Davis and that group,' " recalls Vander Plas.

For the Ludvigson, the experience was educational at best.

"Dale Davis goes up for a shot and I kind of help out and I block the shot, and I said, 'Get that shit outta here.' And he got it back, gathered himself, went up, and dunked it. And Ben Johnson fouled him. And Ben turns to me and goes, 'Don't talk shit. Don't talk shit!' "

That basket was one of ten that Davis would make as he rolled up 20 points in the second half, 30 for the game, to go with 14 rebounds in 38 minutes of play. Davis's otherworldly performance gave the Phoenix its first loss, and even with an otherwise terrific game by UWGB's guards, including a career-high 21 points from Martinez, Clemson closed out a 75-68 victory.

As Colorado's Joe Harrington had done after the previous game, Cliff Ellis, Clemson's coach, educated the local media.

"A lot of people won't realize this is a good win. People who know basketball know Green Bay has a good team. This is a big win for Clemson."

The loss itself wasn't demoralizing for the Phoenix.

"It wasn't one of those losses that we were too concerned with, because we knew we had played well, on the road, against a very good Clemson team," explains Dick Bennett.

But the bigger concern was the extent of Hill's injury. X-rays showed the wrist was broken, and after surgery a week later which revealed a torn tendon, the team learned Hill would be out for the rest of season. Hill was awarded a medical redshirt because he had played in only five games, but the injury was devastating.

"It's a huge loss. He's a critical part of our team," Tony Bennett said. "But that's one of the things about sports and life, you have to learn to deal with losses."

"That was kind of a big hit to the team, because Larry was playing very well. He gave us that added dimension of that low post presence," Martinez explains. "I think we would've been a lot better off with him in the lineup that year than without."

With no Hill, the team's younger big men would have to fill in.

"It meant that guys like Jeremy Ludvigson and Logan Vander Velden – they had to step up," notes Vander Plas. "Jeremy got a lot more time. If Larry doesn't get hurt, Jeremy doesn't play."

Thankfully, the Phoenix had a full week off before playing their second Division II opponent of the year, SIU-Edwardsville. The easy victory improved UWGB's record to 5-1. With six more days of rest, the players finished their first semester coursework and finals.

Windy City Upset

UWGB was 1-1 in its showcased nonconference matchups, with two big ones left. First up, a semester-ending trip to Chicago on December 21, 1990, for a Friday night date with DePaul as part of the Blue Demons' Old Style Classic.

DePaul was a storied basketball program that had known just one coaching family for nearly fifty years. Ray Meyer began as head coach in 1942 and continued in that role for forty-two years, turning the Blue Demons into an independent powerhouse. During Meyer's final years, DePaul made the NCAA tournament seven out of nine years, all while trotting out future NBA stars including Mark Aguirre, Terry Cummings, Dave Corzine, and Tyrone Corbin. Despite the program's dominance, Meyer had graciously agreed to play UWGB when the Phoenix was a Division II program. They met seven times in the 1970s, and the Phoenix under Dave Buss had somehow managed to top Meyer's club on two of those occasions.

When Meyer stepped down in 1984, his son, Joey Meyer, picked right up where his father left off, taking the Blue Demons to the NCAA tournament in each of his first five seasons. His 1989-90 club was the first in seven seasons to miss the NCAA tournament, but had made it all the way to the NIT's Elite Eight before losing to the same Saint Louis team that beat UWGB in the second round.

With all five starters back, including uber-talented juniors David Booth and Stephen Howard, the 1990-91 Blue Demons appeared poised to return to the Big Dance. Meyer's team had been ranked as high as #25 in the country two weeks earlier, before dropping back-to-back games at Louisville and at home against #6 UCLA.

De Paul's Midwestern roots and the fact that the game was being televised on The Sports Channel, UWGB saw the game as its most significant in a long time.

"This is the most important game since Green Bay has turned Division I. That is how we're approaching it," Johnson stated before the game. "DePaul knows about us. This will show what level we're at, where the program is."

"I grew up watching that team, always loved that team," recalls Martinez, who had dreamt of playing for DePaul. "When we were going to be playing them, it was a big deal for me."

"They had history there, and you knew about DePaul because DePaul played against Marquette, and I grew up watching them," notes Rondorf. "It was a great tournament and a good opportunity again to showcase who we were as a basketball team against really good talent."

In a clash of styles that was becoming familiar to Bennett's teams, Joey Meyer wanted DePaul to speed up the game, run the floor, and press whenever possible, while the Phoenix practiced a deliberate, slow-paced game.

LeMoine again received the start, and though he was in primarily for his defense, he unexpectedly delivered some offense. He scored two baskets in the opening minutes to help the Phoenix snag a quick 8-4 lead. He then helped the Phoenix defense go on lockdown, holding DePaul without a made basket for nearly eight minutes, all while Tony Bennett caught fire, scoring 10 of the team's first 19 points and helping the Phoenix expand the lead to 19-8.

The officials were active with their whistles, and in spite of stellar defense, DePaul was in the bonus with more than nine minutes to go in the first half. But Tony continued to dominate, adding a nifty scoop layup, a three-pointer, and an assist to Martinez as time expired to help UWGB finish the first half strong, up 28-20.

Twenty minutes in, and it was the Phoenix guards who looked like NBA prospects. Tony Bennett was unstoppable, piling up 15 first-half points and five assists to go along with Martinez's seven points and three assists. The defense had also done its job, holding DePaul to just 27% shooting, but nine free throw attempts and an eight-rebound advantage allowed the Blue Demons to hang around.

LeMoine picked up his fourth foul just four minutes into the second half, while Johnson, Vander Plas, and Ludvigson each had three fouls. As the fouls piled up, the gap shrunk, and with 12:20 to play, DePaul took its first lead on a David Booth fast-break dunk. Vander Plas picked up his fourth foul on the ensuing possession, and one inbounds later, Ludvigson had his fourth, putting DePaul in the bonus for the final 12 minutes.

Steam poured out of Dick Bennett's ears and froth dripped down his chin, but it wasn't until Tony picked up a charging call with 9:55 left and UWGB up 41-36 that Dick Bennett finally blew a gasket and picked up a deserved technical. DePaul tied the game and continued forward from there to build a four-point lead with 3:43 to play.

The game felt like it was slipping away, but Tony Bennett and Martinez would not be denied.

Tony kicked it off with a nasty crossover move that ended with his three-pointer swishing through the net. A possession later, Martinez was fouled and hit two free throws, and another possession after that, he found Tony on the right baseline for an open jumper that the lefty again swished. Just like that, UWGB was back up 55-52 with 1:58 left.

Two poor defensive possessions gave DePaul the lead back at 56-55 with 58 seconds left. But again, the Phoenix guard tandem would not be denied.

UWGB broke the Blue Demons' press and worked the clock on the game's penultimate possession. With 23 seconds left and Tony blan-

Tony Bennett listens as his father, Dick, provides instruction during a game at the Brown County Arena. (University of Wisconsin-Green Bay Archives)

keted, Martinez got the ball on the right wing and immediately dribbled to the middle of the floor, where four Blue Demons converged on him. Undeterred, Martinez released a running floater in the lane that somehow missed the outstretched hands of three DePaul players.

It was an iconic moment. The ball hung in the air for what felt like an eternity before swishing through. With fifteen seconds left, UWGB had reclaimed a 57-56 lead.

Dick Bennett threw DePaul a curveball defensively by switching back to his standby 1-3-1 zone for the final possession. Meyer's plan was obvious, and with five seconds left, the Blue Demons got the ball to their star, David Booth. Johnson was all over Booth, who had little option but to try a spin move and toss up a 12-footer.

Booth's shot bounced harmlessly off the iron, and Johnson grabbed it as the clock struck zeros. Tony pumped his fist in a display of raw emotion as the Phoenix players yelled, hugged, and high-fived the win.

"For us as a basketball team and a basketball program, that legitimizes you. You went to DePaul, beat DePaul on their floor in their tournament," remembers Vander Plas. "In about a three-week stretch, we knocked off Colorado and DePaul, and you're like, 'OK, we might be able to do this.' "

Ludvigson lauded the team's success, noting, "That was a big win for us – that was a big signature win in their own tournament."

"Big" wasn't enough for Johnson, who called it UWGB's "biggest victory since going Division I." Johnson further praised his good friend Tony Bennett, who had played spectacularly on a major stage, scoring 28 points on 12-of-21 shooting to go along with seven assists, calling him "the best player on the floor by a mile."

But most of the post-game attention was on the other half of the team's dynamic backcourt –Martinez and his "magical shot."

"John's shot was blessed," proclaimed Dick Bennett. "That was as tough a shot under as difficult circumstances as I can remember one of our players being in."

But for Martinez, the shot wasn't necessarily out of the ordinary.

"I used to shoot that shot all the time," he explains. "Every now and again in games, but in practice, I mean I used to *live* on that shot, where I drive into the lane, kind of rise up, and then just float it over the person. When the play broke down, it was just more instinctual for me. Looking back, you realize the significance of the shot and the win in general, and I think that kind of put us on the map a little bit."

Joey Meyer praised Martinez afterwards, stating, "Bennett is a great guard, but we did a decent job on him. Martinez is the one that beat us."

Meyer elaborated a day later: "I'll trade eight of my guys on the bench for (Tony Bennett) right now. He could play in the ACC or the Big Ten. He beat up on us, and to have Martinez play like a Big Ten guard with him made it really tough."

The win over DePaul completely overshadowed the team's letdown a night later. Southern Illinois had somehow knocked off the other tournament favorite, Oklahoma State, setting the stage for a rematch of the 1990 NIT game. UWGB gave up a double-digit lead and lost to the Salukis 70-64 despite a whopping 30 points from Tony Bennett. It was a sour end, but Tony's 58 total tournament points earned him Old Style Classic Tournament MVP honors.

"People who were debating, 'Hey, can this kid play in the NBA?' That kind of gave them a little taste," Johnson says. "You know, this kid's pretty dang good. He deserves a look, he deserves a really strong look and a crack."

The Phoenix closed out 1990 with an overtime win against Central Michigan. UWGB played lethargically and actually trailed 51-47 with less than two minutes to play. But the Phoenix scored on all eight possessions in overtime en route to a 67-59 win.

Ugly as it was, the victory put UWGB at 7-2 just four days before its final major nonconference battle against Nebraska.

A Rope, A Tree

It didn't matter that January 2, 1991, was an otherwise ice-cold, return-to-work Wednesday in Green Bay. With a disappointing 6-10 Packers season officially in the books, local residents flocked to the Brown County Arena to witness UWGB's magical run. For the first time in program history, the Phoenix prepared to host a ranked team at the arena.

A capacity crowd of 5,937 fans crammed in to watch UWGB take on the #22 Nebraska Cornhuskers, who were sporting a premium 12-1 record. They had skill and a whole truckload of size, with 7-2 Rich King, 6-10 Tony Farmer, and two other players over 6-8, in addition to 6-7 All-Big Eight Freshman Eric Piatkowski. That kind of height would put Bennett's pack defense to the test.

The hometown fans did their part right from the start. "The crowd was phenomenal, the setting was everything you'd want it to be," Dick Bennett said.

The hype for the game may have intimidated the UWGB players early on, as Nebraska, sporting their red uniforms with white trim, got off to an 8-0 start and built the lead to 22-12 with 9:46 left in the first half. But UWGB settled into a groove on both ends of the floor, and was able to get within five points at halftime, down just 31-26.

"We were the much better team. We played a lot better than they did; we weren't intimidated by who they were," says Rondorf. "It was one of those deals where we're playing against a team that's ranked in the top 25. 'Let's go out there and prove that we're good enough.' And we certainly did."

UWGB further trimmed the margin after the break and eventually took the lead, building it to as many as four points with under 10 minutes to play. Nebraska came back and tied the score at 51-51 with 6:23 left, and the game remained very close from there.

The intensity never wavered from the crowd, which went crazy every time something positive happened. But while a loud home crowd can sometimes sway an officiating crew, this game had Big Eight refs who may have showed their allegiance in crunch time. Inexplicably, the Phoenix racked up three technical fouls, all of which were dubious.

"Those three technicals were, by far, the worst calls that I remember," adds Rondorf.

Vander Plas was the victim of the first one in the second half. "That's the only game I ever got a technical," he says. "I remember making a play, scoring, and I didn't say a word. And Coach Bennett said, 'What'd you T him up for?' And the ref said, 'He looked at me funny.' "

Rondorf's technical had the same fishy smell to it.

"The guy was posting me up and he threw an elbow or something like that," Rondorf says. "It was like the technical out of nowhere. I wasn't an-

UWGB's Scott LeMoine battles Nebraska's Beau Reid for a rebound during a hotly contested Cornhuskers victory at the Brown County Arena on January 2, 1991. It was the first time the Phoenix hosted a nationally ranked opponent. (University of Wisconsin-Green Bay Archives)

imated to the point where I was showing up the ref. I was just – it was almost like frustration or whatever it was. And he gave a technical and I just remember thinking, 'For what?!' "

The third technical, with UWGB up 62-61 and less than a minute to play, proved to be the nail in the coffin. After a Nebraska three-point attempt from the right wing bounced short off the rim, the Huskers' Tony Farmer grabbed the ball and made a put-back over LeMoine, giving Nebraska a 63-62 lead.

Then the insane happened.

"I was pissed at myself because I didn't get the rebound," LeMoine explains. I don't know why, but he takes the ball and shoves it in my chest. He was like, 'Take it, take it.' He wanted me to quickly take it out of bounds. I took the basketball and I just kind of was like throwing the ball back toward the baseline."

Video replays showed it was a light toss, but the ball bounced off Nebraska's Carl Hayes. The official immediately blew the whistle and called LeMoine for the team's third technical foul. "I think that was maybe like my second technical I'd ever gotten in my life," LeMoine adds.

The crowd, already aggravated, were now incensed. The fans made their disapproval known, booing and initiating a dangerously taunting chant of, "A rope, a tree, hang the referee."

With 40 seconds left and a one-point lead, Nebraska went to the line and made both technical free throws for a 65-62 lead. UWGB, out of options, fouled on the Nebraska technical inbounds, and the two additional free throws grew the lead to 67-62 with 26 seconds left, effectively ending the game.

The fans were on the edge of insanity, sparking Dick Bennett to take action.

"Our fans were just nuts about the officiating – and it was terrible – I said (to the Brown County deputy), 'You have to get their coach and escort him out, kind of protect him.' And they did, they got him out."

After the game, Nebraska coach Danny Nee accused the fans of throwing things at his players on the sideline.

"It was wild behind the bench. They were going crazy. I'm going to talk to Dick about that. When he comes to Nebraska, that won't happen."

It was little consolation that the Nebraska players were classy in victory, with Clifford Scales noting "the two guards for Wisconsin-Green Bay were much quicker than the guards for Wisconsin," and guard Beau Reid calling UWGB "as well-coached as any team we've played to this date."

The players would say the right things after the game, but the fans had a legitimate beef. "The chance (to win) no longer existed after the call was made," Dick Bennett commented after reviewing the tape. "I'm very frustrated. Anger isn't so much the appropriate feeling, even bewilderment isn't appropriate anymore. Just frustration. It was an opportunity that came and went, and we couldn't do anything about it."

Nevertheless, UWGB had pulled off huge wins against national brands like the Colorado Buffaloes and the DePaul Blue Demons in the same non-conference season. Those wins, and admirable efforts against Clemson and Nebraska, gave UWGB its highest profile and most impressive start in school history.

At 7-3, the Phoenix's nonconference resume was rock solid. If paired with a quality conference showing, UWGB would have a case for an NCAA at-large bid or, with at least a top-three conference finish, lock up a return to the NIT.

Chapter 8

Home Court Advantage
(1990-91 - Part 2)

A great home court advantage has the ability to get into the heads of opponents, elevate the intensity of the home team, and even sway officiating. It's no coincidence that the best teams in college basketball history have been incredibly successful on their home floor.

But not all competitive environments are created equally. Community size and make-up, tradition and history, school size, recent team success, availability of competing interests, arena location and construction, and even beverage options can shape a team's home court advantage, and in the process, alter the course of a team's future.

Conference Realignment

Something was in the cold winter air of Green Bay in 1991 – a sense that Dick Bennett's program was on the verge of something special. Phoenix faithful felt it, and the crowds proved it. Through five home games, attendance was up more than 6%, and games like Nebraska showed the crowd could be impactful.

And yet, in some ways the fans at Phoenix games were still learning how to best support their team. The fans and team were dancing with each other, searching for a more cohesive groove. With the conference schedule looming and a date to host the Mid-Continent Conference tournament in March, achieving that symbiotic synchronization, and soon, was more critical than ever.

It bears repeating: you can play your way *out* of the postseason in the nonconference, but you cannot guarantee a tournament bid without taking care of business in the conference. The previous season, the Phoenix did precisely what was needed to get to the postseason, going 8-1 against teams they should beat, and splitting against the top two teams.

With the team's arch nemesis, Southwest Missouri State, now in the Missouri Valley Conference, and Northern Iowa rebuilding, the Mid-Continent picture seemed even clearer in 1990-91. It would be a two-team race between UWGB and newcomer Northern Illinois.

Dick Bennett wasn't ready to declare his squad a favorite, but did agree about the Huskies, noting: "There's only one team that appears it could do what Southwest did, move away from the pack, and that's Northern Illinois."

It was hard to shake the sense that, even at 3-6, Northern Iowa was still dangerous. Beyond that, the conference was a mess. The only other slot that seemed settled was Valparaiso at the bottom.

Conference realignment was again a hot topic as the NCAA prepared for its convention during the second week of January. The landscape of college athletics was changing. Major schools like Miami, Florida State, and Penn State agreed to join power conferences: (Miami to the Big East in 1991; Florida State to the ACC in 1992, and Penn State to the Big Ten in 1993. While football drove these changes, the college basketball world was also evolving.

Perhaps the biggest change had been the creation of the Great Midwest Conference in 1990. The conference, set to begin play in 1991-92, included teams from the Midwestern Collegiate Conference (Marquette and Saint Louis) and Metro Conference (Cincinnati and Memphis State), as well as independent DePaul and former Sun Belt school UAB.

With the MCC and Metro losing schools, both conferences explored expansions or mergers. Meanwhile, rumors swirled that the Missouri Valley Conference was looking to add an additional one to three teams, and one of the popular names being tossed about was Northern Iowa. If the Panthers left, it would leave the Mid-Continent Conference scrambling for teams as well.

On top of conference uncertainty, UWGB learned in early January 1991 that Tory Smith was academically ineligible for the rest of his freshman year. The loss wouldn't hurt the team's regular rotation, but was a disruption nonetheless.

Experimenting with the 1-3-1

Dick Bennett had settled on a rotation through the first ten games that saw just seven players getting double-digit minutes (Tony Bennett, Ben Johnson, John Martinez, Dean Vander Plas, Scott LeMoine, Jeremy Ludvigson, and Dean Rondorf). With a more concentrated roster, the Phoenix looked to ride its momentum right through the Mid-Continent season.

As expected, UWGB started the conference season collecting a trio of wins over the middle of the pack. It began on January 5, 1991, with a 70-63 victory over Western Illinois. Surprise, surprise, it was guard play that led the way. Tony was unconscious, scoring 36 points on 14-for-20 shooting, while Martinez recorded a double-double of 16 points and 12 assists.

But the game was most notable for Dick Bennett's decision to go to 1-3-1 zone defense with 13:30 left in the game. Trailing 44-37 and looking for a spark, Bennett put Martinez at the top and Tony on the baseline, with Vander Plas roaming the middle. Five minutes later, UWGB was back on top for good.

"It was the difference. It slowed our motion offense," remarked the Leathernecks' coach, Jack Margenthaler, on UWGB's 1-3-1 zone. "We just stopped moving. It was the real difference in the game, besides a guy named Tony Bennett."

Dick Bennett was more pragmatic about the defensive switch, calling it a desperation move, and noting, "For once, for all the wrong decisions I've made, I kind of stumbled onto a right one."

Regardless of the reason, Bennett was becoming more comfortable with, if not reliant on, the 1-3-1 zone when he felt his team needed a lift. Indeed, he went back to it the next game at Northern Iowa. This time, the zone failed to produce, with the Panthers able to knock down three three-pointers during the four zone possessions. Northern Iowa had exploited the zone's weakness – three-point shooting.

Tony Bennett was again brilliant, scoring 17 of the team's 19 second-half points, including 11 during the final eight minutes. His highlight move came with UWGB up two and 30 seconds to play. Tony put a nasty crossover, behind-the-back move on Northern Iowa's Cedric McCullough, launching a fade-away three-pointer that hit the back of the rim and fell through the net. The triple helped UWGB to a 59-58 victory. It was Dick Bennett's 250th career win, and gave UWGB a 9-3 record.

UWGB's third-straight win came in its home conference opener and again involved the 1-3-1 zone. In front of a crowd of 5,733 fans– the fourth-largest crowd for a UWGB Division I home game – UWGB started sluggishly. But once it went to the zone, the Phoenix extended its lead from two points to nine in just five minutes, creating a deficit that Eastern Illinois couldn't close. Tony Bennett, dubbed the "premier player in the league" by Eastern Illinois coach Rick Samuels, again led the way with 29 points on 10-for-15 shooting, and Rondorf added 17 points.

With the 72-62 victory, UWGB stood at 10-3 overall and 3-0 in the conference.

Home Woes

A still respectable 4,857 fans arrived for a matchup with the 3-9 Valparaiso Crusaders on January 14, 1991. It was the second-lowest turnout of the year, and for good reason – Valparaiso was the conference's bottom-feeder.

Tony Bennett was dealing with back spasms coming into the game, and Dick Bennett decided to rest him. The team responded adequately in the first half, but the offense fell into a dumpster in the second half, while Valparaiso caught fire and went on a 17-2 run.

Dick had no choice but to put Tony on the floor with 13:33 left and his team down 35-27, much to the joy of Valparaiso. "We knew if he came in, they were getting desperate," said Valparaiso's Tracy Gipson.

Valparaiso was right to be happy. Tony wasn't able to muster anything close to his normal effort, partially for the injury and partially a response to the box-and-one defense Homer Drew deployed. Somehow, the conference's worst team pulled out a win on the road against the conference's best, 58-55.

Afterwards, Tony took the loss on himself: "I made a mistake, I asked to go in and ended up hurting us more than helping us."

The loss was embarrassing, but with a road game against Northern Illinois looming, the team had to plow forward.

A New Rivalry Begins

By mid-January, Northern Illinois was rolling, while Cleveland State had matched the Huskies with a surprising 4-0 start.

Five days off helped Tony's back, and while there was no doubt he'd play against Northern Illinois on January 19, there was uncertainty about how limited he would be. A standing room crowd of 6,060 Huskies fans hoped the answer was "quite a bit."

The showdown was set to be televised on The Sports Channel, and the atmosphere in Chick Evans Fieldhouse was as electric as any mid-major could ask for. The Huskies had won eighteen of their past nineteen home games, and UWGB's loss to Valparaiso did little to dispel the notion that these were the Mid-Continent's two best teams.

Northern Illinois's head coach, Jim Molinari, was in his second season at the helm, and had amassed an impressive 29-12 record. His team had a loaded senior class that included Donnell Thomas, a double-double machine and the team's scoring leader, and Donald Whiteside, a lightning-quick guard with a dynamite shot and a candidate for the Naismith Trophy, awarded to the best senior 6 feet or shorter.

Tight man-to-man pressure defense prevailed in the first half. With points at a premium, the arena had a high-intensity, playoff-like atmosphere. Neither team led by more than one possession through the first fifteen minutes, and it wasn't until Rondorf scored seven straight Phoenix points and Martinez sank two free throws with 2:45 left that UWGB opened up the first four-point lead of the game, 28-24.

Which lasted just one possession.

Two Whiteside free throws and an Andrew Wells layup tied the game back up at 28-28 with 1:27 left to play, and the Phoenix regained a 33-31 halftime lead on a Vander Plas buzzer-beating three-pointer.

The edge-of-your-seat action continued in the second half, with each possession worth its weight. It seemed that both teams were copies of each other, and as it was in the first half, neither team took a significant lead.

In a game like this, trying to find just one turning point is impossible, but an early candidate would have to be a rare four-point play turned in by Johnson with 13 minutes left to help UWGB snatch back the lead at 43-42. The emotion of the moment carried over to the next possession, where Logan Vander Velden grabbed a critical rebound, was fouled, and jumped up and down with a fist pump of emotion. Martinez hit a jumper from the left baseline, and UWGB was up 45-42.

Five minutes later, the score was tied at 57-57 with 1:30 left when UWGB put the ball in the hands of its hobbled star. Tony Bennett started at the top of the key, did a spin move on his defender, and worked his way all the way to the bucket for a left-handed layup, giving the Phoenix a 59-57 lead that finally would stick.

After a timeout, UWGB went into its now-common 1-3-1 zone. The Huskies clanked a long three-point attempt and Vander Plas hit two free throws. A Vander Velden dunk after a final Huskies miss capped a big 63-57 Phoenix win.

The players hugged at center court, and Dick Bennett gave a double-fist pump to the 200 or so UWGB fans sitting behind the bench. The game was, in a word, *intense*, featuring an astounding twelve ties and twenty-two lead changes – numbers almost unbelievable when you consider there were only forty-three made baskets. Indeed, no team ever led by more than four points until the final five seconds.

"For us, it's bigger (than DePaul)," remarked Vander Plas afterwards. "We finally stood the test against a conference team that was supposed to be the best. Every year against Southwest Missouri State, we'd fight for thirty minutes, then let it slip away."

A dejected Dick and Tony Bennett leave the Brown County Arena floor following a poor performance in a 50-48 loss to Akron on January 29, 1991. (University of Wisconsin-Green Bay Archives)

UWGB won its next two road games, first at the lowly Chicago State Cougars, then at Cleveland State. Tony Bennett and Martinez shined in both – Martinez scoring 20 in the first game and Bennett 30 points in the second.

By the last week of January, UWGB returned home to the Brown County Arena with a postseason-worthy 13-4 record, and 4-1 in the conference.

Unzipped Lips

As the schedule progressed, 1990-91 increasingly became a season of two teams – Northern Illinois and UWGB. And as Molinari's club kept winning, the pressure mounted on Bennett's club to keep pace. However, UWGB buckled under that pressure in a home game against their emerging nemesis.

Akron had bolted out of the gates with a 7-2 non-conference record, but was struggling in conference play, setting a Mid-Continent record for futility by scoring only 30 points in a game against Northern Illinois. And yet, visiting Green Bay on January 29, the Zips pushed and bullied the Phoenix all over the floor. UWGB was down early and often, and though it made a late run, missed layups and unforced mistakes cost the Phoenix in a 50-48 defeat.

The Phoenix shot just 31% and saw no help from their usually reliable star, with Tony Bennett going a poor 3-for-13 from the field. The bad home loss killed any hope the Phoenix had of an NCAA at-large bid.

Worse yet, for the first time since the 1988-89 season, UWGB had lost two consecutive home games. Feeling the fans and the program were not on the same page, Dick Bennett vented his frustration. In a stunning display and with a scolding tone, Bennett went right after the crowd.

"We always have spectators, but we don't always have *fans*. I'd like more *fans*," he said. "A huge crowd that sort of waits for things to happen is a very difficult crowd to perform in front of. We have those exciting settings on special occasions, but by and large, it's very quiet."

His frustrations drew the front page of the sports section the following day. In addition to publishing Bennett's grievances with the fans, the article highlighted a number of alleged reasons for the "quiet" environment, including a small student section, the team's style of play, great expectations, and even the pep band.

Bennett was playing with fire. During the Dick Lien years, the team never drew more than 2,000 fans per game over the course of the season. But under Bennett, attendance had risen every year.

Season	Ave. Attendance
1985-86	1,462
1986-87	3,045
1987-88	4,138
1988-89	4,757
1989-90	4,889
1990-91 (8 games)	5,143

In fact, season ticket holders now accounted for over 5,000 of the roughly 5,600 available capacity in the Brown County Arena. While UWGB was drawing more than 5,000 fans per game, only Northern Illinois (3,270 fans/game) and Akron (3,006 fans/game) were averaging even half of the Phoenix's draw. Alienating his growing fan base now could torpedo his team's home court advantage, ruin any positive growth, and destroy a key revenue stream for the university.

Which is why, thirty years later and with the benefit of hindsight, it's still difficult to tell if Bennett's move was lunacy or psychological genius. The case for the former needs no explanation, but there are clear parallels with Bennett's approach to the fans and his approach in motivating his own players. One of his strengths as a coach was pushing his players hard, often questioning their heart and dedication in hopes that he might strike a nerve and motivate the player to prove him wrong. Green Bay is and always had been a prideful, blue-collar town that doesn't like to be told what it isn't.

Community Response

Bennett did not have to wait long to see the effects of his words. The team's next home game just days later saw a raucous crowd of more than 5,700 bring their voices. With the cheerleaders holding up signs with "Coach Wants Noise" on them, the sold-out crowd gave several standing ovations to the Phoenix during the affair.

Tony Bennett drives around the Western Illinois defense as Ben Johnson (left) looks to set a pick during UWGB's 77-50 victory on February 2, 1991. (University of Wisconsin-Green Bay Archives)

Lifted by the vocal support, UWGB responded with one of its best outings in years, shooting 55% from the field in a crushing 77-50 win over Western Illinois. It was the team's largest home conference victory since 1988, and the first "no-doubter" win against a Division I school all season, allowing Bennett to rest his starters.

"I thought the atmosphere was absolutely marvelous. It gave our defense the shot in the arm it needed, and we hit the shots we needed. The crowd was a major factor tonight," praised Bennett afterwards. "Our fans have always responded when we give them something to respond to. That's all I can ask for."

Johnson agreed: "When you go to a university and see a college basketball game, that's the kind of atmosphere you expect. The crowd was excellent."

On a Monday night two days later, nearly 5,000 fans made it the arena to give the team another lift over Northern Iowa. UWGB had a seven-point lead late, but Northern Iowa tied it with less than 3 minutes to play.

That's where Martinez reminded everyone he was the team's second threat. Martinez launched a crossover, fade-away three-pointer from the right wing very early in the shot clock – a shot Bennett hated in every sense. But the ball found nothing but net.

"If it's in, he's a hero. If it's out, you might question it. But sometimes you have to take those," summarized Tony Bennett.

The crowd went bonkers and spent the rest of the game standing, clapping, and screaming for their team, giving the players an emotional lift to close out the Panthers, 72-67. Vander Velden was the surprise of the game, tallying 12 points in 31 minutes of action, including a dunk in the final minutes that brought the house down.

It was no surprise the Phoenix won a game in which Martinez played well. The sophomore guard was becoming the team's barometer, with UWGB 7-1 in games he scored more than a dozen points, and a lesser (though still impressive) 8-4 when he scored less.

Martinez's scoring rise came at the expense of Vander Plas, whose scoring was down slightly (9.7 ppg as opposed to 10.8 ppg the previous season). But this played right into Bennett's vision, and with his own growth, Vander Plas accepted his role.

"The blocker role, you have to assume a servant's mentality," explains Vander Plas. "I just embraced it. I thought, 'If we're going to win, someone's got to do this, and my shoulders are wide and I can set a double screen for just one person. So go get Tony and John Martinez open, and let's play.'"

The victory brought UWGB's record to 15-5 overall and 7-2 in conference, trailing only Northern Illinois's 9-1 conference mark. The day after the Northern Iowa game, the Phoenix received incredible news – it had gained a vote in the AP Top 25 poll for the first time in school history, joining Northern Illinois (who had four votes) on the list.

The ecstasy was short-lived, as the Phoenix managed to bungle away a road game to the conference's third-place team, Eastern Illinois, on February 9. UWGB had a 47-42 lead with less than seven minutes to play, but Eastern Illinois, the nation's second-ranked three-point shooting team at over 44%, went to its strength and hit several long-range bombs to take charge and hold off a late Phoenix surge. The Phoenix was now in a virtual tie with Eastern Illinois.

At 15-6 with six regular-season games to play, Bennett was in no mood to discuss life after the conference tournament: "I don't think we're setting ourselves up for postseason play."

The more level-headed of the Bennetts, Tony remained optimistic: "If we put 20 wins on the board, we should be in good shape."

Tony did what was needed on February 12 to get UWGB's sixteenth win of the season against UIC, posting 21 points, seven assists, and four rebounds in an all-around spectacular effort.

But perhaps the best news was that the Phoenix was getting healthy, with Vander Plas's ankle and Vander Velden's back both improving just in time for the fast-approaching Northern Illinois rematch.

Rockin' and Rollin' in the Dick Dome

Prior to February 1991, it had been the rarest of occasions when UWGB had managed to sell standing room only tickets, always just a few hours before the game. That changed the week UWGB prepared for Northern Illinois.

For all the hype and intrigue around the season's earlier match again Nebraska, this heavyweight fight was certain to be the biggest home game in school history.

The Huskies' sheer dominance throughout the regular season amplified the epic feel, supported by their presence at #31 in the *USA Today* poll and #35 in the AP poll. With nineteen wins and just two losses to Minnesota and UWGB, the Huskies were seriously flirting with at-large consideration from the NCAA. Jim Molinari's teams were disciplined, and his Huskies were second in the country in scoring defense, holding opponents to 55.1 ppg and less than 38% shooting.

Team officials knew well in advance that the Saturday, February 16, game was going to set attendance records at the Brown County Arena. By Wednesday, the ticket office had already sold 100 SRO tickets. On Friday, that number had climbed to over 300, leaving less than 200 SRO tickets for the day of the game.

By tip-off, the new attendance record was set. A crowd of 6,279 sandwiched into the Brown County Arena, covering the entire floor space around the court and filling every nook and cranny in the facility. No one complained – this was one of those games you had to be at.

If it was possible, both teams played even more deliberately and methodically than in the first affair, which accentuated the value of each possession. The anxious crowd hung on every shot attempt and exploded with every positive Phoenix play.

The game was tied 30-30 with 15:30 left, and then, for the first time in nearly sixty-five minutes of basketball between the teams that year, one team went on a run.

In a span of five possessions, Northern Illinois made 5-of-6 free throws, a 10-foot jumper, and a Donald Whiteside three-pointer, all while UWGB committed one turnover and missed two shots within six feet. The 10-2 run helped Northern Illinois take a 40-32 lead with 11:46 to play.

Bennett's words from a month earlier rang in the fans' ears, and the crowd rose to the occasion, turning in its best performance on a night the team needed it the most. The Phoenix's response began with Tony Bennett drilling a three-pointer. Then, Johnson and Tony combined for a steal, which Johnson followed with another three-pointer. When Vander Plas hit a long jumper to tie the game, the crowd exploded as though it had just witnessed a Packers Super Bowl win.

The volume somehow increased, as Tony hit three three-pointers in a few-minute stretch, his third (and fifth for the game) coming from five feet behind the line to put UWGB up 52-49 with 3:37 to play. The crowd was in pure ecstasy, towels waving, people screaming, backs patted in raw emotion. UWGB shut down the Huskies from there, winning 61-53.

It proved to be a seminal moment in Dick Bennett's tenure in Green Bay, and the coach was thrilled with the support: "There was a tremendous amount of emotion that favored us. When that occurs, the hustle was on our side."

The arena had been so crammed that the fire marshal would institute new rules for the conference tournament, ensuring the attendance record set in the Northern Illinois game would last as long as the building. Tony Bennett, who finished the game with 21 points including 12 of his team's 29 points in the last 11:30, was also impressed. When asked to summarize the experience, Tony grinned and provided the quote of the year: "Rockin' and rollin' in the Dick Dome."

Finishing Strong

Cleveland State's win over Eastern Illinois in the middle of the following week made it likely that UWGB would finish no worse than second in

A record Brown County Arena crowd erupts as Logan Vander Velden secures the ball after a steal as Jeremy Ludvigson watches during UWGB's 61-53 victory over Northern Illinois on February 16, 1991. (University of Wisconsin-Green Bay Archives)

the conference, and probable that it would finish no higher than that as well. With four regular season games to go, UWGB focused on getting to the 20-win mark, a resume-builder for the NIT committee.

Due to a scheduling quirk, UWGB's next two games were road matches on consecutive days, first at UIC and then at Akron. In typical mid-major fashion, the reason was that the Brown County Arena was scheduled to host a circus. This created a domino effect, leaving Akron with the choice of which date to play the Phoenix. The Zips strategically insisted that UWGB travel to Akron the night after playing at UIC for back-to-back road games.

UWGB knocked off UIC in a thrilling 89-81 overtime game witnessed by a paltry 1,104 fans in Chicago. Tony Bennett continued his record-breaking ways, setting UWGB's Division I single-season scoring record with his 33-point output, while Vander Plas turned in one of the most productive efforts of his career, racking up 20 points, eight assists, and six rebounds.

One night later, UWGB got revenge against the Zips, both for its earlier loss and the scheduling fiasco, winning in relatively easy fashion, 61-52. Tony was huge, scoring 22 second-half points on a combination of scooping layups and long jumpers, all while upping his conference-leading scoring average to 22.1 ppg.

The wins guaranteed UWGB at least a second-place finish in the conference, meaning the earliest it could play Northern Illinois in the tournament would be the championship game. It also was the team's nineteenth win with two to play.

Returning home for the last home game of the regular season on Monday February 25, UWGB put together another exceptional effort, collecting an 11-point win over Cleveland State in front of 5,847 fans. Sophomore Dean Rondorf gave the team a lift with 16 points.

But it was the team's other Dean —Vander Plas — who the crowd directed its "Dean, Dean" chants in recognition of the senior's stellar career. The linebacker-turned-forward was thankful for the fans, and the program's commitment to him and his style of play: "It put an exclamation point on four years of work. All this was a dream come true. The fans, it's good to know they appreciate my style of play."

UWGB finished the regular season with a forgettable win at last-place Valparaiso, extending its winning streak to six and a 21-6 overall record entering the conference tournament.

Getting past the 20-win mark remained an important milestone for Dick Bennett. "There's a lot of tense days ahead, and I'm just really happy to get twenty," he noted. "Twenty is significant."

A Place to Call Home

The Phoenix had closed out the season with five consecutive home wins, undefeated at the Brown County Arena since Bennett made his statements about the fans. The timing couldn't have been better, with the conference tournament coming to town.

Over the past month, the Brown County Arena had transformed from a tough venue to a darn-near impossible one. The uniqueness of the building itself, coupled with its location, adult concessions, and raucous locals, all coalesced to create a treacherous atmosphere for visiting teams.

From a facilities perspective, UWGB's main advantage was that at least the players knew what they were getting in to. The since-demolished arena itself was simplistic – an unassuming, white-roofed cylinder with sombrero-shaped seating along the sidelines, and temporary metal seats positioned along the baselines for the school band and small student section. The interior walls were dark blue, and behind the bleachers hung huge, dark curtains that created a challenging background for unfamiliar shooters.

"It was not the easiest place to shoot," noted future Phoenix shooter, Ben Berlowski, "Some guys had a hard time with picking up the depth perception with that arena."

"I had trouble being consistent in that place," added Berlowski's future teammate, Chris Westlake. "It was a dark backdrop and I just couldn't get myself locked in to the target."

The arena served as a multi-purpose facility, leading to challenges with the constant set-up and take-down.

"My junior year, we're out there doing a warmup and I finally took Steve Swan aside and said, 'Look it, the rim is not straight,' " recalls Eric LeDuc. "And he's like, 'You know what, you're right.' "

Further, the arena was usually cold, and not just because of Wisconsin winters. Rather, below the basketball floor was an ice hockey rink.

"The ice underneath the floor, your toes would always be freezing because the floor would never warm up," remembers Johnson.

"Guys sometimes were like, 'Is this a slippery spot here? Or is this a dead spot over here?' " notes Berlowski. "We would bounce the ball over the floor, trying to figure out which spots were dead, which spots were slippery."

And then there were the teams' dressing areas.

"The locker rooms were about 12 by 14, so there was nowhere to change," says Mike Karisny.

"It was basically a square room with a toilet and a chalkboard. Like a portable chalkboard that you'd just put some chairs in there," notes Scott LeMoine.

"The locker rooms themselves were like 100 degrees. We had to open – pry open some of the windows for pre-game talks because it was so hot in there," remarks future Phoenix guard Gary Grzesk.

The plumbing within the facility mirrored the heating system in terms of quality and consistency (or lack thereof).

"After the game was even more funny, because we had those four showerheads, and I think two out of the four worked," describes Berlowski. "And it'd be like hot water for about twenty minutes, and then it would go to cold. So we were always stripping down, rushing to make sure we could get some hot water before we had to go meet our parents, do an interview, or something."

"At one point, we were complaining to Chancellor Perkins because the water in the showers was trickling out and it was cold," remembers Grzesk. "So not only were you taking a cold shower, you could barely get enough cold water to come out of the showerhead."

None of this seemed to be of interest to the coach.

"If we complained about anything, Dick didn't take kindly to that," remembers LeDuc. "He essentially would lose his mind if you complained about showers not being hot."

With both teams facing the same challenges, it was an advantage for the Phoenix players to anticipate and prepare for what they were going to encounter. And of course, none of this mattered to the adult clientele attending the games. These folks bought what Bennett was selling, and embraced his philosophy.

"Coach was like Vince Lombardi," notes Westlake, "and I think it was a huge identity thing for Green Bay to be a blue-collar type of team like we were. I think everyone in Green Bay identified with that, identified with Coach Bennett, our style of play, how much we bought into it. And they bought into it."

"It was just an adult crowd, which was one of the keys to our success," states Dick Bennett. "It was an intense crowd, and so they helped us incredibly, and we became kind of the darlings of the community and of the area."

"The guys who follow GB basketball were the auto guys who were fixing cars, you know these small businesses, who wore the brown, white, and green jackets," notes Berlowski. "Green Bay is an interesting town. Once they bring you in and they kind of feel comfortable with you, then they support you."

The Brown County Arena's secret weapon may have been the liquid courage it supplied its working-class crowd.

"You could almost smell a little bit of the beer when you came in," remembers Karisny.

"The fact that they served beer, that was huge," notes Tony Bennett. "Packer fans knew how to get rowdy."

"Because they sold beer at the Brown County Arena, the crowd would get a little wild," recalls Dick Bennett, "There's nothing quite like the old Brown County Arena. I mean, it was a place made for crazy occurrences."

One of the craziest groups was seated in Section F, right behind the opposition's bench. The group was legendary for getting under the visitor's skin.

"That group that used to sit behind the visitors' benches? Oh man, they were *so* rough. We would talk to the teams afterwards, and every team was like, 'Man we hate coming here. They are all over us the entire game," says LeMoine.

"The Section F people right behind the opposing bench, they saw we were getting good," recalls Tony Bennett., "They could see something special brewing."

The fans came to love the plodding, but effective style of Dick Bennett's clubs and proved they were smarter than the average fans.

"The fans of Green Bay were so intelligent, they understood our system, how we played, what our strengths were," notes Grzesk. "You would hear them as much on the defensive end when you were trying to get a stop as you would when we would score."

"They were absolutely incredible. I always said they always gave us at least a five- to eight-point advantage," notes Johnson. "They were rabid, they were on it."

"It was the toughest ticket to get," states Karisny. "In talking to people from other (teams), they said, 'Man, that arena was — we couldn't stand it there. It was the toughest place we had to play.' "

"People hated to come there. They hated and loved it," summarizes future Phoenix star Jeff Nordgaard. "They loved the story and listening to people behind the bench, but they also obviously hated all the excitement and energy for our team and against them. It was a dump, but it was great."

"It was kind of like catching lightning in a bottle," is how LeMoine describes the arena. "We got good and we were really good at home, and those fans that just caught on and were diehards. We were one of the few teams in Wisconsin that was doing really good, and so it was just cool."

"The Brown County Arena was — still is, one of the most special places I've ever been at," states Vander Plas. "I remember walking out on that floor and just thinking, 'Wow.' We were lucky to play in the time we did with Coach Bennett. They used to call it the Dick Dome, and it was an amazing place. I remember the security people, the sheriffs, the fire people, just were ecstatic that we were doing well. And it was packed. I mean it just was electric in the place, and it was a really fun place to play college basketball. There wasn't a venue I played in that was as electric as those fans made us feel."

To the Extreme

That home court advantage was forming at the perfect time of the Phoenix, which were hosts for the 1991 Mid-Continent Conference Tournament.

Prior to the start of the tournament, Tony Bennett was named Mid-Continent Player of the Year, having led the conference in scoring at 22.0 ppg and three-point shooting at 53%, while finishing second in assists at 5.0 per game. Northern Illinois's Jim Molinari was named Mid-Continent Coach of the Year.

March 3 was a Sunday, and fans trickled in to the Brown County Arena throughout the afternoon to watch the four games of the quarterfinals. Those who arrived early for the 1 pm game saw the top-seeded Northern Illinois Huskies cruise past UIC, 77-52, with five players scoring in double digits. The second game, the 4-5 seed matchup, was much closer, with Northern Iowa knocking off the newly revived Cleveland State Vikings, setting up a Northern vs. Northern semifinal.

UWGB was the third game on the slate, and by tip, some 6,117 fans were jammed in. It was the program's fourth standing-room-only crowd of the season, and the second-largest crowd ever to witness a game at the Brown County Arena, behind only the Northern Illinois game from a few weeks earlier.

Akron, the Phoenix's opponent and only conference team to have won at the arena, never saw what hit them. Dick Bennett gave LeMoine the start to counteract the Zips' best player, Pete Freeman.

"Coach told us three things," Vander Plas said. "Get back on defense, play good defense, and don't rush on offense."

The crowd provided every bit of help, picking right up where the regular season left off.

"I heard there were 100 less people here tonight (than for the Northern Illinois game)," remarked Rondorf, "but I thought there were about 500 more. It was just crazy."

Bennett's strategy of using LeMoine on Freeman and packing the lane to prevent easy buckets, worked like a charm. UWGB held Akron without a point for the first six minutes, racing to a 7-0 lead behind cheers with every defensive rebound and made basket. The lead grew to 26-9 with 5 minutes left in the first half, and by halftime UWGB held a commanding 36-17 lead behind 13 first-half points from Tony Bennett.

Five minutes into the second half, the lead had expanded even further to 52-25, and the Phoenix was able to start resting their key players. LeMoine had been brilliant, holding Freeman without a first-half basket and a meaningless nine points for the game. Freeman became so annoyed by LeMoine that midway through the second half, he threw the ball at his head and was charged with a technical foul.

The rout was on, and when it was finally over, UWGB had smashed Akron, 85-61. The win served as sweet revenge for the early season loss and seemingly ensured UWGB at least an NIT bid.

"We won that one easily and that gave us the confidence," remembers Dick Bennett. "I think getting by that first game at home really – I could see the kids relax."

Some of the fans stuck around for the fourth matchup of the day, watching the third-seeded Eastern Illinois Panthers win a curiously close game over sixth-seeded Western Illinois. Panthers guard Steve Rowe had a career high 32 points, setting up a UWGB vs. Eastern Illinois semifinal.

Semi-Sweet

Fans arrived early the next day for the Northern Illinois vs. Northern Iowa semifinal, hoping for a Northern Iowa upset. Those outlandish dreams looked like they might actually come true for a while. That is, until Northern Illinois's Donald Whiteside hit a clutch, last-second three-pointer to force overtime. From there, the Huskies pulled away and locked up their spot in conference championship game against the winner of the headline matchup, UWGB vs. Eastern Illinois.

Somehow, even more fans packed into the arena than the day before, with 6,187 folks making the game. This new number became the second-highest attendance for a game at Brown County Arena, and the team's fifth standing-room-only game of the season.

Eastern Illinois coach Rick Samuels noted before the game that one of his biggest concerns was how to stop UWGB's secondary threats, such as Vander Plas. And though the coach could develop a game plan for the big senior, his team was largely helpless against the fan base. Unable to yell over the noise, Eastern Illinois resorted to using signs to indicate plays to run.

The Panthers were a much better team than Akron, but there was nothing they could do to stop the Phoenix. It started with a long Tony Bennett jumper from the right baseline off the opening tip. The strong start continued with layups on four of the next five Phoenix possessions, and baskets on eight of its first nine possessions for a 16-6 advantage.

The frenzied crowd was overjoyed, and the margin grew to 14 by the half. While Eastern Illinois did cut the lead to single digits later, the outcome of the game was never in doubt.

Johnson and Martinez combined to hold Steve Rowe to just one point and no made baskets for the night.

As for the Phoenix attack, Tony Bennett showed why he was the conference's player of the year, scoring 22 points on 9-for-12 shooting, and Vander Plas added 17 points. The performance was an efficient and crowd-pleasing affair as the Phoenix skated into the championship game with a 63-54 win.

"Don't ask me about the crowd," Rick Samuels told reporters after the game. "How'd you like to write your article with 60,000 people yelling at you?"

"It's a living hell playing here," remarked Eastern Illinois guard Gerald Jones. "You have to outplay Wisconsin-Green Bay players and their crowd."

Hoop Dreams

The final of the Mid-Continent Conference's premier matchup rightly had the highest stakes of the trilogy, with the winner taking home a guaranteed NCAA Tournament bid. Both clubs were deserving, but this was mid-major basketball, and that meant Tuesday's duel could very well spell the NIT for the loser.

This game was important. Really important. It represented the Phoenix's best shot at getting to an NCAA Tournament, and it would do so in front of 6,000-plus home fans against its biggest rival of the 1990-91 season.

A win would justify the years of dedication and work. It would give UWGB bragging rights throughout the state of Wisconsin. It would spotlight the already-pulsating Phoenix in the national media's eyes. It would validate Dick Bennet's coaching career.

Most importantly, a win would give them a chance at immortality as the school's first NCAA Tournament team. Beating any team three times in a year, let alone one as good as the Huskies, is no small feat. Northern Illinois, chasing its school's second NCAA Tournament appearance (the first coming in 1982), was thrilled with the rematch.

"We'd love to face them again, show them who's No. 1," said Huskies center Randy Fen before the game.

Guard Mike Hidden went further: "I want to play them again this year. I want to play them next year, and I want to come back and play them in an alumni game."

"I want them more than they want us," retorted UWGB's Ben Johnson. "We concern ourselves with our game plan, what we need to do to win. Once we start worrying about other people, we'll be in trouble."

For Vander Plas, UWGB's lone senior, the game had a little extra incentive. "Personally, I was just hungry to keep my college career going as long as I could, because I knew whenever that ball went – that last buzzer sounded – I was done."

ESPN's Clark Kellogg and Wayne Larrivee joined forces in Green Bay to broadcast the championship. It would be the first of a double-header for the network, ironically scheduled to be followed by UWGB's old nemesis, Southwest Missouri State, playing (and losing to) Creighton in the MVC championship.

The players did their best to avoid the pregame media circus.

"Clark Kellogg came up to me before the game and asked me how to pronounce my last name," remembers Vander Plas. "I just remember gruffing at him, 'Vander Plas,' you know, like, 'Leave me alone, I've got work to do.'"

Vander Plas wasn't alone in feeling tight.

"Everything was riding on it," recalls Dick Bennett. "We were a little tense."

The Phoenix had good reason. On top of the stakes, its opponent was no pushover.

"They were legitimately good," Bennett says. "They had a tough (player in Donnell Thomas). He wasn't so big in terms of height, probably 6-6, but he was really a player. Strong, wide body."

"They had Donald Whiteside, Stacy Arrington, and a couple other guys that went on to play a lot of years in Europe that were really, *really* good," adds LeDuc.

"Those guys were athletic, they were strong," notes Rondorf. "Certainly more athletic than we were."

With the new fire codes in place, the recorded attendance at Tuesday's championship game was 6,197 fans. But many on hand would swear the actual number was higher, topping the official record set earlier in the year against the Huskies.

"It was like a done deal. At that point in time, we felt like, on our home court, we were unstoppable," says LeMoine. "Northern was the second-best team, and we owned Northern at that time."

This game did not follow the mold set by the first two battles. While the intensity was high, this game would be one of runs and the first one belonged to the Huskies.

It began with Tony Bennett missing a seven-footer from the right baseline, Martinez missing a layup from the right side, Vander Plas having a layup swatted, and then missing a pair of bunnies on the next possession. Tony would miss his next three shots in a start that was eerily similar to the 1990 championship game.

"They bottled him up, and he probably was tight," remembers Dick Bennett.

By the first television break, UWGB found itself down 7-1, having missed their first six shots. And though Johnson and Martinez were able to pitch in over the next few minutes, the deficit grew to 13-5.

It took ten minutes of play to get their legs, but once they did, UWGB's players regained the momentum in a hurry. It started with a Vander Plas left-handed layup off a picture-perfect inbounds pass from Martinez that turned into an and-one. On the other end, Jeremy Ludvigson delivered a poster-worthy rejection that led to a Vander Plas basket – albeit following a Martinez air ball – cutting the score to 13-10. Vander Plas pumped his fist as he ran back, amping up the crowd.

"We knew that the road to the NCAA Tournament had to go through Green Bay," states Vander Plas, "and I just remember thinking, 'We're not going to let this one get away.' "

Clark Kellogg commented on the noise in the moment, saying, "I don't think this crowd has ever left. They have been absolutely fantastic. Even when their team was struggling early, they were still very much a part of it."

By the third official timeout with 6:34 left, the score was 15-10 Northern Illinois, but the Phoenix had hit its collective stride. A Ludvigson layup and Rondorf three-pointer tied it at 15-15, while Vander Plas, from the bench, faced the crowd with his towel and lifted his arms in jubilation. A few moments later, the half came to a close with the Huskies holding a 19-17 lead, but UWGB holding the momentum.

Spread Your Wings

Northern Illinois's 6-5 forward Mike Hidden, with help from Whiteside, had done a remarkable job shutting out Tony in the first half. The younger Bennett had gone 0-for-6 as part of the Phoenix's 28% shooting struggles from the floor.

"I think Tony felt, 'I've got to come through – I must come through for our team,' " recalls Dick Bennett. "But probably like any kid who's sort of your leader and maybe your best player, they don't realize you've got some good people around you who will carry the ball until you get yourself squared away. And that's essentially what happened."

"We didn't shoot it very well in the first half, but we felt like we were in control, because we were just grinding it out on the defensive end," adds Vander Plas. "They were bigger, they were better athletically than us, but our team was better together."

The Phoenix defense duplicated the Huskies' efforts by holding "D-Train" Donnell Thomas to two points and limiting the Huskies to 38% shooting.

Tony Bennett and John Martinez (20) set sail on a fast break during the 1991 Mid-Continent Conference tournament championship game. (University of Wisconsin-Green Bay Archives)

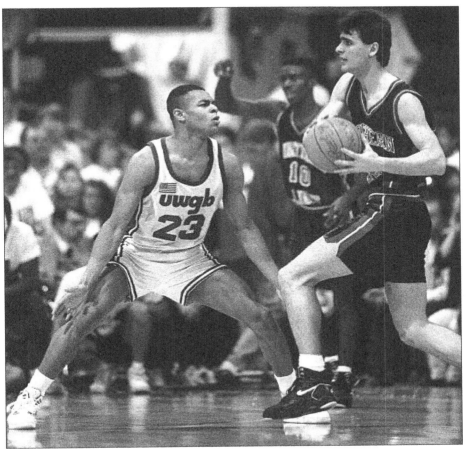

Ben Johnson (23) set the defensive tone for the Phoenix during the 1991 Mid-Continent Conference tournament championship game. (University of Wisconsin-Green Bay Archives)

"Ben Johnson played a huge role because we put him against Thomas," explains Dick Bennett. "And Ben really just never let him touch the ball."

Meanwhile, Martinez had submitted a subtly impressive offensive performance. As the teams returned for the second half, Kellogg credited Martinez with a "real solid" first half, but reminded everyone that "they need Bennett to get off that donut."

Martinez found Tony open on the right baseline for a three-pointer that found nothing but the bottom of the net, tying the game at 22-22. It had taken three more minutes of action in the second half for Tony to get on the board, but once he did, there was no putting that genie back the bottle.

He added a pair of free throws after a Donnell Thomas basket, and then scored on a spin-move drive to the left to give UWGB its first lead of the game, 26-24 with 14:13 left. Seven straight points made it clear the Phoenix's star was back.

The teams traded leads multiple times over the next five minutes. Then, with a 32-31 lead and 9:20 to play, Tony took a pass from Johnson at the top of the key, four feet behind the three-point line, and buried a three-pointer to give UWGB a 35-31 lead and sent the audience over the top.

"The atmosphere that was Brown County, and just the noise and how loud it was and the excitement was great," remembers Rondorf. "I think that gave us certainly an advantage, because I think it took Northern out of their game a little bit."

A Ludvigson tip-in, two free throws from Rondorf, and a fast-break layup by Martinez seemed to bust the game open, 41-34 with 6:55 left entering an official timeout.

A few moments later, Tony penetrated, drew a triple team, and hit Ludvigson for a layup and foul.

"Tony Bennett dropped me a pass, and I went up and laid it in and got fouled, and it's kind of where you're like, 'OK, we're going to win this game and go to the tournament,' " recalls Ludvigson.

Tony worked to keep his emotions in check: "We kept saying to each other on the court with five minutes left, just stay focused, just wait, we can celebrate after. You didn't want to think about it too soon, but it kept coming into the back of your mind."

The lead extended to 49-37 with 3:15 to play thanks to a pair of Vander Plas free throws. Then, after a stop, UWGB worked the shot clock down to 7 seconds before Johnson dished to Vander Plas, who converted a layup while being mugged by the Huskies' Lipinsky. Vander Plas displayed raw emotion, giving two fist pumps and screaming in ecstasy, eliciting a euphoric soundtrack from the audience.

"The whole crowd was chanting 'N-C-A-A ... N-C-A-A,' " Ludvigson recalls. "It was deafening. You had tingles going like, 'Oh my God.' It was crazy."

"It was deafening in there," comments Tony Bennett. "That championship game against Northern Illinois was unbelievable."

Vander Plas made his eighth free throw of the game with 2:27 left, giving UWGB an insurmountable 52-37 lead. Mayhem ensued, with Wayne Larrivee declaring "the coffin has been nailed here in Green Bay." (A predecessor to his later-trademark "There is your dagger" phrase he would use as the Packers' radio play-by-play man).

"All of a sudden, we start to creep away from them, and there's about two minutes left and I'm looking up at the scoreboard," remembers Vander Plas. "I remember thinking, 'We're going to win!' "

Incredibly, in the biggest game in UWGB history, the Phoenix played virtually error-free, committing just one turnover, intentionally, in the closing seconds.

"We had zero turnovers in the championship game until the end. We were holding the ball. There was no time left and (the official) made a five-second call for holding the ball. And that was the turnover," remembered Dick Bennett. "It was the most incredible ball-handling exhibition you'd ever want to see."

A possession later, Dean Rondorf dribbled out the final seconds of the game, throwing the ball in the air as the clock struck zeros. UWGB finished with a 21-3 run during the game's final 8:33 to win the conference championship, 56-39.

They had done it, reaching the mountaintop and securing the program's first ever NCAA Tournament bid.

"I'll never forget all the people rushing the floor," Johnson says. "I remember almost passing out, there were that many people. It was just special to bring that to the city of Green Bay and the campus and the community and all that. That was pretty dang cool."

Vander Plas, who earned all-tournament honors with a game-high 18 points and eight rebounds, was all smiles.

"I've never been hugged by so many people in such a short amount of time," he says. "Magical moment, as the Brown County floor was just full of people. If I could write a hand-written thank you to everybody that was there on those three nights in a row, it was just amazing. I think even if we weren't playing our best, they would've figured out a way to get us home. It was special."

"I'll never forget Chris Yates dumping the Gatorade bottle over Coach Bennett," laughs LeMoine. "He was not happy about that. Water all over the floor, and just everybody on the floor celebrating."

Quickly recovering, Dick met his son for an emotional embrace.

(From left) Tony Bennett, John Martinez, Jeremy Ludvigson, Dean Rondorf, and Ben Johnson celebrate as the clock hits zero, confirming the first trip to the NCAA tournament for the UWGB basketball program. (University of Wisconsin-Green Bay Archives)

Tony Bennett hugs his father, Dick, on the court after the Phoenix beat Northern Illinois to earn the program's first trip to the NCAA tournament. (University of Wisconsin-Green Bay Archives)

"The memory I have is just seeing that court part after we won it, and then just getting to embrace my dad," remembers Tony, who would take home tournament MVP honors. "I've got that picture in my office. That moment was like, 'We did it, we got this thing.'"

Martinez, who carried the load in the first half while Tony struggled to find his groove, agreed.

"It was one for the ages for sure. Having it on our home court and winning the tournament. To accomplish that goal was awesome, and to do it on your home court, even more so."

"It's probably my top game I ever played certainly in my career," states Rondorf. "The outcome, where it took us, and just being able to experience that at home, you know what I mean? It was just great, absolutely phenomenal."

Molinari, whose Northern Illinois club was still hopeful of getting an at-large NCAA Tournament bid, was gracious in defeat. He complimented the crowd's efforts, noting, "It was a great atmosphere. I don't think the Bulls would have beat Green Bay tonight."

Chapter 9

The Big Dance
(1991 NCAA Tournament)

Millions of eyes turn their television sets to ESPN, CBS, and affiliates each March, watching the greatest open-style playoff tournament in major sports. Neutral floor match-ups see audiences rallying behind underdogs in close games, creating concentrated electricity.

NCAA tournament performances are the pinnacle of college basketball careers, and when lightning strikes, it can leave an impression that lasts forever. Indiana State's 1979 run to the championship game with Larry Bird immediately comes to mind, but others, like #14 Cleveland State's 1986 Sweet Sixteen appearance, #16 Princeton's near-miss against top-seeded Georgetown in 1989, and Bo Kimble's Loyola Marymount heroic Elite Eight run in 1990, honoring their fallen teammate, Hank Gathers, achieved immortality without a true championship run.

The NCAA tournament is an opportunity for one shining moment. And for a mid-major program, it may be its single shot at creating a legacy.

Westward Bound
In typical mid-major fashion, UWGB had no choice but to focus attention on the financial ramifications of its position. The conference tournament, a rousing success for UWGB, the city of Green Bay, and the Mid-Continent Conference (especially given the magnitude of the nationally televised championship game), looked to net the conference $20,000-$30,000.

Meanwhile, the Phoenix were rooting hard for Northern Illinois to secure an at-large bid. Having two teams from the Mid-Continent get in would land UWGB a $110,000 payday, and while the amount would be insignificant for a power conference school, it was like manna from heaven for UWGB.

Putting the athletic program's financial struggles in perspective, UWGB had to rely on a local radio station (WNFL) to run a fundraiser just to obtain the $1,600 necessary to fix the school's dilapidated mascot costume. Every dollar mattered as Dan Spielman crunched the numbers.

Meanwhile, Dick Bennett became an instant hot commodity for the

UWGB fans show their enthusiasm after the Phoenix wrapped up a berth in the 1991 NCAA tournament. (University of Wisconsin-Green Bay Archives)

national media, handling calls from ABC and CBS in the days following the team's win. The players took two days off before meeting back for practice on Friday, a week before they would likely play their first-round NCAA tournament game.

"We had extra time to prepare, that's a big deal," notes Bennett. "Our tournament ended like two weeks before the tournament, so we had a whole week to practice before the selection. We were gung-ho, we were ready. We had great practices, spirited practices."

Anticipation was at an all-time high, with the early money on the Phoenix receiving a seed somewhere between 12 and 14. Finally, on Sunday, March 10, 1991, the team met at the Ramada Inn in Green Bay to watch the NCAA Selection Show.

"It was pretty wild," Bennett says. "We sat together, the team and all the fans were gathered behind us."

UWGB had to wait until the final four seeds were revealed before seeing its name on the screen.

"All of a sudden, we saw our names come up and playing Michigan State," recalls Dean Vander Plas. "I just remember thinking, 'We can beat them.'"

"When you looked at them on paper, and probably on the court, certainly more athletic than we were," admits Dean Ronforf. "(But) it was an opportunity again for us to prove that we belonged."

UWGB had received a 12 seed and was being shipped to the West Regional for a Friday matchup in Tucson, Arizona.

"I wish for our fans' sake it could have been closer," remarked Tony Bennett. "But I hear the weather's pretty nice, so it won't be all bad. They will be watching on TV."

"I think every kid that has a dream to play Division I basketball hopes that someday they'd be able to play in March Madness," says Vander Plas.

"To sit there with a bunch of people that are my most dear friends and listen to your name get called and say, 'Hey, you're going to go to Tucson and you're going to play Michigan State, who has a future Hall of Famer on it' – it was pretty cool."

The Spartans were a worthy opponent, though the team had underperformed. At the start of the year, Michigan State had been ranked No. 4 in the country, but finished third in the Big Ten with a solid, if unspectacular 18-10 record.

For Dick Bennett, the matchup was less significant than the accomplishment of making the tournament. "I mean, at that point, you don't care who you play – you're in. We thought it was a good draw."

To the excitement of UWGB's athletic department, the Phoenix's conference brethren, the Northern Illinois Huskies, had indeed received an at-large bid and were seeded 13th, set for a matchup with fourth-seeded St. John's.

Like Dick Bennett, Jim Molinari was excited for both programs. "I take my Christian beliefs very seriously. I just thank God that he let Dick and I get our first bids the same year."

Meanwhile, neither Marquette (11-18) nor Wisconsin (15-15) received bids, the latter settling for an NIT invite. It turned out the Phoenix never needed a regular-season matchup with the Badgers or Warriors after all.

If You Can Play, You Can Play

As a Midwestern team, the Spartans represented an interesting matchup for the Phoenix. "We've always compared ourselves to the Big Ten," remarked Scott LeMoine. "We've always said, 'I wonder how we'd do if we played those guys?' "

"The best part of all of that was they were a Big Ten team, which automatically made us the Cinderella and would excite our fans, would give us some leverage with the arena crowd," explains Dick Bennett. "Here we are, a team that Wisconsin would not play, and here we're going to go against a Big Ten team who was better than Wisconsin."

One thing Bennett refused to do was reach out to UW coach Steve Yoder or the Badgers' athletic department for any game film on the Spartans. Bennett deflected questions on the matter, stating he didn't want to put Yoder in a tough position. And though few accepted that excuse as likely or sufficient, Bennett had always preached preparing the same way for every opponent, and it wasn't part of his practice to spend time on film study.

"I did not watch tape on our opponents," he says. "I didn't do that until my last day. I so focused on our own team, and I let my assistants take care of the scouting, always. Tony isn't like that, but I am, I was."

"Coach Bennett was more focused on what we needed to do to win than really worrying about what the opponents did," notes future Phoenix guard Gary Grzesk.

"We never watched film. We were going to get better at what *we* do. Screw what everyone else does, we were going to be great at what we do," remembers LeMoine. "The only time we ever really got much as far as scouting reports was like right before the game."

"Coach Heideman, like for five minutes, would go over who's guarding who and tell you a little bit about the player, like right before you go out and play the game," notes Ludvigson. "We hardly ever talked about the other team."

"Other than that pre-game, chalk-talk kind of thing, we never really did any specific team game planning," explains Eric LeDuc. "Dick's favorite thing was you play against the game. 'Quality basketball knows no divisions.' He had a real John Wooden kind of approach to it where you play your game. You don't really adjust to people."

The team didn't need film to know that the Spartans' attack started with All-American forward Steve Smith. Smith was 6-5 and averaged more than 25 ppg – a cold-blooded assassin and leader of the club. After Smith, Heathcote would start Matt Steigenga, a 6-7 junior forward who could run the floor, and Mike Peplowski, a 6-10 load of a center. The guard-driven Phoenix lineup would have to fit through a forest of Spartan arms on every possession. In spite of the size difference, Bennett saw similarities in both teams' styles and strategy.

"We knew they would man-to-man us, and we thought we could screen them and get our shooters open. And of course we relied on that against everyone. We thought it would be a half-court game, because they liked that. They were physical, that didn't bother us. And we knew they weren't going to be able to press us. We knew it was going to be a grinder, and we actually were pretty good in those kinds of games."

Heathcote was in agreement, saying at the time: "They play a slow-down style; very, very deliberate and they're a good defensive club. It's going to be one of those meat-grinder games where each possession is an adventure."

The biggest question for UWGB was whether it could contain Smith. Bennett planned to stick with his defensive principles.

"The most obvious and percentage-wise the soundest (strategy) is to pack it in – get a lot of people in and around the lane to help one another, but to stay squarely in front of a guy like Steve Smith. Be on him, stay right in front of him so that you can at least blunt his quick dribble, his quick move into the lane."

As expected, Ben Johnson drew the task. He was respectful, but confident in his own ability. "He's a very skilled athlete, and at 6-5 or 6-6, any time he has the thought, he'll probably be able to shoot over me. I think I can bother him a little. I'll go wherever he goes, make him earn everything. I'm not going to give him any room, crowd him."

Bennett tagged Vander Plas to guard the 6-7 Dwayne Stephens.

"He said, 'Dean, you've got Stephens, he's 6-7, 260 pounds. It's one of the only guys this year you're going to guard that's going to be just as strong as you,' " remembers Vander Plas.

Bennett also gave Ludvigson the start, needing the freshman's size to counteract the Spartans' Peplowski. "Coach Bennett takes me for a walk and says, 'I'm starting you tonight,' " Ludvigson recalls. "When he told me that, I was like, 'Whoa, damn. Here we go.' "

Tony Bennett would guard Mark Montgomery, the Spartans' 6-2 point

All-American forward Steve Smith was the unquestioned offensive star for Michigan State during the 1991 NCAA tournament. (Michigan State University Archives and Historical Collections)

guard, which left, amazingly, 6-0 John Martinez guarding the 6-7 Steigenga. Right down the line, every matchup favored the Spartans in height and possibly in athleticism.

Dick Bennett coaches up Logan Vander Velden during the Phoenix's February 16, 1991, victory over Northern Illinois. Listening in are assistant coaches Tom Brown (from left), Steve Swan and Mike Heideman. (University of Wisconsin-Green Bay Archives)

"It will take a full game of us doing everything we can do to the best of our ability on both ends of the floor, and that's saying a lot, but it can be done," said a confident Dick Bennett. "There's going to be somebody, why not us?"

Tucson

A day before the game, UWGB took the floor in Tucson to perform a walk-through and get acclimated to the arena. Impressing no one, Bennett's squad focused on boring defensive drills and free throws. Afterwards, they found themselves star-gazing as some of the country's best put on a basketball exhibition.

"(Undefeated) UNLV was down there, Georgetown was down there with Alonzo Mourning. Michigan State was down. I mean we're sitting there watching all those teams practicing, and was like, 'Dang, this is sweet,' " remembers LeMoine.

"I remember Tark (UNLV coach Jerry Tarkanian) coming, sitting on the bench and not saying a word," adds Vander Plas. "They had t-shirts on that had a seatbelt painted on them, and on the back it said, 'Buckle up, you're in for a ride.' And they just went to dunking for an hour straight."

UWGB easily sold out its allotment of 250 tickets for the game within one day, and a chartered plane of 150 fans made it to Tucson for the game. Meanwhile, the residents of Green Bay were bananas in anticipation of the game, with bars and restaurants gearing up for record turnouts. In addition to the food industry, community clothing stores helped the coaching staff with their wardrobes.

"I remember Prange's, I think it was, gave our coaching staff green sports coats," says Vander Plas. "The ugliest green. I watch that game now and think, 'God, are those ugly,' but they all had their green sport coats on."

Naturally, the Spartans were the favorite, but media pundits acknowledged UWGB's credibility. During ESPN's Championship Week, Jim Valvano reminded everyone that conferences like the Ohio Valley and Mid-Continent routinely featured teams that could get through the first round.

In addition, two coaches that had seen both teams during the year felt the Phoenix had a shot. Central Michigan coach Charles Cole said the teams were very evenly matched, while Nebraska coach Jeff Smith gave UWGB at least a one-in-four chance to pull off the upset.

Bennett had prepared the team for precisely this moment.

"One of the phrases that Coach Bennett always used to say was, 'Respect everyone and fear no one,' " Ludvigson says. "We had that mentality and we believed it."

"It kind of goes back to Tony saying, 'We're not far off, we're right there,' " recalls Martinez. "I always had that same mentality, so for me, it was just another game that we should win."

Johnson, the team's emotional leader, summarized it by stating: "I really don't think we're satisfied with just showing up to the Big Dance. We do want to make a little noise when we're there. We have a system and we believe in that system. I think if we can just play within ourselves and play within the system, we'll be fine."

The Big Day

Fans trickled into the University of Arizona's McKale Center early Friday morning for the first game of a marathon four-match first round. Team warmups were brief and uneventful, nerves creeping in slightly.

Greg Gumble and Quinn Buckner had the call for CBS and watched the Phoenix dip into a 5-0 hole in the first three minutes. Though fearless, the Phoenix were getting an early taste for the Spartans' height.

"I was guarding Mike Peplowski – they called him the Mountain with Legs. He was about 6-10, 300-something," recalls Ludvigson. "The first time down the court, we kind of bumped into each other and my whole arm went numb. True story. Welcome to the big time, right?"

In spite of the slow start, the Phoenix remained crisp with the ball and sharp on defense. Its first basket came on a Tony Bennett drive-and-dish to Ludvigson, who converted on an old-fashioned three-point play. After a Steve Smith jumper, UWGB worked the shot clock down until Vander Plas found himself open at the top of the key. He squared himself and confidently launched a three-pointer – one of just six attempts he would have from long distance all season – that banged home to cut the deficit to 7-6.

Not surprisingly, defensive rebounding proved to be a major issue for the Phoenix. The Spartans snagged offensive rebounds on four of their next five possessions, converting all into each put-backs to establish a 17-11 lead midway through the first half.

The game could've gotten away from UWGB with this rebounding disparity if the Phoenix hadn't gotten some timely scoring. First, Rondorf made a short jumper. Then, after a rare Phoenix rebound, Tony Bennett knocked down another three-pointer. Michigan State's lead was just 17-16.

It was at this point that Heathcote, a coach intimately familiar with

Tony's game, made a switch.

"They made a very intelligent defensive assignment," explains Dick Bennett. "They put (Dwayne) Stephens, big (6-7) muscular kid on Tony, and then they really bottled him up."

With Tony on lockdown, UWGB turned to the other half of its back-court and Martinez delivered, knocking down a three-pointer from the left wing to give the Phoenix its first lead at 21-19.

The Spartans continued to score over the next few minutes, but UWGB had hit a groove and scored on nearly every posses-sion. The hot streak culmi-nated with Martinez bury-ing another three-pointer – UWGB's eighth straight made basket – to forge a 30-25 advantage with less than five minutes left in the first half.

"The shots went in, and so you do gain con-fidence," notes Rondorf. "You just kind of tune ev-erything out and when the shot's there, you just take it. And they were going in that game."

UWGB maintained a seven-point lead as the Spartans came down the floor for the final first-half possession. Smith took the ball at the top of the key, dribbled all the way to the left baseline, and lifted for

Jud Heathcote led Michigan State to prominence for 19 seasons from 1976-1995. (Michigan State University Archives and Historical Collections)

a shot over Rondorf as the clock flipped to zeros. With no time left, the shot found nothing but the bottom of the net to cut the Phoenix's halftime lead to 35-30.

Michigan State had abused the Phoenix on the boards, converting nearly 75% of its missed shots into second-chance opportunities. On the other end, the Phoenix was shooting an unsustainable 80% from beyond the arc, with three-pointers accounting for 24 of the team's 35 points. Both teams were excelling at what they did best, while failing miserably at de-terring their opponents. It was hard to imagine both clubs sustaining those numbers for another twenty minutes, but the unfolding drama had cap-tured the attention of the ever-expanding crowd, which was starting to side with the underdog Phoenix.

Peplowski came out and scored the Spartans' first four points after the break. A few possessions later, Michigan State retook the lead on a fast-break layup and an and-one conversion by Steigenga, 39-37. Things went from bad to worse a moment later when the Phoenix fouled Steigenga while dunking. His made free throw gave the Spartans a 44-39 lead and a 14-4 run in the first five minutes of the second half.

All the momentum the Phoenix had was gone and it would've been easy to fold, conquered by the bigger and more gifted Big Ten team.

But while Peplowski continued to have his way on the inside, the two Deans stepped up for the Phoenix. First, Rondorf buried a pair of three pointers from a nearly identical spot on the right wing, and then Vander Plas hit a long two-pointer from the top of the key and two free throws shortly thereafter.

"What I didn't expect," Dick Bennett says, "was Dean Vander Plas had a remarkably good game. And for some reason, we were able to get him the ball in open areas and he scored."

In just three minutes, UWGB had swung the lead back in its favor, 49-46, and now had the crowd on its feed in full support of the upstart 12 seed.

Like an EKG, a valley followed every peak, and the Phoenix were in danger when Tony picked up his fourth foul. Dick sat his star, but the Phoenix was somehow able to maintain a lead. Tony returned later, and as the clock ducked under 4:00, Johnson took a pass from the double-teamed guard and buried an open three-pointer, giving UWGB a 56-52 lead.

1-3-1 Zone

Crunch time was officially upon both clubs, the fate of their seasons resting on the final moments of the matchup in Arizona. The good news for the Phoenix was it had held Smith scoreless in the second half. But his teammates, namely Peplowski and Steigenga, owned the inside.

So with a four-point lead and 3:52 to play, Dick Bennett decided to pull out an old standby from his bag of tricks – he switched to the 1-3-1 zone. Tony would run the baseline, Martinez the top, and Vander Plas in the center. Ludvigson was on the right side and Johnson on the left.

"He had this sign that he made (with his hands). It was like a little teepee sign. He put his hands above his head like a Christmas tree," recalls Johnson.

"Sometimes I called it a victory zone, where if we got a lead and I wanted to slow the offense down, make them take more time to get a shot, that was the thought behind it," Bennett explains.

The first defensive possession in the 1-3-1 saw Smith get a wide-open three-point look from the right wing. His shot clanked off the rim and was tipped out of bounds by the Phoenix, but the uncontested look was strike one for the 1-3-1 zone.

On the subsequent inbounds, Michigan State set a double screen on Johnson to free Smith again on the wing. The All-American was too good to miss twice, and his three-pointer cut the Phoenix lead to just 56-55.

UWGB answered with a Vander Plas left-handed layup attempt that bounced three times on the rim before dropping through, making it 58-55 UWGB with 2:30 to play.

With the Phoenix still in the 1-3-1, the Spartans worked it again to

Smith, who got the ball five feet beyond the arc. This time, Ludvigson was standing on the three-point line in defense, but nothing would stop Smith from firing away. His shot was true again. Game tied 58-58 with 2:08 to play.

The 1-3-1 had failed the Phoenix, and in a heartbeat Michigan State had regained control. "All of the sudden it just – we thought we could catch them off guard, and you know, they banged a couple of angle threes," remembers Tony Bennett.

"We had kept Steve Smith in check, and then we went to the zone, and Steve Smith looked at us and he went *whack, whack*, from the wing – two threes in a row," acknowledges Johnson. "The momentum all shifted after that."

"Steve Smith hits two jumpers that are probably twenty-five to twenty-seven feet – what I remember, they were bombs – and it just totally changed the complexion of the game," adds Rondorf. "Now it became almost like a nervous energy for everybody, because now the game's tight."

Rondorf took an uncharacteristically early shot on the next possession that was too strong, and Michigan State grabbed the rebound. Back in the man-to-man, Johnson was now glued to Smith's hip. When Smith finally did get the ball and shot yet another three-pointer with 1:10 left, Johnson was in his face. This time, Smith's shot was short and the ball bounced off Steigenga out of bounds.

After everything that transpired in the first 39 minutes, UWGB now had the ball with the game tied and destiny in its own hands. For a team that had won seventeen games that year when tied or trailing with less than 5:00 to play, UWGB felt like it had Sparty right where it wanted them.

With the game on the line, it seemed inevitable that Tony Bennett would take the shot. Tony got the ball on the left wing with thirty seconds left, guarded by Smith. He put a move on Smith and shot-faked, getting the All-American to soar past him.

But Peplowski had rotated over and jumped as Tony lifted for his shot, forcing him to adjust. The ball bounced harmlessly off the rim and into Michigan State's hands. Heathcote called a timeout with 23 seconds left, content with a tie game and the final shot of regulation.

As it was with UWGB, the final Spartans shot was certain to be taken by their star. Michigan State inbounded the ball, and with eight seconds left, Steigenga guarded by Martinez, handed the ball off to Smith. Smith dribbled to his right, smothered by Johnson more than thirty feet from the basket. With four seconds left, Smith crossed over between his legs outside the three-point line, coming back toward the middle, Johnson still in his hip pocket.

With three seconds left, Smith, who hadn't squared to the basket, pulled up suddenly for a long two-point attempt. Johnson, anticipating the drive, reacted quickly and jumped to contest the shot, but the ball was already gone. It hung in the air for a full second before swishing through the basket.

Ludvigson, like his teammates, was just focused on boxing out. "All I was worried about was making sure Peplowski did not tip it in to win the

Tony Bennett looks for an opening in the Michigan State defense during the Phoenix's 1991 NCAA tournament game in Tucson, Arizona. (John W. McDonough / Sports Illustrated via Getty Images)

game – like I was like fighting for my life to keep him off the glass."

"I was right under the basket to see it go through," remembers Martinez. "You're hoping it's going to hit the front part of the rim or bounce off and you know you're just watching it come through in slow motion. And you're just like, 'Alright, well, that's the end of our season.' "

"I knew I wasn't going to zone," Dick Bennett recalls of the final moments. "We pretty much stayed straight up on everybody else, and Ben was on Smith. He just made that little jerky move. He kind of hesitation-dribbled and made the shot."

"Steve Smith, I mean, he's an NBA Hall of Famer. He's pretty stinking good," states LeMoine. "He took the basketball and he was going to finish it."

In 1991, no one seemed to notice that the clock had a full second left as the ball swished through the net. That final second ticked off, the buzzer sounded, and the game was over. Final score, Michigan State 60, UWGB 58.

"It's just a sick feeling," Tony Bennett says. "You know it's over. It hurts. It's bad. You know that's the end of the year. You're so close. Boom, it happens. It's like somebody dropped a weight on you."

"Having Steve Smith hit that shot, it just hurts right when it happens," says Logan Vander Velden. "It was an amazing shot."

"I was in disbelief," adds Rondorf. "I couldn't believe that we had lost, couldn't believe our season was over, and couldn't believe it just ended that way."

"I thought Ben Johnson was going to be good on Smith, and he *was* good on him," remembered Vander Plas. "Myself, John Martinez, Dean Rondorf – we shot lights out. We had a shot, we just had a shot, and Steve Smith made a play."

LeMoine agreed. "We had a chance to put them away to start the second half and we didn't. And that gave them life. That gave them hope. We talked to some of those guys after the game and they were like, 'Dude, half-time, we were like done. We were ready to go pack it up, and then when you guys stopped scoring, and we scored a couple of times, we were like, alright, I guess we can play.' "

The decision to go to the 1-3-1 zone with just under four minutes to play that still haunted Dick Bennett three decades later.

"It cost us the tournament game. I thought it would stymie Michigan State, but it didn't," he says. "As time wore on, I was bothered more and more because the fact that we might have won it had I not gone to that zone. And so it ate away at me long after it was over. Right after, everybody was congratulating us, but shortly after that it sunk in that we could have won that game."

It was a tough call for Bennett, but one that, at least objectively, was supported by historical success. "We'd done it, we'd been successful. We'd taken teams out of their comfort level of going against our man-to-man, put them in the 1-3-1," maintains Rondorf.

"It's hard to say if that was the difference or not," LeMoine says. "Obviously, if he had to do it over again, probably would've stuck with the man-to-man, because we knew how the other one turned out. But those are the plays where you either look like a genius or you look like you made a dumb choice. Who knows? You know, you live with those decisions."

Tony Bennett took the blame on himself. "Look, I couldn't hit the broad side of a barn. They tightened up on me defensively in the second half. That was part of the issue more than going to the 1-3-1. In hindsight, you'd probably say, 'Well, let's just stay matched up,' but who knows if they would've done that in man-to-man. I guess you never know."

No Regrets

Many of the players, the loss aside, remained hopeful about the future.

"We were right there to pull the game out, but you know it just wasn't in the cards for us that year," Martinez says. "But as a sophomore, man I had nothing but just enthusiasm and excitement going into the next couple of years."

"I think we were just happy to be there and didn't really have expectations of winning," remembers Ludvigson. "If we would've beat them, we would've played that UNLV team, and that would've been ugly."

"In general, that whole experience was great for our program," Johnson says. "It showed people that Bennett Ball's alive, and it's a good style and a good brand of basketball. Can't all be Memphis running up and down the court, and that's a good style, too. But for our group, that's the style that worked."

"That really did kind of set the tone for the next, really, five or six years. Just thinking that, you know, we *should* be playing these games, we *should* have a lot of people here, we *should* be on the verge of going to one of the tournaments," states LeDuc. "That really pushed it to the point where it became an event in Green Bay. At that point in time, the Packers weren't very good, and people wanted to come and see a successful team."

"We all kind of felt like we were going to be back next year," remembers LeMoine. "The person that we felt the worst for was Dean Vander Plas, because we knew he wasn't going to get another chance."

"It was really tough to walk back to that locker room," admits Dean Vander Plas. Steve Smith's buzzer beater signaled the end of the line for UWGB's resident leader, one of the program's all-time greats.

"We could be really bad if we tried to do things individually, but as a team, as a pack, we were so much better. And Dean was a big part of that," notes Rondorf. "Phenomenal career, phenomenal person, great friend, and great teammate."

"You talk about a good player, oh my gosh. He was ahead of his time," states Tony Bennett. "You could play small ball, and he was so versatile with his shot, his drives ... he was *really* good. He was undersized, but in today's day and age, I think he could've played at a higher level."

Dick Bennett raves about the intangibles Vander Plas had brought to the club. "He was really only 6-5, but he was tougher than heck and he embarrassed a lot of big people in his career. Everybody misjudged him from an opposing standpoint. They would look at him and think that he's not very tall, he's probably not 6-5, though he was. He's probably not very quick, but he was. He was incredibly strong, had terrific hands and reactions, and he had a confidence level that never let him down."

A lot of that confidence came, Vander Plas felt, from his coach. "When I got there – and it's true honesty – I was one selfish kid. Coach saw something in me that nobody else saw. Not even me. And that servant's heart that he preaches, that he absolutely won't detour from, has allowed a pretty average athlete from Oostburg, Wisconsin, to have an amazing life."

It certainly was a productive career for Vander Plas. "I think I'm still the only person in the 1,000-point club at GB that didn't average double-digits for their career. I just played in so damn many games you eventually had to get there."

Midwestern Triumphs

Midwestern mid-majors continued their assault on the established powers in the 1991 NCAA tournament, managing a handful of earth-shaking upsets. Creighton, an 11 seed MVC school from Omaha, Nebraska, pulled off a first-round upset over New Mexico State, while a 14 seed Xavier squad pulled out a monster first-round win over Nebraska before falling to UConn in the second round. Topping both of those efforts was Eastern Michigan, a MAC school and fellow 12 seed that pulled off two victories, making the Sweet Sixteen before losing to eventual Final Four participant North Carolina.

For its part, Northern Illinois gave St. John's everything it could handle before falling by seven in its first-round matchup in Dayton, Ohio. And oh by the way, 15 seed Richmond shocked the nation by beating second-seeded Syracuse in the first round before losing to John Chaney's Temple Owls in the second round.

Chapter 10

Star Power
(1991 Pan-American Games)

Transcendent talent is unforgettable, and though rare, not any less exciting at the mid-major level than at major programs. Star power drives viewership and media attention, giving networks a reason to broadcast games regardless of outcome. That visibility is what every mid-major desires to promote awareness, and ultimately recognition, of its program.

The opportunities are rare, so when such a star shoots by, mid-majors grab onto them with both hands and enjoy the ride.

Tony Bennett

There was little doubt when he first set foot on campus in 1988 that Tony Bennett would be UWGB's offensive leader. Three years later, that prediction had become a reality. When coupled with eleven others who accepted roles and supported the betterment of the team, the combination was a hit.

"(Tony was an) awesome shooter, big-time talent," notes teammate John Martinez. "It definitely helps to get some standout players ... you just knew going into the game what you're going to get out of them."

"You need at least one hell of a great player. If you look at any mid-major, they had one just outstanding diamond in the rough player," notes Scott LeMoine. "And then you have to have a lot of guys that just kind of know their role and accept their roles."

"We definitely had the formula of one star, kind of a team that had a lot of third-, fourth-, fifth-year players that had all played together, and a system that was difficult to prepare for," adds Eric LeDuc. "You had all the raw materials to be a team that nobody wants to face."

With the Phoenix's 1991 NCAA tournament appearance, Tony's talent was beginning to do more than help his team secure wins. He was earning national praise while elevating the program's status itself.

He'd already impressed opposing coaches, like Nebraska's Denny Nee. "He'd be a star with Georgetown, he'd be a star with Nebraska, he'd be a star with UCLA," Nee commented. "Tony Bennett can play at any level

Tony Bennett received star attention from the national media for most of his college career. Here he is interviewed by ESPN's Clark Kellogg following UWGB's victory in the 1991 Mid-Continent Conference championship game. (University of Wisconsin-Green Bay Archives)

anywhere. Anyone who doesn't think he can doesn't know a thing about basketball."

Now, NBA insiders were taking notice as well.

"He's one of the smartest kids I've seen," noted NBA scout Marty Blake. "He is a pro prospect. I'll make sure everybody sees him and that he gets invited to the post-season tournaments."

Jerry Reynolds, Sacramento's general manager, asked, "How many juniors are better than he is at that position? Probably several, but not too many. All he needs to be is in the top five or six point guards (to be drafted in the first round)."

Tony's stock would continue to rise as he embarked on an off-season for the ages, thanks to the 1991 Pan American (Pan Am) Games in Havana, Cuba.

Shattered Dreams

For decades, Olympic basketball – at least from the American viewpoint – represented the ultimate international showcase of amateur talent. Every four years, the USA would send twelve of its top college basketball players to compete, and more often than not, beat, the world's best. The US would use the Pan Am Games, held the year before the Olympics, to pressure-test the American roster.

Looking back on the previous decade, the US had put together a who's-who roster for the 1983 Pan Am Games, including the likes of North Carolina's Michael Jordan and Sam Perkins, Chris Mullin of St. John's. That team went undefeated and propelled five Pan Am team members onto the 1984 US Olympic team, joining rising stars like Georgetown's Patrick Ewing and Indiana's Steve Alford in winning the 1984 Olympic gold medal.

Three years later, it was college superstars including Navy's David Robinson and Kansas's Danny Manning who played on the 1987 U.S. Pan Am team, and then continued on to the 1988 Olympic team. That 1988 US team was criticized as a "failure" for having only secured the bronze medal, Team USA's worst-ever finish at the Olympics.

With history as a guide, the selection of the 1991 Pan Am team appeared to have major implications, particularly in setting the stage for the 1992 Olympic team.

That is, until early in 1991, when the international basketball governing authority, FIBA, modified the rules for competing in the Olympic Games. The move by FIBA was clearly a response to the unfair standards previously in place, which allowed countries like the USSR to use "professional" players while banning the US from doing the same. That distinction became impossible to reconcile when the US team fell to the USSR in the semifinals of the 1988 Seoul Olympics.

Nevertheless, overnight, the US was suddenly allowed to use professionals. That fateful February 1991 FIBA decision will forever be remembered for initiating the 1992 Dream Team – the greatest collection of basketball talent the world had ever, and likely would ever, see assembled.

But Gene Keady, head coach of the 1991 US Pan Am team, had a different perspective: "In the past, a strong performance in the Pan Ams was considered incentive to be invited to the Olympic squad. These guys are the first who have almost no chance for the Olympics because the team we send to Spain (in 1992) will be dominated by NBA players."

The decision also stung him personally. "As a coach, I've always had that hope of coaching our Olympic team. Now that job is going to be given to NBA coaches, and all a college coach can look forward to is being an assistant. This is probably my last shot as the coach of a national team."

Even with the professional shift for the 1992 Olympics, the US still intended to take amateur talent to the 1991 Pan Am Games. Nevertheless, for college players like Tony Bennett who would be vying for a spot on the Pan Am team, the news stung. "A dream of mine always growing up was, 'I want to make the Olympic team.' And I thought that (making the Pan Am Games would be) a huge step for me to maybe play on the Olympic team the following year," he remembers. "Well lo and behold, that's when they decided to take (professionals). So (1991 was) the last amateur team."

Tryouts

Joining Keady's coaching staff for the 1991 Pan Am Games were Don Monson (Oregon), Randy Ayers (Ohio State), and Bob Chipman (Washburn), while other legendary college coaches, like Mike Krzyzewski (Duke), Jim Calhoun (UConn), and Roy Williams (Kansas), offered their services as consultants or advisors.

That staff invited sixty-six of the nation's top college players for team tryouts in April 1991. One of those invitees was Tony Bennett. The list was, in a word, impressive, including UNLV's Anderson Hunt, Ohio State's Jim Jackson, Indiana's Damon Bailey, and Seton Hall's Terry Dehere.

Tony Bennett signs basketballs for young fans inside the Phoenix Sports Center. (Mitchell family collection)

Fifty-one of the invitees showed up at camp in Colorado Springs. The schedule included morning and evening workouts on Friday and Saturday, a morning workout on Sunday, and a scrimmage Sunday night, with cuts scheduled for Monday April 30. The top 15-25 players would be invited to return for further practices in July on Purdue's campus, while the remaining players were free to play in the second-tier World University Games in England on a team coached by P.J. Carlisimo of Seton Hall.

Dick Bennett remained lighthearted when asked about Tony's chances. "If they want to keep a small guard, his chances are excellent."

But once the camp started, it quickly became evident that Tony's game fit with Keady's style. As a seasoned, defensively sound guard who could shoot and distribute the ball, Tony seemed to meet Keady's definition of "complete." And he had a knack for winning. Tony's teams (which switched between each game) went a perfect 5-0 during the camp's scrimmage sessions.

So it shouldn't have come as a big surprise that Tony was among the seventeen players who made it through the first round of cuts and were invited to join the final set of practices in July. The praise for Tony's play was immense.

"He was the best point guard without question," noted UConn's Calhoun. "He understands his abilities and the game, and his ability to know where the four other players were at all times was exceptional."

Bruce Weber lauded Tony's completeness: "He can create offense. He can play pressure defense and get some steals, and he can handle the ball well."

And for Xavier coach Pete Gillen, it was a done deal. "If he stays healthy, he's definitely on the Pan Am team. He's a Gene Keady-type player."

It was just the first of two waves of roster cuts, but getting past the first round was a major accomplishment for UWGB's star guard. "It's really an honor," Tony remarked. "Working with these coaches and these players is a dream come true for me."

Dick was also proud. "I think all of us should have a little more spring in our step today. All of our players and coaches have helped prepare him for this honor."

Keady was high on Tony's potential for the team, even before the remaining seventeen took the floor at Purdue that summer. "It would be a real shock if he didn't start or play a prominent role. That's why we kept him," Keady said. "I'd say he's got a great shot at starting."

Prior to the team's second camp, Keady sent his players a letter asking them to be in peak physical condition when they showed up on campus. His letter conveniently left out the fact that Mackey Arena would be a sweltering 90 degrees each day they took the floor. Psychological or not, it was a factor on which Keady didn't want his players focusing. "If that's a problem, the heat and not being able to take it, then we probably won't be able to compete. So, we probably won't discuss it a whole lot."

The second set of tryouts officially started July 15, 1991, with three exhibition games set for late July followed by the Pan Am tournament in early August. The heat in Mackey Arena bothered some, but not Tony. The undersized guard from mid-major UWGB performed admirably, showcasing his playmaking, shooting, and tough man-to-man defense.

By the end of a week and with the first exhibition in the books (a 114-100 win over a regional amateur team, the Lafayette Hustlers), Keady had cut three players: Doug Christie (Pepperdine), Robert Horry (Alabama), and Elmore Spencer (UNLV). Four days later, Keady made his final two cuts, letting go of Byron Houston (Oklahoma St.) and Tom Gugliotta (North Carolina State). Both would be alternates, which meant Tony Bennett had made the 1991 Pan Am Games team.

"Mike (Heideman) and I drove down to West Lafayette to watch the final trial," remembers Dick Bennett. "I realized then that Tony was going to make that team. Gene really liked him for one thing, and he played well, so I was very thrilled."

Keady wasn't the only person Tony had impressed.

"He's one of the few point guards I know that are as quick as Bobby (Hurley). Tony's that quick and has a very, very good jump shot from outside," remarked college basketball royalty, Christian Laettner of Duke. "We see what he does in practice, we see how good a player he is. The only reason he's not as known as the rest of us is because he's not in as big of a league. He can go to any school and play. He's very good."

Duke's Grant Hill, Tony's roommate during the camp, was also all praise: "He's just a good person and a good player. He's real quick, he works real hard, he can shoot real well, and he knows the game. You can tell he's a coach's son."

In the end, Tony Bennett had found himself in one of the rarest and most exclusive clubs in the world. He was now a member of a team that boasted one of the most famous alumni networks of all time, including Hall of Famers Jerry West and Oscar Robertson (1959), Willis Reed (1963), JoJo White and Wes Unseld (1967), Bob McAdoo and Paul Westphal (1971), Robert Parish (1975), Isiah Thomas, Kevin McHale, and Ralph Sampson (1979), Michael Jordan and Chris Mullin (1983), and David Robinson (1987).

In typical fashion, Tony stayed focused on the end goal. "My first goal was to make the first cut, and the second goal was to make the team. Now I hope to get a chance to win a gold medal."

Destination Cuba

Tony would be playing alongside eleven of the best college basketball players in the country; players who would go on to be high NBA draft picks and enjoy impressive professional careers. Eight of the twelve came from either the ACC, Big Ten or Pac-10, with three from the national champion Duke Blue Devils, including Laettner, the 1991 Final Four Most Outstanding Player and a future member of the Dream Team.

"Grant Hill and Laettner and Walt Williams, we had a heck of a team – Jimmy Jackson. Yeah, that was big time to be able to play with those guys, being from more of a mid-major, low-major, however you want to say it. And it just was great," Tony remembers.

1991 USA Pan American Team

Tony Bennett	G	6-0	UWGB
Terry Dehere	G	6-4	Seton Hall
Grant Hill	F	6-7	Duke
Thomas Hill	G	6-4	Duke
Jimmy Jackson	G	6-6	Ohio State
Adam Keefe	F	6-9	Stanford
Christian Laettner	C	6-11	Duke
Eric Montross	C	7-0	North Carolina
Tracy Murray	F	6-8	UCLA
Mike Peplowski	C	6-10	Michigan State
Clarence Weatherspoon	F	6-7	Southern Mississippi
Walt Williams	G	6-8	Maryland

Tony was, without a shadow of a doubt, the least famous name from the smallest school on the team. In spite of the talent pervading the roster, he had earned significant favor with the coaching staff and had a chance of getting lots of meaningful playing time.

But with a roster this loaded, Tony had to adjust his mindset: "If you screw up, you'll probably get pulled, because they don't have to have you in there. So you just let it all out. It's almost like you have to find a new level of intensity."

Team USA was set to begin play on August 3, 1991, against the host country in a game televised on ABC. The US would play three more group stage games before the medal rounds. And while all games would take place at Havana's 13,000-seat Sports City Coliseum, the US team was to be shuttled back to Miami, Florida, in between games.

Showing his supreme confidence in Tony, Keady pegged him as a starter for the first game, a sold-out affair. In traditional Dick Bennett fashion, he was a wreck watching the game via the national telecast. "I was nervous all day. And this was a very tense affair."

Tony, on the other hand, was much more relaxed. "Shoot, Fidel Castro is twenty paces away from me as we're playing Cuba in the first game, and national anthem's there, and he's

Duke superstar Grant Hill was one of many future NBA players on the 1991 United States Pan-American Games team. (Department of Special Collections and University Archives, Raynor Memorial Libraries, Marquette University)

got his armed guards behind him. And I'm like, 'Boy, I remember learning about him at Green Bay Preble or at PJ Jacobs where I was at Stevens Point in the history books, and here I am now.' You know, just kind of a surreal experience."

The game itself was closer than the Americans would have hoped, with Cuba hanging within two points with under 1:30 to play. Keady had Tony on the floor with the game in the balance and he delivered, making a layup on a critical fast break with 1:13 left to give the US a 90-86 lead on its way to a victory.

Jimmy Jackson and Laettner led the way with 22 and 19 points, respectively, but Tony's six points, all late in the game, proved critical.

"He looked like he belonged," noted Dick Bennett. "I thought he played well when his team wasn't playing well, and that was important."

"It was quite a win because of all the circumstances," remarked a gruff Keady. "It was a game that could've gone either way."

Keady's temperature rose a few degrees in the next game against Venezuela, and after Jackson missed a put-back attempt, Keady kicked a movable billboard in front of the US bench. But just as the Phoenix would respond to Dick Bennett's antics, so too did the US squad to Keady's, finding its groove and easily settling in to a 91-66 victory. Tony was again a starter and had a solid nine-point effort in a game that saw everyone on the American roster score.

The Americans' third game resembled the first, with the squad in trouble late against Argentina. Clinging to an 80-78 lead with less than three minutes to play, Keady again looked to Tony to provide a spark and the youngster again delivered, this time hitting a critical three-pointer that extended the US lead to five points on its way to an 87-81 victory. Jackson again led the way with 17 points, while Tony reached double figures with 10 points.

"I think we're finding out these guys are great players. They're older than us. They're all men. They've played together for a long time," Tony said of the competition level. "People wonder why we're not dominating. There are some excellent teams over here. We have to play well to beat them."

The US had no problems in its fourth contest, rolling over the Bahamas 116-58. Tony started and scored just two points, but was an assist machine and welcomed the opportunity to have some fun. "We had more fun in this one, throwing loops and fancy passes, dribbling high and looking away. Not real fancy, but a little fancy, for me anyway."

Perfect in the group stage, the US moved on to the medal round, and along with Brazil and Puerto Rico, were the top contenders to take home hardware. In the quarterfinals on August 13, the American squad cruised past Venezuela 111-104, setting up a date with Puerto Rico in the semifinals.

Tony acknowledged the significance of the moment. "I have a chance to do something so special, to have memories when I'm sixty and know I was able to play in the Pan Am Games. I'm basically living out a dream."

The Medal Round

The Puerto Ricans were for real, touting two former NBA players in Jose Ortiz, a 6-11 former All-American, and Ramon Rivas, a former first-round pick of the Boston Celtics. Prior to the semifinal matchup, Keady was concerned about their experience.

"We've always known they have an excellent team, one they have been developing for a few years, putting it together with an Olympic and Pan Am gold in mind. They are very experienced, very hungry, and very deep. They have a lot of talent, and that is a dangerous combination."

Puerto Rico coach Raymond Dalmua was predictably confident. "Our guys are veterans. They're more physical than the United States is now. The US players are young. They don't know how international basketball is played yet. They're used to the clean way the game is played in the United States. But they don't call over-the-top here."

The Americans were dealt an enormous blow just two days before the game when Jackson was diagnosed with a stress fracture in his left foot and ruled out for the rest of the tournament. Far and away the team's best scoring threat having averaged 18.2 ppg on a nearly insane 67% shooting,

Jackson was devastated: "I set a goal to be on the team and to play in the gold medal game and to play the best I can play. But now it's a different perspective, watching from the sideline when I was so close to being in that game."

Keady knew the pressure Jackson's injury would put on the team, but emphasized that his club was full of players capable of rising up. "I think the strength of this team is its depth and character, so it's really going to get tested now. We've got good kids and hopefully somebody will step forward and take his place."

For the semifinals, Keady turned to future Hall of Famer Grant Hill. As great as Hill was, he was unable to completely fill in the hole Jackson had left. The US led by ten points in the second half, but were held scoreless for nearly four minutes late in the contest, allowing the Puerto Ricans to get back into the game. Without their offensive leader, the Americans looked out of place when the score evened and proved unable to rise up to the Puerto Rican challenge. In the end, the Americans folded 73-68, crushing their dreams of playing for a gold medal.

"I keep thinking, 'What if we had Jimmy?' It would have been interesting," said Tony Bennett. But with just one day off before the bronze medal game, he knew the team had to refocus quickly: "I don't want to stop here. I hope the team comes out like crazy on Saturday. You have to play for what's left."

As the Puerto Rican coach had predicted, his team was more physical than the Americans. "They know how to do the shoving and pushing," Keady said after the game. "That's not what I call cheating, it's just a matter of international experience. It's a compliment, not an excuse."

Keady could publicly weather the heat he was taking stateside for the loss, but inside, the coach was devastated. The one player on his team that saw the pain he was going through was Tony Bennett, and the Phoenix guard resolved to console his coach.

It was a gesture that Keady never forgot. "He came up to my room seeing if I was OK," remembered Keady. "That's the first time that's happened to me in twenty-seven years of coaching. He's a first-class kid."

The bronze medal matchup against Cuba was the US team's final game together and last hope at winning a medal for their country. Unfortunately, the officials played an active role in the outcome as a handful of Americans fouled out, including Tony. "It was a terrible call," Tony remarked of his fifth foul. "After the game, the referee came up to me and said, 'My mistake, no foul, forgive me.' I never had a referee do that before."

Nevertheless, the Americans exerted dominance from the start and had the horses to coast to a relatively easy victory, 93-74.

For the tournament, Tony led the US squad in assists and finished second in steals, more than satisfying the role Keady expected from him.

There was no greater way to prepare for his final season at UWGB, and the experience fueled more talk about Tony's potential NBA future. A Golden State Warriors scout, Sam Schuler, debated Tony's quickness, but felt that "he showed enough" to earn a shot.

The Sacramento Kings GM, Jerry Reynolds, noted that Tony's play "answered a lot of questions," and said, "I can tell you right now I wish we had him. I really think he can play in this league. I'll be surprised if he doesn't."

His pro prospects ripening, Tony relished the Pan Am Games experience. "I'm still very proud. There's still some disappointment, but we were put in the toughest situation possible to win the bronze medal, playing Cuba in their place. It was very intense and I thought we did a good job. We have nothing to hang our heads about."

Chapter 11

Avoiding Complacency
(1991-92 - Part 1)

One of the greatest challenges any team can face is maintaining hunger and drive after achieving some success. Those motivated by external forces such as fame, notoriety, or personal accomplishments can easily find themselves becoming complacent, satisfied with a taste of success.

In contrast, maintaining a competitive desire requires a strong internal drive to constantly improve, and an unwillingness to be satisfied or compromise. Satisfaction from simply meeting milestones cannot be enough – a team must remain intrinsically motivated. And in most cases, those teams must hate losing more than they love winning.

***

Expectations were not merely high for senior Tony Bennett in 1991-92, this was the year the Phoenix was expected to fly.

The program had been building to crescendo for three years, turning potential into postseason realities. It seemed a given that UWGB would repeat as a Mid-Continent Conference representative to the NCAA tournament, perhaps even pulling an upset. This was the culmination of Dick Bennett's dream that began when he took the job in 1985, and became a reality with his freshman class in 1988. This team had big plans.

"The expectations were high, and I think we knew how good we could be. And I think we *were* that good," comments Logan Vander Velden, a sophomore on that team. "(We had) a strong senior class and a lot of good, strong pieces, and we were playing at a very high level."

"Tony always used to say, 'We're right there. We're close. We're not too far off to get to the Final Four,' " adds John Martinez. "I actually believed it, because I felt the same way and I felt like as a player, I could contribute to a team that could get us to the Final Four. Always felt that way, never had a doubt."

"Here's what it comes down to in the NCAA tournament: who's hot, and who's healthy," states Tony Bennett. "If you're hot and you're healthy,

The five seniors on the 1991-92 UWGB roster ham it up at the start of the season. Clockwise from left: Tony Ciaravino, Scott LeMoine, Tony Bennett, Chris Yates, Ben Johnson. (University of Wisconsin-Green Bay Archives)

and you get good matchups, then you can do stuff. And I thought that team had the makings. I thought the experiences we had faced up to that point, all those experiences of playing in the NCAA tournament, going against bigger teams, figuring stuff out – I think we were one of the scariest teams to have played."

One Loaded Roster

The reasons for optimism were obvious, as the team returned nearly every piece from the 1991 NCAA tournament team. Four sure-fire starters were back, beginning with the coach's son, Tony Bennett. His summer Pan Am Games experience had not only honed his craft, it had fueled his drive to be the best.

"Tony worked harder than anybody I can ever imagine working on his game," says Jeremy Ludvigson. "After practice, coming back in at night and shooting and shooting and shooting and working on his game ... Tony just worked his butt off."

"There wasn't a guy that worked harder in any of the sports at Green Bay than Tony did," notes Dean Rondorf. "Tony spent so much time in the gym, so much time perfecting his craft, he deserved all the accolades, all the praises he got."

This wasn't to say his father made his life easy.

"He was probably the hardest on Tony," recalls Gary Grzesk. "Tony had the most ability, but he was also Coach Bennett's son. The combination of Coach wanting to push the best player on the team and not show any favoritism toward Tony led him to be so hard on him."

"At times, it was difficult to be around them because there was so much tension," admits Eric LeDuc. "He would put so much pressure on Tony that there were times you would think, 'My God, is he mentally going to be able to adjust to it?'"

But Tony had welcomed that pressure when he signed on with UWGB.

"I gave him the green light to do it," Tony said of his father. "I said, 'I want to be great, so you have a green light to push me. You take me where I need to go.' He was a master of pushing the right buttons and dangling me over the edge."

Tony also proved a much calmer Bennett than his dad, which did not go unnoticed by his teammates.

"Tony was never the vocal leader," observes LeMoine. "I don't think he ever really wanted that, especially with his dad being the head coach. He just did his job, and he did it very well."

Tony would even go so far as to inject levity into practices, offsetting his father's gruff demeanor.

"In a shooting drill, Tony might make eight out of ten or nine out of ten from three, but it was the one that he missed that Coach Bennett would criticize," Grzesk recalls. "I remember him shooting one time and I was rebounding, and Coach was yelling at Tony, and Tony kind of winked at me. I think he missed the next one on purpose just to upset Coach Bennett even more than he was."

The ying to Tony's yang was his good friend and defensive stopper, Ben Johnson.

"Tony was the ice and I was the fire," remarks Johnson. "Tony was cool, calm – just like he coaches. Poised, smooth – GQ smooth – calm under fire. (But) sometimes you need a guy that's going to stir the pot and get guys going. That was my job, and that was the role coach gave to me."

There was no denying that Johnson was the heart and soul of the Phoenix.

"He led by example. There was no taking a drill off with Ben. There was no three-quarters speed. It was all out, all the time, and you had to be ready, because he was going to bring it," remembers LeMoine. "Like, 'Man, I don't want to go 100%. We've been going for an hour, hour and half, come on dude.' No, Ben wasn't going to let you get away with that."

Martinez was also back, and by the 1991-92 season, things were really clicking for the junior guard.

"I just remember watching some games (as a sophomore) and I'm like, 'Man, I am just running like 100 miles an hour,'" he recalls. "Then it started to slow down a little bit. Definitely my junior year is kind of when that all took place."

His teammates noticed the change. "John was just so good that if he could get to the basket, he could get to the basket and finish. If he had to deliver a pass, he could deliver a pass," explains Rondorf. "He was that security blanket that you knew you were always going to have there. John was just such a confident, even-keeled guy."

Though somewhat under the radar from being in a mid-major program, Bennett and Martinez were one of the best guard tandems in the nation.

"We could shoot, we could handle it. We were both 6 feet, whatever, 5-11, we weren't size-wise, but we thought our backcourt could compete against anybody," states Tony Bennett. "John had that ability where he could make some plays off the dribble, find people. We both played as two scoring point guards, and I just thought it was huge for our program."

Coming in as the fourth starter was junior Larry Hill. Hill's athleticism was undeniable, and in the five games he'd played in 1990, he had delivered high production. Nevertheless, though he had returned healthy from his broken wrist, Dick Bennett remained skeptical.

"He's not a sure thing. I think he has what it takes, and we certainly have a need for what he has to offer," Bennett remarked before the season.

After the top four spots, there was more uncertainty. Rondorf, who had performed admirably against Michigan State in the tournament game, was likely to get regular minutes in the rotation for his shooting and offensive prowess.

LeMoine was in the mix for playing time at center, due mostly to his defensive prowess and his error-free play. "As I watched tape, I became more impressed with what he did (last year)," noted Dick Bennett. "It would be nice if he could finish a little better, but he doesn't make mistakes."

Meanwhile, big men Ludvigson and Vander Velden had banked starts as freshman, seen significant playing time in meaningful games, and improved over the past year. Critically, both had used the offseason to bulk up and adapt to the more physical college game.

"I just ate everything – I mean, I ate six times a day, lifted, protein shakes, peanut butter and jelly sandwiches," recalls Ludvigson, who put on forty-five pounds in the offseason. "Timing was right for my body to put on that mass."

Rounding out the big men were two sophomore transfers: Eric LeDuc from Army and Jeff Zavada from Marquette.

Bennett was excited about LeDuc's potential. "He told me, 'Hey, I think that you could play a lot, and you could even work your way into the starting lineup if you continue to do what you're doing in practice and be that energy guy and know your role,'" remembers LeDuc.

Zavada was more of a known commodity as an in-state talent from the

UWGB's 1991-92 roster was a veteran unit. Back row: Jeremy Ludvigson (44), Eric LeDuc (52), Scott LeMoine (45), Logan Vander Velden (32), Larry Hill (24), Dean Rondorf (30). Front row: Tony Bennett (25), John Martinez (20), Ben Johnson (23), Tony Ciaravino (21), Mark Andres (31). (University of Wisconsin-Green Bay Archives)

Bennetts' old central Wisconsin stomping grounds.

"I knew Jeff from Stevens Point, knew his family," Dick Bennett says. "He contacted us and clearly wanted to come our way. It was not even a matter of trying to recruit him or convince him. Bringing him in was almost a no-brainer. The only thing that concerned me was is he going to feel like, 'Hey, I'm coming from Marquette in the big time, I certainly should be a starter.' And he did start some games, but I didn't see him as a full-time starter. I saw him coming off the bench."

The bottom of the roster featured senior Chris Yates, returning from his year away, along with sophomore Mark Andres and twenty-six-year-old walk-on Derek Ballard.

And then there was Tony Ciaravino, the fifth senior on the team and member of Bennett's signature class. Ciaravino had accepted a lesser role on the team and found himself buried on the depth chart. To his credit, Ciaravino never quit and challenged Tony Bennett every day in practice.

"One of the better shooters I've ever seen," states Tony Bennett. "One of *the* best teammates that I've had. And he was just so fun loving. That group really evolved and Tony was an important part of it, even though he doesn't maybe show as much statistically."

Jeff Nordgaard was one of three redshirts along with Gary Grzesk and Tory Smith. In contrast to Nordgaard and Grzesk, both of whom were logical candidates to sit a year, Smith's redshirt was a sign of the program's lack of sophistication. The coaches intended to redshirt Smith as a freshman, but he had been inserted into an exhibition game that inadvertently cost him the chance to redshirt. As such, Smith had been an official member of the 1990-91 team, logging a total of nineteen minutes. It had been a wasted year, but Dick felt it could be salvaged by redshirting him in 1991-92.

Talented as they were, team members also genuinely liked each other.

"We would kill each other in practice, but when we walked off the floor into the locker room, we were all buds for the most part," LeMoine says. "We didn't really carry any of the stuff that happened on the court into the locker room, which I thought was cool. "We hung out in the commons together. We had a little area where we would just kind of chill between classes. Our girlfriends all hung out with us, too. It was like a big family."

Knock You Down and Build You Up

Dick Bennett bolstered his own staff, replacing graduate assistant Tom Brown with Woody Wilson as his new assistant coach and head of scheduling. Wilson spent the previous six season as an assistant at Evansville, but his coaching career actually began in the high school ranks in Wisconsin, much like Bennett's. Unsurprisingly, the two had crossed paths in their past lives.

"I coached my very first game against Woody Wilson at Dodgeville. It was two years after their state championship (in 1964)," Bennett says. "I remember Woody, after the season, said, 'You know, a number of us were talking, and we thought that you would have a better season than you had, because you had pretty good players.' That was Woody."

Tough as he was, Bennett was far from foolish. With Mike Heideman, Steve Swan, and Wilson, the coach had strategically stacked his bench with assistants who provided a delicate, but needed balance to his own explosive persona. And on cue, when Bennett would tear his players down, the assistants would build their confidence back up.

"They were amazing," notes Johnson. "Balancing, buffering, just always being there for the guys and being sounding boards. They never coddled us, but we always knew we could go to them if there was something really majorly wrong. Coach Bennett was the fire and the driver and the motivator, and the other guys were the listeners and the thinkers. They had the softer side of things to smooth out, clean up some of the messes that he made."

"They were coaches that you could go to and talk to about anything," adds Martinez. "When Coach Bennett was maybe getting a little too passionate at times, they would get things settled down a little bit and just kind of keep everybody on the same page."

"Coach wanted to create that gap. He was one of those coaches who wanted to create that coach-player gap, and he had his assistants fill in to coddle us when things weren't going well," explains future Phoenix player Ben Berlowski.

"They always had Coach Bennett's back and validated what he was trying to do, but they were much more quiet," Ludvigson says. "Much more reserved and took a little bit of a backseat when it came to leading the practice. They were a little bit quieter than (Dick Bennett) was. There's only so much room for somebody snapping on you."

Top to bottom, players to staff, the 1991-92 UWGB men's basketball team was shaping up to be one of the greatest collections of talent in school history and a national force at the mid-major level.

Dodging a Knight-mare

The Phoenix's nonconference schedule included a few signature games, including a home game against Colorado, a road rematch against Nebraska, and an invitation to Purdue's Boilermaker Invitational with a chance at a game against the host.

Even with three major games on the books, the biggest surprise of the 1991-92 Phoenix schedule was a matchup that never was. Through chance, UWGB had received a call late in the scheduling period from college basketball royalty, the Indiana Hoosiers.

"Coach Knight and Coach Bennett are friends," remarked Indiana trainer Tim Garl. "We heard Wisconsin-Green Bay was looking for a game. I mentioned it to Coach Knight, and he said he knew Coach Bennett and would like to play him. In the last few years they've come into the national limelight, and obviously having Tony has brought them publicity. And Coach Knight is always interested in playing good teams."

Tony Ciaravino shoots in front of (from left) Dick Bennett, Mike Heideman, Otis Chambers, and UWGB sports information director Chris Sampson. (University of Wisconsin-Green Bay Archives)

The offer represented an opportunity for Dick Bennett to face off against the single greatest influence in his coaching philosophy. The General's impact on Bennett went back decades:

"(Knight) was maybe a year or two older than me, and I was coaching high school ball when he left West Point to go to Indiana. He was very much in demand as a clinic speaker. There wasn't a lot of college ball on TV or anything like that, and so most of the ideas that you would kind of cling to were stuff you picked up at coaching clinics around the country and in coaching magazines. "I couldn't even count the number of coaching clinics I went to, and I always tried to go where Knight was on the staff of that clinic. I always felt like he shaped the way the game was played more than any individual, with the motion offense, and the help-side defense, and ball pressure and so on. The words he said or the thoughts he had, it was almost like he was picking my brain. When he'd speak at a clinic, I could just feel myself thinking that way. So I would have to say that he influenced me the most."

But the Indiana game would also mean UWGB would have had to move a conference game, something Bennett stood firmly against. The failure to make it work came as a disappointment for both coaches. But while UWGB was unwilling to move a conference game, the Phoenix did agree to drop a nonconference matchup against Central Michigan to lock in a fourth signature game, a road date against fellow mid-major Butler on ESPN. Since Central Michigan was also entered in Purdue's holiday tournament, this move caused minimal distractions. In between, UWGB's schedule was considerably softer than the previous year. With its schedule set, UWGB became the hottest ticket in Green Bay.

The Phoenix Suns Gorilla and the UWGB Phoenix mascot welcome a young fan to the Brown County Arena. (University of Wisconsin-Green Bay Archives)

"There was no question that people just couldn't get enough of us," Bennett recalls. "I had a weekly TV show with (former Packer) Larry McCarren, and even *that* was kind of popular."

Boasting arguably the most entertaining team in the city, UWGB had increased season-ticket sales to over 5,000, a rise of more than 400 from the previous year and at a level that was nearly capped out. The sales increase was critical for a basketball program that brought in approximately 40% of the school's athletic income. And with an athletic department that was generating razor-thin 1%-3% margins on a $1.5 million budget, every dollar counted. It wasn't a guaranteed recipe for longevity, but in cash-strapped times, the success generated by Bennett's squad was keeping the school's athletic programs afloat.

The Green Bay Packers' extended struggles aided the program's increased attention. The Packers had followed up a disappointing 6-10 campaign in 1990 with one of the worst seasons in franchise history, finishing 1991 with just four wins.

Nevertheless, the Packers were and always remained huge supporters of the Phoenix program.

"Bob Harlan and Mike Reese started the Phoenix Club that raised considerable money to allow us to do different things," Bennett explains. "Bob, of course being president of the Packers organization, was very much behind our program. I can remember a number of the Packers coming to the games. And I remember (head coach) Lindy Infante speaking at our banquet when we hosted the tournament. We had a good relationship with the Packers organization, and they really got behind us."

In 1991-92, that symbiotic relationship created a perfect storm for UWGB.

"I can't say whether the fact that the Packers didn't do quite as well made it easier for us – I never like to think that way," adds Bennett. "All I know is the city was on fire for the Phoenix, for the Fighting Phoenix."

"Though we defended and we were sound and all that, we were fun to watch," notes Tony Bennett. "I think it was fun, and like, 'Wait, this was a Division II team a few years ago, and look it, they're coming, and they're starting to play with the big boys now?' The way it was built, the way the program we embodied, what the community was about, maybe even having played high school ball in Green Bay myself, it was just kind of a cool following. We kind of came from the ashes, as they say."

The Anticipation

The newly acquired Wright State Raiders helped refresh the Mid-Continent Conference, filling the void left by Northern Iowa, who had joined the Missouri Valley Conference to reunite with their rival, Southwest Missouri State. Wright State had been far and away the best independent team available, having averaged eighteen wins over the past four seasons while drawing more than 8,000 fans per game in geographically convenient Dayton, Ohio.

With the Panthers gone and Northern Illinois in a rebuilding mode, it seemed a foregone conclusion that UWGB would be returning to the Big Dance in 1992. National magazines like *The Sporting News*, *Dick Vitale's Basketball*, and *Street & Smith* all sang the Phoenix's preseason praises, while the AP writers even managed to give UWGB five votes in the preseason poll. It seemed like a natural, if not fantastic, progression.

"The program itself was kind of transitioning into becoming a very good program top to bottom, year in and year out," notes Martinez. "We felt like this was going to be our best opportunity to really do something. And I think everybody else was on that same page."

"Certainly losing Dean (Vander Plas) was a big challenge, but for the most part, we were losing one guy," explains Rondorf. "So yeah, we had high expectations, because we knew we could compete with all those, the Nebraskas, the Colorados, the Michigan States."

To cash in on the anticipation and build excitement for the season, the school decided to host a Midnight Madness event on October 14, 1991. More than 700 fans turned out to the Phoenix Sports Center to watch the squad engage in a series of low-key contests, instruction from Dick Bennett, and a mini-scrimmage. The fans got more than they expected when Vander Velden turned a routine slam-dunk into a shattered backboard – the first in the complex's history. Even Bennett was impressed, saying with a smile, "Barkley couldn't have done better." It was a rare light-hearted moment for the serious coach.

Along with the Midnight Madness celebration, UWGB had two exhibition home games to appease the local ticket holders as much as tune-ups for the regular season. Both games were largely forgettable Phoenix wins, save for the comical memory of LeDuc's first minutes as a Phoenix player.

"The first exhibition game, I'm anxious, I haven't played a game in a year, and (Coach Bennett) comes down the bench," recalls LeDuc. "I thought he told *all* of us to go in. And he had *NOT* told me to go in. So I checked in, played like two possessions up and down the court, then he pulls me out and comes over and he's like, 'Who told you to go in?!' And I'm like, '*You* told me to go in!' 'I didn't tell you to go in!' I'm like, 'You told me to go in!' And then you've got Steve Swan, who was saying, 'Okay everybody, settle down.' Everybody's intense, even though it's an exhibition game."

Exhibition or not, Bennett had no tolerance for mental mistakes. This team was not about to lose focus.

I Hear the Train A-Comin'

A confident, savvy, and experienced UWGB club attacked the 1991-92 season with a vengeance. It began on November 23, where, in front of the school's largest crowd ever for a home opener, the Phoenix rolled over Southeast Missouri State (not to be confused with the far-superior Southwest Missouri State) by 28 points. The game's only speedbump was the delay in delivery of the team's home white jerseys, forcing the Phoenix to play a rare home game in road greens.

Three days later, UWGB stomped the MAC's Toledo Rockets by 28 points, followed on November 30 by a 20-point victory at Texas Southern in Houston. Three games in, and the Phoenix had held all three opponents to less than 20 points in each first half.

Finally, a week after the Texas Southern win, UWGB had its first real test. The team went to West Lafayette to play in Purdue's Boilermaker Invitational. Tournament officials had conveniently put Bennett's team in the opposite half of the holiday tournament opener from the hosts, matched up against traditional mid-major challenger Central Michigan. Though the Chippewas were a better squad than any of UWGB's previous opponents, the Phoenix still won by 10 points. The victory set up the Phoenix for a date against the host Boilermakers on December 7.

History was not on the Phoenix's side. UWGB was a combined 1-5 against Big Ten opponents under Bennett, the lone win coming years earlier. But with the Phoenix perfect on the season and with its brand red-hot in Wisconsin, a local television station bought the rights to broadcast the game.

Purdue, meanwhile, came in with a 3-1 record, having most beaten Prairie View A&M by 46 points in the tournament opener, 103-57. Coach Gene Keady had replaced three starters from the 1991 NCAA tournament team, and its only loss had come on the road at the hands of #13 Oklahoma State.

Dean Rondorf (left) dives for a loose ball during UWGB's 55-45 victory over Central Michigan in the semifinals of the Purdue Boilermaker Invitational. (Purdue University Archives)

The Boilermakers also boasted a ridiculous home court advantage, with 50 wins in their past 54 home nonconference games, and an amazing 280-53 overall record at Mackey Arena. Within those 280 wins were a number of victories over Wisconsin, which hadn't won at Mackey Arena in twenty years dating back to 1972.

"This was a big deal for our guys, to go to a holiday tournament," notes Dick Bennett. "And I know Tony was jacked up for it. He wanted to play well in front of Gene."

Indeed, the game was a reunion of sorts for Keady and Tony, who had formed a tight bond during the Pan Am Games.

"I loved playing for Coach Keady, and he was such a good man," Tony says. "Just knowing him and wanting to play well in Purdue, a well-respected program. That's a raucous environment. I mean, you talk about intense, that place!"

Keady talked about Tony's strengths before the game, noting: "What set him apart was his character. He was a hard-nosed kid that wants to win. He gets the ball to the open people and he wants to score himself."

UWGB took the floor in their road greens, ready to test their mettle against one of the Big Ten's best. And from the opening tip to the final buzzer, the mid-major Phoenix proved every bit as tough as any opponent Purdue would face all year.

UWGB built a 21-11 lead with 12:00 left in the first half before taking a nine-point lead into halftime. UWGB's offensive production, particularly its shooting, was just a whole lot better than Purdue's in the first half.

To Dick Bennett's delight, the second half mirrored the first. Purdue mounted a minor comeback, but the experienced Phoenix squad was way too polished to give away a lead. With amazing ease, the Phoenix coasted to an impressive 69-53 victory.

"They played really aggressive, but that didn't worry me because we had really good guards in Tony and John, and we were a good ball-handling team, period," Bennett says. "We just outplayed them. We never really let them get in the game."

The players rushed the floor and hugged, as the Phoenix had knocked off one of the premier programs in the Midwest on their home turf. It was the first win for UWGB over a Big Ten team since 1986, and it gave the Phoenix a prestigious holiday tournament championship to brag about.

Logan Vander Velden has been reminded of this game ever since. "Living in Indiana now, people still talk to me about that game. To beat a major school from a major conference who is generally usually a perennial power – yeah, it is a big win, especially for our program."

"We beat them by sixteen on their floor, and did it easy. I mean, it wasn't like it was really ever a game. That's how good we were, and that's

Tony Bennett maneuvers between Purdue's Cuonzo Martin (22) and Travis Trice (3) during UWGB's 69-53 victory over the Boilermakers in the championship game of the Purdue tournament. (Purdue University Archives)

how good we executed," states Johnson. "A lot of that was John and Tony. You couldn't guard the two. They were slippery and skilled, and could both shoot it and make plays. It was like, good luck with that."

Tony was named tournament MVP, having scored 20 points in each contest, and viewed the win as a catalyst for the team's future success: "It's the start of something special. We proved we can play against a quality team."

Still riding the high from the Purdue win, UWGB took the floor in a rematch against Texas Southern two days later. Unlike the November game played in front of just 300 fans in Houston, this time UWGB was at home, which meant 5,500 strong cheering on the home team at the Brown County Arena. The Phoenix put together another complete performance, beating the Tigers 57-42 behind 23 points from its senior star, Tony Bennett.

The players returned to school for a two-week hiatus to complete finals. Even with the game break, Dick Bennett worked his team hard and the players welcomed the opportunity to return to real action on December 21 against lowly Chicago State. Vander Velden got his first start of the year, but it was Hill who scored a career-high 20 points as UWGB cruised to a 19-point victory.

UWGB improved to 7-0, the best start in school history, and moved UWGB into the top 30 in the UPI poll and #31 in the AP poll. But Bennett wasn't buying the hype: "Were it not for the fact that we had an easy preconference schedule - it was the easiest we've had - we caught teams when they were down, teams with new coaches, teams in their first year of Division I."

Nevertheless, the Phoenix had a nine-day break to prepare a huge December 30, 1991, showdown against the Big Eight's Nebraska Cornhuskers.

Aw Shucks

Nebraska had a shell of the team that had stolen a victory from the Phoenix a year earlier. The Cornhuskers had the challenge of replacing four starters, three of whom had gotten shots in the NBA.

Nevertheless, the Cornhuskers had put together a nearly flawless 8-1 record to start the season, including wins over USC and Wisconsin – the latter coming by 19 points. Their sole loss came at the hands of #22 Michigan State, but with Eric Piatkowski now a sophomore, this year's version of Nebraska was actually more athletic and complete than its predecessor. In fact, Nebraska would go on to earn an at-large bid to the NCAA tournament.

For the Phoenix, the taste from last year's debacle was still fresh in the players' minds.

"We looked on that game (last year) as one that could put us on the map. Well, we get to face Nebraska again, and maybe get a little revenge," remarked Ludvigson pregame. "We'll be the underdog as far as strength and quickness and everything. But with our team game, we can make up for that."

Ludvigson was confident, but the Phoenix was playing hurt. Tony Bennett had bruised his thigh, and though he would play, was limited in his capacity. The starting lineup of Tony, Hill, Martinez, Johnson, and Lud-vigson took the floor in front of a full house of 14,239 screaming Nebraska fans – each one looking to create a hostile environment every bit as intim-idating as what UWGB's Section F had been for the Phoenix a year earlier.

Six minutes into the game, the Huskers settled in to a 2-3 zone that seemed to frustrate the Phoenix. Over the next five minutes, UWGB played sloppy offensively and continued to turn the ball over, giving the Huskers easy opportunities to get on the board. Tony did his best to keep the team alive with a couple of important three-pointers midway through the first, but when he cooled, the Cornhuskers kept their foot on the gas. Nebras-ka's 6-8 senior forward Dapreis Owens was a force on the boards, and the Cornhuskers seemed to knock down everything they had in front of them in taking a commanding 45-28 halftime lead.

It was the worst half of Phoenix basketball in nearly a full calendar year, and it was a wake-up call. Dick Bennett railed on his club in the locker room, and the team responded with a second half that demonstrated its resilience. Tight man-to-man defense led the way in stymying the Huskers, while a more balanced offensive strategy led to greater involvement and scoring contributions from Johnson, Hill, and Rondorf.

Rondorf recalled the effect their play had on the arena. "Their crowd was into it, and I remember the one individual play – I think I caught the ball in the corner and I made a three. And it was one of those deals where they were really loud, and it was like the collective 'aww,' ... like the whole air just got blown right out of the gym."

Another three from Tony Bennett and the deficit was down to eight points. The Huskers felt their lead slipping, and a few moments later near-ly fell off the rails. With the lead down to 60-53, Tony and Nebraska's Ja-mar Johnson both hit the floor for a loose ball. Johnson grabbed Tony by the waist and pulled him backwards while trying to jump over the top, and the officials whistled Johnson for the foul.

The crowd went crazy, but nowhere near as wild as Nebraska coach Denny Nee, who barked at an official for a solid ten seconds. In light of the quick technical fouls issued a year earlier, it seemed obvious that Nee would get T'ed up. Only this time, the official swallowed his whistle. A dis-gusted Dick Bennett vented his frustration afterwards. "An official has to step up and make that call. The official just stood there and took it."

UWGB would never get closer than five points and Nebraska closed out the Phoenix for a 76-68 victory, handing UWGB its first loss of the season. Nebraska's fans rushed the floor in celebration.

"It was a big deal for them to win, and they're kind of crazy out there," Bennett says. "Dan Spielman got into it with a bunch of their fans trying to stick up for us, protect us. That's what I remember. Dan was down in the middle of the floor, we're trying to get off to our locker room, and he's like a one-man escort."

Back in the locker room, the players accepted the loss and felt it gave the team an opportunity to reset.

"This takes the pressure off us. We're supposed to be the team that's not supposed to lose," remarked Martinez. "We know we can be beaten now. The pressure's off our shoulders."

As they had a year earlier, the Cornhuskers were gracious in victory, letting the Phoenix know just how much they respected them. "They'd be in the top four (in the Big Eight)," stated Nebraska starter Chris Cresswell.

"No one in the Big Eight moves the ball and is as patient as they are," agreed Eric Piatkowski. "They'd finish at least in the middle of the Big Eight."

Big Eight Swing

The Phoenix had a golden opportunity to prove those statements true just three days later when the Big Eight's Colorado Buffaloes came to the Brown County Arena. These Buffaloes entered the game 7-2, with hopes of contending in the Big Eight and being a postseason team again.

In front of a sold-out home crowd, UWGB more than lived up to the praise by proving to be a more polished and vastly superior team. The Phoenix defense was superb in the first half, holding the Buffaloes to 28% shooting from the field and a mere 16 points. The defensive effort also prevented Colorado from getting into its full-court press, freeing up UWGB's offense.

The cumulative effect of stellar defense and a more up-tempo offense helped UWGB build a 14-point lead at the half and expand that to 19 points midway through the second half.

It was Tony Bennett's deep three-pointer with 4:30 to play that sealed the game, putting the Phoenix up 57-42 and allowing UWGB to glide to a relatively easy 69-60 victory.

UWGB had its best shooting night of the season, connecting on 59.4% of its shots while holding Colorado to a dismal 1-of-14 on three-point attempts. Ben Johnson was the "fire" in leading the defense, gathering five steals on the night, while his pal, the "ice" – Tony Bennett – handled the offense.

"(Tony) was so good," remembers LeDuc. "He'd get people to commit one way, and then he'd run them off a double or a staggered screen. Within a couple minutes of a game, teams that hadn't played us before, they'd start arguing with each other, they'd start bitching and complaining, like, 'You're supposed to switch.' 'Call that screen out.' I just remember all of us taking so much pride, almost like an offensive lineman. Just pounding people, just grinding them away."

As they had with Nebraska a year earlier, the home crowd made an impression on their Big Eight opponent.

"There's just some rowdy fans up here," said Colorado center Greg Price. "It's all in fun, but I don't know if I've ever seen fans get on refs that much as a group. That was a little different."

"It was a great college atmosphere. That's how it's supposed to be," commented Colorado assistant coach and former North Carolina State guard Dereck Whittenburg. "I played and coached in the Atlantic Coast Conference. It's the same atmosphere, only louder with 10,000 to 12,000 more fans."

One man who was not so happy with the fans was Colorado head coach

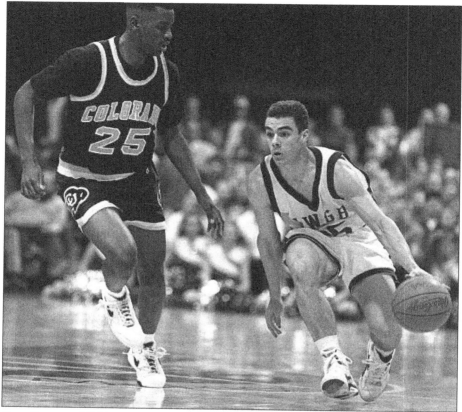

Tony Bennett dribbles past Colorado's Randy Robinson during UWGB's 69-60 victory at the Brown County Arena. (University of Wisconsin-Green Bay Archives)

Joe Harrington. A Phoenix fan harassed Harrington as the coach was being escorted off the court after the game. Harrington, in no mood, turned to face the fan and inadvertently collided with an officer, resulting in the officer being drenched with water.

It took Dick Bennett's intervention to help clear things up.

"The poor Colorado coach got into it with that crew right behind him, and he got arrested after the game," Bennett recalls. "They had him up against a wall and they were going to cuff him in the locker room. Somebody came in our locker room and said, 'Coach, you'd better get into the Hall of Fame area, they've got (Harrington) up against the wall and they're going to handcuff him. I went in there and I talked to the Brown County Sheriff and talked him out of it."

Nevertheless, any question about this team's drive to build on the previous season's success had been answered by a stellar 8-1 record with two wins against quality majors. It was UWGB's second win in consecutive years against the Buffaloes, and evened the team's record against the Big Eight to 1-1 on the year.

Dick Bennett's team was beginning to make a habit of slaying giants.

Chapter 12

Overcoming Adversity
(1991-92 - Part 2)

In college basketball as in life, disruptions come in all forms. Accidents happen, people make mistakes, and as always, the wheel of time continues to turn. These moments are not to be brushed aside or ignored, but rather represent the most prized opportunities to gauge state and character. Adversity is where you best define the measure of a program and its constituents.

Unexpected challenges cut to the core of a team, exposing its moral and ethical base with unapologetic fury. Those built on shaky footing, with shifting ideals and shallow promises, will stumble when the ground quakes. It takes a program rooted in principles to weather storms and stall tall.

Full Steam Ahead
"They might be the first team to go undefeated in the conference, and that's saying a lot," pontificated Valparaiso coach Homer Drew about the Phoenix prior to the start of the conference schedule. "I don't think they will; I think someone along the line will beat them once or twice, but they're that good."

And it was true – this UWGB team was playing at a level that few mid-majors ever had, and it seemed that nothing could derail the inevitable. "We know what it takes," noted John Martinez. "We're not going to be really satisfied unless we make the NCAA tournament."

But before earning a repeat trip to the Dance, the Phoenix needed to take care of its conference responsibilities. And that's precisely what it did in its first four games.

Mid-Continent play began on January 4, 1992, at Cleveland State, where the white-hot Phoenix cruised to an 11-point victory. Two days later, UWGB grabbed an early 21-point lead at Akron in a game that had the makings of another blowout. The pesky Zips did fight back, but a pair of game-winning free throws from Logan Vander Velden with eight seconds left gave UWGB its second conference win, 62-60.

The latter victory came in front of a dozen NBA scouts who watched Tony score 20 points, bringing him to within 23 of UWGB's school record for career scoring. Not that Tony was paying attention – he had no idea how close he was to the school record until the morning of the third conference game, when he and Ben Johnson heard it mentioned on his father's *The Dick Bennett Show*. "I just gave him a wink and he raised his eyebrows, and we left it at that," remarked Johnson.

With a record on the line, 5,800 fans packed the Brown County Arena on January 11, 1992, to watch Tony Bennett and the Phoenix take on new conference foe, Wright State. UWGB gave the Raiders a clinic on fundamental basketball, beating them with solid screens, patient offense, help defense, and crisp box-outs. Tony scored a smooth 14 first-half points, while Martinez, Johnson, and Tony Ciaravino combined to go 7-of-7 from the field.

The Phoenix were so efficient that, with the rout on and UWGB comfortably up 39-16 at the break, the fans were in danger of seeing their star ride the bench for much of the second half despite being a mere nine points from the school record. To the fans' delight, Dick Bennett opted to keep Tony in to start the second half. His son was quiet through the first five minutes as the Phoenix held a 44-24 lead, before coming alive after a timeout. Tony buried a trio of three-pointers in less than 90 seconds, the final shot coming with 11:55 left in the game to give his team a commanding 55-24 lead and sending him into the record books as the school's all-time scoring leader with 1,918 points. The crowd went bananas and gave Tony a standing ovation as the senior went to the bench a minute later. For the game, Tony finished with 25 points in 26 minutes of action, shooting an efficient 8-of-10 from the field, including 5-of-7 from three-point range.

The ever-nervous Dick Bennett appreciated the benefit of having a huge lead when witnessing his son's career accomplishment. "Were the game tight at that point, it would have been hard to enjoy it," he says. Instead, UWGB coasted to a 63-44 win, setting another school record with its thirteenth straight Division I home win.

Two days later, UWGB again steamrolled a conference foe in front of another standing-room only home crowd. This time it was Brian Hammel's Northern Illinois Huskies who took the beating, 58-43. It was another balanced performance, this time with junior Larry Hill provided a solid 13-point effort. The win gave UWGB a 12-1 record and a 4-0 start to the conference schedule.

Hollywood Script

The victory over the Huskies set the stage for an epic mid-season, non-conference showdown with fellow Midwest mid-major Butler University at historic Hinkle Fieldhouse in Indianapolis. "That was a big one because it was at Hinkle Fieldhouse, (and) *Hoosiers* wasn't that far from being released as a movie," remembers Logan Vander Velden.

The game, booked for 11 a.m. on Saturday, January 18, marked the first regular-season game that UWGB would play on national television. "For us to play on ESPN, a regular-season game – I mean it just shows you how

Scott LeMoine elevates for a mid-range shot during UWGB's 63-44 victory over Wright State on January 11, 1992. (University of Wisconsin-Green Bay Archives)

different it was back then and how we were fighting for everything," Tony Bennett explains.

ESPN had negotiated the game prior to the season and had given the play-by-play assignment to one of its top *SportsCenter* talents, Dan Patrick, at his personal request. "He didn't do a lot of play-by-play," notes Dean Rondorf. "*SportsCenter* was big back then. ESPN was kind of coming into being the worldwide leader in sports. And he was there. I think we all knew about Dan."

Patrick, a humorous sports personality, poked fun at the matchup. "You do a Butler/Wisconsin-Green Bay game, and I would say 99 percent of college basketball fans couldn't tell you two players on both teams. In fact, probably have a hard time telling you one player on Butler's team."

But Patrick was no average college basketball fan. He knew Tony Bennett's name, even if he wasn't overly impressed with his game. "Nothing special about Tony Bennett jumped out at me except he's like John Stockton. You look at his numbers after the game and say, 'He had that kind of game?'"

The day before, Patrick, a former Division I basketball player himself, showed up to the Phoenix shoot-around and had no problems showing off his own game. "I remember him shooting around with us and him having a pretty good shot," recalls Jeremy Ludvigson.

For all the attention on ESPN and Dan Patrick, UWGB still had a game to play and its MCC opponent, Butler, was pretty doggone good. Coach Barry Collier had guided the Bulldogs to an 11-4 record, with a stout 6-1 home tally. Three of the four losses came at the hands of Big Ten opponents, but the team had a recipe for success: they were an unblemished 9-0 when outrebounding their opponents, and also had their own sharpshooter they expected to lean heavily on in Darin Archbold.

Johnson drew the task of matching up with Archbold, and ultimately helping UWGB try to control the pace of the game. The Bulldogs played a pressure man-to-man defense and liked to run when they cleaned up on the boards. From the start, the game proved to be an old-fashioned head crusher between two elite mid-majors.

"It was just a hard-fought game. I think we were the same types of programs," remembers Martinez. "It was just good, hard-nosed, old-school basketball."

Defense controlled early, and Butler's 33-28 halftime advantage was the largest lead either team would hold the entire game. The first half saw solid performances from both team's stars, and not much else. Tony Bennett led the Phoenix with 10 points and three assists, while Archbold carried the Bulldogs with 12 points. Aside from those two, both teams struggled to get any real rhythm. Scariest of all, Butler held a decided advantage in rebounding, 22-14.

As the second half got underway, the spotlight remained firmly focused on the teams' two best players. Tony Bennett turned to his passing game, with Hill and Martinez being the major beneficiaries. Hill owned Butler's J.P. Brens inside, scoring 15 second-half points mostly on layups, while Martinez did much of his damage from beyond the three-point line in racking up 12 second-half points.

Defensively, Johnson played Archbold well, holding Butler's sharp-shooter to just 39% from the field. Though Archbold still got his 22 points, Johnson kept the Butler star off the free throw line and limited his opportunities.

The UWGB effort in the second half impressed the announcing crew. "Safe to say looking at Wisconsin-Green Bay, they will probably be headed back to the NCAA's," remarked Patrick during the telecast as the teams were tied at 46-46. "They remind me a lot of Pete Carril's Princeton teams. Very frustrating, patient, drive you crazy, and a team you do not want to play."

In a game with eleven ties and four lead changes, no one was surprised to see a 61-61 score with 3:30 left to play. The next three minutes mimicked the first 37, providing pure drama with every dribble and pass. UWGB took a three-point lead on a Hill and-one layup, giving the big man his ninth straight point for the Phoenix. Butler succeeded in cutting the deficit to one before it again expanded again to three, courtesy of a pair of Tony Bennett free throws with 30 seconds left.

"His father said that the one thing his son knows how to do: Win basketball games," commented Patrick as Bennett sank his attempts. "One scouting service ranks Dick Bennett's son as the best senior point guard in the *country*."

And so, it all appeared to come down to a final possession for Butler. If the Phoenix could get a stop and a rebound, they'd have a chance to ice the game. The Bulldogs worked the ball around, but Johnson was on Archbold like glue. Rather than force the ball into their best player, the Bulldogs found Jermaine Guice for an open three from the top left wing, and Guice delivered, burying the triple to tie the game 66-66 with 12 seconds left.

Though UWGB had not gotten the stop it needed, the Phoenix still had the ball with a chance to win. Showing his trust in his team, Dick Bennett opted not to take a timeout, instead relying on his son to orchestrate the final seconds. Tony did not disappoint.

"You should hear (former Butler assistant coach) Thad Matta tell that story," Tony Bennett recalls decades later. "I looked over at my dad, and I was like, 'Is he going to call a timeout?' He looked at me and he looked at me and just gave me this like, 'Proceed, go ahead.'"

With his father's approval, Tony dribbled up the left side of the court, crossing the midline with six seconds to play. Guarded by Guice and with the seconds ticking away, Tony pounded the floor with three hard dribbles in his left hand before making his move.

"He just kind of played with the ball out there and I'm thinking, 'What are you gonna do?'" says Dick Bennett. "He was really out there, and he lofted one, and I'm thinking, 'Oh no, we've got to get a better shot than that.'"

"It's what I used to do to guys in high school all the time," Tony explains. "All I wanted to do was get a clean look. I knew if I could get a clean look, I had a good chance. And so it was just, I just sensed like, 'He's not going to be ready for this, quick cross-over pull-up. He's going to think I'm gonna attack and drive.' So I shot it just a touch early."

With four seconds left and Guice on his heels, Tony elevated nearly 30 feet from the basket and let his final shot fly. Guice, reeling from the crossover, raised his hand helplessly as the ball flew over it.

The ball hung in the air for two full seconds before splashing through the net.

The shot put UWGB up 69-66 with 1.4 seconds to play and prompted Patrick to remark, "Well, if Tony Bennett is going to play in the pros, you got a good idea of him taking an NBA three-pointer."

The Phoenix bench went crazy, and Martinez and Eric LeDuc bearhugged a fist-pumping Tony as the team headed to the bench. LeDuc stole the subsequent inbounds pass, and it was over. UWGB had come up with yet another massive victory, this time on national television on the shoulders of their future NBA talent.

"Having Tony hit the shot, just almost the same kind of shot that was in the (*Hoosiers*) movie, to win that game," recalls Vander Velden. "I'll never forget that one."

"Tony's shot from like 40 feet, that was awesome," states Martinez. "Just another great game, a game where we got some exposure."

"We all knew he's the best guy on the floor. We weren't arguing that, *ever*," says LeMoine. "We thought we were pretty good, but at the end of the day, we knew Tony was the guy and he could get it done."

The game was huge for the program's visibility. "Just kind of another building block into becoming, you know, *known*," remarked Ludvigson. "Who's UWGB? Well, we're starting to do some cool things."

"Dan (Patrick) talks about that game all the time ... probably about once a year he'll bring it up because of the place, because of how it ended," notes Rondorf, a loyal *Dan Patrick Show* listener. "When someone talks about a game that happened twenty-five years ago or longer that you played in, it's like, 'Okay, that's kind of cool.' "

"That kind of brought some legitimacy to the program. And I think for any mid-major program, that's a big deal," LeDuc says. "When you have those moments – especially then, when there weren't as many games on TV. You wanted to take advantage of those moments knowing that you don't get a ton of them."

UWGB was now 13-1, having won six straight games. With a 4-0 conference record with 12 conference games to play, the Phoenix appeared unstoppable.

Prophecies

After the Butler high, the remaining regular-season schedule appeared to be a formality. UWGB was the best team in the Mid-Continent, and it really wasn't close. The only real questions remaining seemed to be: (1) Could it move into the top 25? (2) Could it finish the conference season undefeated? and (3) How high would its tournament seed be?

The final three games in January 1992 essentially constituted a basketball tour of the state of Illinois, with the Phoenix first playing in Chicago against UIC (January 20), then traveling to Charleston for a game against

Eastern Illinois (January 25), before finishing in Macomb against Western Illinois (January 27).

UWGB won all three, though closer than it would have hoped. In the first game, Tony capitalized on the momentum from his national buzzer-beater by pouring in 25 points and four assists, coming up with the game-winning steal and assist with 0:50 left to give UWGB a 70-66 win over UIC.

He followed that effort with a monstrous 37-point outing, playing all forty minutes and shooting 13-of-18 from the field as UWGB beat Eastern Illinois 74-70. The close win was the team's sixteenth in its last twenty-one games decided by five points or less, and improved UWGB to a staggering 15-1, putting it on the cusp of cracking the top 25.

Tony had been riding a hot streak, but had seen little support from his teammates. After the game, Dick Bennett said what was on most people's minds: "I've been watching it for the last four years, and if we don't have Tony, we don't win. I don't think there's any mystery to it, and I don't think anybody would resent my saying that after so many years of it."

And so the discussion began in earnest – what seed would the Phoenix get?

"If they run the table, they would probably be an eighth seed," remarked college basketball analyst Mike Francesca. "If they lose anywhere from two to three games, they'd probably be a nine or 10 seed. They won't make it any higher than that. If they were any higher than that, I don't think it would be fair."

Northern Illinois coach Brian Hammel was in general agreement: "With the type of team and coach they have, it would be tough to keep them out of the NCAA's unless the bottom fell out, and I don't think that's going to happen." But Hammel did provide one caveat: "They've been lucky with injuries so far, and if somebody gets nicked up, who knows how that could affect their chemistry."

Hammel's words echoed in Bennett's ears. "I kept thinking something crazy could happen," he recalls. "But in my heart of hearts, I knew something crazy *had* to happen for us to stumble, because we were really good."

Hammel's warning proved prophetic just a game later against Western Illinois when Tony Bennett bruised his pelvis four minutes in and had to sit out the rest of the way.

Fortunately, the Phoenix got solid play from Hill (19 points), LeDuc (13 points and eight rebounds), and Martinez, enough to capture a 65-53 win and move to 7-0 in the conference and 16-1 overall.

"Everyone's always 'Bennett, Bennett, Bennett.' It's not really Bennett," remarked Western Illinois guard Rich Townsend. "I know (Martinez) is in a league with that guard from UIC (Kenny Williams). Martinez is solid."

"We wouldn't have won without John, that's for sure," remarked Dick Bennett after the game. But his thoughts were also on Tony. "I feel bad. He was at the top of his game. I've seen too many good players get hurt."

After the Western Illinois game and amidst uncertainty over his playing status, Tony was announced as one of the fifteen finalists for the prestigious Naismith Award, given out to the most outstanding college basketball player in the country. Though he had virtually no chance of winning the award over the likes of Christian Laettner (Duke), Shaquille O'Neal (LSU), or Jimmy Jackson (Ohio State), his inclusion on this list was a tribute to his impact on the game and further proof of the increasing national presence of the program.

The celebration was short-lived, as Tony's injury ultimately cost the Phoenix its first conference game on February 1 against Akron. Though not 100%, Tony suited for the game, and as the score remained close, Dick had few options.

"I did not plan to use Tony as much as I did, but I had no choice," he said afterwards.

Though hampered with his lateral movement and explosiveness, Tony found ways to get open and score while the rest of his team went cold, scoring the team's final 10 points including a jumper with 0:23 left to give UWGB a 62-61 lead.

It looked like the Phoenix

Childhood friends Tony Bennett (left) and Ben Johnson provided veteran leadership for the Phoenix. (University of Wisconsin-Green Bay Archives)

was about to avert disaster, but on Akron's final possession, its star player, Ray Coleman, collected his own miss and made a short put-back. Tony missed a shot as the buzzer sounded, giving Akron the 63-62 victory.

Whether as a strategic attempt to divert attention from his son or genuine disgust at the arena set-up, Dick kept his post-game comments focused on the lack of game clocks in the Brown County Arena and the impact it may have had on Tony's final attempt.

"We've been griping for clocks at the end of the thing since I've been here. Tony could have probably gone to the hole," Bennett said. "Save a buck, lose a game."

Less than a week later, the Brown County Arena confirmed the addition of game clocks on the floor for the following season.

With a 16-2 record, the loss had a minimal impact on UWGB's postseason dreams, but did drop the team in the polls, re-setting their efforts to crack the top 25.

"As that small mid-major school, it would've been nice because there wasn't a lot of mid-major guys that were getting recognized as the top 25," remembers Rondorf. "We certainly knew there was a buzz around there, but I don't ever remember being disappointed by not being in the top 25."

Back on Track

UWGB responded by rattling off three straight wins. The first was the largest Division I win in school history, with a recovering Tony Bennett helping the Phoenix down Cleveland State 92-53. The next was a closer affair, though the Phoenix put down Northern Illinois 78-70. The third was a win over UIC in which the Flames' Bob Hallberg deployed a five-guard lineup. The strategy backfired as Hill had a field day, scoring 25 points on 9-of-10 shooting, mostly on layups.

"It was a matter of his 6-8 against their 6-1 or 6-2," remarked Johnson. "He's going to win that battle nine out of ten times."

UWGB shot better than 50% for the night straight game. More impressive, the Phoenix held its opponent under that mark for the eighteenth time that season. The win brought UWGB's season record to 19-2, and all but officially crowned the Phoenix as regular season Mid-Continent Conference champions.

"Our team is earning my respect," said Dick Bennett. "It takes a lot for me to say that."

On top of that, Tony was a runner-up for *Sports Illustrated's* player of the week based on his performance, and the *Chicago Tribune* prepared a major story on him for print the following week. Meanwhile, the team moved up to #28 in the AP poll entering a matchup at Wright State.

UWGB experienced a lull at Wright State on February 15, running into a buzz saw known as Bill Edwards to experience its largest loss since December 1989, 80-62.

"The last game we were dominated like this was so long ago I can't remember," remarked Dick Bennett. "This reminded me of that first year."

But as it had after its first two losses, UWGB rebounded quickly and dramatically, finishing February on a wicked three-game bend.

First, UWGB stomped the conference doormat, Valparaiso, by 28 points for its twentieth win. By halftime, the score was 39-18, and Dick Bennett was able to clear his bench. Meanwhile, Tony's four assists put him on top as the Mid-Continent Conference's all-time assists leader.

UWGB followed with an 82-47 beat down of Western Illinois. A capacity crowd of 5,897 fans saw UWGB clinch the school's first conference regular-season crown with its backcourt leading the charge. Tony scored 20 points and Martinez delivered a double-double of 17 points and 10 assists.

"This particular championship was a long time in coming," Dick Bennett said. "I don't forget the years when it didn't look like we would get here, and I don't forget the guys from the beginning teams who really worked to get us in this position."

Two nights later, the Phoenix finished its February schedule with a resounding 67-52 win against Eastern Illinois. "If I had one, I probably would have (thrown in the towel)," remarked Eastern Illinois coach Rick Samuels. "The game was decided in the first five minutes."

Dick Bennett tried to keep his club sharp by pointing out some of the weaknesses after the game, but it carried little weight with the players. "We could have played a little harder, but it's kind of hard when you're up that many points," said Martinez afterwards.

It was the seventh time during that UWGB took a 19+ point lead into the half. With the team's final conference game a full week away, UWGB was peaking at the right time and it seemed nothing could hold this team back.

Seven days later, the entire complexion of the season turned on its head.

Tremors

It began with trouble for a player not even on the Phoenix's active roster. Tory Smith, UWGB's redshirt sophomore, was arrested on February 25, 1992, on three counts of delivering cocaine and one count of conspiracy to deliver cocaine. Smith was taken into custody and trial set for June.

His measurable contribution to the team's success was negligble at best, but Smith was a valued and well-liked member of the team. Chris Yates took the news hard, noting shortly after, "I cried a whole day. I couldn't help it. I saw myself in Tory."

"It's not easy for anybody. We all know Tory very well," noted Martinez after the arrest. "He's not only a great basketball player, he's a great person."

Even Dick Bennett seemed shaken. "Tory is a valued member of the team. He was close to all of us. I have not known many more dedicated basketball players," the coach said. "But more than that, there will be deep concern for him as a person. None of us are robots or computers. We're affected by this."

The news united the team in their affection for Tory, but there was a clear disconnect regarding their level of surprise. After the arrest, some players began connecting dots on the warning signs they'd seen.

"He drove a nice car on campus, wore nice clothes, but I don't think anybody knew to the extent that he was involved with dealing drugs until he got arrested," noted redshirt freshman Gary Grzesk.

"This guy's got a brand new Ford Eddie Bauer Explorer. And he told me, 'Oh, my grandpa this that and the other,' got it for him or whatever," recalled redshirt Jeff Nordgaard. "I had no clue. I was naïve coming to school."

"He was flashing it a little bit," said Ludvigson. "He was a good guy, everybody liked Tory, but I kind of knew he's probably involved in some stuff like that."

Nevertheless, the coaches "were pretty oblivious to that," admitted Ludvigson.

"He had some friends who came across, moved into the Green Bay area, and as I learned after the fact, began robbing drug houses," explains Dick Bennett. "He'd find out where there was a party where a lot of drugs were being sold, exchanged, whatever, and they would raid them and clean up."

Tragic as it was, Smith was not the last Phoenix player to get into trouble. A mere five days later, Yates was arrested for armed robbery following a four-month police investigation. The pair of thefts allegedly included a little over $400 in cash, jewelry, some stereo speakers, and a Nintendo system.

Similar to Smith, Yates's contributions to the Phoenix in 1991-92 were not substantial, but the second criminal incident in under a week rocked the program and community to the core. Dick Bennett was beside himself. "The detectives had come and talked to me, and I said, 'Oh my, no, no. Your information is wrong.' Tory's the guy I defended perhaps more. I just felt like, 'No, he loves the game too much. He wouldn't fool around with this.' With Chris, I didn't know, because Chris was frustrated."

As his players attested, Bennett's pain was real.

"Coach Bennett put so much time into our lives, that on a personal level, he felt like we were an extension of his family," says Rondorf. "When things like that happen, I think Coach thought that was a poor reflection on who he was. That affected him. I think he looked at it and said, 'How could these two individuals make these poor decisions?' "

UWGB Associate Chancellor Don Harden was concerned about the potential backlash and spoke out publicly in support of Dick Bennett's character. "Dick has done everything he can to give both Tory and Chris a wonderful opportunity at an education and to be taught basketball by the best teacher I know in the game," Harden said. "You can only help people so far as they want to be helped. There was virtually nothing even a Dick Bennett could do."

The arrests raised a justifiable concern that the team may lose focus. "It didn't affect us in terms of depth or our commitment," noted Bennett, "but it may have bothered a couple of our individuals. I know it bothered Tony."

As if two arrests weren't enough, the University of Wisconsin had fired Steve Yoder the very same week. Inevitably and immediately, Dick Bennett's name was mentioned as a prominent potential replacement, along with UW-Platteville's Bo Ryan and a trio of high school coaches.

All of this served as backdrop to the Phoenix's final regular-season game.

Earthquake

The Valparaiso game on March 2 was supposed to provide some relief from the off-court troubles facing the Phoenix. UWGB was a stellar 22-3, raging through the past three games and leaving no doubt it was the best team in the conference. Meanwhile, Valparaiso was 5-21, with a pathetic two conference wins.

Supercharged fans brought signs reading, "Oh No, Dick Won't Go." The first five minutes of the game were relatively uneventful and close.

Then, tragedy struck.

It happened innocuously enough, with Tony Bennett sending an inbounds pass to Martinez on the right wing. Martinez faked right, dribbled left into the lane, and began his patented floater – the same shot he'd used to down DePaul a season before.

"My go-to move was I drive into the middle of the lane and I go off two feet and then I just kind of drop the ball over," Martinez says.

This time, there was no one home for the Crusaders defensively, and it threw off Martinez's rhythm. "It was so wide open that I didn't go off of two feet. I jumped off of my left foot and just did a regular layup, because nobody was even there to try and block the ball. That in itself was just unusual, because I never do that off of one foot into traffic."

In the midst of the move, a Valparaiso defender lost Vander Velden under the basket, and looking disoriented, stepped toward Martinez as he came down.

"I just remember going up and wondering like, 'Why is this guy not trying to take a charge or block the shot?' " Martinez recalled.

The result was catastrophic. "When I came down, he was positioned to box our guy out and that's when my knee kind of … that's when it just popped," remembers Martinez. "I didn't know I tore my ACL. I didn't know the extent of the damage. I just knew at that point it was not a good situation."

Martinez was on the floor a full two minutes while the training staff looked at his knee. "This was unlike anything I'd ever experienced," said Martinez. "I knew right then and there that I was done."

Martinez's friends, Ludvigson and LeDuc, carried him off the floor.

"You could just kind of feel the life being sucked out of Brown County Arena, and really, that was kind of the turning point of the season," recalls Grzesk.

"John did so many things," notes Rondorf. "John handled the ball, John passed on time, on target. And it freed up Tony to do so many different things. And John made everybody so much better. That was one of those ones that was like, 'Okay, everyone's got to step up now and try to fill a little bit of what John did.' "

At least that night, the Phoenix rose from the ashes and did just that.

In one of the most dominating performances ever witnessed at the Brown County Arena, UWGB held Valparaiso to just 25 total points on a scant eight made field goals. The defense forced twelve turnovers while outrebounding the Crusaders an astounding 45-17 and holding Valparaiso to a pathetic 18.6% shooting. Offensively, the Phoenix got a monster 30-point game from Tony Bennett, including 10-of-19 from the field and 6-of-8 from the three-point line, capping a 69-25 victory.

But afterwards, the team heard the news. Doctors confirmed that Martinez tore his ACL and was done for the year.

"That was a significant blow to our team, that program, and you know even a little bit our psyche," remembers Johnson, "because we knew how good John was and when Tony would get subbed out, you knew John could take the controls and run the team just as well. I'm telling you, he was slick as slick."

"Crushing. I felt so sad for him, and terrible for him. It just didn't feel right. Like, you know, just that whole thing," says Tony Bennett. We were playing good ball and we just knew. And you're like, 'Ugh.' "

"He was considered as good as Tony within the team," states Ludvig-son. "And so when he went down, that was certainly a big blow."

"It was like somebody just stuck a pin in the balloon and it just popped," adds LeMoine. "Everybody was riding high, like this is our year, we were rolling. And when that happened, it just caught everybody off guard. Like, 'No, this isn't supposed to happen.'"

Picking Up the Pieces

There was no time to mourn the loss of Martinez, as the team took the court two days later for its final regular-season game. In a scheduling quirk, UWGB's senior night would take place against the dual-affiliated NAIA and Division II UW-Parkside.

A packed house came to support the senior class, and the Phoenix did not disappoint by delivering a 33-point victory. The veterans enjoyed a relatively easy affair, with senior backup Tony Ciaravino netting 15 points and Johnson grabbed nine rebounds.

But it was the other Tony – Tony Bennett – who got the crowd on its feet with chants of "Ton-ee, Ton-ee." With three minutes left in the game, Tony pushed the ball up the floor on a fast break and suddenly stopped, pulling up for a deep three-pointer that he buried. "I knew that was the last time I'd ever show my appreciation to the fans for all the support they've given me," Tony remarked. "I wanted to show that I can get a little wild and crazy."

It was a fitting farewell from the home fans to the greatest senior class the Phoenix had ever known.

And for all the trouble UWGB had endured over the final ten days of the regular season, UWGB still managed to close with an astonishing 24-3 record that included wins over a Big Ten team, a Big Eight team, and Butler on ESPN. The Phoenix's only losses had been by eight on the road against NCAA-bound Nebraska, a one-point loss on a last-second shot in a game in which its star player was injured, and an aberrational mid-year letdown against a red-hot Bill Edwards and Wright State.

Dick Bennett's team boasted the second best scoring defense in the nation (55.2 ppg), also finishing the year second in three-point percentage (46.1%), sixth in field goal percentage, (51.4%), and ninth in scoring margin (13.9).

Tony's play, in particular, had been off the charts. He finished sixth in the NCAA in three-point percentage, having connected on 50.3% of his shots from distance. Even more impressive, with a 49.4% career three-point shooting percentage, Tony was very likely to finish his career as the all-time Division I leader in career three-point percentage and was just 44 points shy of the Mid-Continent Conference career scoring record.

He was named Mid-Continent Conference Player of the Year for a second time just prior to the conference tournament, and became one of just five Mid-Continent Conference players to be selected First Team All-Conference three times in his career. Tony's work ethic in the classroom also paid off, as he was also selected as a First Team GTE Academic All-American in 1992.

Ben Johnson (right) displays the stellar defense that was his calling card during a senior night victory over UW-Parkside. (University of Wisconsin-Green Bay Archives)

"I'm not the most gifted student, but I worked hard. I'm sure there are people more worthy than me," Tony said of the award. "That's incredible."

Mid-Continent Blues

The Phoenix took to the road, heading to Cleveland State's Henry J. Goodman Arena for the start of the Mid-Continent Conference Tournament on March 8, 1992. In spite of Martinez's injury, the team appeared to be peaking at the right time, having finished on a five-game win streak with an average margin of victory an other-worldly 31 points per game. Winning the conference tournament was certainly the immediate goal, but talk of a deep NCAA Tournament run intensified with every passing day.

As the top seed, UWGB earned the right to play the #8 seed Western Illinois in the tournament's opening match. It was hardly a cakewalk, but against a dramatically inferior opponent, the Phoenix still managed a 22-point victory. Tony dropped in 17 points, putting him just 27 points away from the Mid-Continent Conference all-time scoring record, while his best friend Ben Johnson added 10 points.

The semifinal matchup against the fourth-seeded Eastern Illinois Panthers would not be so smooth. Eastern Illinois had proven to be a tough adversary for UWGB in the team's first game in January by taking the Phoenix to the wire, but Dick Bennett's team had figured things out and easily dispensed with the Panthers in the rematch.

On this day, however, UWGB came out flat. Dead flat.

Eastern Illinois jumped in front early, extended the lead to double digits in the first half, then to as many as fifteen in the second half. Even with a 20-point, 11-assist performance from Tony Bennett, UWGB was unable to keep pace and was upset, 75-65.

"John was gone and we really struggled and got beat in the semis by Eastern, who had a great game against us and had a very good team," states Dick Bennett. "We just weren't the same. We didn't have the same spring to our step. Everything was off on the floor."

In an instant, UWGB's hope of obtaining an automatic bid to the NCAA Tournament had evaporated.

Making Their Case

"This one stings. But there's no sense getting down on ourselves," remarked Johnson after the semifinal loss. "We didn't back into twenty-five wins. Hopefully that will be respectable enough for an at-large bid."

It was now a waiting game for UWGB. Its resume was stellar – a 25-4 record and a #42 power ranking in the USA Today, including an 11-2 road record with wins at Purdue and Butler, as well as at home against Colorado. They had a Naismith Award Finalist in Tony Bennett, and had performed admirably the year prior in the NCAA Tournament against Michigan State. They had won each of their final six games by double-digits prior to the loss to Eastern Illinois. And three of the Phoenix's four losses came at the hands of teams that would be playing in the postseason.

There were factors working against the Phoenix, but nearly all of them were outside of the team's control. The Mid-Continent Conference, for its part, was experiencing a down year, and the Phoenix didn't record a single win over a team likely to get an at-large bid to the NCAA. The loss in the conference semifinals was also a black mark.

But historically speaking, the Phoenix were solidly locked in the tournament based on record alone. No team with twenty-five or more wins and four or fewer losses had *ever* been left out of NCAA's Tournament since the field expanded in 1985. Beyond that, UWGB's 86.2% winning percentage was better than any team that had ever been left out of the tournament.

UWGB's ace in the hole was their marketable talent in Tony Bennett. All objective factors pointed to a team likely to get somewhere between a 10- and 12-seed. That didn't stop rumblings that in spite of the team's epic season, the Martinez injury could influence whether the Phoenix would even get a bid.

"One of the shows were doing pros and cons of 'Will Green Bay get into the NCAA tournament,' " recalls Martinez, "and *I* was listed as one of the reasons that we wouldn't. It's bad enough that I'm already hurt and can't play, and then I'm just like, 'They better not.' "

But that didn't stop the media from stirring the pot. And yet, as the final week played out, UWGB's confidence grew as a number of bubble teams experienced significant losses, including South Florida, Minnesota, Arizona State, Villanova, and Pittsburgh. (Only South Florida would make the tournament out of that group.)

"Every one of us (knew we'd get in). Like, we were just waiting for our name," states LeMoine. "Our resume – we made the NIT (in 1990), we won a game in the NIT before, we almost beat Michigan State. You know, we were rolling off wins our senior year."

Dick Bennett, never one to count his chickens, expressed his anxiety: "I'm very nervous, of course I am. The thing that's disappointing or frustrating is that one game – one game – *ONE GAME* – can affect everything we did all season," Bennett said prior to the selection. "You teach and believe that what you do over the long haul, if you do it well, is what matters."

Unforgiveable

The Phoenix Dunkers Booster Club arranged for a viewing party for the team at the 50 Yard Line, a bar in Green Bay, to watch the Selection Show, and invited fans to join the team. "There were like 500 people there, and we were in a separate room for the pairing," Dick Bennett explains. "I just said, 'We'd rather not watch it with everybody, but we'll be in this back room, then we'll come out afterwards.' "

"They had a huge reception with a lot of the administration, players, coaches, cheerleaders, band," recalls Grzesk. "At the reception, everyone was wondering what seed we were going to be, where we were going to go."

The mood at the bar was jovial, the fans eager to see who the team would get a chance to square off against. But as the pairings continued to flash with UWGB's name absent, anticipation turned first to doubt and then to fear.

And suddenly, the final pairings were announced and reality set it. The selection committee had snubbed the Phoenix.

"That was just an absolute shock to everybody," LeMoine says. "When they stopped reading names, everybody was like, 'Okay, when's the next list coming? We're in that next list.' And they're like, 'No, they're done,' and we're like, 'Holy crap.' "

"That was one of the most empty, hollow feelings I can remember here," notes Grzesk. "It was dead silence for five minutes after."

"We watched that whole painful process and then had to go out," recalls Dick Bennett. "Everybody was just so bummed by the whole thing. It was just – it was a *horrible* feeling. That's as bad as I can remember feeling in connection with a season. Here we are, 25 and 4, and we don't get invited."

"It was a shock, and I don't know why we ever decided to have the viewing party when we weren't sure," adds Tony. "That was a hard one, it was like, 'What?!' "

Roy Kramer, the SEC commissioner and chairman of the selection committee, attempted to explain the inexplicable, starting by questioning the strength of Mid-Continent. He also relied on the Martinez injury as an "extenuating circumstance" that "would be a factor with Green Bay." But most ridiculous, Kramer displayed an appalling lack of competency by referencing the absence of Chris Yates – who averaging six minutes and two points per game – and a redshirted Tory Smith as additional factors that could affect UWGB's potential.

Kramer went through ten factors that he said the committee looked at in comparing the final eight to ten teams, but his dog-and-pony show rang hollow for UWGB, particularly when the Phoenix checked most of his specific boxes. Kramer summarily dismissed the Phoenix with the worthlessly shallow line, "There's 25-4, and then there's 25-4."

His comments cast doubt on whether he had bothered to watch a single moment of UWGB basketball in 1991-92. And his decision didn't sit well with anyone.

"To base the decision on one game, which seems to be the case, I question that," remarked Tony Bennett at the time. "It's frustrating because I thought we had a great year. We did everything we could."

"We were really going to be a tough out, especially for a team that maybe didn't take us seriously or only had a day or two to prepare for us," states LeDuc. "Then John gets hurt, and that was just such a body blow."

"Because John wasn't there for some of the games, you don't take away those wins. The schedule's still there; we still went out there and performed," remarks Rondorf. "You work your way up to get some recognition for the school that you love, and you put so much time and effort in, and then all of the sudden ... Maybe it's lack of maturity, but someone tells you you're not good enough ... I just felt that we were, at the time, one of the best (64) teams."

"Back then especially, I don't know if the committee really got to know teams," notes Vander Velden. "I think they just looked at the mid-majors and if they didn't win their conference tournament, it was really hard to get a bid. We thought we had a strong enough resume to get it, but it was really, just – it was devastating."

"We felt very slighted. We were 25-3 at the time we lost that (Eastern Illinois) game. That's a good college team," laments Johnson. "You can't deny them, just because they don't win their conference tournament, the right to go to the NCAA tournament. They always talk about your body of work. Well, that's a pretty significant body of work. You've got to reward that for what they did, and not how they stubbed their toe in one game."

The injustice incited anger, helplessness, and frustration within the program. "That left a permanent scar on our coaching staff," Heideman recalled years later. "I think that has spurred us. We've always told our kids ever since, 'Don't count on an at-large bid. We have to win our way into the tournament.'"

"I didn't think it was fair at all," states Dick Bennett. "In that period of time, the big conferences didn't want to give the small schools any kind of credit. I thought there was some real bias there."

"You know, that's twenty-some years ago," concludes Johnson. "They weren't listening then, and they certainly aren't listening now, because not much has changed."

Consolation Prize

Later that evening, UWGB was invited to play in the NIT. Their prize? A matchup against a very talented 23-8 Manhattan Jaspers squad. And as was the case every year, the Home and Garden Show had already booked the Brown County Arena during the NIT's opening-round window, forcing the Phoenix to travel to New York.

The game would be played in Manhattan's Draddy Gymnasium, a cramped 3,000-seat facility that could be a challenge for opponents when filled to capacity.

"Trust me, the NIT would've much rather had that game at Brown County and sold 7,000 seats than what we had at Manhattan," notes LeDuc. "It's literally in the middle of Manhattan. It's a high school gym on the third floor of a physical education building, and it's just a different environment."

It was an ironic twist that UWGB's second trip to the NIT had similar, but reversed, storylines to its first. In 1990, Southern Illinois was the team that felt snubbed despite a record twenty-six victories.

"Everyone was flat, like this isn't supposed to be. We're supposed to be in the NCAA tournament; we're supposed to be on TV and fighting for that. Not this," says LeMoine.

Manhattan's first team all-conference forward, Keith Bullock, and excellent guard tandem of Russ Williams and Charles Dubra provided match-up problems for the Phoenix. Meanwhile, the Jaspers played a tough, pressure man-to-man brand of defense and, like the Phoenix, could be very patient with the basketball.

With two healthy guards, the Phoenix may have matched up better, but as the game approached, there were doubts UWGB could even muster one. The Phoenix had been holding onto a major secret – Tony Bennett was experiencing back spasms, leaving his status in doubt. "Even on the plane ride, he had things to support his back because it was in such bad shape," Grzesk confirms. "I didn't think there was any way he was going to be able to play."

Johnson remembers the excessive padding Tony was wearing. "He looked more like a hockey player than he did a basketball guy."

"He just couldn't be explosive again and he carried that into the tournament," Dick Bennett says. "We lived and died with the great play of our two guards, and now we're down to a half a guard."

With few options, Bennett tagged senior Tony Ciaravino to start for the second time in his four-year career. It was a short-lived move. Four minutes into the game and with an early 4-3 lead, he replaced Ciaravino with Tony Bennett.

"Tony Ciaravino started and gave it his best shot," Dick Bennett says, "but without Tony, the game, and that particular game, we would've been beaten badly."

Tony Bennett played through back pain to gamely compete in UWGB's 67-65 loss at Manhattan in an NIT first-round game on March 19, 1992. (AP photo / Peter Morgan)

Tony Bennett would play every remaining minute, delivering perhaps his greatest performance.

The Phoenix offense hardly resembled the team that had galloped through the conference schedule. The team had no penetration threat and had to rely almost exclusively on the deep ball, with three-pointers accounting for 41% of its shots.

The game had already featured six lead changes and three ties in the first ten minutes, with Rondorf hitting a pair of threes while Manhattan's Charles Dubra hit three himself, helping Manhattan to a 15-14 lead. Tony hit his first three-point attempt with 6:47 left in the first half, and connected on two more before the half closed. His third triple, with less than a minute to go, was a record-breaker, giving him the all-time Mid-Continent Conference scoring record. Nevertheless, Manhattan carried a 35-28 lead at the break.

While Bennett and Rondorf were carrying the load for the Phoenix, it was Manhattan's three-headed monster of Bullock (11 points), Dubra (9 points), and Williams (8 points) who were pushing the home team.

That seven-point cushion quickly evaporated in the second half. Tony Bennett hit two three-pointers right out of the gate, and then his sixth and seventh of the game a few moments later. In fact, Tony scored 14 of UWGB's first 16 points in the second half, lifting the Phoenix back into contention.

But it was Tony's eighth three-pointer of the game that put UWGB on top for the first time in the second half, 57-56. And he added a long jumper

Eric LeDuc looks to pass against the Manhattan defense during the Phoenix's loss in its 1992 NIT opener. (AP photo / Peter Morgan)

on the next possession, extending the lead to 59-56 with 4:43 to play.

Manhattan was able to grab the lead back when Bullock knocked down a shot in the paint, taking a 62-61 lead just 1:33 to play. But on the ensuing possession, Tony dribbled to his left, stepped back, and knocked down his school-record ninth three-pointer of the game, retaking the lead 64-62 with 1:03 to play.

It was Tony's tenth straight point for UWGB and gave him 36 for the game.

"Tony's game, it was crazy," remembers Rondorf. "He hit *everything*."

"He just put on perhaps one of his finest performances, at least offensively," Dick Bennett says. "His performance lifted me incredibly."

After a Manhattan miss, Rondorf went to the line and hit the first of two free throws, extending the Phoenix lead to three. But his second attempt was long, and Bullock grabbed the rebound for the Jaspers.

As the clock ticked under a half-minute, Bullock caught a pass on the left baseline and spun to the middle for an open layup. He missed the bunny, but grabbed his own rebound, went back up, converted, and was fouled.

The gym went crazy as Bullock stepped to the line, a chance to tie the game with just 20 seconds left. His free throw was perfect, tying the game up at 65-65. It would come down to a final Phoenix possession.

UWGB broke the press, and Rondorf handed the ball to Tony Bennett with eight seconds to play. The Phoenix legend took three dribbles to his left beyond the arc before Manhattan brought a double team, forcing Tony back to his right and into the waiting body of the Jaspers' Carey Edwards. There was contact, and in the mix-up, Tony lost control. The ball bounced perfectly into the hands of Manhattan's Carey Edwards.

"I just saw it slip away right there. I'm lying on the floor as the guy's running down, and I'm looking up at the clock thinking, 'Maybe there's no time,' " Tony remarked after the game. "But that's not the way it was."

"He tried to spin-dribble across half court, and they wisely had two guys on him," explains Dick Bennett. "They tried to deny him. Everything they did was geared to stopping him, and then in that last run, he brought it down hard and tried to spin. There was contact, there was a bump, but he lost the ball – it was a bad turnover."

Edwards sprinted the length of the floor, and with two seconds left, delivered a game-winning dunk to pull off an improbable 67-65 Jaspers victory. After UWGB's final desperation pass was intercepted, the crowd stormed the floor.

Aftermath

In a game that he almost didn't play, Tony Bennett experienced the highs of setting school and conference records, and the low of a solitary error that marked the end his team's season and his career.

"I thought that was one of the most incredible individual efforts I've ever seen," remarked Manhattan coach Steve Lappas. "I'd like to have a bad back like that."

Dick Bennett agreed: "I've never seen him better. I've seen him quicker, stronger. But to just keep stepping up and knocking it down when he had to, I've not seen him better."

For the team, the Manhattan game marked the excruciating end to what was otherwise an exceptional season.

"We limped to the finish line," admits Johnson. "It was probably time for the horse to go out of the pasture and be put to sleep. But still, you know, it's your last game of your senior year, you want it to be more, you want to keep trying to squeeze something out of the orange."

"I remember all of us staring at each other after the game, and then the realization hit, like 'It's over.' We were just kind of looking at each other like, 'Oh, shit. We're done,'" adds LeMoine.

"Disappointing *end* to the season," Ludvigson points out. "It was a great year, and we thought we were going to do some good things, but we didn't have much margin for error. If we played bad, we could get beat by anybody, and we did that year."

"To kind of have it all fall apart at the end, and with John's injury right before the conference tournament," comments Vander Velden. "It was disappointing for that year to end that way, but the way that it ended also helped propel us."

With the final chapter written, the only thing left to ask was the big 'What if?' What if John Martinez hadn't gotten hurt?

"I think that team could've played with dang near anyone in the country ... because we had enough size, we had enough athleticism, our guards, we were as good as anyone in the country," Tony Bennett states. I believe that – I *know* that. Having played in the NBA, watching it, and I see that. No question. Had he not gotten hurt, who knows what our team was capable of."

"You had Tony, you had Ben, we had other guys that really were good. And I think it was definitely a Sweet Sixteen team," pontificates LeDuc. "It always depends on the draw, but I thought we definitely could've made some noise. And especially with the way that we shot the ball that year, there was really nobody you couldn't beat."

"Making the Sweet Sixteen or Elite Eight, I mean that was definitely within grasp, without a doubt," adds Martinez. "I would be surprised if we *didn't* make the Sweet Sixteen. We were kind of rolling along at that level."

End of an Era

The Manhattan game was the grand finale for the greatest class that Dick Bennett had ever assembled at UWGB.

"It was certainly a tough one," remembers Rondorf, one of two redshirted members from that stellar class of 1988. "That's Tony (Bennett) and Ben (Johnson)'s and Scott (LeMoine)'s and Tony Ciaravino's last game, the guys that I came in there with."

Senior Scott LeMoine's career with the Phoenix peaked during his junior year when he started 14 games and recorded 40 blocks, though LeMoine had played meaningful minutes in every season, and recorded seven starts as a senior. His senior teammate, Ciaravino, was fondly remembered as a fierce competitor who worked hard to keep Tony Bennett on his toes.

"He made me better having to guard him and play," Tony says. "He got me probably chewed out by my old man more than most guys because he was an unreal shooter and just a tough kid, and big, huge heart. When we start talking about okay, what kind of people make a program, and the essence, the fiber of who they are, their character – he's right at the top of the list with that."

For everything Ciaravino and LeMoine gave the program, it was undeniable that the loss of best friends Ben Johnson and Tony Bennett cast the largest shadows.

"Ben Johnson was a big influence on me," remembers Ludvigson. "Showing me the ropes and teaching me how to play the defense and the attitude and all that good stuff. I think Ben Johnson was as big a mentor to me as anybody."

Johnson finished his career second on the school's all-time steals list with 166, and with Ciaravino, attended a camp in Chicago in the summer of 1992 to display his skills to overseas scouts. Johnson eventually found a home playing – and ultimately excelling – in an Australian professional league for years before entering college coaching.

"(At UWGB), you learn to work hard every day, and that's kind of how I've tried to live my professional life," Johnson says. "You try and help where you can help, and leave programs better than what you've found them. I think it's all about the mark you leave on the sport and how you impact kids' lives. That's what I took away from my college experience, you know Dick Bennett and Mike Heideman, Woody Wilson, Steve Swan, Tom Brown – they were great mentors for me, and obviously I've tried to be that for the kids that I've worked with over the years."

That left Tony Bennett. The greatest player and role model in school history.

Like Ben, Tony had been a leader, but influenced more through his actions than words. "Tony was a little more kind of quiet," comments Martinez. "He showed more just by example than anything."

"Tony was the quintessential teammate. He could care less about his individual accomplishments. He was 100% team," states Mike Karisny. "He put the team ahead of himself, at every turn. He lived it and breathed it, and he had every right to *not* do that. But not once did I ever see him put himself ahead of the team – never. His humility carries forward. That's the word that comes – his human nature to accept mistakes of others, to accept what is, but expect more from himself. It still to this day provides me with real-life examples of how I hope to live my life."

Tony's work ethic propelled his game and that of his teammates.

"No exaggeration, I don't remember anyone in college basketball, and maybe not many people since then, that were as good at the things Tony was good at," says LeDuc. "In terms of setting people up, running them into the double and triple screens that we'd set for him, and just plain not missing. If he got his feet set and you gave him a second to look at the basket, he barely missed."

"Trying to shut him down, like in practices and stuff like that ... he was good every day. Like he didn't have an off day," recalls LeMoine. "I don't think he ever once lost at knockout. Like, it just didn't happen.It was crazy.

You just didn't see him have a bad shooting day."

"He was so efficient on the offensive end and such a great player," Grzesk says. "I definitely took my lumps and learned how to be a good defender by chasing him through all those screens in the motion."

"He made everyone around him better, because of what he could do offensively," adds Rondorf. "He was such a good player and he could hit the clutch shots, and he was so good at it. So I was fortunate enough to play with a guy like that and then fortunate enough to see what he's doing right now (in coaching)."

Tony Bennett became the most decorated player in school history, collecting accolades and records throughout his tenure. He finished his four years as both his school's and the conference's all-time leader in scoring (2,285 points) and assists (601), as well as third in school history in steals. He was also a three-time first team all-conference player, and two-time Mid-Continent Conference Player of the Year. During his senior year, Tony was named Honorable Mention All-American by the Associated Press and GTE Academic All-American of the Year, and in April 1992 was awarded the Naismith Award, given to the outstanding senior college basketball player 6-feett tall or less.

But perhaps his most well-known and long-standing statistical achievement was finishing his career as the NCAA Division I all-time leader in three-point shooting percentage at an astounding 49.7%. This is even more impressive when you consider that he was the primary offensive weapon on his team, routinely being subjected to double-teams and unique pressure defense tactics.

All of this left no doubt where Tony was headed.

"There were probably twenty NBA scouts (at Manhattan) to watch Tony, and that was one of the first times where it became obvious and evident," recalls LeMoine. "It was completely obvious that Tony was headed to the NBA."

NBA Draft

Tony's road to the pros began with pre-draft camps in Orlando and Chicago. His performance was decent, but not exceptional, and ultimately appeared to slightly dent his draft stock. By draft day, it appeared possible he would slide to the second round.

His most hopeful scenario was to land in Chicago, as the Bulls had interviewed him and held the #27 pick. But on draft day, that pick came and went and Tony was still on the board. "That's when I saw the tension on Tony's face. That was stress," observed Johnson, who watched the draft show with his best friend.

That stress lasted just eight more picks before the Charlotte Hornets snatched him up. Tony would have a chance to compete for a backup role to Tyrone "Muggsy" Bouges, the winner of the Naismith Award in 1987.

The Hornets' pick came as a massive relief for Tony. "We were all going crazy and high-fiving, and there were some tears," Johnson says. "It was very special."

"Had I not gone there, I'm not sure I would have been drafted," Tony remarked at the time. "I've always been the underdog in everything. Maybe I am again, but I'm going to battle for everything I'm worth."

In the end, Tony joined Ron Ripley as the only Phoenix players ever picked in the NBA Draft. Unlike Ripley, Tony would go on to make the Hornets' roster, become the first UWGB player to play an NBA game, and enjoy a productive three-year career in Charlotte.

Tony treasured the influence his family and friends had on his career path.

"To go through it not only with obviously my dad being the coach, my family being able to watch, but my best friend, Ben Johnson. We were teammates and roommates, and that was special."

Johnson agrees, and takes great personal pride in Tony's achievements. The years of pick-up games, one-on-one battles, and physical practices were more than an important opportunity for Tony to refine his craft – they were sacred memories.

"I wasn't as talented or as good as he was, but I was every bit as competitive, and so that pushed him and made him better. That type of intensity and someone that you care about and are passionate about, and are pushing yourself to be the absolute best every single day as a college athlete. Those were special times for us as you look back on it."

"Shoot, we shared something really special, helping Coach Bennett build a program and putting it on kind of the national map for that period of time. It was good and special to be the first to do it at Green Bay."

Offseason Drama

The offseason in 1992 was a rough one, and it started in April. With Tony Bennett's career completed and the Wisconsin Badgers' job open, UWGB risked losing its coach.

"That was something that was being thrown out there that (Dick) could potentially leave," Ludvigson says. "That was definitely a concern."

One week after the Manhattan game, Dick Bennett officially withdrew his name from consideration, feeling Wisconsin was already committed to Stu Jackson. And sure enough, on April 1, 1992, the Badgers hired Jackson to be its head coach.

"He had talked to us as a team and basically said that he was going to be staying," recalls Martinez. "And so, there was little to no concern, at least from us as players."

"I'll be honest, we were probably naïve enough to not really think about it," notes LeDuc, adding with a laugh, "The main concern was – and I say this in the best possible, nicest way – the main thing was, 'Was Dick going to lose his mind over Tony leaving? What was that going to be like?'"

The program then spent the summer focused on the legal matters against two of its players. Tory Smith stood trial in early June and was found guilty on multiple drug charges. A month later, he reached a plea deal for a second set of offenses related to an alleged armed robbery. His sentencing was delayed until September, where he was given fifteen years in prison for his crimes.

Unlike Smith, the facts in the Yates case were less clear, with conflicting testimony and nefarious actors. The jury took more than eleven hours to deliberate, but ultimately found Yates guilty on one of the robbery charges and innocent on another. In October, Yates, continuing to plead his innocence, was sentenced to five years. Yates's story would take a tragic twist a decade later under drug-related circumstances.

Then, by mid-summer, the team received more bad news. Martinez's ACL surgery had been delayed until July as he finished up his classes, and that meant he would have to redshirt and miss an entire season.

"(It was) the hardest thing I've had to deal with in my life," he says. "Basketball was everything to me; that's kind of what got me out of a bad situation growing up. Kind of kept me in line, to stay out of trouble, stay out of gangs, stay out of, you know, all that stuff. And when that happened, that was kind of like the whole dark side of my experience at Green Bay."

But Martinez educated himself and accepted his fate.

"I just kind of learned that you can come back from it. It'll take, at that time it was like a good nine months to a year before you even start doing any kind of playing back on the court. I was willing to do whatever it took to get back on the court."

Chapter 13

Passing the Torch
(1992-93)

Nothing lasts forever, and college basketball players are no exception. Every year, one class graduates and a new class enters. A great player can impact a program for a few years, but all players must move on.

Reloading beats rebuilding under any theory, and the easiest way to do that is with steady class sizes and equal talent distribution, minimizing the impact of any single-season loss, assuming players play out their eligibility. But even with the best intentions, these factors are often beyond a coach's control.

The best teams focus on what they can control in anticipation of the inevitable. They foster a culture of mentorship and growth so that when it comes time to pass the torch, the next class – few or many, talented or otherwise – will be prepared.

Family Ties

Even without John Martinez, Dick Bennett still returned plenty of experienced players in Larry Hill, Dean Rondorf, Logan Vander Velden, Eric LeDuc, and Jeremy Ludvigson, as well as eligible transfer Jeff Zavada. By design, these players had spent years growing in the system and learning from the classes before them.

"You were all recruited by the same coach, so you became – it was like family, it was like siblings," comments Dean Vander Plas. "The older ones were required to help the younger ones grow up in the process."

"Success kind of breeds more," notes Dick Bennett. "Because you've done it and because the formula has been established and these guys buy in, they become your best teachers, your best motivators. They teach. Once you have a core group of kids who have bought in and especially that have enjoyed some success, they're going to teach. When guys come in as a freshman, they are made to play the right way, or at least the right way for that system."

1992-93 Freshman Recruiting, Part 1

Replacing a foursome as strong as Tony Bennett's class would be no easy feat. That restocking process actually began in the fall of 1990 as Dick Bennett recruited players for his 1991 class. He targeted two players in the early signing period, but his top candidate, Shannon Smith, spurned the Phoenix for Marquette. Unfazed, Bennett struck gold with his second.

Gary Grzesk (pronounced "Gresh") was a left-handed, two-sport athlete at Wauwatosa East High School, excelling as both a soccer player and a basketball guard, averaging 14 points and 4 rebounds as a junior. Grzesk's father had played under Al McGuire at Marquette in the 1970s, and that background instilled confidence in Gary.

"Coming out of a suburban Milwaukee school, I was thinking I was good enough to play at (UW-) Madison or Marquette," recalls Grzesk. "As a natural high schooler, you think you're better than you really are."

But Grzesk drew little attention from anyone his junior year, and during the summer of 1990 he attended a camp in Green Bay. The visit gave Grzesk a unique, and painful, opportunity to demonstrate his toughness to the Phoenix coaches.

"I ended up dislocating my finger in the middle of one of the games during the camp, and I went to the trainer and they popped the finger back in and I went back and finished. I think that had a little bit of an impression on Coach Bennett."

It did indeed, and Bennett extended him an offer that fall. The challenge for Grzesk was whether to accept early or wait and see if he had any options on the pitch.

"Soccer actually kind of came naturally to me, and I really enjoyed playing it. It was a very tough decision," recalls Grzesk. "I thought I might even go to a school to play both sports."

Ultimately, the competitiveness of basketball and a full-ride offer convinced him to sign with UWGB in the fall of 1990.

Bennett was unable to fill his second spot until just before graduation in 1991 when he signed Jeff Nordgaard from tiny Dawson, Minnesota.

"It was a real small town, no stoplights or anything like that," explains Nordgaard. "Everything revolved around what was going on with high school teams."

Like Grzesk, Nordgaard was a two-sport star at his high school. And also like Grzesk, Nordgaard had an athlete's pedigree, being the son and grandson of college football players. He excelled as a quarterback on his high school's football team, leading the state of Minnesota in yards and touchdowns as a senior. He believed his future was on the gridiron.

"You know, 6-foot-6 forwards are a dime a dozen in basketball, but 6-foot-6 quarterbacks with a strong arm are not out there as much," he states. "I didn't really foresee when I was a junior or senior being a college basketball player."

Nordgaard received some football interest from schools such as San Diego State and Wyoming, but no scholarship offers. Frustrated, Nordgaard turned to basketball. The problem was, that late in the year, most Division I and II schools had filled their scholarships, leaving only Division

III options. That is, until fate stepped in. There are humorously conflicting memories on how Nordgaard landed at UWGB.

"Coach Heideman and Coach Swan came to watch me at the Minnesota state tournament, and they had gone back to Coach Bennett with an assessment," Nordgaard says. "The story I get from Coach Heideman and Coach Swan is that Coach Bennett asked, 'How are his feet?' I wear size 18s, I'm not overly quick, obviously, but they go, 'They're slow.' And he said, 'We don't need another Vander Plas!' "

Bennett tells it differently:

"I sent (Heideman and Swan), and they came back and said, 'Oh, he's a good player, but he's a little too slow for our needs.' And so I didn't think anything of it. I didn't go to see him myself. And then I went to the Final Four, and (ran into a coach from Minnesota). He cornered me and said, 'Have you seen this Jeff Nordgaard from – it's a little school, he played for his dad.' And I said, 'Well, my assistants did and they just didn't think it was a good fit for us.' He says, 'Oh man. He's really good.'

"So I called and got all these tapes sent. And I watched. I remembered sitting in my office and I watched – oh, I don't remember how many, but at least two or three – and I walked into Mike's office and I called Steve in there, and I said, 'Now tell me, what's *not* to like about this Nordgaard?' "

As Nordgaard puts it, "The truth is somewhere in between." Regardless of where that is, he signed with UWGB, his only Division I basketball offer, in May 1991.

Rising Expectations

Seeing both recruits on campus only heightened the coach's hopes. Regarding Grzesk, Bennett noted, "He's a banger and he can do a lot of things. He's another one of those who plays better than he looks."

Grzesk had hopes of developing into an all-around player, but as he readily admits, "Shooting never game naturally to me. I was always kind of a pass-first team guy, and my shot never really developed as much as I would have liked."

Meanwhile, Bennett initially pegged Nordgaard as a blend of the linebacker-like Dean Vander Plas and the scrappy Jeremy Ludvigson. But upon seeing him at fall practices, Bennett quickly elevated his assessment.

"I don't know if I'd ever seen a more versatile offensive player. He had those long arms, big hands, he could help you on the perimeter with the ball, he could go inside against anybody," recalls Bennett. "He was such a quality guy; he could block shots; he could rebound; he could take it in the lane."

But with the returning talent on Bennett's 1991-92 team, he chose to redshirt both players. They bonded instantly with teammates and learned from the core Bennett had groomed.

"The first day we're playing pickup, everybody's kind of like, 'Ooh, he (Nordgaard) is pretty good!' He's dunking on people and not backing down from anyone," remembers Eric LeDuc. "We played physical, guys had a little bit of an attitude, and he just stepped right up and was like, 'Nah, I'm not backing down to anybody. I'm good.' "

Jeff Nordgaard puts up a shot against Butler during the UWGB's 74-64 victory on December 12, 1992. (University of Wisconsin-Green Bay Archives)

Meanwhile, Grzesk was busy soaking up what he could from Tony Bennett and Ben Johnson.

"You're there practicing, and you're learning even by watching," Grzesk says. "That was a pretty special group with great leaders."

It was Johnson who Grzesk's game most resembled, and as Johnson's career came to a close, both saw an opportunity to continue a legacy.

"I think what really good leaders do is they know that it's not about them, but it's what they leave behind," says Johnson. "I just thought it was really important that someone continue what we had done, and I knew Gary was a similar player to me, and I knew he could handle the heat. He could handle the pressure. He could handle the expectations and demands that Coach was going to have for the program and on him."

"At the end of the banquet that year (1991-92), all the seniors get up and say their senior speeches," Grzesk recalls. "And Ben kind of looked over to me and said, 'G, you're the next me.' "

"He knew exactly what that meant," notes Johnson. "He took it and ran with it, and did a lot better job than I did, because they were amazing after Tony and I and Vander Plas. We kind of lit the torch and they kept it going and took it to another level."

"He was kind of passing the torch of that defensive role player to me, although Ben was much more complete than I ever was," Grzesk says. "But I kind of saw myself in the same role as Ben Johnson."

1992-93 Freshman Recruiting, Part 2

Grzesk and Nordgaard were ready for action in 1992-93 following their redshirt season. Joining those two would be a pair of true freshmen, creating a foursome that would become the most successful class in school history.

The first signing came in the fall of 1991 when Bennett went after Milwaukee Rufus King High School's point guard, Eric Jackson. There were a number of potential hurdles in signing Jackson, not the least of which was his rising stock as a point guard for the defending state champions. Further, Jackson was a 3.4 GPA student looking for an engineering program, which UWGB could not offer.

Jackson was a top talent, and seeing an opportunity to snag him, Marquette offered him a scholarship in October 1991. But insiders knew Jackson was keen on the Phoenix, respecting the levels to which the program had risen.

"With Eric, we recruited hard, got him up, and his father was a coach and we sold the family on that," Bennett says.

In possibly the biggest recruiting coup of Bennett's career, Jackson spurned the Marquette offer to sign with UWGB. The Phoenix had not only landed a top-notch recruit within the state, but they had also to beaten out Marquette to do so.

"Eric Jackson was probably as critical of a piece as any," Grzesk states. "To get an African-American kid from the Milwaukee city schools to come to Green Bay when he had multiple Division I offers was really pretty amazing."

As he had the year before, Bennett waited until the end of the year to lock up his second spot, this time with an undervalued Ben Berlowski of Janesville Craig High School in southern Wisconsin. Of all of the incoming freshmen, Berlowski was most familiar with UWGB before being arriving.

"I went up to a basketball camp in eighth grade, and I saw Dick Bennett and Tony for the first time," Berlowski explains. "I saw Tony do dribbling drills, shooting drills, and I was absolutely in awe. I came back to Janesville, and people would make fun of me because I said, 'Tony's going to be one of the best (high school) basketball players in the state.'"

As a sophomore at Janesville Craig, Berlowski, a 6-2 guard, was playing with major Division I talent. Three of Berlowski's older teammates went on to play college ball: Robb Logterman would join Marquette in 1990-91, and brothers Jim and Dave Jackson would play at Virginia Tech.

Berlowski had learned to be scrappy against that level of talent. While he first stirred interest within the Phoenix coaching staff at a BC All-Star Camp, the excitement was fleeting. At the start of his senior year, Bennett's staff sent him a rejection letter.

"They said they thought I wasn't tall enough. They thought I was a little bit bigger, but I wasn't as big as they thought. And I lacked lateral quickness," Berlowski recalls. "I was *pissed*. I was furious. Like, lateral quickness? What the (bleep) is lateral quickness? So I played my senior year with a chip on my shoulder."

By January, time was running out for Berlowski.

"I wanted to play Division I basketball so bad, and the only way I knew I could get there was to try and get to the state tournament," he says.

As luck would have it, Janesville Craig did make the state tournament, where the Cougars ended up playing, of all teams, Milwaukee Rufus King and Eric Jackson. Berlowski had a strong performance in a losing effort, re-igniting Bennett's interest.

"Dick Bennett called up Eric and said, 'What do you think of this guy?' and Eric's like, 'Shit, I'd rather play *with* this guy than against him,'" Berlowski says.

With an endorsement from Jackson, Bennett extended the offer to Berlowski, who didn't have to think twice.

"I knew I wanted to play for Dick Bennett always," he says. "I wanted to be part of that family. I had a chance."

Fast Friends

With Grzesk, Nordgaard, Jackson, and Berlowski all in hand, Bennett had merged a four-man freshman class who were all were slated to play in 1992-93. Bolstering the likelihood of success, all four bonded quickly.

It began with Grzesk and Nordgaard.

"It was already set up he was going to be living with a couple upperclassmen and I was going to be living in the dorm with Logan (Vander Velden)," remembers Nordgaard. "Gary and I then went four more years and were roommates the rest of the four years, and it was great."

Berlowski and Jackson also immediately clicked.

"Eric Jackson and I had a great relationship. We roomed together," recalls Berlowski, "I would play Air Supply or my music, and he's like, 'Man, let's get some real music here,' and he'd be blasting Tupac and NWA and everything else. We'd play Super Tecmo Bowl for hours, talking trash. We had just a lot of good memories sitting around, hanging out, bonding – and just philosophizing."

The two pairs came together largely due to state tournament encounters with Grzesk. In 1991, Grzesk's Wauwatosa East squad had eliminated Berlowski's Janesville Craig team from the state tournament, a game that turned on a critical foul Berlowski committed near the end.

Jackson's Milwaukee King team then got the best of Grzesk's undefeated Tosa East squad in the championship, an outcome saved by a critical Jackson three-pointer.

"When Eric moved into the dorms in Green Bay, he was putting up posters on the wall, and there was one from the *Milwaukee Journal*," notes Grzesk. "It was a picture of his game-tying three-pointer at the (UW) Fieldhouse in the state championship game. "The clock reads 0:00, we're up three points, King is losing by three, and he's holding his follow-through. I had just run by him to contest the shot and I'm kind of looking at the ball in the air, and it was the perfect picture."

"We ended up as great teammates the next four years together, so I think we all jelled and got along pretty well pretty quickly," concludes Grzesk.

The four became tight. "We hung out a lot," Nordgaard says. "Us four together was a nice crew."

Filling Out the Roster

Bennett added two final pieces to that recruiting class. First, he signed Sam Maddox, a 6-5 forward from Ohio. Maddox was a wiry player with good athleticism, and though he had been a sixth man on his high school team, he had managed to get Division I offers from three other schools. Maddox would redshirt his freshman year.

Second, Bennett added Gary Thomas, a rare junior college transfer from Nebraska. Thomas, a 6-3 guard, had been productive, netting 21.6 points and 9 rebounds per game as a JUCO, and impressed Bennett with his scoring mentality.

Heading into the fall, the only roles clearly defined were those of the team's two seniors, post player Larry Hill and forward Dean Rondorf. Hill, the team's top talent, had erupted as a junior and had the makings of a potential first-team all-conference player and dark horse NBA prospect.

"My very first day at GB, I went down the lane and tried to do one of my finger rolls that I would get away with all the time in high school, and Larry Hill put that in like the fifth row," Berlowski says. "And then I tried to do it again, and he did the same thing. And I'm like, 'Alright man, this is a different level.' "

"I had every belief that if he didn't play in the NBA, he was for sure going to have a long, long successful career in Europe, because he was a legit 6-7, 6-8, long arms, and just strong," remarks LeDuc.

Dean Rondorf was also looking to build on a strong 1991-92 campaign, and was sure to be one of the offensive focal points of the team. But behind Hill and Rondorf, the team was very green.

"We had a good class of the Jeremy Ludvigsons, the Eric LeDucs. And Jeff Nordgaard was, I believe, a redshirt freshman that year," Rondorf says. "There were guys that were there, but not a lot of guys who had a lot of playing time. And so it was all kind of new."

We're Talking About Practice

Dick Bennett was always been maniacally focused on perfecting the basics and playing fundamental basketball. And he believed that effort starts with practice.

"Though our style was very simple, and just based on execution, it's a hard way to play," noted Bennett, "Everybody knew who we were, they knew how we played, and we weren't going to outthink anybody. We had to out-execute them. And that's a hard way to go. It's a pure way to play and it's not so talent-oriented, it's system-oriented. It's very team-oriented, and that runs against the grain for a number of guys."

"I know it's gotten criticized over the years, but our style is made to win at that level against the superior competition," notes Tony Bennett.

"We just (never) beat ourselves," adds Grzesk. "We were very sound defensively, we took care of the basketball, took good shots. It's a lot of coach talk, but it's what wins games and ultimately what wins championships."

"He wanted such value in taking care of the basketball, making sure you get the best look and the best shot. Get the ball into the guys' hands who've got the best chance of making it from a percentage standpoint," notes Berlowski. "How Dick Bennett taught us, with angles, and taking care of the basketball and closing out, contesting every shot, and boxing out, doing these little things."

Bennett was so committed to excelling at those little things that he created a "Winner's Chart," where he tracked items that did not show up on a standard stat sheet. Bennett would tally those metrics, and at the year-end banquet, he would hand out various accolades like the Ball Pressures Award, the Shot Challenges Award, the Screener Award, the Charges-Taken Award, and others, motivating players who may not have had a scoring role on the team.

"You quickly picked up on how to play Dick Bennett basketball," Ludvigson says. "How to play physical, how to play hard, help defense."

In spite of his straightforward strategy, most recruits were shocked by the transition from high school to Bennett Ball. Tony Bennett is the first to admit the transition from high school to college was difficult: "I don't think you can prepare – even as I lived it and watched it – then all of the sudden you go there, and it's the intensity, the volume of work, how hard it is."

"I went to one of (Bennett's) camps at UW-Stevens Point and sat in a defensive stance for a week straight," Dean Vander Plas says sarcastically, "so I knew what I was getting myself into."

But, as Mike Karisny notes, "Practices became like a dry-run for the games. If you had a bad week of practice, you weren't playing. It was so important to him to form things that he wanted. He used those as dress rehearsals."

"Nothing is ever half-way," explains LeDuc. "The message that was loud and clear from the first day I got there is don't bother showing up if you think you're going to coast today. You're going to get ran right over if you think this is going to be half-ass effort day. It was a frustrating thing sometimes with Dick, where it was not about the result, it was about the process."

On top of the already-challenging practice regime was the fact that Bennett was rebuilding with inexperienced talent. Throw in an NCAA rule change pushing back organized practices from October 15 to November 1, and the fall of 1992 was setting up to be a nightmare for the Phoenix players.

"That's when they moved the date back like fifteen days," remembers Berlowski, "so Dick Bennett felt we had to get double the work. So my first experience was two-a-days. I felt like I was in a military boot camp."

The daily schedule became an almost unwieldy grind for many.

"We're up at 5 a.m., we're back there at 4 p.m.," relates Ludvigson. "You get up at 4 a.m., you're getting yelled at, working your butt off, you're going all day, you come back, do it again. Nine, 10 o'clock at night you get home, you go to bed, and you get up and do it again. That was hard. I mean that was really hard."

"I remember our 6 a.m. workouts, preseason, just getting up and doing aerobics and cardio. Oh my gosh, those were brutal," recalls LeMoine. "Just brutal."

Jeff Zavada was no fan, either, "I don't get going until the last fifteen minutes of practice, and by then he's been yelling at me for an hour and fifteen minutes."

The result was the most intense preseason of practices the university had ever seen.

"We got our asses worked off in the preseason. I mean, we were like a track team," says Ludvigson. "We ran and ran and ran and ran. I think Coach Bennett knew we weren't going to be that good, so it was tough."

Over The Edge

The most significant moment of the 1992-93 season took place before a single game was played. Just two weeks into practices and without any warning, Larry Hill quit the team.

"All of the sudden, he stopped showing up for morning practices," Berlowski says. "He wasn't answering his phone or whatever, and we're worried about him."

"I can remember distinctly going to his house after practice and just being like, 'What the hell, dude? What are you doing?' And he's like, 'I don't think I want to do it,' " says LeDuc.

"We tried to convince him to stay, to come back, but he had to walk away. If that's what he felt he had to do, that's what he had to do," says Vander Velden.

The move was disheartening for all, but none more so than his remaining original classmate, Dean Rondorf.

"Certainly for selfish reasons, I wanted Larry to be there. But I think as a team, we wanted Larry to be there too because we had spent so much time with him and he was such a big part of our life, and just, you know we all loved him."

"What killed it for him was we had 5:30, 6 o'clock practices," notes Nordgaard. "He wasn't waking up at that time. And truthfully, there were plenty of classes missed by a lot of us because we had to go to basketball practice at 6, and instead of going to our 8 o'clock or our 9 o'clock, we went home and slept. It was a failure, I think."

The departure of Larry Hill destroyed all expectations surrounding the 1992-93 team. Gone were the top four scorers from the year before (Bennett, Martinez, Hill, Johnson), along with one of the team's top rising talents (Smith). The only sure thing was Rondorf, the team's eldest leader.

"Dean definitely stepped up," says Ludvigson. "We ran a timed mile at the beginning of every year, and I think he was the first one in. You could tell he was working on it, and he was going to be a leader."

After Rondorf, the team had little identity and even less experience.

"Once you realize it's going to be hard to have a really successful season, your goals adjust accordingly," states Dick Bennett. "We hoped that some of our younger players would develop, and that we would continue to recruit."

One of the few silver linings was that the door was open for the freshmen, and in particular the freshman guards, to step up.

Notes Grzesk: "We kind of got pressed into a point guard by committee with myself and Eric Jackson that year, which was good."

Bucky Sighting

It took just one game for UWGB to appreciate that 1992-93 was unlike its past few seasons. A road affair against Southeast Missouri State was close late in the second half.

"I remember sitting there at one of the timeouts and talking to Jeremy (Ludvigson) and being like, 'Well, we're going to win, you know, we always win these games. It's always close, and in the last 3-4 minutes, we figure out a way to win by five, win by seven,' " says LeDuc. "And we lost ... I remember just kind of looking at each other after the game and being like, 'Holy shit, we actually lost a game? How did that happen?' "

The team couldn't dwell on the loss, as its next opponent game was the Wisconsin Badgers. The same Wisconsin Badgers program that had steadfastly refused to play UWGB for more than a decade.

"When Tony was playing, we were probably the best team in the state, at least that's what people thought and we sure felt that way," states Dick Bennett. "I really wanted to play both Marquette and Wisconsin, and they would not play us in those years."

"I don't think they wanted to play us because they weren't as talented," adds Rondorf. "I believe we could've beat them with the Vander Plas teams, all four years that Tony was there, or at least two or three of the years that he was there."

"We were upset, still *are* upset (30 years later). Because for us, we were the young, snotty nose, little brother," reflects Ben Johnson. "We were really good, and we would've loved to have had an opportunity to play against Marquette or Wisconsin during that stretch of time. But you know, it's not what the ADs wanted to see happen, that's for sure."

With the Phoenix's best team graduating, the Badgers' athletic department finally relented amid public pressure, agreeing to a matchup in early 1992. It was long-awaited satisfaction for the Phoenix coaching staff.

"What it means is more important than the game itself. It means they respect us enough to want to play us," Bennett said at the time.

Assistant coach and scheduling manager Woody Wilson echoed that message. "They said they respected our program and thought it would be good basketball in our state, and they took the step to do it."

With the game finally on the books, Bennett had to face the reality that his team was overmatched. "Wisconsin had a good team, and we were afraid – we were concerned that we were going to get blown out."

But that didn't mean the Phoenix weren't chomping at the bit for the opportunity.

"Your blood gets flowing and you get a little more emotional," remarked Rondorf. "I think that's what this program needs and Wisconsin needs."

"The chance to play both (Wisconsin and Marquette) was big, especially for us Wisconsin players," recalls Vander Velden. "Those schools being as big as they are, being prominent, and how you always want to play, I think first at Wisconsin, second at Marquette. Maybe not being recruited by them puts a little chip on your shoulder. And being able to go play them and show them what you've got is always good."

Despite a surprising opening-game loss to lowly Loyola (Chicago), the talent scale tipped dramatically in the Badgers' favor. Junior guard Tracy Webster was outstanding and freshman post player Rashard Griffith was certain to be a load, but the true gem was sophomore sensation Michael Finley.

"Michael Finley was a phenomenal player, we knew right away that he was going to be an NBA ball player," says Berlowski. "They had a lot of good talent."

The Wisconsin Fieldhouse was nearly full with 11,494 fans for the intrastate matchup, many being friends and family of the Phoenix. When it finally came to show time, UWGB channeled its years of pent-up emotion and produced an outstanding effort from a group of relative unknowns. The young Phoenix team showed significant resolve, and on this night, played defensive like a typical Dick Bennett club. UWGB was patient on offense and exploited an advantage in the post, where Zavada was able to routinely get excellent position on the block.

In addition, Nordgaard flashed some impressive offensive skills, scoring six points in two minutes, including a nifty layup and a long two-pointer. The latter put the Phoenix on top 32-30 with the first half winding to a close. And though the Badgers ultimately snatched the lead back as the half expired, UWGB was hanging tough with the Big Ten big brother.

The Phoenix continued to leverage Zavada in the second half and Rondorf caught fire. The score remained close, leaving the Phoenix right where it wanted to be heading into the stretch.

With under 2:00 to play, UWGB had a one-point lead and the ball. The favorite was on the ropes. But, as so often happened during this era, for-

Freshman sharpshooter Ben Berlowski puts up a jumper during UWGB's 68-47 triumph over Eastern Illinois on February 1, 1993, at the Brown County Arena. (University of Wisconsin-Green Bay Archives)

tunes turned with the squelch of a whistle.

On this occasion, Rondorf set up to post on the left side of the floor against Jason Johnson. Johnson tried a swim move over Rondorf's left shoulder and locked Rondorf between his arm and body, pulling Rondorf to the floor. Johnson had initiated the contact, but the official standing on the baseline sprinted in and signaled Rondorf for the offensive foul.

"It was a bad call. It was right in front of our bench, and they called me for a push off," recalls Rondorf. "I just remember thinking, 'Are you kidding me? I cannot believe you're making that call right now.'"

Johnson's first free throw attempt bounced off the back of the rim, touched the top of the backboard, and floated through the net. His second attempt missed, but there was a tie-up on the rebound and Wisconsin retained possession. Webster got the ball alone on the wing for a three-pointer, giving the Badgers a 68-65 lead with 53 seconds to play.

UWGB managed a pair of possessions with a chance to tie the game, but came up empty both times, falling to Wisconsin 70-65 in an outcome that was much closer than anticipated.

"We were very competitive against them, so it reinforced what we were doing," Bennett recalls. "We were worthy. Had we been at home, I think we would have won. Let's put it this way: we didn't get any breaks."

But for the team's senior leader, the missed opportunity stung.

"I didn't get recruited at Wisconsin. I don't think anyone on Green Bay's team ever got recruited at Wisconsin," Rondorf says. "You always think that you're just as good as these guys. We had the opportunity to do it, and didn't."

The Phoenix followed up the Wisconsin loss with a nightmarish 25-point whipping at Colorado. It was the team's worst loss in five years, and gave Bennett's team an 0-3 record for the first time since 1986-87.

"The worst butt-kicking I ever experienced," remembers Ludvigson, "It was like a layup line. These guys from Colorado were going up, tapping their shoes, dunking it, going off the backboard, dunking it. It was ugly."

"Just got our asses kicked," admits LeDuc. "I had been familiar with that feeling at Army, but that was the first time at Green Bay where I can remember, too, Going back to the hotel that night thinking, 'Man, that's a really crappy feeling. I don't want to do this anymore. We just can't get embarrassed.' "

Explosive Personality

The strain of the season was wearing on Bennett, and he took it out on his team. During a December 12, 1992, home game against Butler, Grzesk was handling the ball when a mental error drew a very public reprimand from his coach.

"I got a long rebound, and rather than milk the shot clock and run the clock down, I don't know what I was thinking, but I went down on a fast break and I thought I saw a Green Bay player out of the corner of my eye. I just threw a pass and luckily it went off the defender and out of bounds, so it was still our ball," remembers Grzesk.

The harmless outcome aside, Bennett was intolerant of the mental error.

"The whistle blew and the arena was kind of quiet and everyone was wondering what I was doing. And almost at the top of his lungs, he yelled, 'Goddamnit Grzesk!' And literally you can hear about 5,000 people in the arena kind of go, 'Oooo,' all at the same time," Grzesk says.

The Phoenix won the game 76-64, but Bennett's screams had been significant enough to be picked up by the *Green Bay Press-Gazette*, which ran a story about the intensity of the moment. For his part, Grzesk harbored no ill will, noting, "I didn't have a problem with him yelling at me because it was a terrible play at a critical time, and we were fortunate to get the ball back and win that game."

The moment was a public example of the overflowing passion Bennett had for perfection. "I had a temper that had a very short fuse, particularly during basketball games," Bennett admits. "I was not in the habit of swearing. To this day, I don't. But the times I have ... my vocabulary shrunk, and it was limited to very undesirable words in the heat of the game."

You wouldn't hear any disagreement from his players.

"There were times where his emotions would get the best of him, and a lot of it was kind of actually kind of funny at the time," John Martinez says.

"He just really cared and had that passion about basketball. And I love it, because I felt the same way."

"People asked me what it was like playing for Coach Bennett. I say it was like Bobby Knight without the swearing," Nordgaard says. "For most guys, he was a negative motivator, meaning he would tell you how bad you are in order to make you mad at him to show you how much better you are than he thinks you are. And it worked for a lot of us."

"As kind as he is off the court, behind the scenes and at practice, people should understand that this was a tough guy to play for," states Karisny. "Fair, but very, very, very tough."

Fueled by his intensity was the coach's Lombardi-esque pursuit of perfection, a lofty ambition that took its toll on his players and his health.

"His expectations of practice were that you were in two places at the same time. You help and you recover. And you know if you don't do that, he's yelling at you," remembers Ludvigson. "The natural thing to say is, 'Well come on, how can I possibly do both?' But he expected you to do both."

"It bothered him when his teams weren't perfect. He took it personally and it affected his health. It affected who he was," notes Rondorf. "He certainly had the nervous energy."

"He had a hard time sitting still at pre-game meals," adds Johnson. "He could barely sit with us and eat, because if anyone giggled or laughed, it'd like be you committed a sin. And, 'You're not ready to play, you're weren't focused, you're not ready to go.' You know, all of that. Like, 'Coach, you know, Martinez just cracked a joke. It's eight hours before the game, you know? Just enjoying?' But no."

With the least-experienced, least-disciplined, and least-talented team he had endured in nearly five years, 1992-93 nearly pushed Dick Bennett to the brink.

Officially Rebuilding

The Butler win was part of a nice four-game win streak the club put together between December 10 and the end of the calendar year. At 4-3, the Phoenix enjoyed its brief moment over the .500 mark. But this Phoenix team was young and inconsistent, and the joy proved short-lived.

Entering the conference schedule, UWGB still carried enough clout to be picked to finish in the top half, but below the conference favorites Wright State, Illinois-Chicago, and Cleveland State. Nevertheless, the first five games saw the Phoenix rack up losses at Cleveland State, at Northern Illinois, and at future Mid-Continent Conference brethren UW-Milwaukee, as well as a home loss against the new-look UIC Flames.

Unlike any Bennett team since 1988-89, this Phoenix team was finding ways to lose, rather than win close games. The poor conference start put the Phoenix at 5-7, looking up at nearly everyone in the conference. On the positive side, Bennett had extreme latitude to try out lineups and build experience with his core group.

Rondorf, as expected, carried the offensive load, scoring 20+ points in four of the first five games. Zavada's play was more inconsistent, but when he flashed, he did so brightly, averaging 12 points over the first seven games.

Bennett also saw his freshmen gaining confidence. For starters, Grzesk had taken the reigns from Johnson and quickly assumed the mantle as the best lockdown defender on the team. Meanwhile, true freshman Eric Jackson was also bagging quality starts, nearly matching Grzesk on the defensive end. While Grzesk and Jackson helped keep the scores low, neither provided much offensive production.

"It was really hard to play when nobody would guard your starting backcourt," observes LeDuc. "They would just leave them both and dare them – just say, 'Hey, if you want to shoot, go ahead and shoot.'"

That's where the other two freshmen stepped up. Nordgaard had a strong showing against the Badgers and was rewarded with a string of starts. He responded with double digits scoring in four of his next five games. Meanwhile, Berlowski was proving to be a capable shooter, scoring in double figures in each of the four nonconference wins. And Berlowski hated to have his abilities questioned.

"Probably one of the most famous quotes that (Bennett and Heideman) had was, 'If you want Ben Berlowski to do something, tell him he can't do something,' " Berlowski says. "I knew I could play at that level, but I also know that I had to do a lot of work. I wasn't the fastest, I couldn't dribble

Jeff Nordgaard looks to score during UWGB's 67-47 victory over Youngstown State on February 27, 1993. (University of Wisconsin-Green Bay Archives)

the best. The one thing I could do – I could work on – was shoot the basketball."

Along with the maturation of his freshmen, Bennett saw the transcendence of Logan Vander Velden. Bennett had opted move the 6-9 junior from his interior post to the perimeter, a decision that set the groundwork for the natural shooter's career growth.

"I had primarily played more of like a four position, and they came to me looking for more scoring. They essentially moved me to a three," explains Vander Velden. "I was more comfortable with it personally, but I also believe it propelled me to my career after college."

The move gave Vander Velden a size mismatch over most small forwards and a skills mismatch compared to power forwards and centers. And it played to his preference of facing the basket.

The move helped UWGB course-correct midseason. With an 0-5 record in games decided by seven points or less, the Phoenix looked to be on pace to drop its sixth against Western Illinois on January 25, 1993. Trailing by three points with under two minutes to play, and as Bennett summarized, "It looked bleak."

That's when Vander Velden took over, first hitting a three-pointer, and then scoring on a second-chance opportunity to give UWGB the lead, 63-61 with 42 seconds left. After a Leatherneck three-pointer, the ball was back in Vander Velden's hands with a chance to finish it off.

"We actually ran the play wrong," Vander Velden says of the fateful possession. "They set the screen on the baseline, so I ended up just going with it. I ended up getting it and hitting the shot."

The 65-64 win was a morale booster, and in a season definable by chunks of games, it helped UWGB put together four more wins in its next five attempts.

A Learning Experience

UWGB split a pair of games during the week of February 15, putting its season mark at 11-9 heading into its other state showdown, this time at Marquette. The Warriors were having an excellent season, and at 18-4, came into the game ranked No. 24 in the country. In his fourth season with the program, Kevin O'Neill had his team clicking toward the NCAA Tournament.

The game was televised on ESPN with Dan Patrick back for another broadcast, but this affair was in front of 14,500 fans at the Bradley Center in Milwaukee and turned out much differently than the Butler game had a year prior.

"The Bradley Center was a different kind of animal to play in. It was an NBA arena," says LeDuc. "I just remember right from the beginning, being like, 'Ooh, we're kind of in trouble here.'"

Rondorf led UWGB scorers with a measly 11 points, while no one else scored in double digits. It was a pathetic affair, with Marquette gliding to an easy 17-point victory. The game proved most memorable for the fans' treatment of former Marquette player Jeff Zavada. They cursed and harassed Zavada, who had an anemic one point in fifteen minutes of action. That behavior irked Bennett, who lashed out afterwards.

"I respect Marquette's coaches and players, but I don't like the people up in the stands calling our kid 'asshole.' That's very poor, particularly when it's a state kid."

The visibility of it – clearly audible on the ESPN broadcast – forced Marquette's AD, Bill Cords, to issue a public apology.

"I talked to (the fans) and said, 'Jeff Zavada is a great kid and doesn't deserve this kind of treatment,'" remarked Cords. "I couldn't get to all of them, but we tried. That is not reflective of Marquette University."

At 11-10 and with a 7-5 conference record, UWGB somehow remained mathematically alive in the race for second place in the Mid-Continent Conference. But a woeful 2-3 mark over the final five games left the Phoenix at a pedestrian 13-13 overall. At 9-7 in conference, UWGB finished fourth for the first time since 1988-89. The season came to a merciful end in the first round of the conference tournament at the hands of UIC in a 46-43 loss.

It was a tough way for Rondorf, the last of Bennett's great 1988 recruiting class, to depart. Rondorf had finally reached his potential as a top-flight scorer and had done his best to lead a floundering team.

"Smart player, very mobile, very smooth. He really was a good player," Bennett says. "I've always enjoyed Dean. He's really a good guy, neat kid. We just didn't have enough to support, to compete successfully."

One of the few silver linings in the tournament game had been Grzesk's play. He shut down the Flames' quick-as-lightning Kenny Williams, holding him to 3-of-15 shooting and a mere 11 points.

"The two games during the regular season, he just torched us and torched me," notes Grzesk. "And then I finally had a good game against him defensively, and I think that gave me some confidence and momentum going into the next three years."

That confidence was a supplement to the intangibles his coach already loved about him.

"Coach Bennett always appreciated two things," Grzesk says. "One, that I played soccer, that I had good footwork, good feet, could move my feet laterally; two, that I was left-handed, so if I was going against a right-handed shooter, it was natural for me to contest with my left hand because it was right there."

Building confidence upon his burgeoning skill set, it appeared Grzesk had indeed taken the baton from Ben Johnson and would be the Phoenix's defensive stopper of the future.

The What-Ifs

UWGB predictably suffered without Tony Bennett, a rare blue-chip player at a mid-major program. Add in the losses of Tory Smith, Larry Hill, and John Martinez, and the 1992-93 team had lacked direction and star-level talent.

"We could play tough at certain times, but we just didn't have a very good team, didn't have the experience, didn't have the leadership," notes Ludvigson.

It wasn't only the loss of key players that factored into the poor season. The program's architect had lost some of his own focus.

"I think Coach Bennett would even say that was probably his worst year as a head coach, because he was partially focused on our team, but also really focused on Tony's career with the (Charlotte) Hornets," comments Grzesk. "We had a lot of close losses and a lot of young guys that were playing, but we never really kind of hit our stride and there was a lot of parity on that team."

Bennett conceded as much a year later. "I was distracted last year more than any year I coached. I was not consistent with the players."

Decades later, Bennett admitted he was having doubts about his ability to resurrect the program.

"We were really down in terms of experience and we just kind of muddled through that year," he says. "I was a little concerned that maybe we had seen our best years. There was a transition where we were without the new group, and of course most of the old group was gone. So, it tends to happen. It's not as easy to reload as they often say at that level."

Bennett had built the pyre in the late 1980s, watched it burn brightly through Tony's era, and seen it quickly wane in 1992-93. He'd added more than enough fuel in the past few years, and now sat back, hoping the coals and sparks were enough to keep the program aflame for years to come.

"It was a trying year," notes Martinez, who spent the season rehabbing. "At the same time, though, once that season ended, a lot of people were looking ahead optimistically for the next year."

"We certainly learned from those experiences, and it made us better the following three years going through it," adds Grzesk. "It was certainly very difficult to go through and have that type of season, but it was also probably the turning point and what led us to have success the following three years."

Whether he believed it or not, Dick Bennett was succeeding in building character, leadership, and selflessness within his program. Impressively, the impact of his Green Bay Way was observable and envied by other coaches, the best of whom sought to learn it from Bennett during this time.

"(Bowling Green coach) Jim Larranaga spent quite a bit of time with Coach Bennett learning about our program and the principles, and then (Butler coach) Barry Collier did the same thing," Grzesk points out. "And you look at what Coach Larranaga did at George Mason after that, and then what Barry Collier did at Butler and turned it over to the following coaches. I think Coach Bennett laid the blueprint out for those guys on how to build one of the best mid-major programs in the country."

"They always call it the Green Bay Way, you know where he introduced those (five core) pillars," states Tony Bennett. "It went from Collier, and then Collier was the AD, and then there were a couple of coaches and then Brad Stevens, and then they called it the Butler Way. Everyone knows about the Butler Way and all that, but that's all from the pillars. They have the five pillars, and that meeting that my dad had with how you build your program."

Tony took the same teachings with him on his coaching journey.

"All those words that Tony says at Virginia," notes Berlowski, "those are all the five principles that his dad gave us at GB. And they're up on the walls at Virginia."

"That's why when I watch Virginia, and I watch the way Tony handles himself, I feel like I'm a part of the Cavalier program," says Vander Plas. "Tony's preaching those same things, and he's going to send people out into the world in a better way than he found them."

Chapter 14

Senior Leadership
(1993-94 - Part 1)

There are few advantages that mid-major programs have, but one place where the little guys have an edge is in relative roster certainty. Mid-majors rarely lose talent to the professional ranks prior to graduation, and while transfers are a risk, few of their players are looking beyond their college careers.

The best coaches exploit this to the fullest, utilizing redshirts, building character, and developing experiences to exploit the advantages that fourth- and fifth-year seniors bring: calm, cool, and collected experience.

The Pack Is Back

The city of Green Bay was abuzz in the spring of 1993, and for the first time in recent memory, it had nothing to do with the Phoenix. The 1992 Green Bay Packers had rebounded from a horrific 1991 to finish the season a shocking 9-7, captained by a second-year kid from Kiln, Mississippi. Brett Favre had replaced the injured Don Majkowski in the team's third game and never looked back, leading the league's signature franchise to just its second winning season in ten years. A bona fide quarterback was half the equation, but hopes skyrocketed when the Packers' general manager, Ron Wolf, landed the NFL's top free agent, Reggie White, in April 1993.

While the Packers were on the rise, optimism about the Phoenix program had been waning since Tony Bennett's class had moved on. Ben Berlowski remembers feeling the chill in the fall of 1992 as his family drove south.

"We stopped at Oshkosh at this sporting goods store, and they had some gear there. They had a couple of UWGB sweatshirts, one was a medium, one was a small. I said, 'Do you guys have any other or more Green Bay gear here?' And the guy says, 'Oh, we're not going to re-order anything. Tony Bennett graduated, they'll never be good again ... Tony, the whole crew's gone, they're done.'"

The 1993-94 UWGB roster included a mix of senior leaders and underclassmen ready to step forward. Back row from left: Eric Jackson (12), Chris Westlake (10), Luke Madsen (14), Gary Grzesk (22), Sam Maddox (21), Ben Berlowski (34), John Martinez (20); Front row: Jeff Nordgaard (33), Jeff Zavada (55), Logan Vander Velden (32), Eric LeDuc (52), Jeremy Ludvigson (44), Pete Wade (30). (University of Wisconsin-Green Bay Archives)

Part of the lack of enthusiasm sprang from the fact that the roster for the 1993-94 UWGB team looked disturbingly similar to that from the dismal 1992-93 team. But bubbling below the surface were three developments that foreshadowed a change: a unique chemistry formed between the fifth-year seniors and talented sophomores, a healthy John Martinez, and the rare addition of a junior college transfer.

Development 1: Seniors and Sophomores

It was a rarity to find a team loaded not just with five seniors, but with five *fifth-year* seniors, all of whom were contributors, leaders, and mentors. That the 1993-94 Phoenix was constructed precisely in this way was hardly a product of chance, but rather the anticipated result of Dick Bennett's deliberate planning.

"I like to grow kids into the program ... let them grow up together," he explains. "They're possibly, probably going to lose, but if they're good kids – and that was clearly our obligation to find good people who had enough talent and that we could bring them together and mold them a little bit – they would grow from the good and the bad."

As Martinez points out, this was one of the few advantages mid-majors had in evening the playing field with the big boys. "Being a mid-major, guys stay around until they're seniors. There's not any one-and-dones coming through Green Bay, so you're going to have a bunch of guys that have played many years together, that believe in each other and the system. When you get all of those things working at the same time, you're going to have a really good basketball team."

Tony Bennett learned this lesson and deployed it in his own coaching career: "It certainly started at Green Bay. Whether it's redshirts or kids getting into their upperclassmen years, that's how we can compete against the Dukes and the Carolinas. That maturity level and having those guys who see that, who have character, I think that's your chance."

"You've got to develop guys, and keep them in the program, redshirt them, keep them for five years, and by the time they're fourth-year juniors and fifth-year seniors, you've got some kids that came in as 6-5, 195, and now they're 6-7, 225. And you've developed some skill," notes Eric LeDuc. "We had a lot of guys that had known each other since maybe we were sixteen, seventeen, and had all kind of grown up together, at least to that point had had some success, had some tough times, and kind of looked at like, 'Okay, this is kind of our time.'"

Not only were the Phoenix loaded with senior leadership, those seniors took ownership and accountability over the destiny of the program, forging titanium-strength bonds with the underclassmen, and in particular, the quartet of sophomores.

"With the leadership we had from the five seniors, I was convinced that we could play with anybody," recalls Berlowski, a sophomore on that team. "The one thing with those guys that was very unique is that we did pull very close together as a group. We all hung out together a lot, so that was always good."

"That's a strong five, and two of them were real leaders," notes Jeff Nordgaard another of the sophomores. "Jeremy (Ludvigson) and Eric (LeDuc) were real leaders."

"Those two guys (Ludvigson and LeDuc) were the best talkers on the defensive end that I've ever been around," agrees fellow sophomore Gary Grzesk. "They would be talking and talking and talking on every possession, so there would never be any miscommunication on matchups or who was helping on certain screens, or where your help was on the defensive end."

"We were of one mind. Everybody was unselfish," states Ludvigson. "Nobody cared who scored. Everybody was equally respected and worked hard and had a voice. When we would come together at the end of practices and put our arms in, it was a one-unit feel, down to the last man. Everybody, *everybody*, got along that year. Managers, walk-ons, everybody liked each other, everybody got along."

"The year before we had been through the ringer together," remembers senior Logan Vander Velden. "By the time that we were seniors, we had a pretty tight-knit team. And I think that year more than any, we were all really close. We did everything together."

Development 2: Here's Johnny

By the summer of 1993, one of those senior leaders, John Martinez, was finally healthy and looked better than ever.

"I think it was the best summer basketball that we had in all my years there," he recalls. "I remember that summer in particular, the games were just another level compared to the previous summers."

"John's biggest attribute was that he made the game easier for everyone else," LeDuc explains. "He was great at getting into the little cracks, and those little dump off passes for a layup. He was just awesome at that."

Even a broken nose he suffered in a collision with Eric Jackson in July couldn't keep Martinez off the court. The time away had given him a new-found purpose, and he felt like everything was clicking.

"(Rehab) was difficult to deal with because you're so used to being around the guys all the time and practicing and playing. (But by summer 1993), I was playing at probably the highest level I've ever played, most confident I've ever played. And I think sitting out for that entire year really helped me mentally to really have the game slow down for me."

Development 3: Ju-Co Rarity

Mid-major coaches often utilize junior college transfers to immediate-ly bolster a lineup with semi-proven college talent. But in Dick Bennett's system of recruit and develop, they were uncommon.

"To interrupt (program continuity) with a JC player can be hard, because you're probably going to replace one of those kids," notes Bennett.

"I think (it conflicts with) the philosophy of redshirting kids," adds Grzesk. "It would make it tough for a kid to come in from junior college and have a great two years."

And yet, the key to the 1993-94 improvement was indeed a rare junior college transfer, Chris Westlake. A 6-3 left-handed guard and the only real addition to the 1993-94 roster, Westlake of-fered UWGB deceptively wicked quickness and skills.

"He was something that we hadn't had at that position really at our time at Green Bay," Marti-nez says. "He was like 6-3, 6-4, a lefty, had a really nice three-point shot, but could get to the basket."

Chris Westlake
(University of Wisconsin-Green Bay Archives)

"Chris was a phenomenal shooter. He had some athleticism that we never really had," notes Berlowski. "Getting to the basket and jumping and dunking on guys. And a white dude doing that, a lefty. He gave us a differ-ent perspective, and he was phenomenal."

That was certainly saying something coming from Berlowski, the play-er most likely to have playing time displaced by Westlake.

"I heard about Chris Westlake through practice many times. You know, 'Berlowski, we have a guy coming here this next year that you won't see the court at all if you don't step up your game!' " recalls Berlowski. "Chris came in and we played in the courtyard, and of course I'm guarding him. And one of the very first times down the court, he jumps basically over the whole team and dunks it, like right on everybody. And right away, everyone looked at me and was like, 'Dude, you ain't getting no time!' "

Westlake's journey to Green Bay started years earlier, when, as a high school athlete in DeKalb, Illinois, he was recruited by then-Evansville as-sistant coach Woody Wilson. Wilson left Evansville before Westlake started, but Westlake stuck with the Purple Aces and had a productive freshman year, shooting 44% from the three-point line.

But when Evansville refused to extend Westlake a scholarship, he chose to sit out one year before joining Rock Valley Junior College in 1992-93. In the meantime, Dick Bennett had added Wilson to his staff at UWGB, and Wilson worked on bringing in Westlake. By the spring of 1993, Bennett realized he needed talent and Westlake had it, so the coach offered him a scholarship.

While UWGB had similarities to the program Westlake had left, there was a glaring difference – the coach.

"Coach Bennett's defensive genius, I guess you'll call it, really allowed you to be in games," Westlake explains. "At Evansville, Coach Cruz was more of an offensive-minded guy and didn't have a complete defensive system. It just wasn't a complete system like Coach Bennett's was."

In contrast to the Phoenix roster, Westlake was more a free spirit, and his "live in the moment" attitude created friction with his controlling coach. The two got off to a rocky start when Bennett invited Westlake to Green Bay during the summer of 1993 to get to know the team. Westlake, focused on his summer job and baseball, never gave the invite a thought. None of that sat well with his coach.

"I got this nasty little short note from him saying that maybe he had made a mistake and, you know, that I wasn't the right guy for their program," recalls Westlake. "He's a competitor, he's trying to win, he's a serious coach, and I'm a young dude who – yeah, I've got some talent, but I'm not a terribly serious person at the time."

And yet, Westlake's talent was undeniable, and he found a home with his new teammates.

"He fit in really well on a personal level. We were all super tight, and from a basketball level, he fit in good. I mean, he was a super talent," says Ludvigson.

Internal Optimism

They may have looked very similar to the 13-14 team from a year before on paper, but by the time the players began practices in October, they were convinced this team had turned a corner.

"We did have a lot of guys back, which could be good or could be bad," remembers Grzesk, "but I think a lot of us improved during that offseason and were certainly motivated to make sure it didn't happen again."

"We had a lot more confidence in each other," comments Berlowski. "We kind of made it this bond and we all worked hard, man. I've got to tell you, all those guys that were on that team, one to twelve, they all put in the work."

Bennett knew he had a special group of players. He eased up on the pressure he'd packed in previous years, relying on his fifth-year seniors to keep the team in line.

"They made a pact that they would not party or drink during the season. And that's quite an accomplishment for a bunch of guys that are going to be seniors in Green Bay," Bennett notes. "They were just incredibly motivated. Just the easiest team that I've ever had to coach. Because of that, and because times were changing, I pretty much let them do whatever they wanted to do."

"We kind of policed ourselves, and all of us kind of developed our own voice," explains LeDuc. "And if he'd start really losing his mind during games, we could essentially tell him to calm down. 'You settle down, we got this.' "

"I don't want to say laid-back, because that might be pushing it," adds Martinez. "He just didn't seem as stressed out. I felt like he enjoyed the team."

For the first time in his coaching career, Bennett even allowed his players to change the team's look.

"We ended up getting black shoes that year, he let us get the names on the back of our jerseys, and he let us design certain warm-ups," notes Martinez. "He just let us do some of the things that he would never have let us do when I first got there in '90."

Healing and Hurting

Martinez wasn't the only one returning from injury. Nordgaard had also endured surgery in the off-season and missed time. And yet, like Martinez, something strange happened when he was injured.

"He came in as a freshman, I remember this gawky, gangly 6-5-and-a-half guy who could barely walk and chew gum," says Ben Johnson. "He really couldn't ... he's not good enough. He's going to have to transfer. He was bad, he just couldn't play."

And then?

"Here's the weird thing – he got hurt. His second year he got hurt, took some time off, I think they casted him up or whatever they did. Then he takes the cast off, and the rest is (history). It's like all the rest and time allowed his body to kind of catch up to his growth plates."

For the first two weeks of practice, it seemed as though Nordgaard and Martinez had both returned stronger, faster, and better than their pre-injury iterations.

That is, until lightning struck a second time on November 11, 1993, less than two weeks before the Phoenix was scheduled to start the season. Martinez, playing at the highest level of his entire career, tore cartilage in his knee that would keep him out of the lineup for at least a few weeks.

"Everybody feels so bad for him," Ludvigson says. "He's such a good player and he's had such bad luck. We can still be good, but let's not kid anybody, his position took us to another level."

To Martinez, the second knee injury was, in a word, devastating.

"That was ten times worse than the original injury," he states. "I remember talking to Coach Heideman specifically and some of the players that I was thinking of quitting the team. My first rehab was the full twelve months. I don't think there was *a day* where I didn't do something to get better with my knee. So when that (second injury) happened, it was like the most deflating feeling. I just felt like it was all over."

Martinez's injury hurt the team's short-term outlook, but it also destroyed any chance Martinez had at joining Tony Bennett in the NBA. Though he hadn't garnered the media buzz Tony had, his coach felt like he had the talent to make it.

"At that point in the NBA time, there was a chance for smaller guards to be looked at," recalls Dick Bennett. "That was a time when John Stockton and Mark Price and a host of other guards were making their mark. John was a very gifted passer and just a good player."

"Before that season, (Coach Bennett) pulled me and Nordgaard aside and he said (he thought we could play in the NBA)," Martinez remembers. "I felt that I was playing at a level that if I would have not gotten hurt and played like that – like I had played that summer and up through the pre-season – if I would've had a year playing like that, I for sure would have gotten a look or a tryout or something."

It was a dark few days for Martinez and the Phoenix in mid-November, but after examining the injury, the team doctor, Dr. James Hinckley, offered a ray of hope. The ligament was only partially torn, and with eight weeks of rehab, Martinez may be able to return and defer surgery for a few months to finish out his career.

"Both options, at the end, are going to require surgery, but I decided to rehab again for eight more weeks, which was the last thing I wanted to do," Martinez says. "I knew I wasn't going to be the same player, I knew that going in. But I didn't realize to the degree it would affect me."

The Gauntlet

UWGB had no time to mourn the now-temporary loss of Martinez. The team's nonconference schedule was by far the best in school history, chock full of major-conference opponents providing an amazing opportunity to shine on the national stage.

For starters, UWGB was invited to Anchorage, Alaska, to play in the prestigious Great Alaska Shootout, a Thanksgiving-weekend tournament with the semifinals and finals covered extensively by ESPN. The tournament, known for its high prestige and top-quality competition, boasted two ACC entrants in North Carolina State and Wake Forest, quality mid-majors in Hawaii, Weber State, and Portland, along with national powerhouse and UWGB's opening round foe in Purdue.

After returning from Alaska, the Phoenix would play in Marquette's First Bank Classic with a chance to take on the hosts in the championship. From there, UWGB continued its challenging run, playing at Wisconsin and then at Bowling Green.

The Phoenix's first home game wouldn't come until game eight against the Pac-10's Oregon Ducks. A patsy against Chicago State a week later would offer the team a tune-up before its first home holiday tournament, dubbed the Great Northern Classic. It was a schedule with little room for error, but bursting with opportunity and visibility.

"Coach Bennett and the staff, they were never afraid to schedule the best teams out there because you wanted to test yourself and see where you were at," notes Grzesk. "Even if you end up losing those games, they would give us an indication of what we needed to work on to be really good."

The Martinez injury put Bennett in an early-season bind, so he used two preseason games to work through his roster.

"We had run our offense prior to that, all of our preparation, with John (Martinez) being the primary ball handler. And so we had to adjust a number of things," Bennett explains. "We then went to an emphasis on our forward play, because we had really excellent forwards in Nordgaard and LeDuc and Ludvigson and Vander Velden."

In addition to testing his roster, the two preseason games helped UWGB adjust to a major rule change the NCAA had implemented. College basketball would have a shorter shot clock duration in 1993-94, decreasing from 45 seconds to 35 seconds. In Green Bay, there was a concern that this might adversely affect the Phoenix's deliberate style of play.

Two 20+ point victories in the preseason showed the change actually had the opposite impact.

"People thought it would hurt us because we would have to shoot sooner, but it actually made it better for us because we wouldn't have to defend quite as long," recalls Nordgaard. "We could defend for 35 seconds even better that we could defend for 45 seconds."

With some confidence in its lineup and repetitions with the shorter clock, UWGB packed its bags for the Last Frontier.

Great Alaska

The Great Alaska Shootout was one of the premier early-season tournaments, along with the preseason NIT and the Maui Invitational. What began as the brainchild of former Alaska-Anchorage coach Bob Rachel in 1978 almost immediately proved more popular than Alaska, or the NCAA, could ever dream.

The inaugural event, initially dubbed the Sea Wolf Classic, saw legendary coaches and programs like Bob Knight and Indiana, Denny Crum and Louisville, and Norm Sloan and N.C. State, converge on the city of Anchorage to play an eight-team tournament. Throughout the next decade and a half, the tournament had been host to nearly every blue blood program in America.

"That was an opportunity for the people of Alaska to see some outstanding competition," recalls Grzesk. "It was a good atmosphere there and a lot of excitement to see all of those teams."

Hoping to carve out a name for itself in the 1993 version, the Phoenix took to the air a few days before Thanksgiving. The first legs of the trip were uneventful, but the team experienced a surprise on its final flight.

"I can't remember where our departure point was, probably Portland or Seattle," notes Bennett, "and then, teams ended up flying up to Anchorage together, and we were on the flight with Purdue, who we were playing in the first round."

"It wasn't a charter, but ... who the hell goes to Anchorage for Thanksgiving? So it was pretty much just us and Purdue and the traveling party," recalls LeDuc.

The two programs took the court on the Wednesday before Thanksgiving in the tournament's second match, a game set for an 11:30 p.m. start

Wisconsin time. The opening game had seen Weber State upset N.C. State, meaning the winner of the Purdue vs. UWGB game would play on ESPN against Weber State, while the loser would get the ACC's Wolfpack.

Two years earlier, in Tony Bennett's senior year, the Phoenix had marched into West Lafayette and won Purdue's holiday tournament in convincing fashion. But this Boilermaker squad was older, wiser, and more talented, beginning with All-American and future Milwaukee Bucks star

Glenn "Big Dog" Robinson and fellow junior Cuonzo Martin. A year earlier as sophomores, Robinson and Martin had propelled Purdue as high as No. 9 in the country, while this year's team began the season ranked No. 21.

Dick Bennett, satisfied with his team's preseason success, stuck with his starting lineup of Ludvigson, LeDuc, Vander Velden, Grzesk and Westlake. Nordgaard, still somewhat unknown, would be the sixth man.

Grzesk, the team's best defender and a fierce competitor, sought out the toughest defensive challenge, but was shot down by Bennett.

"I wanted to guard Big Dog, but he was like 6-8 and he played forward for them," recalls Grzesk, "so Eric LeDuc ended up guarding him."

For all the effort the team had poured into the offseason, none of that manifested itself in the first twenty minutes of action. Quite to the contrary, UWGB was woeful, shooting a paltry 25% and digging itself a nearly inescapable 39-24 hole.

Worse, the Phoenix had been star-struck, particularly by the Big Dog.

Purdue's Glenn "Big Dog" Robinson was one of the best players in the country and a future star for the Milwaukee Bucks. (Department of Special Collections and University Archives, Raynor Memorial Libraries, Marquette University)

"One of the first plays of the game, he got on the wing, and he kind of got a couple of hard dribbles to the lane, and I remember thinking, 'I've got this, I'm good, I square him up,'" LeDuc says. "I remember him going up, me going up, and him just kind of continuing to go up. And just kind of like hanging and like hitting a 10-footer, and thinking, 'Yeah, that's not what I expected!'"

"He shot a jump shot when I was sitting on the bench, and he must've had a 40-inch vertical it seemed to me, he jumped so high," adds Berlowski. "And coming out from the second half, they did an alley-oop and he came out of nowhere and just crushed it on our whole team. I'm like, 'God, there's a level of talent that I really didn't see much before.' Like, 'Wow, this guy is big-time.'"

No one would have guessed that at halftime in the first game of the year, more than 3,000 miles from home and after midnight Wisconsin time, UWGB would experience a season-altering turning point. But that's exactly what happened.

"We go into the locker room before the coaches are even in there. We're like, 'Let's go.' Collectively, among ourselves, we're like, 'We are not going to have a season like we had last year,'" says Vander Velden. "Right then and there, we were determined that we were going to be better."

"I think it was a defining moment, that game against Purdue," recalls Westlake. "There's just so much pride, I guess, personal pride individually between the teammates that, I don't care who we're playing, we're better than being down (fifteen points) at halftime. And so we came out and really gave it to them in the second half."

To a man, the Phoenix's intensity level ramped up, and the club that had quietly receded into the bowels of Sullivan Arena at halftime was replaced by a rejuvenated band of upstarts intent on rewriting the narrative.

UWGB chipped away at the Boilermaker lead, getting the game back to within eight points midway through the half, and then remarkably cutting the deficit to just one point with 3:33 left. Ludvigson was particularly impressive during that stretch, providing an offensive boost when needed.

Unfortunately, for all the fight UWGB brought, the best player on the floor showed in the final minutes why he was one of the NBA's top prospects.

"Big Dog just decided to take over, and when he did, it was done," recalls Nordgaard.

Robinson scored 13 of Purdue's final 15 points on his way to a game-high 28 points. In the end, it was the Big Dog's dominating finish that put Purdue over the top, narrowly escaping with a 74-69 win over the Phoenix. Nevertheless, the resolve the Phoenix brought in the second-half was electrifying.

"I remember at halftime being very concerned that we looked like we did not belong," remarks Bennett. "At halftime I remember saying, 'We cannot win this game. I'm not concerned about winning the game, I'd like to see if we can play.' We just played, and by God, we almost won."

"When you have a moment like that, it does give you a lot of confidence," adds Westlake. "When you're playing against a very, very good team that, 'Hey, we might be okay. You know, we might be pretty good.'"

The Purdue Boilermakers were good – really good – and went on to win the Great Alaska Shootout. Keady's squad would be perhaps the best of his career, finishing the 1993-94 season No. 3 in the country, compiling a 26-4 regular-season record, earning a Big Ten championship, and getting all the way to the Elite Eight.

Alaskan Hospitality

As was the Great Alaska Shootout tradition, all teams had Thanksgiving off and were invited to enjoy the natural sights as well as dinner with the locals.

"We took a couple of trips, went up to a glacier as a team, and then we went to these host families for Thanksgiving," recalls Vander Velden. "The family that we went to, you walk out their backdoor and you saw the mountains. I'm an outdoors guy anyway, and I've wanted to go back to Alaska ever since."

A day later, UWGB hit the floor again for a matchup against the ACC's North Carolina State Wolfpack.

"Going from a Big Ten team to the ACC is what you come here for," noted an excited Dick Bennett before the game.

His players were riding the emotional high from a quality second half against Purdue, and despite the loss, seemed as confident as ever.

"I remember talking to John (Martinez) on the phone and him asking about N.C. State," Ludvigson says. "I said, 'I think we're going to beat them.' And he goes, 'Really?! You're that confident? You just think you're going to beat N.C. State?' And I'm like, 'Yeah, I think we're going to beat them.'"

The Wolfpack were coached by Les Robinson, who previously had guided mid-major East Tennessee State to NCAA Tournament appearances in 1989 and 1990. As often happens, Robinson's success drew prying eyes, and he was poached from the Southern Conference to succeed the great Jim Valvano at N.C. State. The job proved harder than expected, and though Robinson had managed to bring the program to the NCAA Tournament in 1991, his teams had finished a dismal 20-37 over the next two years, good for seventh and ninth place in the ACC, respectively.

Robinson's 1993-94 bunch showcased sophomore Todd Fuller, a 6-11 center, and Lakista McCuller and Curtis Marshall, a pair of junior guards who each averaged double figures. Bennett tweaked his starting lineup, subbing in Nordgaard for Vander Velden. The start had extra meaning for Nordgaard, whose grandfather had been a basketball and football player for N.C. State.

It took only minutes to see who the better team was. In an amazing display, the underdog Phoenix raced to an 11-2 lead just five minutes into the game and dominated every facet, making the most of its high-profile chance. UWGB built a 16-point lead midway into the first half and expanded it to 50-27 with just under 10 minutes to play in the game. From there, the Phoenix coasted, securing an impressive 76-56 victory.

"I don't think N.C. State had any idea of who Green Bay was or how good we were, and probably underrated us. And we ended up blowing them out and playing really well," states Grzesk, who had managed to hold McCuller to a scant seven points.

"We had a huge chip on our shoulder because we were all kind of embarrassed that we lost number one (to Purdue)," explains Westlake. "We kind of took that out on North Carolina State. They were never in the game. And for us to not ever let North Carolina State in the game, what did we beat them by, like 20? That's impressive for a mid-major team like us."

For the second game in a row, the ambitious Ludvigson proved his worth, leading the team in scoring with 15 points on 7-for-14 shooting.

"It isn't like he's shooting the lights out," noted Bennett, "but he's also following up and getting one or two tip-ins."

Better Than Their Record

The victory sent UWGB to the tournament's fifth-place game against yet another major-conference opponent – Wake Forest, also from the ACC.

That 1993-94 Wake Forest team, fresh off a Sweet Sixteen season, was the real deal, returning future NBA talent Randolph Childress at point guard and senior Trelonnie Owens at forward. Fortunately for the Phoenix, Childress was hampered by injury and unlikely to play, but Wake also started a little-known freshman center – Tim Duncan.

"He was a freshman," recalls Berlowski. "He could barely walk and chew gum. I mean he wasn't the player that he developed at all at that time."

Green or not, Duncan would play a whopping forty minutes in a game that would take forty-five minutes to complete.

Both teams played a slow-paced, half-court offense and stingy man-to-man defense, predictably ensuring neither team built a huge lead. Nordgaard flashed an inside-outside game early in the affair, scoring eight points in the first ten minutes.

"That's where we kind of saw Jeff's ability," Ludvigson says. "We came together and said, 'Okay, let's get him open, get him the ball. He can score inside.' "

Wake led 24-23 heading into the locker room and the second half remained just as tight, with the score knotted at 39-39 halfway through, and Wake holding a one-point lead, 45-44, with 4:35 to play.

The Deacons then opened a two-possession advantage thanks to back-to-back baskets by Travis Banks. Vander Velden returned the favor with a pair of layups, the first courtesy of a beautiful pass from Westlake, and the second on the receiving end of a Nordgaard pass. With 21 seconds to play, UWGB found itself with the ball and down just two.

The Phoenix went back to the Vander Velden well and the senior again delivered, converting a layup with 10 seconds left to tie the game, all while being fouled. Vander Velden had a chance add to his game-high 20 points and give the Phoenix the lead, but his free throw was short and Wake Forest grabbed the rebound.

"They came down and my guy beat me baseline and missed like a 12-footer," Westlake says of the final possession. "Thank God, thank God, otherwise I would still have that on my conscience."

With the game tied at 52, the teams geared up for extra time. UWGB took the early lead on a long jumper by Nordgaard on the first possession, followed by a Ludvigson baseline jumper on the second. After another stop and already up 56-52, UWGB looked like it was poised to put the game away when LeDuc found Ludvigson under the basket for an easy layup. Only Ludvigson was called for an offensive foul, wiping out the basket.

"They called a BS push-off on me underneath," he says. "I was fending him off with my forearm, which was a really ticky-tack call."

The whistle was doubly painful as it sent Travis Banks to the line on the other end for a pair of free throws, which he converted. One call flipped a six-point lead into two and killed the Phoenix's mojo. UWGB missed its next three shots, while Wake Forest went to the line on each of its next two possessions and hit a running jumper on its third. After a few security free throws, Wake had escaped with a 61-58 win.

After the game, Vander Velden was hard on himself. "We lost to Wake Forest in overtime because I missed a free three at the end of regulation."

But for LeDuc, the call on Ludvigson was the real turning point.

"I'm still bitter about it – getting screwed against Wake Forest on a terrible offensive foul call against Jeremy. Or we would've ended up 2-1 in that tournament with beating two ACC teams and barely losing to a Big Ten team."

The questionable call aside, Ludvigson was brilliant in the tournament, averaging a team-high 14.7 points and earning a spot on the All-Tournament Team. And he and LeDuc had begun to see a potential rising star.

"Against Purdue, we both noticed that Jeff (Nordgaard) had a knack for scoring inside," Ludvigson recalls. "Eric and I were like, 'Jeff, we're going to get you open.' It kind of changed to where we were looking to get him open first, and we would feed off of that."

A sixth-place finish and a 1-2 record is hardly anything to boast about, but the Phoenix made the most of the trip.

"Being able to come back on Purdue, win a game, and then playing Wake Forest to overtime, we were confident, and I think it showed," notes Vander Velden.

"Even though we went 1-2 on the trip, to have that type of competitiveness and a chance to win those games against really good teams gave us a lot of confidence going forward," remarks Grzesk.

Martinez, stuck listening from Green Bay, sensed the team's growing confidence.

"The fact that the team was able to do what they did in Alaska just kind of proved the point that this team was ready to do something and that this was going to be a big year."

Broken Shields and a Sixth Shooter

UWGB drove down I-43 to Milwaukee a week later for the program's second early-season tournament, this time at Marquette's First Bank Classic. The Phoenix were matched up with mid-major Detroit Mercy in the first round, with a chance to play the host in the tournament championship if they could survive. Detroit was in its first year with new coach Perry Watson, a former Michigan assistant, and despite an 0-2 start, were considered a contender in the MCC.

Much of that was based on the play of guard Tony Tolbert, a transfer from Michigan. Tolbert had been a bench player for the Wolverines, but at Detroit, he was the man, coming off a junior season averaging 20.4 points per game. Grzesk drew the defensive matchup to start, but Tolbert made everyone do a double take.

"First thing I remember about that game was Tony (Tolbert)," remarks Ludvigson. "Gary Grzesk was all proud of his defense, and I remember after the game we were just lighting him up that he got just abused."

Tolbert was unconscious, hitting everything in sight, and prompted Bennett to do the unthinkable – switch Grzesk off of his assignment. "That's probably the first (and only) time that year that I had to get switched off of an opponent," Grzesk recalls.

Westlake and Jackson each took their turns with Tolbert, but he torched everyone en route to an epic 41-point performance.

The problem for Detroit was it had no one else, and for the second consecutive game, the Phoenix headed to overtime. This time, extra time was better to the Phoenix as it sprinted away to a 74-63 win.

Ludvigson proved again to be one of the team's leaders, scoring 17 points on an efficient 8-for-11 shooting. But one of his misses with just over a minute left nearly overshadowed his night.

"I go up for a dunk and I threw it over the rim, and Ben Berlowski caught it on our bench," Ludvigson says. "I missed it bad, and Coach Bennett just freaked out."

Berlowski had been relegated to the bench most of the game and did little to ease his coach's temper when called upon a moment later.

"There's two seconds left, we're up by like five points, Coach Bennett looks down the bench and goes, 'Ben, come in and get in the game.' And I looked at him like, 'Really, you want me to go in there for two seconds?' And I looked away," relates Berlowski. "I'll never forget that, and he chewed me out in the locker room afterwards."

Bennett may have had his gripes with Ludvigson and Berlowski, but he'd found something golden with Vander Velden. The senior led all Phoenix scorers with 22 points doing so coming off the bench.

"I had been in and out of the starting lineup as a junior, and then coming into the senior year, he decided he was going to bring me off the bench and I just kind of got comfortable with it," explains Vander Velden. "I actually liked coming off the bench because it was a little bit less intense for me."

Vander Velden was the first player to ever ask Bennett not to start, and like a lucky chemist stumbling upon a magic elixir, Bennett quickly realized his good fortune.

"He loved coming off the bench. He's one of the few guys that preferred that, because he clearly could've started, was arguably one of our two or three best players," remembers Bennett. "And what a lift he gave us, game in and game out. I could put him in for anybody. I mean literally ... I could take any of our big kids out or any of our wing players out. He was clearly just invaluable because he automatically gave us a lift, he could stretch the defense. Along with John (Martinez), he was our best perimeter shooter. And he could pretty much shoot over people from any spot on the floor. So it was just a tremendous lineup for us."

UWGB's Jeremy Ludvigson (44) gets off a shot over Marquette's Jim McIlvaine in the championship game of the 1993 First Bank Classic in Milwaukee. The Phoenix won a tightly contested nailbiter, 46-45. (Department of Special Collections and University Archives, Raynor Memorial Libraries, Marquette University)

Take It to the Bank

Without a doubt the most satisfying part of beating Detroit was the rare date it earned UWGB with the Marquette Warriors.

"Wisconsin and Marquette were never going to come up to Green Bay to play, so you had to go on the road on your opponents' court to just to have an opportunity to compete," notes Grzesk. "We got an opportunity to get the matchup that we wanted to play an in-state team in Marquette and a team that when you're fighting for respect as a mid-major, you want to play the best teams out there."

"We thought it was really important, *I* thought it was really important that we make a good showing down in Milwaukee," Bennett says. "And Marquette had a nice club that year."

The 1993-94 Warriors had been flirting with the Top 25 early in the season and as Bennett noted, were talented, beginning with senior center Jim McIlvaine. At 7-1, McIlvaine presented match-up challenges for everyone, and his backup, 6-11 sophomore Amal McCaskill provided little relief. In addition to the big men, Roney Eford, a sophomore guard, was good for 10 points a game, as were a pair of seniors familiar to many of the Phoenix players.

"Damon Key was a (senior forward) for Marquette that John Martinez played with – they were both the same year in high school where they had an undefeated season," Ludvigson says. "John always used to mess with us and be like, 'Damon's gonna just do work on you guys.' "

Meanwhile, Key's teammate, senior guard Robb Logterman, was a former prep teammate with Berlowski at Janesville Craig.

Marquette's talent-laden starting lineup outplayed the Phoenix over the first seven minutes, putting the Warriors up 14-5 courtesy of seven points each from Eford and Logterman. But just when it looked like the game might get out of hand, UWGB proceeded to play quite possibly the best twelve minutes of defense in school history.

For a dozen minutes constituting the remainder of the first half, the Phoenix held Marquette to two points on 1-for-13 shooting. Offensively, UWGB hardly lit the world on fire, but steadily chipped away and eventually took the lead. And then, on the final possession of the half with under 10 seconds left, Berlowski dribbled left, then spun back to his right and knocked down a jumper over his high school teammate, Logterman. The basket gave UWGB a 24-18 lead going into the half, visibly aggravating Marquette coach Kevin O'Neill as he headed to the locker room.

By sheer coincidence, the NBA's Phoenix Suns were playing the Milwaukee Bucks the following night in Milwaukee, and the league's reigning MVP, Charles Barkley, was taking in the game courtside. Years ahead of his media career, Barkley was interviewed at half, and offered his candid analysis: "I think (UWGB's) playing great defense. The main thing, Marquette just has to speed it up and take advantage of the talent level. I think obviously a better team, but they're playing right into Wisconsin-Green Bay's hands."

Of course, Barkley's appearance itself was a motivating factor for UWGB.

"We're seeing Barkley and Danny Ainge sitting on the court," remembers Westlake. "We're like, 'Hey, we want to play good, you know. We don't want to be chumps.'"

Marquette took Barkley's advice and stormed back in the second half, taking the lead 29-28 is less than five minutes. From there, neither team took a two-possession lead for more than twelve minutes, and for a long while it appeared that the first team to 40 would hold the upper hand. Marquette reached that threshold with three minutes to play when Logterman hit a short jumper for a 40-38 lead.

Vander Velden responded by hitting two two-pointers on back-to-back possessions, putting the Phoenix back on top 42-40 with less than two minutes to play.

"Logan just got on a streak for a while there," remembers Grzesk. "Charles Barkley was kind of hitting the guys next to him and slapping high fives and couldn't believe how well Logan was playing."

A moment later, Grzesk was fouled on a layup attempt and hit two free throws. For the first time in fourteen minutes, UWGB had a two-possession lead, 44-40. The state's Cinderella was ready to try on that slipper and see if it fit.

Marquette had two short layup attempts on its next possession, but somehow missed both, and Nordgaard emerged from a mass of bodies with a critical rebound. Down four, Marquette had no choice but to foul, and the player with the ball in his hands was the same one who had spent the critical moments of the Detroit game on the bench – Ben Berlowski.

And yet, the normally reliable Berlowski missed the front end of the one-and-one. Marquette's Eford knocked down a long two-pointer on the Warriors' next possession, and seconds later, an ill-advised foul sent Damon Key to the line. But the normally reliable Key also felt the pressure, and hit just one of two attempts. UWGB retained its miniscule 44-43 lead with less than 10 seconds to play.

Marquette again was forced to foul, and again Berlowski went to the line. This time, with no teammates to rebound and the crowd deafening, Berlowski proved his worth, burying both free throws to give UWGB a 46-43 lead.

Logterman got a good look for a tying basket, but missed, and a meaningless McIlvaine layup as time expired was not enough. LeDuc took the ball and threw it into the air as the clock ran out, the scoreboard reading: UWGB 46, Marquette 45.

The Phoenix players danced with joy, celebrating the team's first in-state victory over a Division I opponent in school history. No one was happier than the team's head coach, a wave of relief washing over him in proving his program's worth to the Wisconsin doubters.

"It was huge," Bennett admits. "There were a number of priests in the pressroom as well as others, and it reminded me of going into kind of a funeral. It was a very disappointed group of Marquette fans. That's when I knew we had a really good ball club."

"It just showed how confident we were playing and how much we believed in what we could accomplish," recalls Vander Velden. "I think Alaska really kind of propelled us to that victory in that (Marquette) tournament."

Vander Velden scored 18 points in the championship game, including eight in the final six minutes, while Ludvigson's play earned him All-Tournament honors for a second straight tournament.

Perhaps the player who took the most pride in the victory was Berlowski, who just a day earlier had garnered scorn from his coach.

"I remember the look that he gave me afterwards. You know what, almost like this love-hate relationship we kind of developed," Berlowski says. "He started figuring that out with me, like I mess with him, he messes with me. He could somehow got that out of me."

The win would look only more remarkable as the Warriors continued to peak later in the season. Marquette would rise to No. 19 in the country, finishing the regular season 22-8 and making the Sweet Sixteen in the NCAA Tournament.

Badger Bust

The nonconference crush of a schedule kept on hitting, with UWGB getting just four days off before a long-awaited rematch with the Wisconsin Badgers. Stu Jackson, in his second season, had seemingly turned the page from the Steve Yoder years and had the Badgers ranked No. 19 in the nation.

A major reason was an improved roster with two legitimate pro prospects in junior Michael Finley and freshman big man Rashard Griffith. The latter had been particularly impressive, logging a 27-point, 12-rebound performance against UW-Milwaukee that caught the attention of UWGB assistant coach Mike Heideman.

"Everything they've written about him is pretty accurate," Heideman noted. "He'll be a dominating player if he stays around. He's an NBA-type player."

Ludvigson was notably nervous for the game, but most of his teammates seemed unconcerned with the Badgers' top players, looking back on their near-victory the previous year for confidence.

"Going in last year, we were wondering if we could play with them. Now we know we can," remarked Eric Jackson before the game.

UW coach Stu Jackson, mindful of last year's fortunate escape, was cautious.

"Green Bay, I think, is definitely our toughest test to this date, and maybe the toughest test we have in the entire nonconference," he said. "I think they're an excellent basketball team. Teams just move the ball freely on the perimeter, but the problem is, they move the ball on

Eric LeDuc (52) comes down with a rebound during UWGB's surprisingly easy 66-46 victory over Oregon on December 18, 1993. (University of Wisconsin-Green Bay Archives)

the perimeter for 35 seconds and end up with nothing. It's the darnedest thing I've ever seen."

In one of the rarest of feats, once the game started, the Badgers appeared to out-Bennett UWGB. The Phoenix succeeded in suffocating Wisconsin, holding the Badgers to just 25 first-half points. But the Badgers' defense was even better, limiting UWGB to a paltry 13 points on 24% shooting. The second half started just as poorly, with UWGB digging a 14-point hole before climbing back to within seven points with just over 13 minutes to play. It would be the closest the Phoenix could get, as Wisconsin went on an 8-0 run on its way to a convincing 64-50 victory.

It was little consolation for UWGB that it held Finley to just eight points. This Badgers team was deeper than one player and were disciplined enough to play shutdown man-to-man defense.

Stu Jackson was clearly thrilled with the quality of the win: "No one's beaten them like this. I'm very happy about that."

"I was very impressed with Wisconsin, particularly their defense," noted Bennett. "They're 100% improved from what I observed last year. They're really a tough defensive team, and if they continue to play that way, they're really going to be a load in the Big Ten."

At 3-3, having played all six games away from home and five of them against major conference opponents, Bennett was positive.

"I said going in, if we play well and come out 0-7, I'd live with it," he said. "We're 3-3, and (Wisconsin) was the only game we didn"t have a chance to win late."

Conference Realignment Hits Green Bay

With one final road game at Bowling Green, it seemed UWGB had weathered the brutal early-season schedule and could settle into a routine. But a few days before the December 11 game, Green Bay received an early Christmas surprise.

UWGB announced that the 1993-94 season would be the school's last in the Mid-Continent Conference. Effective in 1994-95, UWGB would be upgrading to the Midwestern Collegiate Conference (MCC), along with Mid-Continent Conference brethren UW-Milwaukee, Wright State, Cleveland State, Northern Illinois, and Illinois-Chicago. The MCC boasted quality mid-major programs like Xavier, LaSalle, and Detroit, all of which would offer a chance to improve UWGB's conference resume and hopefully avoid injustices like the 1992 NCAA snub.

The move would cost the Phoenix between $10,000 and $20,000 in fees to leave the Mid-Continent, as well as any NCAA share the school might earn if they made the NCAA tournament in 1993-94 (upwards of $80,000). But the MCC was seen as a significant basketball upgrade and also offered UWGB an automatic bid in men's soccer – something the Mid-Continent Conference couldn't match.

"I consider it, and I think everybody considers it, a step up," commented UWGB athletic director Dan Spielman. "It's better known nationally; it's perceived as a better league."

Bennett expressed skepticism over the potential impact. "It's not like we're moving to one of the major conferences. But because more good teams have done well for that league, its prestige is better. I don't think there's an appreciable difference, but it's perceived with more respect."

Whether distracted by the news or fatigued from the schedule, the Phoenix's road trip to Bowling Green proved more difficult than anticipated. Playing its fourth road game in eight days, UWGB looked sluggish against Jim Larranaga's club. But Berlowski played well in the second half and came up with a huge basket on the team's final possession to help the Phoenix to a 52-49 victory.

"Berlowski had a big second half against Bowling Green and just really showed that, hey, if we need somebody to get tough baskets down the stretch, he can do it," states LeDuc. "He's undersized and maybe doesn't look like he should be all that good, but he's good."

And so, after one of the toughest nonconference road stretches any college basketball team faced that season, UWGB was sitting at 4-3.

"We would have taken that in a minute," noted Heideman. "We'll be delighted to get back to Brown County Arena and play before our fans."

The Boys Are Back In Town

UWGB's first regular-season home game took place a week before Christmas against yet another major conference foe, the Pac-10's Oregon Ducks.

The good news? Martinez was cleared to suit up, and even though he likely would not play for another week or two, his presence gave the Phoenix a huge psychological lift.

If anyone needed convincing that the 1993-94 Phoenix were for real, this game gave it to them. UWGB grabbed a four-point lead at the break, and quickly extended that to double figures in the second half behind a tremendous defensive effort that held Oregon to just 28% shooting. "They were the most physical basketball team I've ever seen," remarked Oregon's coach, Jerry Green. "They were very physical and super-coached."

The result was a shocking rout. The Phoenix crushed the Ducks, 66-46. It was UWGB's second victory against a major conference opponent on the season. That feat, which had once seemed aspirational, was now becoming almost commonplace.

The Phoenix returned to the Brown County Arena on December 27, 1993, for a game against lowly Chicago State. The big news —Martinez would play, though Bennett was committed to restricting his star guard's minutes. He played half of the game, dishing six assists and scoring eight points, including a jumper with just under 10 minutes to go that had the bench going wild despite the eventual 44-point margin.

"Overall, I did what I wanted to do," said Martinez afterwards. "My defense was the only thing I'm not happy with. I'm not where I want to be. I have to keep working on the knee and the leg, and maybe with that some of the quickness will come."

"Even if he doesn't score or get an assist, the other players' confidence elevates when he's on the floor," remarked Bennett. "It's a gift, and he's always had it. He has the capacity to make the other kids around him better because of his passing."

"Playing and winning some of those competitive games *without* John early on probably helped us as well in that 1994 team," theorizes Grzesk. "All of the sudden, Nordgaard had a greater role, a bigger opportunity to score, and Logan Vander Velden was all-tournament at the Marquette tournament."

Great Northern Classic

As 1993 came to a close, the Phoenix prepared to host the program's first holiday tournament, dubbed the Great Northern Classic. The dream was to gather three other top-quality mid-major programs, giving UWGB two strong home games and an event from which their team, opponents, and fans would all benefit.

For Bennett, the man for the job was undoubtedly his newest assistant, Woody Wilson.

"He was one of the all-time great promoters," Bennett says. "He could talk people into scheduling, he was tremendous. And he did the lion's share of the scheduling. We couldn't offer the big guarantee that they would get at other places, but believe me, coaches want to get in tournaments that they have a chance to win."

Wilson was one of the unsung heroes of the Phoenix program.

"He was the restricted earnings coach, so he barely drew a salary. He was in a closet that was turned in to an office at the Phoenix Sports Center," remembers Grzesk, "There was barely any room to sit down, and then he had decks of VHS recorders stacked on top of each other. He would make a highlight film for me based on who I was going to play, just on that individual player."

For the inaugural tournament, Wilson helped bring in the reigning Colonial League champions in East Carolina, one of the top MAC contenders in Eastern Michigan, and the Big Sky's Eastern Washington. The opposition quality was a credit to the $25,000 guarantee that UWGB was able to offer, thanks to sponsorships by Employers Health Insurance and Pepsi.

There was a curious buzz around the arena on December 30, 1993, as 5,500 fans packed the dark, beer-stenched

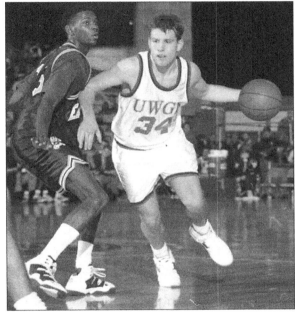

Ben Berlowski drives against East Carolina during UWGB's 60-43 victory in the championship game of its Great Northern Classic at the Brown County Arena. (University of Wisconsin-Green Bay Archives)

dome. Following the pedestrian 1992-93 season, UWGB's blue-collar fan base had taken some coaxing to return. But with early season wins over teams from the ACC, Pac-10, and in-state rival Marquette, and with Martinez returning to action, the arena was charged with anticipation.

"Having John back was like kind of having a Brett Favre come back on the field," notes Berlowski. "The fans and the players got a natural lift because he was just a natural leader."

Martinez's return gave Bennett the option to bring Grzesk and Berlowski off the bench for the opening matchup against Eastern Washington. Martinez teased his talents while easing his way back with 10 points and four assists in the first half, while Vander Velden led the team with 11 points.

But with Eastern Washington's quick guards hurting UWGB early,

Bennett went back to his two bench sophomores for a second-half spark, and they responded. Berlowski hit back-to-back three-pointers that turned a one-point lead into seven, while Grzesk provided his trademark lockdown defense. In the end, UWGB turned a close halftime effort into a relatively easy 58-44 victory.

"Gary can look ugly sometimes on offense, but he's Mr. Intangible," stated Bennett afterwards. "It became apparent that unless somebody stopped that good little point guard, they were going to beat us."

Grzesk remembers the lasting impact the game had on his career.

"I came off the bench and ended up shutting him down," he recalls. "I ended up starting the rest of the year after that because I think Coach Bennett didn't want to sacrifice the defense. Just his principles and his beliefs."

Bennett reinserted Grzesk in the starting lineup for the championship matchup. That game, set for New Year's Eve, pitted UWGB against East Carolina, which had knocked off Eastern Michigan the night before.

UWGB's bench again provided a huge boost. Nordgaard led the team with 14 points and nine rebounds, while Berlowski scored 13 points. In a contest that was never in doubt, UWGB's 60-43 win gave the hosts the inaugural Great Northern Classic championship.

Berlowski was named tournament MVP on the strength of his 8-for-12 shooting and 21 points. He was joined on the all-tournament team by Nordgaard and Martinez. Martinez had actually led all Phoenix scorers with 23 tournament points, but he was still adjusting to a new normal.

"I just remember how slow and how like just my legs felt heavy," he recalls. "I felt like I was at 25, 30 percent during that tournament. "I was just so anxious to get back out there like I didn't really care how bad it was going to be for me. I was just excited to be back out on the court, so that kind of like overshadowed any feeling of me getting reinjured or being too slow."

"John was clearly our leader, our go-to guy, and there was just a super calmness about him," comments Westlake. "He was a lot slower than he had been in the past, but he had this savvy, the intuition, the sense to change speeds when he had the ball, and when he was moving without the ball, and he was real sly about it, it really brought everything together."

Afterwards, East Carolina coach Eddie Payne became the first on the season to discuss the Phoenix's potential.

"I would think (UWGB) will win their league, from what I've seen of the power rankings and all. They have an excellent chance not only of going to the NCAA tournament, but they could win a game or two."

Chapter 15

Striking Gold
(1993-94 - Part 2)

In recruiting, there are stars and there are role players. And at the major college basketball level, most coaches have a good sense for what they are looking at and acquiring during the recruiting process.

But mid-major recruiting requires a coaching staff to focus on the overlooked, to seek out players thought to be too slow, too weak, too short, or otherwise so flawed as to not be worthy of playing major college basketball. Inherently, mid-majors have to gamble. A lot.

Placing bets on unknowns is a high-risk, low-reward proposition which, on average, leads to a team of sound role players with little top-end talent, and at worst leads to dysfunction. To beat the curve, great programs have to push or win more often than not, and at least on occasion, hit the jackpot.

Reading the Tea Leaves

UWGB entered January 1994 with a remarkable 8-3 record – remarkable both in its success against the competition, and also in the way it was achieved, specifically with a truly balanced identity. Seniors Logan Vander Velden and Jeremy Ludvigson had provided the most consistent offensive production, but eight different players had scored in double figures at least once.

But behind that success, Dick Bennett remained frustrated. It started with Chris Westlake, who had shown flashes of off-the-charts athleticism but was struggling with his shot. Even more critically, Bennett ripped sophomore Jeff Nordgaard, who had faded after a strong start.

"I don't think he is hungry enough and doesn't hunt the shot enough," remarked Bennett.

"Dick didn't think (Jeff) played enough defense, and sometimes I think thought he was a little bit of a back-talker because Jeff always was a little bit of a smart ass," adds Eric LeDuc.

Bennett's concerns aside, UWGB was dominating defensively, holding its opponents to just 54.4 points per game, good for second in the nation (behind Pete Carril's Princeton Tigers). And while UWGB had been tagged as a middle-of-the-pack Mid-Continent team before the season, by the time the conference season was ready to start, it had moved into true contender status along with the loaded UIC Flames.

"They're shutting down people defensively. Without a doubt they're playing the best ball in the conference," remarked Western Illinois coach Jim Kerwin.

Birth of a Legend

Kerwin's Leathernecks, at 2-5 on the year, were UWGB's first conference test on January 8, 1994. Twenty minutes into the affair, it looked like Kerwin's club was the team with the defensive prowess rather than Bennett's Phoenix. Western Illinois held a commanding 31-17 lead, having stunned the Brown County Arena crowd by limiting UWGB to just 25% shooting in the first half.

"They outhustled us early," Bennett remarked. "Thank heaven there's a halftime so you can at least regroup."

It was during that halftime on a cold Saturday evening that the Phoenix found its future in the form of the 6-7 sophomore from Dawson, Minnesota.

"The turning point for Jeff was the home game against Western Illinois," remembers Gary Grzesk. "We were losing at the half, and we were kind of embarrassed on how we were playing. And then something clicked for Jeff where he just got the ball

John Martinez (20) and Gary Grzesk anchored the UWGB backcourt in the 1993-94 season. (University of Wisconsin-Green Bay Archives)

on the block and scored a number of times."

"I just remember at halftime, Dick coming to me, Jeremy, and Nordgaard ... and they're like, 'Run this screen for screener, do this triangle game with the three of you,'" explains LeDuc, "and it was like, 'Oh my God, this is going to work!'"

Fresh off the recent criticism from his head coach, something transcendent occurred for Nordgaard.

"I vividly remember at halftime thinking to myself, 'How am I going to get out of Brown County Arena without having to see anybody?' " he recalls. "And then the second half, I don't remember now what had happened, but I think I made my first six, eight shots and had 23 points in the game. Martinez helped me. He would get me easy buckets by penetrating and just drop it off to me. But I kind of got in a groove. That game I found out, 'Okay, I can be a go-to guy.' "

Nordgaard went 7-for-7 from the field in the second half as he tallied a career-high 25 points, 23 of which came in the second half including 13 in a row at one point. His individual brilliance carried the Phoenix, which overcame an 18-point deficit to win its sixth game in a row with ease, 60-48.

Remarkably, the Western Illinois contest changed the entire trajectory of both the Phoenix program and Nordgaard individually.

"The rest of that season, the offense – although it ran through John – it went through me as sophomore, a third-year sophomore," remarks Nordgaard. "It was that Western Illinois second half that kind of changed the season and my career."

"From that point on, he was almost unstoppable on the block," agrees Grzesk. "That was probably the turning point in his career, and once we had another scorer to go along with John Martinez, that obviously made us a really good team with some scoring inside and some perimeter scoring with John."

The Start of Something Good

UWGB parlayed the Nordgaard find to win its next three conference games, beginning with its old nemesis, Northern Illinois. With a six-point lead late, Ludvigson took a pass from Grzesk and swished his first three-pointer of the season, effectively finishing off Northern Illinois.

Nordgaard and Ludvigson both led the way with 13 points and six rebounds each, while Martinez continued to contribute despite his limitations, scoring 11 points and dishing four assists.

A few days later, Nordgaard continued his ascension, tallying 21 points and seven rebounds against Youngstown State, all while Vander Velden sat nursing an ankle injury. And when the Phoenix needed it the most, their quiet senior leader, Martinez, provided the dagger, making three critical free throws in the final ten seconds to hold on for a 69-67 victory.

On January 17, 1994, UWGB came out stronger at Cleveland State. The game turned in the first half when Ben Berlowski scored seven of UWGB's next nine points to drive the Phoenix's lead to 13. UWGB pulled away from there, devouring the Vikings 78-56 for its school-record-tying ninth straight win, improving to 4-0 in the conference and 12-3 overall. Nordgaard led UWGB in scoring for the fourth straight game, this time with a double-double of 14 points and 12 rebounds.

"If you got (Jeff) a crack, chances were he was going to make it," LeDuc says. "And he just had such long arms and big hands that it didn't matter if guys were bigger than him, he could get shots off. He could get to the hoop, he could score; everything just kind of took off."

UWGB dropped a winnable game at Wright State on January 22, 1994, when the Raiders' Andy Holderman hit a three-pointer with less than five seconds left for a surprise 53-51 victory.

"The game at Wright State, we didn't play as well as we could have, and I think Wright State played very well," notes Grzesk. "But (our) team was very competitive. We did not handle losing very well and wanted to have a special season."

Indeed, the seniors pulled the club together and two nights later, the Phoenix rebounded to beat a middling Eastern Illinois team by seven points. Martinez, knocking off a little more rust with each outing, finished with a season-high 18 points, going 4-for-7 from beyond the arc.

On January 26, 1994, in the team's final of five straight road games, the Phoenix put together its best conference performance, downing UW-Milwaukee 64-42. Nordgaard continued his tear, recording another double-double with 17 points and 13 rebounds as UWGB exacted revenge for a difficult loss the year previous year.

"We didn't make a big deal of (last year) coming into the game, but essentially we're the same team. There's only one new guy, and everybody knew it," remarked LeDuc.

Black Shoes and a New Attitude

There was no doubt about it, at 14-4 and with wins in eleven of its past twelve games, UWGB was on a roll. The Phoenix's 6-1 conference record put it in a tie for the conference lead looking ahead to its next two home opponents, the upstart Valparaiso Crusaders and the loaded UIC Flames.

With the recent success came a wave of Phoenix fans rushing back to the Arena on January 29 for the showdown against Valparaiso. The 5,994 in attendance was the most the team had seen at a home game since it won the Mid-Continent Conference Tournament against Northern Illinois on March 5, 1991.

It was another masterful defensive performance by Bennett's team, limiting Valparaiso to just 33.3% shooting. LeDuc contained Valparaiso's best player, Casey Schmidt, to just 13 points. Meanwhile, Nordgaard continued to impress, scoring 23 points and grabbing seven boards as the Phoenix tabbed a 63-50 win.

Valpo coach Homer Drew, always a class act even in defeat, praised the Phoenix following the game noting, "They're playing, I think, the best defense in the nation right now."

Drew wasn't far off. UWGB ranked second in the nation by the end of January 1994, holding opponents to just 54.4 points per game.

Two days later, UWGB's fiercest conference competition, the stacked UIC Flames, came to Green Bay in a battle to break the first-place tie. The Flames were unquestionably the most talented team in the conference. Like the great Northern Illinois team in 1991, UIC had an NBA-prospect forward in Sherell Ford, and a silky-smooth point guard in Kenny Williams.

"(UIC) was just an overall great team," elaborated Martinez. "I had a

Jeff Nordgaard plays physical defense during UWGB's 53-51 loss at Wright State on January 22, 1994. (Courtesy of Special Collections and Archives, Wright State University)

lot of respect for Kenny Williams, their point guard, and Sherell Ford was just a really talented individual player that could just make plays on his own."

As if the conference lead wasn't motivation enough, the game carried with it an additional incentive, courtesy of a softening Dick Bennett.

"We were picked what, fifth or sixth (at the beginning of) our senior year in the conference, and we're all like, 'That's BS,' " remembers Jeremy Ludvigson. "So we made the deal with Coach Bennett, 'Hey, halfway through the year, if we're in first place, can we get black shoes?' And he agreed to it. I don't think he thought we could do it, honestly."

"(We) just wanted to do that and get out of green and white shoes," adds Vander Velden. "Everyone was going to the black shoes thanks to the (University of Michigan) Fab Five."

Sure enough, with first-place on the line, the UIC game marked the midway point of the conference season. And with style on the line, UWGB put together one of its strongest defensive performances of the season.

Bennett was uncharacteristically tight with his bench, playing six of his players (Nordgaard, Grzesk, Martinez, LeDuc, Vander Velden, and Berlowski) at least nineteen minutes. LeDuc again played solid defense, holding Ford to 17 points, while Grzesk kept Williams to 13 points – a combined 15 points below their season averages.

Still, the game was tight throughout. UWGB was able to take a six-point lead into the locker room, but UIC quickly tightened up the game, tying it at 39-39 just five minutes into the second half. The teams traded baskets the rest of the way, with Nordgaard having a lot of success on the inside.

"They play in front of the post on defense. That makes guys like me hungry for the ball," remarked Nordgaard, who scored most of his 25 points from the paint.

Holding a tenuous 61-60 lead and just over three minutes to play, the Phoenix defense put a lid on the rim. UWGB blanketed the Flames possession after possession, challenging every pass and shot, and grabbing every rebound in holding UIC scoreless the rest of the way. A Nordgaard layup with 1:45 left stretched the lead to three, and from there the Phoenix put away the Flames from the free throw line, making eight down the stretch on its way to a convincing 71-60 victory. The win created separation in the conference race, but for the players, it was all about the shoes.

"We get back in the locker room, and the whole room is chanting, 'Black shoes are in the house, black shoes are in the house.' And Coach Bennett comes walking in, and he's kind of like, 'What's going on? What's going on?' and Coach Swan had to explain it to him," Ludvigson says. "He was like, 'You guys look slow enough already!' But he let us do it."

"How little it took to please them," Bennett recalls with a laugh. "That wouldn't fly today, but wow."

Post-Season Pontifications

The shoes aside, the Phoenix was now 16-4 overall and sitting alone in first place in the conference at 8-1. The conversation inevitably shifted to the postseason.

"We all think about it," remarked Nordgaard, unabashedly attacking the topic. "We were planning our spring break and saying, 'We're not going on spring break; we're going to the NCAA tournament.'"

The postseason discussion only intensified over the first two weeks in February as UWGB rattled off four more wins. The first two took place at home against Youngstown State (69-58) and Cleveland State (83-62). In the latter, Nordgaard posted a new career-high 27 points.

"The team's starting to realize he's our go-to-guy," noted Ludvigson. "Whether he finished it or kicks it back out, we're looking to go through him."

The Phoenix also polished off its next two opponents on the road, first at Western Illinois (66-48) and then at Northern Illinois (73-70). Western Illinois's coach, Jim Kerwin, raved about Nordgaard's performance. "The media has spent this season writing about several other players in our league, but there's no better player than Nordgaard."

February also saw Martinez begin to regain his old form as chief distributor. Ludvigson, who scored his career-high 24 points at Western Illinois, gave all the credit to his teammate.

"He was just giving me the ball on a platter, and all I was doing was just taking it and laying it in," Ludvigson noted. "He was just setting me up like crazy ... and he'll remind me about that, too!"

With a 20-4 record overall and at least six games more to play, UWGB was quickly venturing from likely NIT candidate to legitimate NCAA bubble team. And by mid-February, UWGB had received a vote in the AP's Top 25.

Northern Illinois coach Brian Hammel was convinced: "There's no question (they should make the NCAA tournament). If they lose in the first round of the Mid-Continent Conference Tournament – and they're not going to do that – they still deserve an at-large bid. They've played quality, and beaten quality."

Relying on Bennett's man-to-man pack defense, the Phoenix had the seventh-best field goal percentage defense (38.1%), as well as the second-best scoring defense (54.8 ppg) in the nation, trailing only Princeton.

"Princeton relies on its offense to keep the score low. Green Bay keeps the score low because they play defense," praised Wake Forest coach Dave Odom. "(Dick) has taught his system as well as anyone in (the ACC) has taught their system. The difference is talent. This league has Duke and North Carolina, and they teach their systems very well. If you put Dick Bennett and his system in the ACC with ACC talent, it's reasonable to believe he'd be just as effective here as he is in Green Bay."

The high praise had little impact in settling the coach's fear of repeating what had happened in 1992. He steadfastly refused to buy into his team's hype, noting, "I know enough that I'm not going to plan. I'm not going to get my hopes too high."

At 12-1 in the Mid-Continent Conference, only two teams – UIC at 10-2 and Valparaiso at 9-4 – looked capable of raining on the Phoenix's dance parade.

And just as it had three weeks prior, UWGB would face those teams in back-to-back games, this time on the road.

In the first game against Valparaiso, UWGB had what can only be described as an off night. The Crusaders implemented a press set to break UWGB's rhythm and take the ball out of Martinez's hands, and their scheme worked like a charm. The Phoenix was within three points with less than eight minutes to play, but when the horn sounded, Valparaiso had taken down the conference leaders 63-56, snapping the Phoenix's eight-game winning streak.

The loss brought the Phoenix back into a tie with UIC for the conference lead, but more importantly, hampered the team's at-large chances.

"They made us stumble, so we almost have to be perfect the rest of the way. That, I'm not sure we're capable of doing," remarked Bennett afterwards.

Two days later on February 21, the conference lead was on the line as UWGB took on the Flames at the UIC Pavilion in Chicago. Unlike the first battle against the Flames, this one turned early.

With UWGB up four late in the first half, Benentt was called for a technical foul for arguing a non-call on Kenny Williams. Bennett stormed the court in anger, and it took Jeff Zavada putting him in a bear hug to restrain the irate coach. UIC turned the tables with the technical, making free throws and converting on the free possession to take a two-point lead.

As they often did, the Phoenix players channeled their coach's outburst to reach a positive outcome. UWGB scored the final seven points of the half to take a 36-31 lead at the break, and continued right on track throughout the second half.

When it was all over, UWGB was able to glide to an 80-66 win. The Flames' two superstars performed better than in the first affair, with Ford scoring 22 points and Williams 18, but the game was never in serious doubt.

Nordgaard led the way for the Phoenix with 23 points, while Vander Velden added 20 points. Meanwhile, the recovering Martinez provided an efficient 14 points on 6-for-6 shooting.

UIC coach Bob Hallberg noted Martinez's importance to UWGB's success, saying, "John's one of those guys who, regardless if he plays good or bad, he's going to use his head. That's a big factor against us."

The win closed out a regular season sweep of the Flames, effectively giving UWGB a two-game lead in the conference standings. At 21-5 overall, it appeared the Phoenix had righted the ship and was back on course for the NCAA tournament.

And then it played at UW-Milwaukee.

Offensive Liabilities

"I'll ask the questions to get this thing started. What happened? Let's start at the top: They had a scheme that I couldn't solve. We got tight," led Bennett at his post-game press conference. "What kind of loss was it? Very damaging. About as damaging as they come ... What could we have done to avoid it? Play harder earlier and smarter later."

UWGB's loss to a middling UW-Milwaukee team on February 24 was both perplexing and alarming. As had become standard, Bennett played two of his prime defenders, Grzesk and LeDuc, together for much of the game.

But UW-Milwaukee's counter – a gimmicky triangle-and-two that left Grzesk and LeDuc open – proved enormously effective. The Panthers held the Phoenix to a season-low 36.5% shooting, and only Nordgaard was able to muster double figures with 17 points and nine rebounds. The loss was a wake-up call to Grzesk, forcing him to confront his offensive limitations.

"That was pretty hard to swallow – the fact that they weren't guarding me and we ended up losing," recalled Grzesk, "That was the first time that stuck out in my mind where a gimmick defense and my lack of offense cost us a game."

The UW-Milwaukee loss brought the team back to reality.

"After the Illinois-Chicago win, we were on top of the mountain," Martinez said after the loss. "We played the whole season and got to that point. To play like this and lose at home, we fell right back to where we began."

Any dream the Phoenix had of an at-large bid had vanished, and UWGB administration began to look ahead at the availability of the Brown County Arena to host an NIT game.

Titletown Once More

With two games left, UWGB focused on securing the regular-season crown and top seed going into the conference tournament. Just two days later, the Phoenix returned to action against Wright State and convinced 5,596 fans, including special guest U.S. Senator and Milwaukee Bucks owner Herb Kohl, to forget about the UW-Milwaukee debacle.

Bennett had been a nervous wreck before the game, biting his nails and squeezing a stress ball as he considered his lineup and team's strategy. By game time, he had settled on Nordgaard, Grzesk, Martinez, Vander Velden, and LeDuc as starters, but through the first nine minutes of the game, that group was only able to build a slim 11-10 lead.

At that point, Bennett made wholesale changes, subbing in his "second group" of Jackson, Berlowski, Westlake, Ludvigson, and Zavada. His bench responded, going on a 19-4 run highlighted by four Berlowski three-pointers.

"I chastised myself for not going with the second unit as much on Thursday (against UW-Milwaukee). I was not going to make the same mistake tonight," Bennett said.

UWGB built on a 14-point halftime lead and ran away to a dominant 80-46 victory. Even UWGB's final bench player, walk-on Rico Rondorf, scored on a slick layup that brought the crowd to its feet with delight.

The win brought UWGB's season record to 22-6 and kept it in a tie with UIC for the conference lead at 14-3. It also meant the Mid-Continent Conference's regular season championship would come down to

Jeff Nordgaard slams one down during UWGB's convincing victory in the rematch with Wright State at the Brown County Arena. (University of Wisconsin-Green Bay Archives)

the final games on February 28, 1994.

UWGB had a home game scheduled against Eastern Illinois, while the Flames had a road game at Cleveland State. A UWGB win or a UIC loss would give the Phoenix the regular-season conference crown for just the second time in team history.

The going was tough early as UWGB appeared to buckle under the pressure. But at halftime and with the score tied at 28-28, the seniors pulled the team together and demanded the squad to return to its defensive roots. With LeDuc leading the way, UWGB held Eastern Illinois to just 6-for-25 shooting (24%) in the second half.

"(LeDuc) was helping, he was covering his man and was on the glass," Bennett. "He played with the heart of a lion."

Even though it was announced midway through the second half that the UIC Flames had lost, giving the Phoenix the conference title, the seniors kept their foot on the gas, leaving no doubts about who the best team was in the Mid-Continent Conference. With a 58-45 victory, Green Bay was Titletown once again.

It was a return to the glory of the Tony Bennett era – a conference championship earned through hard work and consistent defensive excellence. This championship, the team's second in three years, was extra special for the senior class.

"What we did before was great, but this is something that's ours," said LeDuc after the game.

The championship also revalidated Bennett's coaching philosophies, fully embraced by his 1993-94 squad.

"I've never had a group that had the servant's mentality in basketball like this group. I think that's why they won," he said.

The conference announced its awards days before the tournament. The top player awards were predictable, with UWGB's Nordgaard named first team all-conference along with Kenny Williams and Sherell Ford from UIC, and Casey Schmidt and David Redmond from Valparaiso. Williams doubled as the conference MVP.

The big surprise came when Homer Drew of Valparaiso was named the coach of the year. There was no doubt Drew had done wonders in turning around a 12-16 club and getting them to a 19-7 finish, good for third in the conference. But Green Bay fans felt that Bennett was more deserving.

"The team was really upset about it, because you know, we're picked fifth in the conference. How can he not get coach of the year? You know, we won the conference?" states Ludvigson. "I remember being in a hotel room with all the guys talking about it, and I remember Eric Jackson specifically was fired up and was like, 'You know, we gotta do this for Coach Bennett tomorrow night. We gotta win this thing.' "

Meanwhile, Martinez also found his name conspicuously absent from the postseason conference honors. His mid-season return had coincided directly with the Phoenix's second-half success, and his masterful play with diminished explosiveness was nothing short of miraculous.

"He gave me so many easy shots with his penetration and making the extra pass that it got my confidence going," remembers Nordgaard. "There's no doubt he had to be frustrated in his head because he wasn't what he had been. But still, him at not full strength was better than almost everybody outside of Kenny Williams in that conference as a guard."

For his part, Martinez took the oversight in stride, exemplifying his unselfish and humble demeanor: "I don't think I had the numbers to get second team. What I do for us is more psychological. Unless you're one of our fans or on our team, it's hard to understand what I do."

Leave No Doubt

The Mid-Continent Conference tournament was scheduled for March 6-8, 1994, at the Rosemont Horizon Center outside of Chicago. For all of the excitement and success the team had achieved over a grueling 29-game regular season, a bad Milwaukee loss meant its ultimate fate was likely to be decided in this three-day stretch.

As the top seed, UWGB drew the eighth-seeded Western Illinois Leathernecks in the quarterfinals. In a three-team race, that top seed also gave UWGB the added advantage of ensuring it would not have to play either of the conference's other two contenders (#2-seeded UIC or #3-seeded Valparaiso) until the championship game.

The quarterfinal matchup was a typical David versus Goliath battle on paper, with the Phoenix large favorites. The 7-9 Leathernecks were hopeful, having finished the season with a strong win over UW-Milwaukee by 15 points.

But none of that mattered. From tip to buzzer, the Phoenix demonstrated its dominance with a 79-39 victory, shooting nearly 60% from the field and an astounding 75% from beyond the arc.

"I don't know how they could play any better. I don't know how anybody can play any better," a baffled Coach Jim Kerwin said.

A day later, UWGB tackled step two in its semifinal match against Cleveland State. Just like the Leathernecks, Cleveland State supplemented a mediocre record with some recent momentum, having won seven of its last eight contests behind strong play from 6-9 forward Sam Mitchell.

"They were in the same hotel as we were, and they were big talkers," recalls Grzesk. "We just ended up blitzing them. Our team was so focused and played so well on both ends that Cleveland State was never in the game."

Every player on the Phoenix roster shot at least 50% from the field, and the game was over before it started. Nordgaard was the leading scorer with 23 points and Martinez added 18 points as UWGB blew out the Vikings 93-63.

It was the team's third win in four games by 30 or more points, and left Cleveland State's coach, Mike Boyd, feeling helpless: "If they play the way they did in the last two games, they're going to walk away with a victory."

Even the jaded Dick Bennett was riding high, lulled back into the dream that the Phoenix had done enough, even without a championship, to potentially get an at-large bid: "I believe (25 wins) is significant for that, with the schedule we've played."

Stoking the Fire

On the other end of the bracket, UIC and Valparaiso won their quarterfinal matchups, and for the third time this season, UIC disposed of the Crusaders in the semifinals. UIC was headed to the conference championship game for the fourth time in six seasons and third year in a row, this time to face UWGB.

For the Phoenix, the season was playing out eerily similar to 1990-91, with the program hoping to beat a top contending team from Illinois three times in one season, including in the conference championship. Back then it was Northern Illinois, now it was UIC.

The Flames, for their part, were confident their time was now. "We've got a great opportunity," remarked MVP Kenny Williams before the game. "We've got our fans, we know Green Bay is going to be tough and we don't mean any disrespect to them, but I really feel this is our tournament."

Williams, along with his teammate Sherell Ford, had been nothing short of spectacular in the tournament's first two rounds. Ford had put together monster performances, averaging 28.5 ppg, while Williams had been even better, averaging 29.0 ppg.

"They were really good. I mean they were *really* good," recalls LeDuc. "For the most part, they were Chicago kids, they were city kids, they were tough, they didn't back down."

It would be the climax for UWGB's fifth-year seniors. Could this unsung collection of largely Wisconsin athletes actually replicate what the Phoenix had accomplished only once in its history?

This team would have to do it in Chicago rather than Green Bay, a fact not lost on UIC's coach, Bob Hallberg. "I'd much rather play here than at Brown County Arena," he said. "There won't be those people sitting behind me drinking beer. As long as they're far away ... I won't be able to hear the insults."

Nevertheless, more than 1,200 Phoenix fans packed buses and carpooled to Chicago. "We had a lot of fans that traveled because it wasn't obviously that far for us," adds LeDuc. "We had, over the course of the year, built up a good rivalry with them, so it was a good environment."

"I don't remember feeling any extra pressure or any realization of how big the moment was," adds Nordgaard. "We just went out there and played."

Schematic Wrinkles

UWGB and UIC were evenly matched clubs, built in similar ways, disciplined and methodical, and extremely polished. UWGB's plan was to stick with their patient motion offense, while UIC's strategy was to work Ford early and often.

Bennett went with his standard lineup of Nordgaard, LeDuc and Ludvigson at the forward positions, Martinez and Grzesk at the guards, and Vander Velden as the first man off the bench. Grzesk would guard Williams, while LeDuc drew the task of containing Ford.

But while the lineup was unchanged, Bennett had a defensive trick up his sleeve.

"We adjusted our defense and allowed total denial on Ford," he explains. "We played him nose to nose, with and without the ball, and everybody else was in our traditional help position. We called it the 'Four Pack.' "

LeDuc proved more than up to the challenge, conceding an early turn-around basket, but forcing a pair of early turnovers that allowed UWGB to build a 9-4 lead by the 12:00 mark. But as would happen time and again, UIC fought back and tied the game in less than a minute.

Bennett needed a spark, and he turned to the team's sixth man to give it to him. Vander Velden connected on a scooping layup with 10:13 in the first half, extending a Phoenix lead to four points, and after a missed layup on the next possession, Vander Velden unexpectedly became gun-shy.

Thankfully for UWGB, Nordgaard was hunting his shot. He made four quick baskets, including three in a row that catapulted the Phoenix to a 19-11 lead with 7:07 to play.

When Bennett rested Nordgaard and put in two of his other sophomores, Berlowski and Jackson, the momentum again swung back and UWGB saw its advantage cut to 21-19 at halftime.

The first half was everything Bennett could have hoped for on the defensive end. UWGB had held the Flames to just 25% shooting and an abysmal 2-for-12 from three-point land. Individually, Grzesk had held Williams to a goose egg – zero points. Though Ford had gotten his 10 points, he also had spent multiple possessions complaining to the officials and losing his composure.

Offensively ... not so much. Nordgaard had his 12 points, but there was little else to latch onto. Bennett directed his halftime fury toward Vander Velden, begging the fifth-year senior to look for his shot and take it when it came.

The conference's two best teams gave every paying customer, regardless of affiliation, their money's worth in the second half. Each possession was critical, and no coach was willing to leave any stone unturned. Bennett even went so far as to suggest an old trick that went over like a lead balloon with his players.

"All of us had agreed that we'd lost that '91 Michigan State game because we went to the 1-3-1. We decided to go away from our defensive principles and play the 1-3-1," remembers LeDuc. "(At a timeout) he's like, 'What about a 1-3-1?' And five of us, at one time, are like 'NO! We're not playing a 1-3-1!' "

UWGB stuck to its man-to-man defense and continued to exploit the trapping defense of UIC for easy buckets, while UIC lived and thrived on mid-range jumpers. Things took a dangerous turn when Martinez caught an inadvertent elbow in the face from UIC guard Jevon Hobbs. Martinez, who had been playing extremely well in forcing turnovers, dishing assists, and knocking down shots for the Phoenix, had suffered a broken nose.

But UWGB's veteran guard had been through injuries before and was determined to gut it out. "I didn't want to come out, so I just kind of, you know how you take your hands and put them together over your nose and you just kind of crack it back into place? So I ended up doing that."

Martinez never even left the floor, and on the ensuing possession, assisted on a turnaround basket by Nordgaard. And yet, as UIC closed the gap to 54-53 with just over a minute to play, the Phoenix felt the momentum shifting to the Flames.

"I can remember with it just being a couple of minutes left that this is slipping away a bit," recalls LeDuc. "And one of the last timeouts, just kind of all looking at each other and thinking, 'I just don't want to play in the NIT. We want to go to the NCAA tournament.'"

Clinging to a one-point lead with 1:30 to play, it was time for UWGB to step up and secure its bid to the NCAA Tournament. And who better to lead the way than the team's unsung hero and voluntary sixth man.

As the clock ticked down near one minute remaining, UWGB worked the ball from Martinez on the baseline to Grzesk at the top of the key, and then to Vander Velden. The lanky forward took one dribble to the left and launched a 14-foot jump shot that hit the back of the rim, bounced more than five feet straight into the air … and dropped flawlessly through the rim to give the Phoenix a 56-53 lead with 1:03 left.

UIC put the ball in the hands of Williams on the next possession, guarded closely by Grzesk. Williams worked to the right, and while Grzesk fought over a screen, the smooth star dribbled once forward, then popped back to launch a three-pointer over the outstretched arm of Grzesk. The shot was perfect, tying the game as the announcers, crowd, and Flames players went berserk.

With just 45 seconds left to play, UWGB quickly pushed the ball up against the trapping defense and worked it around until it came to Vander Velden on the left wing. This time, his shot clanged hard off the back iron, but LeDuc was able to stretch for the rebound and knock the ball out to Grzesk, who called timeout with 19 seconds left.

Bennett told his team to anticipate the trap and implored them to get the ball to the middle, opening up the offense. Bennett's guidance was spot-on.

"They trapped us at half court, and Jeff (Nordgaard) got the ball in the middle, and I was on the weak side," explains Vander Velden. "When he got it, I was left. There wasn't anybody there. I just went to the basket, and he found me."

"(Nordgaard) hit Logan cutting down the lane, and it was a bang-bang play," adds Grzesk. "The basket went in, and they called a (blocking foul on UIC)."

"Could've gone either way on that one," said Nordgaard. "I mean, it was one of those things. That was the right call, but you know how it is."

In an instant, Vander Velden had put his team up two with a chance at three. He felt certain he was not at fault: "I'll take the call, don't get me wrong," he said. "Could it have been a no-call? Possibly. (But) I *know* I didn't charge."

Dick Vitale, breaking the game down on ESPN afterwards, agreed. "I think it was a great call for this reason: the official made it with authority. There was no hesitation on his part. Some people will say questionable, but he made the quick call."

Vitale, having some fun with it, added, "Vander Velden. Logan. I love that name baby, he's going to make my All-Name Team!"

Vander Velden stepped to the line and knocked down the free throw, putting UWGB up 59-56 lead with just 12 seconds left. But UIC was not likely to go without one last heave.

Immediately after the free throw, the Flames got the ball to Williams, who set up on the right side of the floor, again working off a screen from Ford. Williams took two dribbles, and with under seven seconds left, lifted from a nearly identical spot as he had scored from just a moment earlier.

This time, Grzesk was there and anticipated the shot. With his arm outstretched, Williams was forced to adjust his shot, adding a hitch just before it left his hands. The ball drew the back iron and clanked out. Grzesk grabbed the rebound, was fouled by Williams, and made two free throws to ice the game. A UIC full-court shot bounced away harmlessly as time expired. Williams dropped to the floor, his face buried in his hands.

Back in the High Life Again

They had done it. For the second time in school history, UWGB had won the Mid-Continent Conference Tournament and was headed to the NCAA Tournament.

Jubilance overcame the Phoenix as the team stormed the court, arms raised. Zavada provided the primary entertainment, lifting her jersey to reveal he had "NCAA" shaved into his chest hair.

"He was going around to everyone's room showing what he did, which was pretty funny," comments Berlowski.

"We were just on cloud nine," Grzesk remembers. "Winning that game, getting the automatic bid, was pretty amazing considering that we had a losing season the year before and did it pretty much with the same guys coming back along with John."

Martinez did his best to enjoy the party in spite of his still-bleeding and painful broken nose. "I really couldn't celebrate like I wanted to because blood was going to start pouring out of my nose," he says. "An awkward celebration for me as I'm jumping around with the guys in the middle of the court, because you can tell that I'm pulling my face away from everybody and trying to keep my head up."

Like Martinez, his senior teammates took extra pride in the accomplishment.

"It was just unbelievable because it was our senior year," notes Ludvigson. "I think I was more outwardly just excited and pumped up and screaming than I was even the freshman year."

Offensively, Nordgaard's 22 points and five rebounds led the Phoenix, but it was Vander Velden's critical surge down the stretch that sealed the victory.

"You know it's funny, I spent most of the halftime chewing on him because I didn't think he hunted the shot enough. Well he fixed me – he hunted it when it counted," Bennett commented in his postgame interview.

"I had not played well up to that point, and I was just struggling. Just one of those things, couldn't get into a groove," Vander Velden recalls. "But for whatever reason, I found it easier to get open down that stretch in the last five minutes. Whatever it was, I just found myself open. I will say this, I was never afraid to take important shots."

For his part, UIC coach Bob Hallberg was all class after the game: "(Bennett) is probably the best coach and the nicest guy in the country. He's also a personal friend. When you lose, it takes some of the sting out, losing to a guy like that."

That mutual respect existed with the players as well. "You know how they say it's hard to beat a team three times? That's why it was a big accomplishment, at least in our opinion," noted Martinez. "They were just a very athletic team, well-coached, and they just played hard, (so) just winning the three games against them that year was a big accomplishment for us."

"I played with (Kenny Williams) afterwards at Marathon Oil, and he told me, 'Man, we hated playing you all. Leading up to playing you guys, and all those screens, we hated it,' " adds Ludvigson. "And I'm like, 'Well, we hated playing you guys, too, because you guys were super athletic and we didn't like playing you guys either.' "

Chapter 16

The Big Dance
(1994 NCAA Tournament)

Scientists say repetition correlates with recollection. The more you hear it, the more you remember it. The principle is as relevant to athletics as it is in advertising or education, and in terms of college hoops, its application is simple. Teams that play in one NCAA tournament game are more easily forgotten than those that repeat.

Each game puts a momentary magnifying glass on a program, which in turn drives public awareness with the media, fans, and most importantly, with recruits. And in the continuously cycling basketball race, the closer you look, the more you're bound to see.

California Dreamin'

The Phoenix enjoyed a few days of much-needed rest after the Chicago trip.

"The beauty of being at Green Bay and getting into the NCAA was you had an extra week to prepare," Dick Bennett says. "You'd finish, and you could give your kids a little time off to rest their legs and then they'd come back fresh, like probably on the Wednesday. And you would work, you would regain your fundamentals, your sharpness, toughness. And then you would get your matchup on the Sunday."

To the fans in Green Bay and students on campus, it was all one big pre-party leading up to the Selection Show.

"I remember (local sports personality John) Maino coming out on campus and did a live shot from Jeremy (Ludvigson) and John (Martinez)'s on-campus apartment, and we were all just excited as can be, going crazy," says Jeff Nordgaard.

While the fans and players relished a few days in the sun, the media immediately began speculation on seeding and opponents. Tim Brando kicked off the conversation during the UIC game, saying: "I wouldn't want to be the fourth or fifth seed that would have to play them."

Senior Jeff Zavada took the fan's approach, less interested in the number and more interested in the pairing: "Whether it's the first round or the second, I'd like to play somebody that's nationally known. If we're going to make a name for ourselves, that's the way to do it."

"We're going to run into a team that doesn't know very much about us, probably not going to respect us," noted Eric LeDuc. "And if we play the way we need to play, anything can happen."

Selection Sunday arrived on March 13, 1994. The Phoenix Dunkers booster club hosted a watch party at The Bar in Green Bay, but conspicuously absent were the Phoenix players and coaches.

"After the incident out at The Bar (in 1992), Coach Bennett said we'll never have a public watching of the Selection Show again," recalls Gary Grzesk. "He invited us out to his house, we had pizza, and Anne made her homemade hot fudge."

Somewhere along the way, the idea of playing the California Golden Bears crept into the conversation.

"We had actually joked earlier in the year about a Cal, you know, a West Coast team, not going to know anything about us, not going to take it serious, and definitely does not want to play the style of basketball that we're going to play," notes LeDuc.

"So when it came out, everybody's looking around at each other like, 'Dude, we got this, we're going to beat them,'" Ludvigson concurs.

Nostradamus would've been proud. The committee had, in fact, sent UWGB to the West Region as a 12 seed, pitted against the Pac-10's California Golden Bears.

"We would have rather gone to California or Florida or wherever else," Jeff Nordgaard says, "but go out to Ogden, let's see what we've got!"

Cal was one of college basketball's hot teams. Just one year earlier, the 1993 version of the Golden Bears had been a Sweet Sixteen team. Then-sophomore Lamond Murray and then-freshman Jason Kidd had exploded on the national scene, upsetting the heavily favored, back-to-back national champion Duke Blue Devils in the second round.

Both were clearly headed for the NBA, with Kidd in the mix as a potential top pick if he decided to come out. And with another year of experience, the 1993-94 Golden Bears were a trendy pick for the Final Four.

If anything, that talk was just additional motivation for the Phoenix. "We were all very confident, 'We can beat them,'" recalls Logan Vander Velden.

"They had Jason Kidd and Lamond Murray, so you would think we would be somewhat intimidated, and then knowing the career that Jason Kidd had in the NBA, you know, Hall of Fame point guard," notes Martinez. "(But) we felt like we could win the game, and we practiced like we were going to win the game."

The swagger the veterans exuded was infectious.

"The seniors really had a lot of confidence about that game," adds Berlowski. "They read up on Jason (Kidd), they followed him. They knew about Lamond Murray as well."

"The confidence came from the five fifth-year seniors because a lot of those guys were on the team that played Michigan State earlier in their careers," notes Gary Grzesk. "We respected everybody, but really didn't fear anybody."

Pack Mentality

Genius or otherwise, the matchup would be a proving ground for Bennett's pack defense. And Bennett knew it.

"Once we got the matchup, I knew precisely what we had to do. We talked about it all week – we had to build a wall in front of Jason Kidd. And we had to just really cheat on the guys guarding the people next to him," he explains. "We were simply not going to let him get to the rim. If he wanted to shoot from outside, we were there to bother him, but that wasn't going to beat us."

"If their player gets around one of our players, there's going to be another guy waiting for them, maybe two," Martinez stated before the game. "Over the course of a game, that wears them down on offense. Then they have to play defense. We run them through a lot of screens, and I don't know if they're willing to battle through that for a whole game."

Though his matchups were set almost upon the announcement, Bennett had some fun with the media when asked whether Grzesk or Martinez would defend Jason Kidd. "What will probably happen is, I'll say, 'Who wants him?' and the guy who forgets to step back will get him."

Predictably, shutdown guard Gary Grzesk drew the lot, but he remembers the decision was not as obvious as it seemed.

"(Cal was) fairly tall at the guard position. They had a two-guard by the name of Monty Buckley that was like 6-5, so if I did end up guarding Kidd, John (Martinez) was going to have to guard him," Grzesk notes. "But in the end, Coach Bennett decided to put John on Monty, and then I ended up guarding Jason Kidd. And then Eric (Jackson) ended up – it was a natural fit – guarding (Lamond Murray)."

Bennett was keenly aware of the height mismatch Martinez would face with the taller Buckley, and for the first time in his career, took it to his senior guard in practice.

"John hated Coach Bennett for this, but that was probably the only time that John really had to do a box-out rebounding drill with the forwards and the post guys," says Grzesk. "But in the end, that's what we needed to do to get ready to play against it."

"Coach Bennett got all over him. First time he's *ever* gotten all over John," remembers Ludvigson. "John was one of those players where Coach Bennett just kind of gave him the ball and let him do his thing. Never yelled at John. Last practice in Green Bay, his senior year, he gets all over John about not blocking out, he's going to have to be ready."

His coach's mood irked Martinez.

"I was in the training room icing my knee, and so was John," recalls Berlowski. "And John's like, 'Dude, did you see what happened today? Coach Bennett *yelled* at me?' And I'm like, 'Yeah?' He goes, 'Dude, I never get yelled at, bro.' "

While Martinez was stretched to his limits, the Phoenix was also balancing a delicate medical issue. LeDuc had been held in isolation, having contracted chicken pox after the conference championship.

"They didn't want anybody to know, because they were afraid if the NCAA found out I had chicken pox, they weren't going to want me to come to an NCAA regional site. So I had to stay home (and) only practiced one day leading up to the tournament," LeDuc says. "It's the reason why, if you watch that tournament game, I'm wearing a green t-shirt under my uniform. Because there's no way in hell Dick would've let somebody wear a t-shirt under their uniform. But by that time I had begun to scab over, and you could see them."

Punky Band of Fellows

Though the Phoenix knew all about California, the same could not be said for its opponent. After hearing of the selection, Cal's star point guard, Jason Kidd, was quoted saying: "I saw them play early in the season at the Great Alaska Shootout, and to tell you the truth, I don't remember *anything* about them."

His high-profile teammate, Lamond Murray, seconded that sentiment, admitting, "I don't know anything about them."

"I *know* they (overlooked us)," remarks Logan Vander Velden, who later played with Murray and received his first-hand account. "(Their coach) was telling them to take us seriously. He was going to put the tape in, and he was like, 'You take these guys seriously. Don't underestimate these guys.' And I know when he put the tape it, they laughed. He admitted they took us lightly."

"They're out on the West Coast, having a very good team, now they're going to play these guys from Green Bay who, I think they referred to us as 'a bunch of workhorses,'" remembers Bennett.

Cal was not alone. The media was equally oblivious to the Phoenix.

One article in particular stood the test of time, at least with Ludvigson: "I'll give you a quote that a writer out in California wrote about us before the game that we used as motivation, and I'll never forget it. He said, 'I'm sure that Ludvigson, Nordgaard and Vander Velden and the rest of the Swedish ski team are a punky band of fellows, but they're no match for California's physicality.' End quote."

The Flying J Motel

On Tuesday, the Phoenix team and around 150 fans rode a charter bus out to Ogden, Utah, taking over a small motel on the outskirts of town. UWGB wasn't the only school from the Dairy State to be placed in Utah. The Wisconsin Badgers had also made the tournament as a 9 seed, matched up with Cincinnati at the same location. Nevertheless, few teams were ranked lower than the Phoenix when it came to assigning lodging.

"Cincinnati, Missouri – those schools were all in downtown Ogden," recalls Grzesk. "We ended up getting assigned outside of the city at the Flying J, which actually kind of fit our team and our personality. We were just kind of a blue-collar group of guys that we were not staying at the fanciest hotel, but were staying at the Flying J *Motel*."

"It was a truck stop," adds Bennett. "It was one of those where as soon as you went out of your room, you were outside. There were no lobbies or hallways, but it was fine."

One thing the Flying J had invested in was the latest in high-tech communication equipment. "I remember getting faxes to the hotel from family, friends from high school. Like, 'Congrats, good luck' faxes!" laughs Nordgaard.

UWGB's blue-collar style was on full display at the team's walkthrough the day before the game.

"All the other teams are doing dunks and alley-oops and stuff, and we're doing defensive slides," Nordgaard says. "People come to watch practice and they're like, 'Really, what? We came to watch this? They're doing defensive slides and closeout drills?' "

The walk-through looked similar to the team's 1991 dry run, but the two squads bore little resemblance after that.

"We relied heavily on Tony in '91 to get the team going," explains Martinez, "whereas the '94 team was completely the opposite. You didn't know who to guard. Anybody could score, and that was a great feeling to have."

Game Time

On Thursday, March 17, 1994, Tim Ryan and Ann Meyers were on location at the Dee Events Center on Weber State's campus to handle CBS's broadcasting duties for the West Region's first- and second-round games. The opening game saw Jim Boeheim's 4-seed Syracuse Orangemen beat the 13-seeded Hawaii Rainbows 92-78, setting the opponent for the winner of the UWGB vs. Cal game.

Bennett put in a fresh stick of gum as he anxiously prepared his team, a scowl on his face. He'd waited three years for another shot at the Big Dance, and wanted to make sure his team made the most of the opportunity.

It would be a clash in styles, with Cal using to an up-tempo style of play, their guards pushing the floor as often and hard as possible. The challenge for the Bears would be stamina, playing at high elevation with a much lighter bench than the Phoenix.

UWGB, ranked third in the nation in scoring defense at 54.7 ppg, planned to stay true to its patient philosophies. The looming questions were whether it could remain disciplined enough to enforce a slower tempo and make enough shots to keep pace.

In their road green jerseys on St. Patrick's Day, UWGB looked to have the luck of the Irish in the early minutes. Nordgaard started the scoring, first hitting a 16-foot jump shot from the left corner, then a runner in the lane. A possession later, LeDuc hit a deep two-pointer to give UWGB a quick 6-0 lead at the four-minute commercial break.

Cal did precisely what was expected. They played a pressing, trapping defense and ran the floor, looking for quick baskets in transition. When UWGB was able to get back, Cal's offense stagnated, with players standing still and very little ball movement.

On the few occasions Cal was able to run, they did so at the expense of ball security, turning the ball over with sloppy passes on several occasions.

UWGB forced seven turnovers in the game's first five minutes. On top of it all, Cal was as cold as ice from the floor.

"I think the start gave us a ton of confidence. I mean, we jumped on them right away, were getting stops on the defensive end, and scoring on the offensive end," Grzesk says. "After that first five minutes, not only (did) we realize we could play with them, but we realized we would have a chance to beat them if we continued to play well."

The Phoenix remained patient, even when forcing turnovers and having numbers in transition, regularly taking the shot clock under ten seconds and often five seconds before putting up a shot. It was a steady build-up for the Phoenix, as Cal committed ten early turnovers and struggled to make anything. By the 7:48 mark, UWGB held a two-touchdown advantage, 21-7.

UWGB's hot shooting eventually cooled off, while Cal took better care of the ball and focused their half-court offense on getting the ball inside. The benefactor was center Ryan Jamison, who converted from both the field and the line in scoring seven points, trimming the 14-point advantage to four with less than 3:00 left in the first half.

The resilience of the Phoenix then came through, with the team scoring six straight points to take a 32-23 lead into the locker room. The pack defense, and Grzesk's individual play, had held Kidd in check, limiting the future NBA star to just eight points and two assists. Cal's speed had been on full display in the opening 20 minutes, but in the high altitude of Ogden, Utah, and with limited bench options, there were warning signs flashing for Bozeman's club.

20 Minutes to Glory

Nordgaard, who led the Phoenix with 10 points in the first half, started the effort in the second half scoring two quick baskets. Ludvigson knocked down a jumper as well, and Bozeman was forced to call a timeout with his team suddenly down by fifteen points to the region's #12 seed.

"We were really handling them that first half, and then coming out in the second half, we came out and scored like two or three quick buckets and they called a timeout," remembers Ludvigson. "We go to the bench and we're just like, 'Wow, we didn't think it'd be this easy.' "

After a Cal miss, Nordgaard found Ludvigson wide open on the other end for another layup, giving UWGB a commanding 40-23 lead just two and a half minutes into the second half. Ever the skeptic, Bennett remained unconvinced: "It's always hard when you get a big lead early. Boy, those are the toughest kind to protect."

Truer words have never been spoken.

The Phoenix exchanged baskets with the Golden Bears over the next few minutes, extending the lead as high as 18 points at 47-29 behind baskets by Nordgaard and Ludvigson. The fantastic period of basketball had awoken the arena, and the crowd now firmly backed the underdog Phoenix.

Meanwhile, Kidd continued to press and push the ball when possible, but was clearly frustrated by (as a local fan during the broadcast dubbed him) Gary "The Blanket" Grzesk. On nearly every possession, Grzesk

Cal star and future Hall of Famer Jason Kidd locks in on UWGB's John Martinez during the Phoenix's upset victory in the first round of the 1994 NCAA tournament. (Richard Mackson/Sports Illustrated via Getty Images)

seemed to have a hand in Kidd's face and forced a number of mid-air adjustments. But while Kidd struggled, his teammate, Lamond Murray, began to get into a rhythm and helped shoulder the offensive load. As a result, Cal succeeded in chipping away at the large Phoenix advantage.

The game seemed to shift when, around the 10:00 mark, Grzesk committed his fourth foul and was forced to the bench. Kidd immediately took advantage, assisting on a three-pointer and coming up with a loose ball on back-to-back possessions. A Murray basket over Vander Velden cut the deficit to 50-47, and Kidd scored on a lightning-quick drive to the basket on the next possession.

"Right away (after Gary was pulled), Jason blew by (us) like two or three times. I remember looking at the bench, like, 'Get Gary back in … we've got to keep this lead. Get Gary back in,' " Berlowski says.

The massive 18-point lead was gone, and Bennett had no choice but to do just that, his team up one point with 7:15 to play.

Even with Grzesk back on the floor, Kidd managed to assist on an easy basket by freshman guard Anwar McQueen, giving Cal its first lead of the game at 51-50. It had been a herculean effort in bringing his team back, but Kidd had orchestrated the rally in a matter of minutes. When viewed from the UWGB side, it looked a little too much like a drastic meltdown.

However, all of the effort was taking its toll on Kidd in the thin air of Ogden. Spent from his burst of adrenaline and not acclimated to the altitude, Kidd struggled to recover, bending over and gasping for breath at every break.

Cal's offense slowed considerably, and though the Bears took a slight lead, the tempo was playing in UWGB's favor. With less than three minutes to play and down one, the Phoenix's patience and experience was front and center.

"That's the point where just the confidence level of our team and the system, playing with each other all those years," states Martinez. "Nobody lost faith; nobody got nervous; nobody would question like, 'Now what?' It was, 'Stick to the plan,' and we did."

Indeed, the Phoenix took the lead when Grzesk found a streaking Nordgaard as he beat a tired Cal defense for an easy basket. It was 57-56 UWGB with 2:29 to play.

Tired and worn, McQueen walked the ball up the floor for Cal for what may have been the Golden Bears' laziest possession of the game. Cal's critical late-game opportunity consisted of zero screens, no movement off the ball, and two passes. And yet Cal was able to tie the game when, after a Murray miss, Michael Stewart grabbed a rebound and was fouled. It was Ludvigson's fourth of the game, putting the Phoenix in the precarious position of having three of its best defenders – Grzesk, LeDuc, and Ludvigson – down to their last fouls.

Stewart made one of two, and with a timeout on the floor, the score was again tied, 57-57, with 2:07 to play. Kidd came up with a huge steal on the next possession, anticipating a pass from Martinez to Ludvigson in the post.

"Jason Kidd got his paw on it, and back in position in like a split second. It was like a blur," describes Ludvigson.

And yet, even with the ball and the momentum, a gassed Kidd nevertheless walked it up the floor with 1:30 left to play.

"The elevation and our depth really played in our favor. We were playing 10, 11 guys regular minutes. They were playing maybe six or seven," notes Grzesk. "You could tell our screening and our physicality and our depth, and the elevation, was taking its toll on them."

Bennett crouched on all fours, nervous as his eyes shifted between the Cal players as they largely stood around while Kidd dribbled it well beyond the three-point line. When the shot clock hit 10, Kidd dribbled toward the baseline and elevated for a shot. But Grzesk was in his face, forcing Kidd to pass instead, something LeDuc anticipated. In a scramble with two other Cal players, LeDuc got his hands on the ball and Nordgaard smartly signaled for a timeout.

"I knew they had the possession toward them, so if it was a jump ball they'd get it," noted Nordgaard afterwards. "It looked like (LeDuc) had possession, so I called the timeout."

With less than 1:00 to play and the score tied at 57, it was UWGB's turn to try and take the lead down the home stretch. Martinez found Nordgaard working off a LeDuc screen, and the sophomore buried a mid-range jumper from the right baseline with just 30 seconds left. UWGB 59, Cal 57.

"It was definitely, at that time, my biggest shot ever, certainly," Nordgaard says.

Bennett remained the most nervous man in the arena.

"I felt bad," he says. "I was really engaged in the game, but I started getting that sick feeling that this wonderful performance, this wonderful year is going to, could end. And I just had that sick feeling."

With 27.2 seconds to play, this was Cal's last best chance to tie or take the lead, its season in the balance. Bozeman took his team's final timeout, wanting to set the perfect play.

From the left wing, Kidd worked through a screen by Murray, dribbling to the top of the key as the clock ticked under 20 seconds. LeDuc showed for a moment while Grzesk recovered from the screen.

"Gary had those tree trunk legs, man, that he could just stay in front and get through screens and stay in front of Jason. It was unbelievable," remembers Ben Berlowski.

With 18 seconds left, Kidd lifted for a long shot from the top of the key. Grzesk, quickly recovering, elevated and challenged the shot, while LeDuc sprinted to the basket, preparing for a box-out. Kidd's shot was short, and LeDuc's positioning allowed him to keep Murray off the boards.

The ball was tipped, first by LeDuc, then by the Bears' Akili Jones, out of bounds. It was UWGB's ball with a two-point lead and just 14.8 seconds remaining. And Cal was out of timeouts.

Cal rushed to set its press as Grzesk inbounded the ball to Martinez in the corner. The athletic Golden Bears came with a well-positioned double-team, but rather than hold the trap, they instead quickly fouled Martinez, sending him to the line with 13.5 seconds left.

This was it. Martinez had two free throws to give his team a two-possession lead in the biggest game in school history. The Phoenix bench grasped hands and sank to their knees in prayer. All five Cal players were lined up along the lane, while only Ludvigson stood in for UWGB.

"They didn't have a timeout, so, you know, that probably would've been a good time (for them) to take one," remembers Martinez. "An extra

The defensive effort of UWGB's Gary Grzesk (22) played a major role in limiting Jason Kidd and the Cal Bears during the Phoenix's 61-57 upset victory. (Richard Mackson/ Sports Illustrated via Getty Images)

couple of minutes of thinking about it, you know who knows what would've happened."

As it was, the senior calmly took the ball, bounced a few dribbles, and launched his first free throw.

"The first shot kind of bounced in. It didn't go straight in. So it kind of like hit the rim a couple of times and went in," describes Martinez. "I kind of just looked at (Ludvigson) and gave him this smirky smile, like I meant to do that type of thing."

Hands reached for the sky on the Phoenix bench, while the crowd roared at the three-point Phoenix advantage. A few seconds later, Martinez adjusted his aim and his second shot found nothing but net. It was now UWGB 61, Cal 57 with 13.5 seconds left.

UWGB set its half-court, man-to-man defense, and Cal, with no timeouts, got the ball to its superstar, who raced up the floor. Grzesk had no hope of stopping the ball as Kidd went to the left, intent on getting a quick layup. But Grzesk had enough speed and intelligence to stay in step and contest Kidd's effort, which may have been the difference. Kidd's shot careened to the left and went out of bounds off LeDuc. Cal retained possession, trailing by four with 6.1 seconds left.

The inbounds pass went from Kidd to McQueen, who found Murray at the top of the key. Murray threw up a prayer with two seconds left that missed the mark. LeDuc secured the rebound, and the fifth-year senior chucked the ball into the rafters as the clock struck zeros.

In the words of Tim Ryan: "Rebound, Upset."

Pie in the Sky

"(LeDuc) threw that thing probably as high as he could, and then all of us rushed into the middle of the court," remembers Grzesk. "It was just one big celebration there at half court."

The Phoenix had done the unthinkable. UWGB's win over Cal was without question the greatest victory in the history of the school, and one that would stay with the team for the rest of their lives. The celebration continued into the locker room, though Bennett maintained tight control over the guest list.

"We're all losing our minds," Ludvigson says. "The media comes into our locker room, and I remember Coach Bennett just getting all kinds of mad and kicking them out."

"The TV people wanted to come into our locker room afterwards and I did not let them," admits Bennett. "They thought I was a little crazy ... but we never did that, and I never did it in any of my years."

The players relished the win in the intimate environment.

"I thought, 'This is perfect. This is where I knew I wanted to be when I got out of high school. This is perfect,' " LeDuc beamed afterwards. "Even after we won the conference tournament, nobody on the team would have been happy unless we had won here. And we're planning on winning at least two games."

"After that game, we showered and we were going to the bus, and I got a call from Mike Holmgren, who at that time of course was with the Packers," Bennett says of the former Packers head coach. "He had been at Cal, and he said he was really happy for us. He had told Cal, because he knew a lot of those people, he said, 'You guys don't know what you're in for.' He had warned them."

Even with the Phoenix win, there was no mistaking who the most talented player on the floor had been, and it wasn't close.

"We played against a lot of good players, but there was only twice that I was on the court that I felt like this player was in a different planet than I was," remarks Ludvigson, "and (one) was with Jason Kidd."

"His speed was what jumped out at me. If he could get the ball in his hands in the backcourt and he took off with it, if you weren't back, there was nothing you could do," recalls Bennett. "He was probably the fastest player with the ball that I've coached against. He just – he could fly."

"Jason Kidd never changed when he was a sophomore in college to (when) he left the NBA," adds Berlowski. "He was the same body makeup, the same speed, the same strength – I mean he was a man amongst boys when he was a sophomore."

All of that just made what the Phoenix defense had done all the more spectacular. With a combination of genius scheme, total buy-in, and a stone-cold stopper in Grzesk, UWGB had shut down a future NBA legend.

"We did make it real hard on Jason Kidd, and he's admitted that himself," notes Bennett. "That was really the team that made me commit to the pack (defense) as being a really good defense."

Central to that defensive performance, and the justifiable recipient of much of the praise, was Grzesk. Grzesk played 37 minutes, nearly all of which were spent holding Kidd to 12 points, including just 1-for-7 shooting from three-point land.

"He turned a first-team All-American into - what was he, 3-for-15?" states Nordgaard. "He locked him up."

"Gary did such a great job of keeping him squarely in front of him that we didn't have to over-help," explains Bennett. "The danger in over-helping against a great player like Kidd is he'll find the open man."

"It definitely gives you that much more confidence as a teammate to kind of do your own thing and not have to worry about in the back of your mind, 'Well, we're going to need to help Gary with Jason Kidd all day,' " says Martinez. "That's just what Gary brought to the team ... even though we had a great system in place, a lot of that credit goes to him individually."

The moment was legacy-cementing, both for Grzesk personally and the Phoenix program.

"It's probably my single greatest memory from my playing days," admits Grzesk. "It was probably the biggest win in the history of Green Bay basketball. It put us on the map nationally, and it proved that quality has no divisions or boundaries, which was one of Coach Bennett's favorite sayings."

"I always say this: Gary's the most underrated and overrated player in the history of UWGB basketball," Nordgaard adds with a laugh. "People that don't know basketball well are like, 'This guy can't shoot – look at his ugly shot. He doesn't do anything out there.' But they don't know how important he is on his defense, and his unselfishness in other ways, too, screens and making the passes.

"But then, because he locked up Jason Kidd, he gets all the credit for that win. And I have people say, 'Oh, were you on that team Jeff?' Was I on that team!? What do you mean? Just because I didn't defend Kidd?!' "

Sweet Dreams

One of the perks of winning a first-round game was the offer to upgrade accommodations. But while many of the players were looking forward to spending the extra time in a much nicer hotel, their old-school coach felt a move was unnecessary.

"We could get Cal's hotel rooms and move to a nice room instead of the Flying J, but Coach Bennett said, 'Nope, we're good here, I like the (coconut pie)' or whatever he said it was that they were serving at the diner there," recalls Nordgaard.

"We were offered that, but we turned it down. It was my decision," Bennett acknowledges. "They had great coconut cream pie – it's the best coconut cream pie I've had to this day."

Bennett let his players enjoy the victory for the rest of the day. The team went out for dinner, and to their surprise found the Golden Bears at the same restaurant. "As we're sitting down, in comes the California team, paraded by us to the back room to have dinner. They had to walk by us at the same restaurant," remembers Ludvigson. "It was crazy."

Afterwards, the UWGB party returned to the Flying J and enjoyed seeing themselves as the lead story that evening on ESPN's *SportsCenter*. For one shining moment, UWGB was on top of the world. After a night of celebrating, the team turned to preparation for its next opponent, the Syracuse Orangemen. This time, UWGB would not be flying under the radar.

"Everybody knows how good this team is," remarked Syracuse coach Jim Boeheim. "I don't think there's any secret about that now.

Boeheim knew what he was talking about. His program had a one-man intelligence department in the form of assistant coach Tim O'Toole. Back in 1990, O'Toole helped recruit LeDuc to Army, and the two had stayed in touch. Guided by O'Toole's scouting reports, Boeheim advised his team to be patient on defense.

"You can't make a turtle run," he said. "If you try to pressure a team like this, they're smart and they'll take advantage of that and get easy baskets. I think you pressure only as much as you have to, and if you have to, it's a gamble."

Syracuse was an entirely different beast than any team the Phoenix had played all year. The Orangemen were exceptionally long and quick, enabling them to play a wicked 2-3 zone that eliminated easy shots inside the arc and challenge perimeter shots. Boeheim's team was one of the smarter squads in the country and had been ranked in the top 25 the entire year.

Sophomore forward John Wallace and tall, lanky guards Lawrence Moten and Adrian Autry were the fire starters for Boeheim's scheme, with forward Lucius Jackson and center Otis Hill rounding out the 'Cuse starting lineup.

"Syracuse was the biggest team I think I have ever played against," remembers Martinez. "These big-time programs, that's the way it is. I mean, you're going to be 6-5 or 6-6 at every position, or taller. And that's the way they were."

In typical Bennett fashion, UWGB had not prepared for Syracuse at all prior to the tournament.

"I never (prepared ahead). My rule was to my last day of coaching in the tournament was always the same, and Tony does the same thing," Bennett states. "I'm sure Mike (Heideman) had watched anyone we might play, but I never went beyond the team we were playing next."

"We did very little scouting of the other team," adds Ludvigson. "It was all about what we're going to do, our game plan, and how we're going to play."

In the case of Syracuse, scouting may have been futile anyway.

"They're playing a 2-3 zone with guys who are longer, bigger," notes Berlowski. "That's a tough zone to play against. Where are you going to find the gaps?"

"In that practice the day before, we worked against a zone," recalls Grzesk. "You can try to simulate it and work on your offense, but until you go against their length, you really don't understand why their zone is that effective."

Perhaps it was naïveté or willful ignorance, but there was no fear in the Phoenix locker room.

"We had already beaten the 5 seed, so I think there was a lot of confidence that we could play with anybody at that time," Grzesk says.

"No one was intimidated. We just did our own thing," adds Martinez. "It's an exciting feeling to play against top-notch (teams) where you can really gauge where you really fit."

Zoned Out

It took just moments for UWGB to realize the Syracuse zone was worthy of the hype, with the Orangemen pestering the Phoenix early and owning the offensive glass. But a long two-pointer by Ludvigson and a three-pointer by Martinez on early possessions helped demonstrate the formula for beating it.

"I've seen Syracuse play that zone hundreds of times. And either you can shoot a three – a deep three because they're so long – or you have to get into the lane," explains Martinez.

UWGB took an early 12-7 lead on a second Martinez three-pointer, but that lead wouldn't last. The hands of Syracuse's defenders were always active, and nearly all lazy passes were prone to deflections and turnovers. On one of those turnovers, John Wallace went the distance and turned in a monster dunk, giving the Orangemen the lead.

"He went up for a dunk from the other side of the court, it seemed like. It was just like, 'Oh my gosh, what is that?!'" remembers Ludvigson.

No place was the talent gap quite as stark as on a series of possessions midway through the first half. First, Berlowski caught a pass from Zavada on the left wing, with no Orangeman closer than the lane. Berlowski gath-

*UWGB's Gary Grzesk (right) guards Syracuse's Lawrence Moten during their sec-
ond-round game in the 1994 NCAA tournament. (Mark Turney / The Daily Orange)*

ered himself and lifted for a shot, but by the time the ball left his hands, the
long Luscious Jackson had recovered.

"I think Luscious Jackson was underneath the basket when I looked
at him, and then when I went to go shoot the basketball, he blocked it,"
remembers an impressed Berlowski.

Jackson gathered it in and fed the ball ahead to Lawrence Moten, who
made an easy layup.

One possession later, a quickly closing Moten made a nearly identical
play on a Martinez three-point attempt. Syracuse's Adrian Autry converted
on the other end with an easy jump shot in the lane.

On the third consecutive UWGB possession, Nordgaard caught a pass
along the baseline and went up for a reverse layup, but his shot was swatted out of bounds by Otis Hill. That series helped Syracuse take a 21-15 lead

with 6:30 to play.

"I can remember the first couple shots thinking, you know, we're going to get good shots, and like guys coming from eight, ten feet away and getting their fingertip on a ball, or deflecting a pass, or blocking a shot," says LeDuc. "We had a little bit of a moment to adjust to it."

Unlike the Cal game, UWGB relinquished control and allowed Syracuse to dictate the pace of play in the first half. Out of rhythm, the Phoenix was sloppy, throwing the ball away, and taking ill-advised shots early in the shot clock. Fouls also played a factor, with the Orangemen spending a significant part of the first half shooting free throws. All of this allowed Syracuse to build the six-point margin all the way into a 37-21 lead with less than a minute remaining.

Mercifully, the Phoenix was able to score five straight to end the half, including a three-pointer by Nordgaard at the buzzer. But if the Phoenix had any hope of making a game of it, they needed to clean up their offense and get after the boards.

Don't Call It a Comeback

Bennett reamed his team at the half, telling them they were not alert, intimidated, and at least a step slow. The lead neither grew nor shrunk for the first few minutes of the second half, but after a Ludvigson layup cut the deficit to eight with 12:00 to play, things began to change.

UWGB's defense tightened its grip, forcing turnovers and taking charging calls, while the Phoenix offense finally made a few baskets.

"To go against that type of length, it took us a half just to get used to it," remembers Grzesk. "And then I think in the second half, the game kind of slowed down for us. We attacked the zone much better, got on a little bit of a roll, and really gave ourselves a chance."

A Nordgaard jumper trimmed the 'Syracuse lead to 52-48 lead with under 10:00 to play, forcing Boeheim to call a timeout. All the momentum had switched to the boys in green and white, with the crowd now thoroughly behind the underdogs.

From there, the game remained within five points the rest of the way, and as the clock ticked under 3:00 to play, Vander Velden found Ludvigson cutting to the hoop for an easy layup. With 2:30 to play, the score was Syracuse 58, UWGB 57.

Syracuse had two chances on its next possession, but came up short on both. With less than 2:00 left, Ludvigson grabbed a rebound and suddenly UWGB found itself with an opportunity to take the lead.

Could UWGB do it? Could it pull off a second upset, and punch a ticket to the Sweet Sixteen?

Martinez would have a golden opportunity. On the following possession, Martinez caught a pass beyond the arc, shot-faked and took two dribbles toward the basket before lifting for his patented floater – the same floater that had downed DePaul three years earlier. But this time, the shot was just short, and worse, Moten grabbed the rebound for Syracuse.

Luscious Jackson was fouled on the ensuing possession and made the first of two free throw attempts with 1:28 left. Otis Hill grabbed his errant second free throw, again giving Syracuse a second chance. The Orange-men dribbled time away, the clock ticking under 1:00 before Adrian Autry nailed a soft floater, putting Syracuse up 61-57.

And somehow, all was not lost, as the Phoenix appeared to answer not once, but twice. First, on a nifty play, Vander Velden found Ludvigson cut-ting as Nordgaard boxed Hill out of the way. Ludvigson has a clear look at a right-handed layup ... but missed the bunny.

But UWGB retained possession after a tie-up, and on the follow-up possession, Berlowski received a cross-court pass with just 40 seconds left. Finding himself on the left wing with the taller, slower John Wallace guarding him, Berlowski shot-faked and easily blew past Wallace toward an open basket. A slow-rotating Hill stepped in toward Berlowski as the sophomore lifted for a layup, which dropped through the basket as the whistle blew. For an instant, it felt like the Phoenix were on the verge of a three-point play.

But that moment evaporated when the official signaled a charge against Berlowski instead. The magnitude of the call was not lost on Berlowski: "It was probably one of the most crucial calls I think in the tournament that year. You know, I thought it should've been an and-one."

Vander Velden shared Berlowski's view. "I've watched it a few times, and if they call a charge they call a charge. But, in my opinion, the ball left his hand (before contact), so the bucket should've counted. That changes the whole trajectory of the game, because we had to foul after that. And so that would've made that game a whole lot different."

Grzesk quickly fouled Autry on Syracuse's ensuing possession, picking up his fifth and exiting the game. From there, Syracuse did enough at the free throw line to close out the Phoenix season, moving on to the Sweet Sixteen with a 64-59 win.

The Orangemen celebrated like they'd taken down a giant.

"One of my memories is how elated the Syracuse team was after they beat us. They were jumping around like they won the NCAA tournament," recalls Ludvigson. "It was kind of respect in a way."

Boeheim was impressed by the Phoenix: "There's nobody in this tour-nament that would have an easy time with them. I'm not trying to be a nice guy, but that's a very, very good basketball team."

LeDuc's connection confirmed those were no idle words. "I was talking to Tim O'Toole, talking to Jim Boeheim (after the game), and really those two saying, 'We're happy we got past you guys,'" reports LeDuc. "Because they did NOT take us lightly. They were definitely ready to play, and pre-pared."

Deep Impact

It was a game of missed opportunities.

"Ben Berlowski's drive, my baseline shot, (and) when Syracuse was shooting a free throw at the end, they got their own rebound," remembers Martinez. "There were like a few opportunities that could've gone the other way, and the result would've been different."

"It didn't go our way," notes Grzesk. "It's amazing what a call here or a call there could do on your perspective."

Of all three, it was the Berlowski call that perhaps stood out as most disappointing.

"It's real hard to get those calls," Bennett says. "But then again, we got the same call in the (UIC) game that got us into the tournament and could have gone the other way."

The loss and its greater implications were tough for the players to swallow. Martinez placed a heap of blame on himself.

"I definitely helped the team that accomplished the goal of getting back to the NCAA tournament, but I also feel like I was the reason that we didn't get past the second round," he says. "When your point guard is playing at, 55, 60 percent at best, you're only going to go so far. They went with me and my two broke knees, and just rolled the dice. And we came close – we almost got to the Sweet Sixteen."

"I wish we could have gotten (to the Sweet Sixteen)," Bennett said after the game. "It became apparent we can play at that level. You start thinking some crazy thoughts, like maybe we can make the Final Four."

In Ogden's other second-round matchup, Missouri rather easily disposed of the Wisconsin Badgers, 109-96. The Tigers continued their streak, beating Syracuse in overtime in the Sweet Sixteen before ultimately falling to Arizona in the Elite Eight.

Meanwhile, Wisconsin's other tournament team, Marquette, pulled off a minor upset in the second round, beating the favored Kentucky Wildcats to make it to the second weekend of action. Duke eliminated Marquette in the Sweet Sixteen, 59-49.

But the talk of the first weekend remained the 12-seeded Phoenix and the 12-seeded Golden Hurricanes from Tulsa, who not only beat blue blood UCLA in the first round, but also knocked off Oklahoma State to one-up the Phoenix. The 5-12 matchup was evolving into *the* trendy first-round matchup for upsets.

"The infamous 5-12 seed, and that was kind of like where we started that thing. We had a big 5-12 upset, then all of the sudden Butler, Gonzaga, these teams started having these matchups," Berlowski points out. "You've got a team that was a top 25 team that was decent against a team that was a top mid-major that was coming in who could compete, and who's will was going to win that night?"

By the time the 1994 NCAA tournament concluded, images of the Phoenix's trip to Ogden were forever ingrained in tournament and program history.

"I still get the chills when I see (the 1994) *One Shining Moment* video because we are in it three or four times," Nordgaard says. "LeDuc throwing that ball up and asking for hugs, and the band and the bird. Every time I see *One Shining Moment* – and I make sure my kids see that, too – it takes me back to that '94 team out in Ogden."

"I think that was probably the pinnacle of it," adds Ludvigson. "The fact that we not only won, but beat a team that was a dark horse to go to the Final Four, that had a couple of lottery picks on it, really cemented us on the map to say, 'Okay, we're a program that really can beat the heavyweights.' In the NCAA tournament, when it really matters, on the big stage, we beat 'em. So I think from a recruiting standpoint, a viability standpoint, that was incredible."

Fifth-Year Goodbyes

UWGB's five fifth-year seniors were the glue that bound the team together. They set the tone, created the attitude, mixed the chemistry, and drove the success. Five distinct souls from different backgrounds, each with unique career paths that intersected in a magical farewell tour.

At the time, Bennett called them "the best group of seniors I've worked with in twenty-nine years of coaching." Decades later, Bennett's attitude hadn't diminished in the slightest: "They were all high-character players and all smart players who understood the game."

His players fed off the faith he had in them.

"He had a lot of respect for who we were as a team and who we were from a senior leadership standpoint that he allowed for some room with those things," Ludvigson notes.

"He gave up some control and let us kind of manage that team. And in a lot of ways, kind of figure stuff out for ourselves," agrees LeDuc. "I think that really helped us in especially close games, where we weren't relying on a coach to draw up plays, or a coach to tell us to rebound or whatever. Everyone was really dialed in and on the same page."

With the blessing of their coach, the five fifth-year seniors all led, some with their selflessness and sacrifice, others more vocally.

"That group of guys, especially Eric (LeDuc) and Jeremy (Ludvigson), they were the glue of that team," recalls Nordgaard. "We saw how they brought us in, and make us feel a part of 'their' team, but they were probably a little more unsung than a lot of seniors might be on a team that is that level."

LeDuc, the transfer from Army, had been an energetic defensive force during his three-year stint with Green Bay. Though he never averaged more than four points per game, he was one of the Phoenix's interior enforcers, leading the team in blocks in both his junior and senior years. He was quick to build relationships, and demonstrated his dedication through the intensity he brought every day to the gym.

"Eric and I were very like-minded. We were very tough, hard-nosed players," comments Ludvigson.

Like LeDuc, Ludvigson also prided himself of sacrificing the individual praise for the team's success. "I was willing to do the little things – screen, rebound, play hard. I was kind of scrappy like that."

While perhaps weaker on defense, Ludvigson had flashed more scoring potential than LeDuc, finishing his senior year as the team's fourth-leading scorer at 8.4 ppg and earning all-tournament honors in both the Great Alaska Shootout and the First Bank Classic. And, as Bennett noted, "Jeremy, I thought, was the most outgoing leader of the bunch."

Ludvigson's unselfishness rubbed off on his fifth-year counterpart, Jeff Zavada. The big man transfer from Marquette had endured his ups and downs throughout his college career, but eventually accepted a lesser role while buying in to Bennett's system.

"He was the leading returning scorer from the team the year before, and he was playing earlier and starting on that team," Grzesk says. "Then he was asked to sacrifice some of his scoring, and starting, and minutes for the betterment of the team, and once he accepted that and bought into his role, I think the team took off."

The team's fourth big man senior was also its quietest. It took him a few years to make an impact, but once he settled in to his sixth-man role, Logan Vander Velden flourished.

"He's a small-town guy, too," notes Nordgaard. "He was a hunter and fisherman, and really an innocent, innocent guy. We became friends and had a good time."

Unlike his classmates, Vander Velden was quite introverted and could be difficult to read.

"He had a phenomenal jump shot, unbelievable skills, he really did," remarks Berlowski, "(but) he frustrated Coach a lot because he could never really tell. Coach could yell at him and Logan just had the same demeanor. You just couldn't get to him. He wouldn't show emotion."

Grzesk loved Vander Velden's ability to get into the zone: "He just would get on these rolls and just kind of carry us. And he had such a unique skill set for a guy who was 6-8, maybe 6-9 to score on the block, step out and shoot the three."

"I wasn't sure about his explosiveness or quickness," Bennett recalls, "but he had one of the most beautiful shots. And at 6-9, he could lift that shot. He had such a touch."

Vander Velden finished as the team's second-leading scorer both his junior (10.3 ppg) and his senior year (10.4 ppg). Few of his teammates would have guessed that he'd take that success and parlay it into a professional career, but that's exactly what he had in mind.

"After our senior year, we'd be out at the bar, having some drinks, and he'd come up and just be like, 'I'm going to make the league next year. I'm going to make the league,' " remembers Ludvigson. "And he wasn't *practicing*. Like, he wasn't working hard on his game. He didn't start for us."

And yet somehow, Vander Velden worked his way through the USBL and eventually fielded a call from the Los Angeles Clippers for a tryout in the fall of 1995. By the end of the preseason, he had shown the Clippers enough to earn a roster spot for the start of the regular season, ironically playing alongside former Cal forward Lamond Murray.

On November 9, 1995, Vander Velden saw his first minutes of NBA action in a road game at Seattle and got his first basket.

"I don't know if it was thundering, (but) my first NBA points did come on a dunk," he remarked afterwards.

Skeptical as they had been, his Phoenix teammates were thrilled for him and enjoyed the opportunity to get in on the fun.

"Even though Logan only played fifteen games in the NBA, Jeremy Ludvigson and I made sure we made two trips to Los Angeles in those fifteen games," notes LeDuc.

"Eric LeDuc and I went out there right away when he made it, and I remember sitting with him at the Key Club in LA," Ludvigson recalls. "We went out there and saw him play against Jordan and the Bulls, and the Orlando Magic and Shaq. We're sitting there in LA, and we met Stanley Roberts and Magic (Johnson), and just surreal. Like, is this really happening?"

The Clippers waived Vander Velden in January 1996, but not before the lanky kid from Valders had reached the pinnacle of professional sports.

The final member of the Phoenix's stellar senior class was John Martinez, the heart and soul of the team and unquestionably one of the most iconic players in UWGB's history.

"John was a special player. I don't know how many people truly appreciated how good he was," comments Tony Bennett. "He was one of the most gifted passers I have ever played with or seen to this day. He just had this innate ability, and you cannot coach it."

"In the open gyms in the summer, when he would go against Tony (Bennett) – when John was healthy – Tony probably practiced and worked and made himself into a pro, but there were a lot of times where there was not that much difference between John and Tony," observes Grzesk. "He was just such a fluid, smooth basketball player, and had a great feel for the game. And he had the unique ability to make everyone else around him better."

"Johnny was the quiet leader of the group for sure. John was so smooth, his ball-handling skills were just incredible," states Berlowski. "He just had a way with handling the basketball and dishing it and finding the open man that was just a notch

John Martinez battled through painful knees to give all he could in the 1994 NCAA tournament. (University of Wisconsin-Green Bay Archives)

above everybody else from a point guard perspective."

"He was a very gifted passer," remarks Dick Bennett. "And he had a style that was just, kind of unique. He never rushed, he didn't look quick, but he just had a smooth style in everything he did. And he was a very accomplished player."

"John's level of passing was unlike anybody I've ever seen, even to this day," remembers Chris Westlake. "He was a special guy. There's players over the years that you play with that you know can do things that you just can't teach, and he's definitely one of those."

Martinez accomplished nearly everything a player could at a mid-major. He played in five postseason games (2 NIT, 3 NCAA), and the Phoenix made the postseason *every year* he played. Yet for fans and teammates, there was always the question of 'what could have been' had Martinez not hurt his knees.

"He doesn't get hurt, he goes to the NBA and makes millions," says Ludvigson. "I mean, he does."

But for an older and wiser Martinez, there's no reason to dwell with sadness on lost hardwood opportunities.

"If I would have never gotten hurt, I probably would have played somewhere," he says. "Even if it wasn't the NBA, it probably would've been like – let's just say it was over in Italy or whatever. And I would have probably lived there, and might still be there. And I would never have met my wife and my two girls. So there's a reason why that all happened. I can't imagine my life without them. So it worked out – there's a reason it worked out the way it did, and I am absolutely 100 percent thankful and appreciative that it did work out the way it did."

Best Ever?

With their five seniors, that 1993-94 Phoenix team had a legitimate claim to being included on the short list of the greatest teams in school history.

Ten years after the Cal game and four years after going to the 2000 Final Four with Wisconsin, Dick Bennett admitted that the 1993-94 UWGB Fighting Phoenix were the best team he ever coached.

"That team was the most together, had the most tools, and the most depth," he states. "I think it would have done well in any league in the country. That team was so solid that you couldn't crack them."

Another twenty years after that comment, nothing had changed: "I've said I think that was the best team I had at Green Bay, and that included when Tony was there. I think this was the most complete team. It was also the most unselfish team, and it was a group of guys that took care of themselves."

"You get (players) to buy in to a team setting, just the same way we had with our '94 team, you'll be in every game. You just will be," adds Berlowski. "That's what Dick Bennett figured out. It doesn't matter how talented on offense. If you can somehow take away – almost like a general from an army or whatever – how can we take this away, and take that way, and strategically negate their firepower. And that's what playing defense like that does."

Much of that success was the team's unselfishness and willingness to sacrifice. Commemorating that impact, Dick Bennett had the word "Servant" imprinted on the inside of their 1994 NCAA rings.

Chapter 17

Adapt and Survive
(1994-95 - Part 1)

Mid-major programs must play the hand they are dealt. Limited scouting budgets and heavy competition put mid-majors in the challenging position of having to make the most of whatever talent they can gather.

Without assurances over the skill level on the roster, rigidity and close-mindedness in approach simply have no hope of sustained success. Consistently winning requires an accommodating system and flexible philosophy that bends with the personnel to accentuate their strengths and shade the weaknesses.

Local Flavor

Big changes were in store for the Phoenix as it began the offseason before the 1994-95 campaign. Five fifth-year seniors had graduated, four of which made up Dick Bennett's power forward and center faction. His tallest returning player? Jeff Nordgaard at 6-6 (6-7 in the media guide).

"We went from one of maybe the biggest teams in the country to overnight, in one class, graduating all those post guys, to one of the smallest teams in the country," comments Gary Grzesk.

Bennett was confident in the talent of his returning junior class, but knew what he needed. The number one, two, and three priorities for the 1994 recruiting class were, in no particular order, height, height, and height.

And yet, as the process unfolded, the Phoenix lost out on a number of their taller targets. Bennett was notably disappointed with his inability to close, stating, "It's been surprising and discouraging how hard it's been."

And so Bennett spent his first two signings on unsung local guards in Green Bay East's Kevin Olm and Ashwaubenon's Ryan Borowicz. Olm was 6-3 and a true point guard through and through, known for his good court vision and ball handling. Meanwhile, Borowicz had greater potential as a shooter, exhibiting great range even at the high school level. Finally, in

April 1994, Bennett added a third to his incoming class with 6-4 forward Gabe Stevens from Stevens Point.

Critics panned these recruits, in particular Olm and Borowicz, but Bennett defended the signings. "They said that about Tony, they said that about Martinez," noted Bennett. "It's typical of the comments you're going to hear from those whom aren't familiar with these guys."

Finally, in May 1994 and just five months before the start of the next season, Bennett finally landed some size. It started with James Daggs, a 6-7 forward from Bristol, Tennessee, who Bennett called him the "most talented frontcourt player" he had landed at Green Bay. "We're hoping he can become one of the best big kids we could ever get."

A few days later, UWGB signed 6-7 Mark Domenick. In a sign of his limited recruiting options, Bennett had pulled the trigger after seeing just one game tape and having a brief conversation with his high school coaches.

Then, as summer began, Bennett made his sixth and final signing, adding a 21-year-old, 6-4 forward. Tom Anderson was a high school dropout, and in typical Bennett fashion, the coach wanted his player to better himself, so he struck a deal – if Anderson got his GED and passed his entrance exams, Bennett would give him a scholarship. Anderson met Bennett's challenge and then some.

The late-season signings were important saves for the coaching staff, and even with them, Bennett continued to double-down on his enthusiasm for Olm and Borowicz: "I refuse to apologize on those kids. John Martinez wasn't recruited and look what he did. Gary Grzesk wasn't recruited and look what he did. Ben Johnson wasn't recruited and look what he did. The biggest surprise to me would be if they *didn't* have great careers."

Shift to Small Ball

As he had proven time and again, Bennett was willing to do what it took to make his team successful. With four upperclassman guards and a complete dearth of rebounding potential, Bennett reinvented his team and modified his entire offensive scheme to suit his changing roster.

"I knew we were going to have to play small, because our tallest guy returning was Jeff Nordgaard," he explains, "so we ended up playing four guards pretty much that whole year."

The move had little chance of success without confidence and leadership, which Nordgaard provided.

"(Before the season), Jeff asked me how I felt about things," remembers Chris Westlake. "And you know, I was discouraged at that moment because I didn't know how we were going to rebound. We're a Division I team, our biggest guy is 6-6. He just simply said, 'You know what, man, we're just going to block out. That's all we're going to do. We're going to block out and we're going to do our best.' And as simple as that sounds, that did it for me."

The Next Generation

Dick Bennett's willingness to adjust was based on the trust he had with his juniors. As for the team's sole senior, JUCO transfer Chris Westlake, the jury was still out.

Westlake had provided glimpses of his potential in 1993-94, but more often than not had played tight, struggling to adjust to Bennett's style and system. As his junior year was winding down, even while the team was making its conference tournament run, Westlake questioned if he would stay with the program. As the team prepared for Cal and the NCAA tournament a week later, Westlake fortuitously hit the gym with a shooting instructor, altering his shot and his fortunes.

"With my middle finger on this valve stem, the ball would come off the outside of my hand sometimes when I shot. But by putting my pointer finger on the valve stem, it came off two fingers – my middle finger and my pointer finger at about the same time," Westlake explains. "He tweaked that, and he made a huge difference in my consistency."

With some encouragement from Grzesk and a newfound shot, Westlake resolved to take his future into his own hands.

The Phoenix needed the athletic Chris Westlake to up his game in his final season with the Phoenix in 1994-95. (University of Wisconsin-Green Bay Archives)

"I had to say to myself that I can't allow Coach Bennett to get in my head," Westlake recalls. "I know how to play, I know I can do this."

The change in mindset would pay huge dividends.

"We thought he'd have more of a role on that (1993-94) team than he did," says Jeremy Ludvigson, "but I couldn't believe the following year."

"That first year, he and Coach Bennett butted heads," notes Nordgaard. "But Chris definitely bought in on that next year, and his athleticism and talent was something that we didn't have on any of our other players."

It was a good thing, too, because depth was another of Bennett's big problems. Beyond Westlake and the four juniors, he had just two returning players who had even seen the court the year before (Sam Maddox and Rico Rondorf), and both had averaged less than five minutes per game.

Bennett would turn to redshirt freshman Pete Wade and true freshman Kevin Olm to be the most likely contributors, but 1994-95 would be a seven-man operation.

In addition to the offensive scheme and personnel changes, UWGB had a named a new athletic director in the offseason, and he was a familiar face. In an unusual hire, UWGB picked former athletic trainer Dennis "Otis" Chambers to replace Dan Spielmann, making Chambers one of – if not the only – Division I athletic director to have a degree in sports medicine. Nevertheless, Chambers was well-liked and the move was a positive one in terms of continuity for the program.

A New Conference

Adding to the roster and administration shakeups, UWGB was joining a new conference, the MCC. UIC, Northern Illinois, Wright State, Cleveland State, and UW-Milwaukee also were moving to the MCC, but it was the existing conference stalwarts that figured to be some of the most intimidating competition.

It began with the Xavier Musketeers, a mid-major powerhouse that had made the NCAA tournament seven times in the previous nine seasons, all under Pete Gillen. Though Gillen had left to take over the reins at Providence, the Musketeers, with new coach Skip Prosser and star guard Jeff Massey, were again runaway favorites to win the MCC in 1994-95.

Meanwhile, with the return of its star guard, Kareem Townes, LaSalle was expected to be the conference's second-best team. The Explorers had only been in the MCC for two seasons, having left the MAAC in 1991-92 after a string of four NCAA tournament appearances in five seasons. While their run in the MCC had thus far produced a dreary 25-29 record, they were expected to be vastly improved in 1994-95. Rounding out the MCC's returning schools were solid Midwestern mid-majors Butler and Detroit, as well as conference doormat Loyola (Chicago).

"It was a clear step up to have teams like Xavier and Butler be a part of it," Nordgaard recalls.

With the increased competition and loss of talent in Green Bay, the preseason polls slotted UWGB in the middle of the pack behind Xavier, LaSalle, and UIC, and just ahead of Detroit and Butler. Nordgaard received token mention as the lone Phoenix selected to the preseason all-conference team, while UIC's Sherell Ford was the early pick to take home the player of the year honors.

"It surprised me a little bit (being picked fourth) in that we have the youngest group and the smallest group and the fewest returning letterman," remarked Bennett.

"We knew we had talent on the team," states Berlowski, "but we weren't sure what was going to happen at all."

Talk of the Town

The Green Bay fan base was back on the Phoenix bandwagon in the wake of its NCAA tournament win.

"It was one of those things where you'd go out to restaurants and people would know who you are and all that. It was exciting," Nordgaard says.

With that excitement came season ticket sales. By October, UWGB had secured more than 4,900 season ticket orders for the 5,500-seat Brown County Arena, marking the fifth consecutive season of at least 4,600 season tickets. The challenge for the administration was scheduling enough quality home games to satisfy the growing fan base.

Assistant coach Woody Wilson put together the best lineup he could, and while the schedule for 1994-95 was no comparison to the prior year's, it certainly included one considerable challenge.

Wilson had put the Phoenix on the road to start the year, with four games in eight days including games at Oregon, a rematch in Madison against Wisconsin, and a sneaky-good trap game at the MVC's Illinois State Redbirds.

Complicating the matter, the program had received a very late request from Marquette to get a rematch on the books. In the era of burgeoning cable sports, ESPN recognized the value in showcasing the two in-state tournament teams and worked hard to get the game booked. To accommodate Marquette, UWGB needed to bump a game it had scheduled with Western Kentucky to the following year. ESPN offered to telecast two Western Kentucky games to get the deal done, including the UWGB-Western Kentucky matchup in 1995-96 on its new ESPN2 network.

"We probably have the worst four-game stretch of anyone in the country," Wilson remarked.

With the schedule set, the team begin its fall workouts. Bennett's enthusiasm increased throughout the October sessions.

"I've been pleased by the shooting of the guys I didn't know would shoot well," he said. "Eric Jackson has been shooting it well. Even Gary Grzesk has done a better job of shooting."

Nordgaard and Grzesk also stepped up to the plate as leaders of the new Phoenix.

"They had the mental toughness and the emotional stability, the mental toughness, for being leaders," remembers Westlake.

The new-look Phoenix soared in its two exhibition games. Nordgaard and Westlake each dropped 24 points against Athletes in Action, while Berlowski added 13 in the convincing home victory. A week later against a traveling Croatian team, Nordgaard scored 24 points while Westlake added 15 in a blowout 77-50 victory.

Bucky Buckwalter, an NBA scout for the Portland Trail Blazers, was impressed: "This Croatian team isn't bad. Green Bay gave them a lesson tonight. Coach Bennett, without question, is one of the premier coaches at any level in the United States. They could surprise some people."

West Coast Woes

As UWGB packed its bags for the season-opening trip to Oregon, Bennett informed the players that they would be playing in white sneakers. Unlike the 1993-94 team's performance-based deal, this year's squad had made an academic-based bet with Bennett based on class attendance. And as of mid-November, they had not lived up to their end of the bargain.

Dick Bennett shouts instructions during a timeout as Chris Westlake, Ben Berlowski, and Jeff Zavada listen on the bench. (University of Wisconsin-Green Bay Archives)

Bennett trotted out his four juniors and lone senior as starters in their road greens, debuting his small four-guard lineup. Given his personnel, Bennett encouraged his team push the tempo, abandoning his patient offensive style. The result was apocalyptic.

The Ducks, a team not drastically different from the one embarrassed by the Phoenix the year prior, exacted their revenge, delivering a 96-71 beat down in front of a raucous 5,647 fans at McArthur Court, Oregon. The 25-point loss marked UWGB's largest defeat since January 1988, and the most points allowed by a Bennett team since Cleveland State put up 103 in 1986. The lone bright spot for the Phoenix was the play of Westlake, who scored 23 points to lead the team in the losing effort.

"We got drilled. We haven't been handled like that in a long time," Bennett remarked afterwards.

Grzesk recalled: "We tried to match talent on talent and play fast with them, and I remember they probably had five or six dunks in that game. I think that probably led Coach Bennett to question what we were doing a little bit, at least from the offensive end."

Two days later, the Phoenix again suited up for a West Coast affair, this time against the Big Sky's Idaho State Bengals. For entirely different reasons, this matchup also resembled an unmitigated dumpster fire.

"In my thirty years of coaching, I've never experienced officiating like this," screamed an irate Bennett.

Six Phoenix players fouled out, including the entire starting lineup. In contrast, not a single Idaho State player fouled out and the Bengals attempted 41 free throws.

The Phoenix's sixth disqualified player was freshman Gabe Stevens, who was called for his fifth foul in just *eleven* minutes of action.

"I felt so bad for him, the poor kid," said a dejected Bennett. "We didn't know what to say to him."

"We barely had enough guys to finish that game," noted Grzesk, who watched the Phoenix fall 87-81 from his seat on the bench.

Two weeks later, still fuming from the game, Bennett penned a letter to the commissioner of the Big Sky Conference: "I didn't ask him to do anything. I just said this thing is bothering me so much that I want you to know how I feel."

Bennett ultimately realized his request to push the floor needed to change.

"There was a little bit of an experiment to go from a half-court, grind-it-out game to more of an up-tempo, pushing it on every opportunity," remembers Grzesk. "After that, we realized we didn't have the depth, it wasn't working for us, did not fit our personality, and we went back to our traditional way of playing.

End of the Road

The weather in Idaho caused problems for the Phoenix, which was slated to take on the Badgers after just one day of rest.

"We got snowed in, terribly cold weather," Bennett recalls. "All we could do was get a flight in to Madison late morning the day of the game. We went to the gym down at the Fieldhouse and shot around a little, and went back and tried to rest, and then get ready to play that night."

Expectations were at a recent low for the Phoenix given its 0-2 start, though the club relished the rare opportunity to play its in-state big brother. Meanwhile, the No. 15 Badgers, fresh off their first NCAA tournament appearance since 1947, had a well-rested Michael Finley and Rashard Griffith they were ready to unleash. The 6-11 Griffith was a matchup nightmare in the post for Bennett's undersized squad, leaving the coach with no option but to put 6-6 Jeff Nordgaard on him.

"I guarded Rashard Griffith because I was the tallest starter," remembers Nordgaard, "(but) he's six inches taller than me and fifty pounds heavier than me."

Bennett instructed his team to abandon the run game and return to the more patient brand of Bennett-ball. This strategy required maximum effort on the defensive side of the ball, so Bennett demanded his team sprint back on defense after any made or missed attempt, conceding nearly every offensive rebound opportunity.

Halfway through the game, those changes had failed to deliver significant results, as the Badgers held a solid 28-18 lead with the Phoenix shooting just 24% from the field. The Badgers expanded their lead in the second half, eventually creating a 16-point advantage midway through the second half. On a clear path to 0-3, it was at this moment that UWGB began to show life for the first time all season.

Over the last seven minutes, UWGB executed a balanced offensive attack from juniors Nordgaard and Berlowski, senior Westlake, and surprisingly, freshman Kevin Olm, while the defense began to put together regular stops. Two Berlowski free throws with 1:06 left cut the deficit to 58-55, bringing the Phoenix to within one possession for the first time in over thirty minutes of play.

UWGB was forced to foul when the Badgers retained possession the next trip down the court, and Wisconsin put away the Phoenix at the line, 61-57. Nevertheless, even while falling to 0-3, the final seven minutes had given Bennett some hope.

"I'm really not upset. It's probably as good as a coach can feel at an 0-3 stage," Bennett said. "I see progress."

Berlowski's 18 points off the bench were an inspiration, as was Grzesk's defensive effort Michael Finley. Grzesk held the future NBA star to just 2-for-12 shooting and 11 points while also forcing six turnovers.

The return to Bennett-ball and total dedication to creating a set defense every possession produced a competitive effort, holding the Badgers to 48% shooting. But it also left the Phoenix with no margin for error on offense, as UWGB grabbed just one offensive rebound.

"That has to set some NCAA record for defensive rebound percentage," remarked UW's Stan Van Gundy. "Green Bay just decided not to send anybody to the (offensive glass)."

As was always the case when the Badgers and Phoenix met, the conversation about an ongoing series took center stage. Van Gundy made his position clear – he wanted no part of UWGB moving forward.

"Let's put it this way," he said, "if there are about 300 Division I teams, there probably are 270 or 280 at least that I would rather play."

Bennett put the ball in Wisconsin athletic director Pat Richter's hands, saying his program would do whatever the Badgers wanted to keep the series alive. But for a man making all the calls, Richter seemed remarkably comfortable dodging the question: "If we can fit it in, we'll do it. Hopefully, we'll be able to work it out."

Surprising no one, Richter and the Badgers passed on renewing the series, and the two teams would not meet again until December 1999 under entirely different circumstances.

UWGB got its first win of the season a few days later, beating Illinois

State 64-58 as Nordgaard, Berlowski, Grzesk, and Westlake scored every point. The win was a good one as the Redbirds were a program on the rise, having finished fourth in the MVC the year before and on their way to a second-place finish and an NIT bid.

"If you really look at it, we only played one bad half of basketball in the trip, the second half against Oregon," remarked a positive Bennett after the win. "Tonight, we had to play with great poise down the stretch."

Winter Bloom

With final exams coming before the holiday break, the players had two weeks to digest the win before their first regular-season home game. Bennett took stock of his team and noted three trends. First, Nordgaard was logging huge minutes against big men, and it was taking its toll.

"I don't see any way he can continue with the ironman," remarked Bennett. "No matter what, I've got to spell him. One of (our) bigger kids has to come along."

Unfortunately, it wasn't going to be Mark Domenick, the player Bennett had signed after just one tape and a phone call. He refused to commit and was drifting more and more out of favor. Two weeks after the New Year, Domenick was ruled academically ineligible and kicked off the team.

And third, though he was hard on his big men recruits, Bennett had nothing but praise for his true freshman guard, Kevin Olm.

"(He's) been nothing spectacular," Bennett said. "He's just been steady. That's how he'll always be. I value his decision making. I value his defense. I value his passing and dribbling."

The Phoenix returned to action in front of a home-opener record 5,646 fans on December 17, 1994, against Jim Larranaga's Bowling Green Falcons. It was a dream scenario for any mid-major fan, pitting two solid programs and all-time coaches against each other in a high-intensity, disciplined affair.

Larranaga had been Bowling Green's lead man since 1986 and had successfully guided the team to consecutive postseason bids for the first time since the 1940s, taking his program to the NIT in 1990 and 1991. His 1994-95 team was riding a four-game winning streak behind the strong play of its spectacular sophomore guard, Antonio Daniels, last season's MAC Freshman of the Year.

In a tight affair, it was true freshman Gabe Stevens who helped seal it for the Phoenix down the stretch, scoring 11 points and grabbing three rebounds in less than ten minutes of action. Stevens's pair of free throws with 9:14 left tied the game at 44-44 and proved to be the catalyst in a decisive 10-2 UWGB run. The Phoenix never trailed after that, bagging a 69-62 victory.

Two nights later, after a 31-point Phoenix win over his team, Morgan State's first-year head coach Lynn Ramage, was impressed with the Brown County Arena atmosphere.

"We've played Georgetown, Iowa ... This is as tough as any place I've been or tougher. I understand they have a tough time bringing people here. I understand."

UWGB followed that with its fourth straight win three days later in the final game before Christmas. It proved almost too easy for the Phoenix in dismantling the 5-2 Mississippi Valley State Delta Devils, 75-53. The UWGB was in control from the tip, leading by 22 points at halftime and coasting from there.

Most impressively, Grzesk and the defense completely shut down MVSU's best player and NBA prospect, Marcus Mann, holding the junior center to just six points. At the same time, Westlake was continuing to impress, scoring 17 first-half points to drive the Phoenix charge.

"I thought Chris Westlake probably had as good of a first half as is humanly possible," Bennett said afterwards.

Holiday Whirlwind

The team had found its way to a 4-3 record entering the Christmas break, and memories of the first three games seemed distant and irrelevant. After a few days off for the holiday, UWGB welcomed new conference foe Butler to Green Bay. It was the earliest conference game in school history, and the program's first MCC game.

Barry Collier was in his sixth season as Butler's head coach, and his Bulldogs were predicted to finish somewhere in the middle to top half of the conference. At 5-4, they had effectively played to their potential through the first six weeks.

Collier had done his homework and had a plan for beating the Phoenix. He recognized that UWGB's offense was consolidated among Nordgaard, Westlake, and Berlowski, and that after those three, the scoring threats were negligible. So he went all in on stopping those three, leaving everyone else open and daring them to beat his club. It was the most dedicated plan of attack Bennett had seen that year, and it worked to perfection.

The Bulldogs managed to keep all three Phoenix stars to single digits, breaking Nordgaard's streak of twenty-two games with at least 10 points. To Bennett's frustration and Collier's delight, no one else stepped up for the Phoenix and Butler won without much of a fuss, 56-43. It was an unceremonious debut for the Phoenix against one of the MCC's mid-level teams and gave the Phoenix an unextraordinary 4-4 record. Afterwards, Bennett took ownership for the loss.

"I thought Butler had an excellent game plan and they executed it well," he said. "I've been outcoached many times, and I'm sure I'll be outcoached many times more."

The Phoenix had an opportunity to change its fortunes two days later in the team's holiday tournament, this year renamed the Pepsi/Oneida Classic. In the tournament's second iteration, Woody Wilson had again succeeded in attracting quality mid-major challengers, and it started with the tournament favorite, John Beilein's Canisius Golden Griffins. Beilein's team had won the MAAC regular season championship in 1993-94, and this squad looked just as strong having already beaten No. 13 Cincinnati. Joining Canisius in the field were the Missouri Valley Conference's Indiana State Sycamores, and Georgia State, a mid-level program from the Trans America Athletic Conference.

Canisius disposed of Georgia Southern in its first-round game, while UWGB buried Indiana State, 74-53. It was a bounce-back 17-point performance by Nordgaard that led the Phoenix, while Pete Wade, in his first significant contribution of the year, scored six points and grabbed four rebounds in eight minutes of action.

The Phoenix's real challenge awaited them in the championship game on New Year's Eve. In another December battle of top-notch, mid-major coaches, this time Bennett came out on top.

Playing its most complete defensive game of the year, UWGB allowed only one Golden Griffin to score in double figures and held Canisius scoreless for a seven-minute stretch early in the second half that turned the tide. Bennett's bunch closed out the holiday tournament with a 17-point championship victory.

Nordgaard took home the tournament's MVP honors with 35 points and 14 boards, but it was fellow all-tournament selection Gary Grzesk who garnered the coach's credit. With an exceptional 16 points, 15 assists, 12 rebounds, six steals, as well as a tremendous defensive performance, Bennett declared, "I love Jeff Nordgaard, but Gary Grzesk is my MVP."

One-Loss Week

Even with six wins in its previous seven games, it was far from clear what the potential of this Phoenix team was as the calendar turned into 1995. Back-to-back games against the 10-1 Northern Illinois Huskies and at 8-1 Marquette, meant the team's day of reckoning was imminent.

It started on January 5, 1995, at the Brown County Arena against Northern Illinois. The Huskies, UWGB's transfer buddy to the MCC, had reeled off eight straight wins to start the season, including six at home before falling at Akron. Prior to the game, Bennett received a letter from one of his former players, Jeremy Ludvigson, who had played the Huskies as a member of Marathon Oil in the preseason.

"He said the team that impressed him the most was Northern Illinois," noted Bennett before the game. "He said they were intense and play exceptional defense. He said they mean business this year."

Ludvigson's assessment proved correct. Harkening back to the 1991 battles, this game was a back-and-forth affair, with points at a premium. With less than a minute to play and Northern Illinois up two, crunch time had officially arrived.

Bennett traded ball handling for scoring potential, putting Westlake in for Olm. Westlake promptly launched a step-back three-pointer from the right wing that could've given UWGB a lead, but it rimmed out. However, Grzesk had his man boxed out on the left block, snatched the loose ball, and went right back up. He layup went through the basket as he was fouled. Eric Jackson's hands stretched to the sky, Grzesk gave a fist pump that would've impressed Tiger Woods, and the home crowd went berserk.

It took a moment to calm himself after the emotion of the play, but Grzesk eventually sank his free throw for an old-fashioned three-point play, giving UWGB a 58-57 lead. After a Huskies miss on their next possession, Jackson finished it off by grabbing the rebound, sinking two free throws, stealing the ensuing inbounds pass, and assisting on a basket to Westlake as time expired.

It was a thrilling moment for the team's junior.

"I've been waiting for a chance to get in and help the team out," Jackson said. "I made good of the opportunity."

It was an exhilarating victory for the Phoenix as a whole, which improved to 7-4 on the year. The needle had been moved in a positive direction as the club was showing signs of consistency and maturity.

Bird Hunting

UWGB's final nonconference test came on January 7, 1995, in the game ESPN had moved mountains to make happen. The newly dubbed Golden Eagles from Marquette were 8-2 and had a new coach to go with their new mascot.

Mike Deane, the former Siena head coach, replaced Kevin O'Neill, who had jumped ship to move to the SEC. Deane was a typical mid-major success story, having taken Siena to the postseason four times in his eight years, including a third-place finish in the 1994 NIT, before moving to Milwaukee.

This made Deane's flippant pregame remarks suggesting the Phoenix were scared to play the Golden Eagles seem a bit ignorant.

"Green Bay tried to get out of the game with us this year. They had a lot of losses to graduation," he said. "If they really want to play us, then they have to play us on our terms."

Bennett, whose team had gone above and beyond to accommodate Marquette, disagreed with Deane and prepared his team to weather a revenge-filled atmosphere. The Phoenix packed the buses early in the morning and headed to the local Perkins for breakfast – the team's pregame meal – before journeying two hours south for their 11:00 a.m. tip.

Digger Phelps and Steve Physioc were at the Bradley Center to broadcast the early bird special for ESPN. The seasoned announcers prepared the audience for a clash of styles, with Marquette hoping to flaunt its high flyers and run, while UWGB would work every possession and slow down the tempo. As Physioc noted, "This game cannot be, really, in the 80s or 90s, or Wisconsin-Green Bay is going to get killed."

Early on, the Phoenix was successful in dictating the tempo against Deane's scheme. UWGB repeatedly got back on defense after both makes and misses, limiting the Golden Eagles' second-chance opportunities. Meanwhile, on every defensive rebound or steal, UWGB would get the ball to Kevin Olm or Eric Jackson, both of whom looked right at home slowly walking the ball up the floor.

As the first half progressed, it was clear the game was settling in at a dangerous pace for Marquette. Grzesk was having his way defensively with Marquette's top talents, in particular guards Anthony Pieper and Tony Miller, who combined for a dismal 2-for-9 from the field in the first half.

Meanwhile, Nordgaard was having just enough success offensively to keep UWGB alive. The combination of Nordgaard's outside touch and polished interior game created match-up problems for the Golden Eagles, who

Marquette's Aaron Hutchins goes in for a layup in front of Ben Berlowski during UWGB's 50-48 victory in Milwaukee on January 7, 1995. (Department of Special Collections and University Archives, Raynor Memorial Libraries, Marquette University)

didn't have a clear defender that could handle both Nordgaard's quickness and his size. The best Deane could muster was 6-11 junior center Amal Mc-Caskill, but Nordgaard routinely made McCaskill look foolish, beating him with backdoor cuts and quicker feet.

Nevertheless, Marquette kept a small, but steady lead throughout the first half, taking a 24-21 advantage into the locker room. Any dreams Deane had of getting the score into the 80s or 90s were history. The Phoenix had shot a disappointing 33% in the first half, but its defense had been up to the challenge, holding Marquette to an equally anemic 32% shooting. And in spite of a major size disadvantage, UWGB had kept the rebounding disparity in check, only trailing Marquette 18-13.

Early in the second half, it was Nordgaard's longer-range jump shots that kept the Phoenix hanging around until Berlowski finally found his spot. Over a two-minute stretch in the middle of the second half, Berlowski scored 11 straight points, including three triples, helping UWGB take a 36-35 lead with under 13 minutes to play. All the while, Berlowski jawed with his defender, Roney Eford.

"Roney Eford talked so much shit to me all the time ... he's like, 'Dude, you shouldn't be on the floor. Dude, you're worthless. Dude, you ain't getting a shot up today," remembers Berlowski, "(but) I'm not afraid to say what's on my mind."

It was an honest self-assessment, and Nordgaard agreed. "(Ben) has that kind of cockiness where he thinks he can do whatever he needs to do."

Berlowski had carried the Phoenix during the middle of the second half, but to the Phoenix's detriment, he picked up his fourth foul with six minutes to play. With UWGB up 40-39, Bennett was faced with a game-defining decision. Determined not to sacrifice the scoring potential, Bennett chose to leave Berlowski in the game.

The move felt dramatic at the time, but over the next two minutes, Marquette worked to ensure it didn't matter, going on a 7-0 run while building its biggest lead of the game, 46-40.

Feeling the game slipping, Bennett called a timeout and set his team straight. The break was timely, as the Phoenix scored on back-to-back possessions, and after a poor three-point attempt by Marquette's Tony Miller, had the ball back.

Down two points, the Phoenix patiently rotated the ball around the perimeter, and with just under 1:30 to play, Westlake dribbled on the left wing while Berlowski worked off of a Jackson screen. Westlake caught Berlowski with a pass in stride and Berlowski connected on a three-pointer right over Miller.

It was a huge moment. Suddenly, UWGB was in the lead 47-46 with 1:27 to play. A Westlake free throw and a Marquette make tied the game at 48-48 with just under 30 seconds to play. UWGB would have a chance for, perhaps, the final shot to beat the Golden Eagles for a second straight year.

Bennett called a timeout, and in one of the greatest strategy sessions in school history, the team set its final play. Nordgaard recalls it in detail:

"Larry Bird is my favorite player of all time. He used to tell people, 'I'm going to get the ball right here and score on you, this and that ...' Coach

Bennett says, 'Alright Jeff, which block do you want it on? We're going to get the ball to you in post.' And Amal McCaskill is guarding me, we're going to still get the ball to me in the post. I'm five inches shorter than he is, makes sense *(laughing)*.

"I said, 'right block,' and he goes, 'Ahh, you know, I think we should go left block, so you can turn in and shoot that jump hook.' I'm like, 'Yeah, yeah, let's do that.'

"So we get out of the timeout and I go up to Amal, and I said, 'I'm going to catch the ball right here, turn in and hit a jump hook over you to win the game.' And he goes 'F*** you, Nordgaard, you suck.' "

Before any play could take place, UWGB had to milk most of the shot clock.

"Eric (Jackson) had to handle the ball by himself for about 25 seconds," explains Westlake. "That might not sound like much right now, but when you're having to manage that situation, I thought that was a big-time moment."

Meanwhile, Nordgaard did exactly what he said he would do and posted up McCaskill on the left block. With eight seconds left, got the ball from Jackson.

"I kind of gave a fake baseline, turned middle, jump hook over his stretched arm," Nordgaard recalls.

The ball swished through the rim, nothing but net. UWGB had a 50-48 lead with 6.6 seconds to play. It was the stuff of legend.

Marquette's final possession was a bust, with Aaron Hutchins air-balling a jump shot as the buzzer sounded. UWGB had secured a massive in-state victory at the Bradley Center on ESPN.

"We really had just kind of found a way to hang in the game until the very end," Grzesk says. "It was a pretty amazing win."

While the native Wisconsinites soaked in the national awe, the intra-state win was less significant to Westlake, whose Illinois roots gave him a different perspective.

"Marquette – they kind of have some history to the program, kind of *almost* big time, but *not really* in my mind," noted Westlake. "If you stood up to them, you know they'd back down."

While Westlake remained unimpressed, the game had changed the opinion of Marquette's head coach.

"This game against Green Bay, I think, is a great game. It's a great test for us," Deane said. "I think it's a natural we continue this game. We will continue this game. It's good for the state. It's good for our program."

The Phoenix had also managed to achieve a scoring anomaly with only three players registering points. Berlowski led all scorers with 22, Nordgaard had 20, and Westlake added eight.

"You were going to count on Jeff, and at that time I had proven that you could pretty much count on me to get mine, too," Westlake says. "And then having Ben right there, that was really when it was all clicking. The three of us had to score really consistently to win, because we just didn't have anybody else."

Bennett provided a glowing assessment of Berlowski in an expose a few days later.

"If the kid were 6-5 or 6-6, we'd probably be talking about an all-American candidate, but the fact is he's more like 6-2," noted Bennett. "He continually comes through in games because he has a fierce determination to get it done. He has already won a lot of games for us this year."

In a span of three days, UWGB's season outlook shifted. The wins over Northern Illinois and Marquette had given the Phoenix a new swagger, and at 8-4, the "rebuilding" label had been ripped off the season, permanently tucked back in the drawer.

Chapter 18

Shooters
(1994-95 - Part 2)

At its root, basketball is a simple game: you try to put a ball in one hoop, and stop your opponent from doing the same in a second. And because those hoops are positioned just ten feet off the ground, player height is a key attribute.

You can't teach size and it can be hard to find. Like a rare gemstone, the tallest of the tall are precious, highly sought, and almost entirely consumed by the rich.

But basketball can be a great equalizer, and height often comes with a tradeoff for ball-handling, shooting, and quickness. So while a wealthy team can control the interior with its giants, the right opponent can capitalize with highly skilled shooters to score from the perimeter and effectively compete against the height they'll never have.

There's Something Happening Here

The most astounding development in the first half of 1994-95 was the emergence of a two-headed deep threat for UWGB. Jeff Nordgaard was a known commodity and was living up to his billing, averaging more than 18 points per game.

Close behind him, senior Chris Westlake and junior Ben Berlowski were becoming the perfect deep-threat duo. The pair were both shooting better than 40% on three-point attempts and equally able to neutralize defenders with their penetration and shiftiness.

"(Berlowski) had a lot of confidence in his shooting and he made big shots," Westlake recalls. "He brought a tiny bit something different as a shooter than I did. It's not something that we ever really talked about, but it sure was nice. That was when we were clicking the most."

"One day it would be me, one day it would be Chris," agrees Berlowski. "I mean, we would battle."

The result was a perimeter presence that complemented Nordgaard's production perfectly. With Westlake's shooting tweaks and Berlowski's natural progression, the pair had developed into a lethal combination to pair with Nordgaard.

Hot January Nights

Two days after the huge win over Marquette, the Phoenix train continued to roll. UWGB collected its fifth straight win while handing the Cleveland State Vikings their fifth consecutive loss. The game turned roughly ten minutes in when the Phoenix put together a massive 24-6 run, and the Vikings never recovered.

Gary Grzesk held Cleveland State's top scorer, Jamal Jackson, to just 11 points, while Nordgaard led the way for the Phoenix with 25 points and 13 rebounds, helping him earn MCC Player of the Week honors. But it was an efficient 13-point performance from Pete Wade in fourteen minutes off the bench that really surprised the team.

UWGB took nearly a week off before heading down I-43 to take on UW-Milwaukee at the MECCA on Sunday, January 15, 1995. Like Butler earlier in the season, UW-Milwaukee coach Steve Antrim was dead set on stopping UWGB's trio of Nordgaard, Berlowski, and Westlake, who were scoring over 70% of the Phoenix's points.

In an attempt to counteract that, Antrim deployed every defensive strategy he had in his arsenal, starting with a 2-3 zone, shifting to a triangle-and-two, and settling into man-to-man. But unlike Collier's Bulldogs, nothing the Panthers tried proved effective, as Nordgaard (31 points), Berlowski (16), and Westlake (13) combined to outscore the entire UW-Milwaukee team, helping the Phoenix nab a 79-58 victory.

The UW-Milwaukee win set up a critical MCC showdown the following night as the 10-4 Phoenix headed to Chicago to play at the 9-5 UIC Flames. UWGB entered with ten wins in its previous eleven games, while the Flames were good for eight of their previous nine.

Four NBA scouts were on hand to watch the Flames' Sherell Ford, and Ford obliged by playing the entire forty minutes of basketball and taking over in the end. After a Westlake three-pointer cut UIC's lead to 63-62 with three minutes to play, Ford swished two outside jumpers over Grzesk and the Flames successfully finished off UWGB, 71-65.

"In the last five or six minutes, one of the things I have to do is take over the game," remarked Ford. "I wanted the ball."

Ford finished with 21 points on a stellar 9-for-12 shooting night, adding in ten rebounds and four assists. Ford's night was determinative, but Westlake continued to build confidence, leading all scorers with 27 points.

"Chris is playing well," commented Dick Bennett. "He has come to grips with some things. He fought himself so hard when things didn't go well."

The UIC loss set the Phoenix back, but only momentarily.

Cerberus

Offensively, the opening weeks of January had been good to the Phoenix. Berlowski (46.3%) and Westlake (49.3%) ranked as two of the country's top three-point threats, and when paired with one of the conference's best players in Nordgaard, were creating a three-headed monster for opposing defenses. Westlake in particular was coming into his own, and credited assistant coach Mike Heideman with his improvement.

"I would come in the gym, not warmed up, and he would say, 'Okay, let's start,' " remembers Westlake. "When you're not warm, it's really hard because you lose your breath right quick and you don't get any warmed up. So that's how I train, and he was the instigator of that."

Westlake, with Berlowski and Nordgaard, helped UWGB rebound with a bounce-back win on January 19, 1995, against nonconference foe Southern Utah, 65-58. In front of just 4,700 fans – the team's smallest home crowd of the year –Nordgaard collected his 1,000th point, while UWGB fought hard in the final ten minutes to create enough separation for the victory.

"I think he is symbolic of our program," noted Bennett. "He is generally outsized, outnumbered, and out-quicked, and yet he somehow finds a way to get it done."

Two nights later, UWGB again pulled out a close game with a less-than-stellar performance, defeating an overmatched Loyola team by six points in Chicago's Alumni Gym. Two critical free throws from Nordgaard in the final ten seconds locked up a second straight win for UWGB, which improved to 12-5 overall and 4-2 in the conference.

Gola the Explorer

A week later, UWGB had its first encounter with MCC stalwart LaSalle, one of the country's premier programs in the late 1940s and early 1950s. Under the guidance of Charles McGlone first, then Kenneth Loeffler, the Explorers racked up nine consecutive seasons of twenty or more wins. In 1952-53, riding the talents of future Hall of Famer Tom Gola, the Explorers earned their first ever #1 ranking, and a year later, defeated Bradley to win the NCAA Championship. The Explorers returned to the NCAA title game in Gola's senior year, but lost to Bill Russell and K.C. Jones's San Francisco Dons.

In 1986, LaSalle made an unusual move, hiring its former women's basketball coach, Bill "Speedy" Morris, to coach the men's team. Morris became the first Division I basketball coach to lead both the men's and women's programs at the same school, and he thrived in the new position. In his first year, the Explorers finished runner-up in the NIT, and in his second year, LaSalle was back in the NCAA tournament for the first of four appearances over a five-year stretch that included a 30-2 team in 1989-90.

LaSalle made the move to the Midwestern Collegiate conference in 1992, and along with Xavier, represented the best of the new conference opponents in 1994-95. This year's version of LaSalle boasted a potent backcourt, led by Paul Burke and potential NBA talent Kareem Townes. And while the Explorers were just 10-7 on the season, four of the team's losses had come at the hands of top-25 teams.

A roaring 5,934 fans packed the Brown County Arena on January 28, 1995, to size up Townes and the Explorers. Early in the week, Bennett had made the decision to start Pete Wade, moving away from his four-guard lineup and giving Nordgaard some support on the front lines.

Five minutes into the game, the move looked like pure brilliance. Wade delivered UWGB's first eight points, driving the Phoenix to a quick advantage that it never relinquished.

"Wade came out of the blocks just the way you dream about," Bennett said. "I don't think he could have played any better than he did the first five minutes."

Everything had clicked for the Phoenix, who amassed a double-digit first half lead and breezed to a 17-point victory. Wade finished with a solid 13 points and seven rebounds, while Nordgaard added 20 points and seven boards. Berlowski scored 23 points off the bench, and Grzesk held the superstar Kareem Townes to just 12 points. Even the crowd had done its part.

"That was a good, electric atmosphere at the arena," Grzesk recalls. "We jumped them right away and probably played as well as we could have against LaSalle."

The first month of 1995 had been good to the program. With the win against a perceived elite, UWGB improved to 7-1 in January and 13-5 overall, looking more and more like they belonged in the MCC. With eight regular-season games to play, the magic number of twenty wins seemed in play for a potential NIT bid.

Building Up

UWGB opened up February 1995 with a pair of victories on the road against top-half conference talent. First, the Phoenix went to Northern Illinois and gutted out a gritty victory against the 13-6 Huskies. UWGB trailed by five a few minutes into the second half, but a timely Dick Bennett timeout righted the ship. With instructions to work the ball to Nordgaard inside and shift to a 1-2-2 zone to mix up its defensive look, the Phoenix scored 10 straight points and closed out the win.

Two days later, UWGB went down to Hinkle Fieldhouse and ripped a victory from the jaws of defeat. The 12-7 Bulldogs built a second-half lead, primarily the result of their defensive game plan designed to use all five players to stop UWGB's top three scorers.

But the Phoenix's two undefended guards, Gary Grzesk and Eric Jackson, provided desperately needed offense, hitting wide open jumpers to help slash the lead. Facing a one-point deficit with 18 seconds to play, Bennett called for his team to spread the floor and isolate Nordgaard in the post. With five seconds left, Nordgaard finally received a pass from Berlowski inside, took one dribble to his left and threw up an awkward, sideways bank shot that somehow went through.

"I don't think I even looked at it after I shot it. I figured it was going in," commented Nordgaard confidently after the game.

Butler had one final shot at victory, but Westlake snuffed it out and UWGB left with a 61-60 victory. Westlake had been a major part of the win, racking up 19 points, all in the second half, and largely on the same play.

"Coach Wilson asked Coach Bennett, 'We'll have Gary set a ball screen for Chris, and Chris will come off and shoot threes from that,' " recalls

Westlake. "I had three or four three-pointers in the second half off of that one play."

The Phoenix were second in the nation in defense (59.5 ppg), and Bennett, unafraid to alter his tactics, had mixed in zone with his man-to-man. At 7-2 in the conference and 15-5 overall, UWGB was still in the hunt for a conference championship. But to do that, the Phoenix would have to win its next game against the conference's top dog, Xavier, and get some additional help along the way.

Knocking Down

The Xavier Musketeers were mid-major royalty during the 1980s and early 1990s. Coaching legend Pete Gillen took over the program in 1985-86 and began a run of NCAA tournament appearances that would be unmatched by any mid-major program until Gonzaga started its run in the 2000s.

The Musketeers made six tournaments in a row in Gillen's first six years, including a Sweet Sixteen run in 1990 that included a second-round upset over the heavily favored Georgetown Hoyas. In Gillen's nine seasons with Xavier, the team won the MCC six times, made eight postseason appearances, including seven NCAA tournaments, and pulled off five NCAA tournament wins. Gillen won over 200 games for the Musketeers before moving to the Big East with Providence in 1994.

Xavier replaced Gillen with his top assistant, Skip Prosser, and under Prosser, the Musketeers were looking even more impressive. With an 18-3 record entering their game with UWGB, Xavier was teetering on cracking the Top 25.

Xavier also had a strong home-court advantage, and it showed when the clubs met for their ESPN showdown on February 11, 1995. More than 9,500 fans rocked the Cincinnati Gardens for a game UWGB would have probably preferred it had been played in total darkness.

UWGB played a respectable first half, and even carried a one-point lead nearly ten minutes into the game. But within minutes in the second half, Xavier busted out to a 16-point lead and systematically dismantled the overmatched Phoenix. The game ultimately turned farcical, and at the end, it was the clearly superior Xavier 76, UW-Green Bay 55.

"Even on made field goals, they would run it down on us so fast, we were barely getting back to set our defense. Just that speed and athleticism was not something we had seen all season, and it kind of took our breath away," Grzesk notes. "They were the one team that we were probably afraid to play."

"Xavier is certainly everything we heard they would be," remarked Bennett. "When you really get whipped like this, there's not much to do but go back and regroup and learn from it."

A day later, the conference received word that both Xavier and LaSalle would be leaving the MCC following the season. The losses would undoubtedly hurt the MCC's credibility, but at least it allowed for balanced scheduling with nine remaining schools.

"I think they have to get the conference schedule consistent so everyone plays home-and-home," Bennett said. "Xavier is leaving, so our fans will never get to see that excellent team come in here unless we get a non-conference game. I was very disappointed."

The Xavier game was an embarrassment, and it changed the team's outlook. Gone were the hopes of winning the conference, and with a team as strong as the Musketeers, dreams of pulling off an upset in the conference tournament seemed far-fetched.

With no rest for the weary, UWGB had to regroup and prepare for another conference dogfight as the UIC Flames came to the Brown County Arena. The Phoenix had swept the Flames in 1993-94, but with a loss earlier in the year, UIC was hoping to return the favor.

"Right now, UIC and Green Bay is a huge rivalry game because of the game last year. We should have won the tournament game," noted Sherell Ford.

Bob Hallberg agreed: "There is a history of Green Bay and UIC being very competitive. I never have to get my guys up for Green Bay. It's been established that you're not going to beat Green Bay unless you play your tail off."

Like their game earlier in the year, the teams were evenly matched and played to the wire. In this affair, Nordgaard forced overtime with a late jumper, but in the extra period, the Phoenix played uncharacteristically sloppy, missing shots, committing offensive fouls, and turning the ball over. UIC, the more disciplined and talented team on that day, made no such mistakes and escaped with a 78-64 win.

"What we did in overtime is inexcusable. I have never, ever seen a team give it up the way our team did," said an angry Bennett. "It's absolutely inexcusable to play the way we played in overtime. There are things we teach, things we stand for. I didn't recognize any of it down the stretch."

Bennett continued to rant after the game. In addition to criticism for sloppy turnovers and poor shot selection, Bennett directed his aggression at Westlake and Nordgaard for failing to lead: "I don't want to pin it on our only senior. I don't want to pin it on our returning all-conference player. But we are not getting a person to step up and just talk to somebody. 'Hey, we've got to get a better shot. Hey, let's stay together on the floor.' "

If the Xavier loss removed hope of a conference championship and earning an NCAA tournament bid, the loss to UIC created doubt about an NIT run.

Tony's Best Move

Tony Bennett's third NBA season came to an early end in late January, 1995. An injury to his foot required surgery and would keep him out of action for nearly three months, ultimately ending his career.

"He worked so hard in the offseason, he just did everything extra, and I think he wore out a lot of the joint tissue," remembers Dick Bennett. "He just basically outworked everybody, and it cost him."

Even before his days at UWGB had ended, it was a foregone conclusion that Tony Bennett's number would be the first retired by the program in its history. However, with the NBA regular season kicking off before and ending after the college season, opportunities to accomplish this had been few and far between.

Now, laid up with an injury, there was a silver lining. The time away from his professional team gave his alma mater the chance to bestow its greatest honor. Athletic director Otis Chambers arranged for Tony to attend UWGB's February 18 game against Loyola.

The event, publicized about two weeks ahead of time, ensured a sold-out Brown County Arena, where more than 6,000 supporters showed up to catch a last glimpse of the program's best. The game drew the fifth-largest Phoenix crowd ever, and the program's largest since Tony's playing days in 1991.

A nervous-looking Tony took the microphone and delivered a speech few saw coming. After thanking everyone for his memories in Green Bay, Tony took a deep breath and said, "The last thing I'd like to share with you guys is this. You know, in my four-year career here, you guys have seen me make a lot of great moves on this court. But what I'm about to do right now is share with you the greatest move of my life."

With that, he turned to his girlfriend Laurel, got down on one knee, and asked her to marry him. In front of a standing ovation from Green Bay's most passionate fans, a smiling and surprised Laurel responded "yes."

It was a move that Tony had run only past his best friend, Ben Johnson, his sister, and UWGB ticket director Marilyn McCarey. Everyone else was in the dark, including his father.

"Honest to gosh, I thought he was going to do something stupid, like a cartwheel or a hand spin," Dick Bennett recalls. "When he reached into his pocket, I thought, 'My Lord, what is going on?' "

The two, personifying the ultimate royalty in Green Bay, walked off the floor of their dark arena kingdom arm-in-arm.

As for the game itself, Dick Bennett brought back his four-guard lineup of Grzesk, Jackson, Westlake, and Berlowski – joined by Nordgaard. It was the group he would ride the rest of the season. Whether it was the lineup change, the emotion of the ceremony, the desire to rebound from a terrible performance, or the harsh words of their coach still ringing in their ears, the UWGB players came out of the gate determined.

Westlake started the charge, hitting a three-pointer at the start, and it snowballed from there. Nordgaard hit a pair of buckets, while Berlowski and Westlake each added a three-pointer, helping UWGB rip off a 14-0 lead over the first seven minutes. While the Ramblers did finally get on the board, the margin never got closer than ten. UWGB snapped its two-game losing streak with a 76-56 victory, rehabilitating the locker room.

Westlake, the man chastised for failing to lead following the Xavier game, was the hero for the Phoenix, scoring 17 points in the first half and finishing with 25 on an even mix of three-pointers and penetrating layups. His relationship with the head coach would remain rocky, but Bennett had succeeded in getting the best out of his shooter, and Westlake knew it.

"Coach knows I don't like my heart being questioned," remarked Westlake. "He wants to build up toughness to where if something goes wrong in a game, you can handle it because you already handled it. It makes you

February 18, 1995, was a big day for Tony Bennett and his family. This was the day UWGB retired Tony's No. 25 jersey, and he surprised even his father by proposing to his girlfriend, Laurel. The jersey retirement ceremony helped make the game against Loyola one of the largest basketball crowds in the history of the Brown County Arena. (University of Wisconsin-Green Bay Archives)

frustrated and it makes you mad, so you play harder. The toughness is there; he just brings it out."

Dick Bennett was a wreck after the game, a mix of emotions stemming from the pride he felt for his son, the regret he experienced for his actions after the Xavier game, and the resiliency witnessed by his current team.

"I come here tonight demonstrating the incredible swings of emotion that are possible in this profession," he said. "It was less than forty-eight hours ago that I probably managed to alienate every family member of every kid who ever played for me, or who played this year. Today, I want to gush over how well they did."

Postseason Push

With three games to play in the regular season, UWGB was sitting tenuously at 8-4 in the conference, 16-7 overall, holding out a slim ray of hope it could still finish second in the MCC. More likely, and with a little luck, twenty wins and a shot at the NIT seemed back within reach.

UWGB's lone senior, Chris Westlake, continued his hot streak against an abysmal 3-20 UW-Milwaukee team. Taking every look he saw, Westlake poured in 28 points on Senior Night while upping his season three-point percentage to 51.1%, tops in the conference and in the top ten in the NCAA. The result was a second consecutive 20-point win for UWGB.

"It was *my* night," recalls Westlake. "I just took a green light (and) took quite a few more shots than I normally would.'"

The defense for the Phoenix – partially owning to a stretch of 1-2-2 zone – succeeded in locking down Milwaukee's top threat, Shannon Smith. Bennett saw the zone switch as necessary, even when it cut against his defensive principles: "We just didn't, couldn't stay with them in the man. It's hard to admit. At this point, we're probably a better zone team than we are a man-to-man."

With seventeen wins, UWGB then played its second-to-last game of the regular season at Detroit Mercy. The Titans had managed to salvage what appeared to be a lost season, and though they carried only an 11-12 record, they had won eight of their last ten games and were still fighting for a top-four spot in the conference.

UWGB was the superior team and grabbed a multiple possession lead early, but was rarely able to extend the lead to more than six points. Detroit rode its momentum as far as they could until some clutch free throws by Berlowski in the final minute helped UWGB get its eighteenth win of the season.

Entering the final regular-season game, a road game at Wright State, Bennett was high on his team's potential.

"We're about as good as we can be at this point," Bennett remarked. "I think twenty (wins) should almost be a lock (for the NIT). We've proven to be a good postseason team."

To get there, UWGB needed to defeat the Raiders on their home floor and in front of more than 7,500 fans, which also meant going toe-to-toe with one of the most enigmatic players in conference history.

Vitaly Potapenko was a 6-10, 270-pound junior center from Kiev, playing his first season of Division I basketball. Ironically, UWGB was no stranger to "The Ukraine Train." Potapenko had actually been on hand to watch the Phoenix as a fourteen-year old during UWGB's Soviet Union trip in 1990.

Now, a still-developing Potapenko was averaging nearly 20 points, 6 rebounds, and 1.3 blocks per game. It was an understatement to say that his size and skill created problems for Bennett's four-guard lineup, but that was nothing new.

"We were very small, I mean we had some real limitations," admits Grzesk. "I think in the media guide that year, they inflated everyone's height by at least an inch or two. I think I had been always 6-3 up until that point. I think if you look in the media guide, I was 6-4. Ben Berlowski, who's probably about 6-1, was listed as 6-3. I think Chris Westlake was listed as 6-3. Eric Jackson, who's 5-11, I think he was listed at 6 foot. Jeff (Nordgaard) was probably listed at 6-7."

Having seen his team measure up in the past, Bennett trusted his process and put Grzesk on Potapenko. The Phoenix's defensive stopper spent much of the game denying entry passes and trying to force outside shots. While his defense was adequate, it wasn't until UWGB switched to a zone with ten minutes to play that the momentum really turned.

With that zone switch, the Phoenix put together a 6-2 run to build an eight point cushion, 59-51. A few moments later, a long Berlowski jumper helped the Phoenix string together ten straight points to put away the Raiders, 75-61.

Potapenko flashed the talent that would later make him a first-round

Jeff Nordgaard (33) flashes in the lane as Ben Berlowski looks to feed him over Wright State's Vitaly Potapenko (The Ukraine Train) during a key MCC game on February 26, 1995. (Courtesy of Special Collections and Archives, Wright State University)

UWGB guard Kevin Olm (13) passes away from pressure during the Phoenix's 75-61 victory over Wright State. (Courtesy of Special Collections and Archives, Wright State University)

draft pick, dumping in 21 points on an efficient 8-for-13 night shooting, though his teammates were woefully inadequate in their support. Thanks to the Phoenix game plan of packing the paint and forcing outside looks, the rest of the Raiders went a dismal 11-for-33 shooting, connecting on just 8 of 30 outside of five feet.

After a pair of mid-February losses to Xavier and UIC, UWGB had strung together four straight victories to get to 19-7, tying UIC for second in the conference. The Phoenix had vastly exceeded the preseason predictions and righted a ship that looked lost when it opened 0-3.

"In this day and age, people don't generally brag about finishing second, but I am," noted a proud Bennett. "At the beginning of the year, I personally thought our fourth-place pick was high. We had the smallest, youngest. In terms of coming as close to their potential as possible, you have to appreciate this group."

A week later, Nordgaard was named to the First-Team All-MCC, joined by Potapenko, LaSalle's Kareem Townes, Xavier's Jeff Massey, and Player of the Year Sherell Ford.

Get to 20 Wins

Conference juggernaut Xavier appeared a lock to win the conference tournament and sew up the MCC's automatic NCAA bid, but the NIT was nothing to scoff at.

Yet again, UWGB's administration saw the Home and Garden Show blocking the Brown County Arena, so Otis Chambers began exploring other local arena options to potentially host an NIT game. The best option quickly became the Kolf Sports Center at hour away at UW-Oshkosh with a capacity of 5,800 fans. Chambers locked up an agreement and informed the NIT they could play there if the need arose.

Critical to that path was a first-round tournament win. As the third seed, UWGB played the first of a quadruple header at Wright State's Nutter Center against the talented, underachieving sixth-seeded LaSalle Explorers. While UWGB was looking for the magical twentieth win, LaSalle's 13-13 season meant its only hope was to keep on winning.

Though both coaches expressed sentiment to the contrary, the matchup heavily favored the Phoenix. As a team, UWGB's defensive average of 59.9 points per game had been tops in the conference and top ten in the nation. Further, it included one of the school's all-time great defenders in Gary Grzesk, and was seemingly tailor-made to shut down one-dimensional, guard-driven teams like LaSalle.

The importance of the Grzesk-Townes matchup was not lost on LaSalle coach Speedy Morris: "Not many teams have shut (Kareem Townes) down. (Grzesk) did a very good job on him, no question. We've played Arizona, Massachusetts, and I think Gary has done as well as anybody."

On the other side of the ball, LaSalle played a difficult 2-3 zone with enough speed to stretch the floor and challenge the Phoenix shooters.

The early minutes of this noon game showed two teams that were playing tight, with the score tied at 8-8 through the first twelve minutes. UWGB's defense hit its stride, holding LaSalle to a season-low 15 first-half points. And with Westlake and Berlowski tag-teaming the scoring, UWGB had a six-point halftime advantage.

LaSalle was able to fight back early in the second half, tying the game at 25-25 with under 14 minutes to play. But Nordgaard, Grzesk, and Westlake put the team on their backs, scoring sixteen consecutive points to build a 41-32 lead with five minutes to play. UWGB closed out the Explorers from there, 54-46, holding LaSalle to its season-low scoring output and worst shooting percentage (25%).

"I'm just delighted to have twenty wins and be playing," Bennett said. "I think it has to be a major factor in (NIT) considerations."

He had no idea how his team's outlook would change in a matter of hours.

March Mayhem

Two hours later, UWGB watched in awe as the #7-seed Northern Illinois Huskies surprisingly dropped the #2 seed UIC Flames from the tournament, 87-83. That meant UWGB would face Northern Illinois in the conference semifinals, avoiding a dreaded rematch with Ford, Williams, and the Flames. But with powerhouse Xavier still in the mix, prospects for a tournament championship remained slim.

That was until the final game of the day. In the most stunning MCC conference tournament outcome ever, the hometown Wright State Raiders, at just 11-16, upset the #25-ranked, tournament-bound Xavier Musketeers.

"You talk about (events where you) remember exactly where you were and what you were feeling at the time?" recalls Grzesk. "Wright State had to play a play-in game just so they had the right to play Xavier. I think they were trailing most of the game, but we were there watching because we had finished playing."

The outcome hung in the balance as the clock left enough time for one last play. Down one point with a final prayer, Wright State chucked a full-court pass to Delme Herriman, who gathered the pass and launched a shot at the buzzer. Herriman's heave, which would become known as the "most famous shot in Wright State history," miraculously found the bottom of the net. Final score: Wright State 71, Xavier 70.

It was as though the Red Sea had parted for the Phoenix. "There were two teams that I don't think that we probably could have beat head-to head, just because they had our number," says Westlake. "Xavier was one of them and UIC was the other one."

In a matter of hours, both roadblocks had been eliminated.

"They (Xavier) were way better than us," states Nordgaard, "so when they got beat by Wright State, when Delme Herriman hit that (shot), we were high-fiving. It was as happy as we were when we beat Cal. I mean, that's how great we felt."

"We went back to the hotel and we were super stoked and we were pumping each other up," Berlowski says. "Like, 'We can pull this off. With how we're playing right now, we can pull this off.' "

While the players were flying high, Dick Bennett remained steady in the face of improving odds.

"I've seen this happen when you look ahead and it backfires," Bennett said after witnessing the Xavier upset. "We still have to win (tomorrow). Northern Illinois will be a very tough game for us. We'll have to play better than we did today."

Serving the Dish Cold

One player who needed no warning about looking past the Huskies was Chris Westlake. Back when he had been in junior college, the lefty had looked to Northern Illinois as a possible Division I home.

"It was the only place I visited personally," he says. "I took a couple of my Evansville tapes and went into the coaches' office there after I had left Evansville, and I said, 'Hey, I'm leaving Evansville and I'd like you to consider me as a student athlete, and here's a couple tapes.' It was one of the assistant coaches, I think, took the tapes, and he set them on the shelf right there in his office as I watched him. And then I think it must've been a couple months later, I followed up, and I walked in his office, and those tapes were still sitting in the same spot where he left them."

The lack of respect cut deep, and though Westlake moved on, he never forgot.

"I'm glad I didn't go there because they didn't have the values that I was looking for. It worked out better. But still, you remember those things as a competitor."

So while the rest of the Phoenix stumbled out of the gate in the semifinal match, Westlake turned in the revenge game of his life.

It started on the first Phoenix possession. Westlake worked off a Jackson screen, caught the ball at the top of the key and drilled a three-pointer, setting a tone that would reverberate for the next forty minutes. Two possessions later, Westlake again worked off a screen, caught a pass at the right wing, and knocked down a second three-pointer. A moment later, he hit his *third* three of the game, this time off the dribble at the top of the key. Two free throws later and Westlake had accounted for all eleven of UWGB's early points.

"I had found a zone that was really probably one of the best moments of – you know, where you're pretty much unconscious," Westlake recalls.

Westlake's onslaught continued throughout the game, and while the Huskies did their best to match him, nothing was going to stop the blond bomber from delivering. His junior teammates eventually kicked their game into gear, each helping deliver the knock-out blow during a key three-minute stretch at the end.

After Westlake hit yet another three-pointer to extend the Phoenix lead to 55-47, a confident Grzesk stepped up and rattled in a 15-foot jump shot. A stop on the defensive end, and Jackson assisted on a picture-perfect pass to Nordgaard, who had gotten behind his defender for an easy layup. On the ensuing Huskies possession, it was Berlowski who came up with a key steal, setting up another Jackson-to-Nordgaard layup that helped UWGB take a 61-49 lead with under three minutes to play. It was all academic from there, with the Phoenix prevailing 68-55.

UWGB was heading to its second straight conference championship game, and the all the talk was on Westlake's career 27-point night.

"People forget how consistent and how great he was as a senior. But that game against Northern Illinois – that's his home town, and they didn't even recruit him," Grzesk says. "I think he set the conference tournament record for made threes."

It was true – Westlake had set an MCC tournament record with seven made three-pointers while UWGB as a team tied the tournament record with twelve. And his revenge was oh so sweet.

The Huskies' head coach, Brian Hammel, stated the obvious after the game: "Everything we tried to do, he seemed to answer. He was hotter than the Hawaiian Islands. We just couldn't stop him."

But if Westlake hoped to hear anything close to regret from Hammel, he was destined for disappointment. Instead, Hammel appeared to go out of his way to backhand Westlake's success.

"We didn't have a need for that type of position. Just because Chris Westlake is a great player for Green Bay in that style, what's one man's food is another man's poison. I know he wouldn't have had that type of career (here). We demand more from our guards as far as ball-handling. The system gets him his shots."

"System guard" Chris Westlake and the rest of the Phoenix spent one final night in a hotel before the conference championship.

Poster Perfect

A lot went right for the Phoenix in the 1995 MCC tournament, but entering the conference championship, the true Cinderella was the Wright State Raiders. Ralph Underhill's team had won just ten games during the regular season, but in a miraculous turn, it had somehow pieced together three straight tournament wins. At 13-16 overall, the Raiders were trying to become just the tenth team in NCAA history to make the tournament with a losing record.

Meanwhile, for the fourth time in Bennett's career, he was coaching in a high-pressure conference championship game. And as it was in his previous three, this championship included the host school, ensuring a raucous environment.

For ESPN, the setting proved idealistic, with 10,000 fans packed into the Nutter Center to watch their hometown upstarts take on the best-coached team in the conference. Along with the Raider faithful, a whopping ten NBA scouts were in attendance, evaluating the mountain of a man, Vitaly Potapenko.

Wright State would play a 2-3 zone, with Potapenko roaming the middle. Despite the size mismatch, Bennett opted to ride his four-guard lineup and insisted on sticking with his man-to-man defense.

"If (Potapenko) were really aroused and they could put the ball in his hands, he was going to damage us. He was going to hurt us on the glass," Bennett remembers. "(But) I didn't worry so much about him on defense. We could play around him that way, and we weren't the kind of team that was going to challenge people at the rim all night anyhow."

As it turned out, Bennett had little reason for concern. The energy of the past three days seemed to put the Raiders in a lull, while the Phoenix rode the wave of recent success, starting with a Berlowski steal on the Raiders' opening possession that ended with the junior going coast to coast for an easy layup.

"I was fired up. I really wanted to go back to the NCAA tournament to kind of redeem myself," Berlowski says.

Nordgaard swished a long jumper from the left baseline on the second possession. After another stop, Westlake buried a three-pointer from the top of the key. Then after a fourth stop, Westlake again connected on a baseline jumper to give UWGB a quick 9-0 lead just three minutes into the game.

UWGB's swarming defense packed the interior, and Bennett demanded every defender to box out, limiting the Raiders to just one shot. The strategy worked wonders, as Wright State committed two quick turnovers and had no more than one shot attempt on each of its first six possessions. The Raiders played tight and their nerves were most evident on a Potapenko free throw attempt that caught nothing but air.

For all practical purposes, it was game, set, match – Phoenix.

The play of the game came late in the first half. With his team up nine, Nordgaard worked off a screen from Grzesk on the left baseline and caught a pass from Kevin Olm. Potapenko, much too slow for the smaller and quicker Nordgaard, clumsily took a step out, while Nordgaard went hard to the basket. The Ukraine Train recovered just in time to foul a fierce Nordgaard as the Phoenix forward rose and delivered a thundering reverse dunk right over him.

"Potapenko had his hand in his chest, and Jeff was just almost eyes length at the rim. Just had a tremendous dunk," comments Grzesk. "(It became) one of the pictures in the *USA Today* or one of the national (publications)."

ESPN loved the jam so much that they opted to show multiple replays rather Nordgaard's successful free throw attempt.

"I have memories of that one," Nordgaard smirks years later.

The rout was on, and UWGB closed out Wright State 73-59, securing the program's second consecutive NCAA tournament bid and third in school history. The unlikely run through the conference tournament exceeded all reasonable expectations.

"I would say this team has achieved more than any I have ever coached. I don't know if there is a close second," Bennett beamed afterwards. Decades later, he added: "They were a real spunky group, I mean they just played their hearts out. And you know, just to win the conference tournament took some real doing."

Nordgaard, who scored 28 points in the championship, was named the tournament MVP, and Westlake took home second team all-tournament honors. In front the NBA scouts, it was the perfect time and place for Nordgaard to have a signature game, but his coach wasn't surprised.

"Jeff was very flexible," Bennett says. "He could go inside and post up and he had those long arms and big hands. He was a great mid-range player because he could put the ball on the floor, pull up, get to the rim."

After the broadcast, Chris Fowler and Dick Vitale couldn't help but recall the Cal victory from a season earlier in forecasting the challenges the Phoenix could present.

"If you can beat Jason Kidd and Lamond Murray, you can flat out play. I wouldn't want to play them in the first round," noted Vitale. "Dick Bennett's club, trouble baby in that first round, keep your eyes on them, they're going to be big-time trouble!"

Chapter 19

The Big Dance
(1995 NCAA Tournament)

Like any big stage, the NCAA tournament has a way of magnifying all things great and small. The gap between earning a bid and playing a game is finite, and yet the sights, sounds, and distractions peripheral to the goal seem to be infinite.

The result can be an onslaught of unexpected feelings and emotions that have the capacity to cloud judgement, distort priorities, and overload the senses. If you want to win, you have to limit distractions and set the proper focus.

Gutter Balls

Just one day after UWGB's conference championship, rumors began swirling that the Wisconsin Badgers were going to fire Stan Van Gundy. Though UW athletic director Pat Richter had twice passed on Dick Bennett, the Phoenix coach's name was again said to be at the top of the Badgers' wish list.

Bennett spent much of the week following his team's conference tournament flatly denying rumors of interest, at one point bluntly stating, "I do not know what the rest of my coaching career is going to be like. I don't know how long it is going to be. But I do know that I am not, nor will I be, a candidate at Madison if there would be an opening."

Bennett's words did little to quiet the growing concern when, on Saturday, March 12, 1995, Wisconsin officially fired Van Gundy.

Dumping the future NBA coach after just one year left a sour taste with many associated with the program. Donnell Hoskins, the Badgers' rising junior guard, stood up for his former coach stating, "I think it's morally wrong, and I'll tell that to Mr. Richter if he asks me."

Stu Jackson, Van Gundy's predecessor, denounced Richter's administration. "The ignorance is what really bothered me. There was a lack of understanding about what it took at that level of college athletics to succeed. And the lack of communication (with administration) was something that bothered me."

Jackson, further frustrated that the haughty Richter hadn't even shown up at the team's year-end banquet, dug in deeper, stating:

"Coaches make public decisions night in and night out, game in and game out, and they always have to face the consequences of their decisions. Yet administrators can always hide behind their office doors when they make a decision. They not only damage their own credibility, but they don't think about the people who have helped them have careers, and that is the kids. For somebody not to be at the banquet for those seniors who have done a heck of a lot for the university – particularly Mike Finley – I think makes the lowest of statements."

In his own trademarked manner, Van Gundy summed it up simply: "I coached for seven months and they're going to pay me roughly a half million dollars one way or another. Don't look at me like *I'm* an idiot."

Ignorant of the hypocrisy, Richter's sole target was suddenly the man he'd twice brushed off without a second look. With, at best, reckless disregard for the position he was placing Bennett in or the impact on the Phoenix team, Richter proclaimed, "At this point, we don't want to take 'no' from anybody, regardless of who it is." When pressed about Bennett's denouncement, he added, "There are some things that have to be talked out."

Richter's desperation, intentional or otherwise, turned attention away from the ongoing success of the state's best team, UWGB.

Texas Two-Step

While Bennett continued to face questions about his future, his team gathered on Selection Sunday, waiting for their dance partner to be announced. When UWGB's name finally came up, they found themselves as a lowly 14-seed headed to Austin, Texas, for a Friday night showdown with a familiar foe – Gene Keady's Purdue Boilermakers.

Though Glenn Robinson had departed from West Lafayette to become the top draft pick in the 1994 NBA Draft, the Boilermakers had still managed to win the Big Ten championship in 1994-95. Six games in and just .500, few would have pegged Purdue for that kind of success, but Keady's squad went 21-3 the rest of the way, including a 15-3 record in the Big Ten. Without the Big Dog, it was Cuonzo Martin, a 6-5 triple threat with his shooting, penetrating, and passing, who captained the team. Behind Martin, the team was remarkably balanced.

"We didn't have expectations to get there," explains Jeff Nordgaard. "We got Purdue and we're like, 'Let's beat 'em.' You know, 'Let's beat 'em!'"

Not unlike the Phoenix, Keady's squad ran a motion offense, relied on tough man-to-man defense, and was perfectly content to grind games out rather than rely on outgunning their opponents.

"It was a tough draw because they were in the Big Ten, very good, played a similar brand to us, but bigger, more athletic, probably more talented at just about position," notes Gary Grzesk. "We were a little bit nervous about the matchup, to be honest, because we'd rather play somebody that's not built the same way we were."

"I thought they were a good team, but I also thought that we could compete with them," adds Ben Berlowski. "They were a team that had Cuonzo Martin, who was a good player, they had (Matt) Waddell, they had some good guards, but I thought we had just as good of players with Chris (Westlake) and me and Eric (Jackson) and Gary (Grzesk) and Jeff (Nordgaard)."

Purdue coach Gene Keady played up his team's perceived semi-underdog role to prepare his team for an NCAA tournament first-round matchup with UWGB. (Purdue University Archives)

This time, UWGB had no hope of a surprise attack.

"We're not going to sneak up on them," remarked Bennett after the selection. "This is a team who does know us, who does respect us. I don't think that was ever the case with the Cal players."

Keady validated Bennett's comments: "They don't scare me. I respect them. I consider (Dick Bennett) one of the finest coaches in the nation. He coaches. He teaches fundamentals. I'm not sure he can't take six kids out of the dorm and teach them."

And as Bruce Weber, a Purdue assistant coach, noted: "The thing that helps us, our kids *know* they're good. They respect them. It's not like we're playing Gonzaga or somebody. They beat us at (home) not that long ago."

With UWGB's success a year earlier, they were a trendy upset pick by some talking heads. Even future Michigan State coach Tom Izzo chimed in, stating, "I would pick Purdue ... And yet, I never count a Dick Bennett team out."

Keady, responding to the media frenzy and seeking to pull every motivational card from the Rolodex, said, "From everything I'm hearing, this will be an upset if *we* win. It's amazing how that works in people's minds."

Keady's proclamation notwithstanding the odds of an upset were against the Phoenix. Entering the 1995 NCAA tournament, history had seen a 14-seed upset the 3-seed just eight times in forty tries. The most recent example was three years old, when East Tennessee State knocked off Arizona in 1992 before being displaced by Michigan's famed Fab Five in the second round.

And yet, even before UWGB took the floor Friday evening, March 17, 1995, history was being rewritten. Early in the day, an underappreciated Weber State team, champions of the Big Sky, knocked off a heavily favored #3 Michigan State team. Weber State, led by senior guard Ruben Nembhard, came back from a nine-point halftime deficit to pull off a 79-72 victory over the Big Ten's second-place team in what would be Jud Heathcote's final game as Spartans coach. Later in the afternoon, #14 Old Dominion, the Colonial Conference champions, took down the Big East champion Villanova Wildcats in a triple-overtime thriller, 89-81.

UWGB hoped to turn the day into a trifecta of 14-seed upsets.

Do-Si-Do

The crowd in Austin was boisterous as the evening game inched closer. The fans had been raucous during an earlier game, demonstrated their passion straight out of the gates as defending champion Arkansas had held on for a one-point victory over Texas Southern. It was the only factor that openly played in UWGB's favor.

In contrast, the lineups and talent clearly favored Purdue. Keady's starters were grizzled and cagey, unintimidated and proud, and veteran. Joining senior forward Cuonzo Martin, senior guard Matt Waddell, and juniors Justin Jennings and Porter Roberts, was freshman center Brad Miller, a talented brute with NBA potential.

With little choice, Bennett chose to ride the same lineup he had used the entire last third of the season, trotting out his four guards in Grzesk, Westlake, Jackson, and Berlowski alongside the team's scoring leader, 6-6 forward Jeff Nordgaard.

As it had four years earlier in the tournament against Michigan State, UWGB faced mismatches at every position. But the toughest defensive draws were Grzesk, who drew Martin, and Nordgaard, who drew the 6--11 Miller.

The game was everything you would expect from a Keady and Bennett contest. Both teams were prepared and fearless, but also patient. The game settled into a slow, plodding pace that, in contrast to all common sense, seemed to endear the fans in attendance.

UWGB got strong production early from their pair of sharpshooters. Berlowski and Westlake delivered deep balls in the first ten minutes, helping UWGB jump on top. Meanwhile, Purdue was doing exactly what was expected – they attacked the paint, hit the offensive boards hard, and played intense defense. The Boilermakers were particularly effective in denying Nordgaard the ball, and it wasn't until seven minutes into the game that he finally took, and made, a shot.

The Phoenix actually held an 11-point lead midway through the first half, but Keady's offensive game plan was balanced and straightforward. Possessions flowed through Martin, while at least three white jerseys crashed the offensive glass. In typical Big Ten fashion, the Boilermakers exploited the size advantage, with their bigs, Miller and Jennings, regularly capitalizing on second-chance opportunities.

By halftime, UWGB's lead had dwindled to just two points, 30-28. The Phoenix had led for the entire twenty minutes, but its scoring had come in bunches and at the hands of shooters who had cooled down after a hot start.

As Dave Sims and Dan Bonner noted on the telecast coming out of the half, "I don't know that Wisconsin-Green Bay can beat Purdue simply with twos, but they sure can with threes."

Three's a Crowd

Two things stood out above all else in the second half of the game. First was Cuonzo Martin, who came alive, scoring Purdue's first six points in the second half and helping the Boilermakers take the lead. Second were the officials, who played a major role in the outcome.

It began with a questionable reach-in call against Grzesk – his fourth foul – with just over 16:00 left. In a bold move, Bennett left Grzesk on the floor, but switched his defense to a 1-2-2 zone to shake up the look and alleviate some immediate pressure on Grzesk.

On the following entry pass, another quick and questionable whistle, this time on Nordgaard for an apparent block when a stumbling Miller stepped into him. Nordgaard shook his head in disagreement, while Waddell drained a three-pointer to give Purdue its largest lead of the game, 39-35.

On the ensuing Purdue possession, the whistles blew again. This time, Purdue's guard Todd Foster steamrolled UWGB's Kevin Olm on his way to the basket and drew the foul. As the announcers noted, "Foster just ran down the middle of the lane, almost ran over Olm. Olm was trying to get out of the way ... he just runs smack into Olm."

With the calls, the game got chippy. UWGB maintained its composure, with the 1-2-2 zone causing problems for Purdue. Westlake, Berlowski, and Nordgaard delivered just enough offensively to keep the game within reach.

"It was a physical game," Berlowski recalls. "There were bodies flying, good box-outs, it was just a real grinder of a game. Just two pretty hard-nosed, blue-collar teams trying to just will it out with hard defense, taking care of the basketball, and taking good shots."

An Eric Jackson deep two-pointer with 3:20 to play cut Purdue's lead to 47-45. And when Nordgaard executed a perfect box-out on the bigger Miller after a Purdue miss to grab the rebound, it appeared the momentum had turned. But when Nordgaard fell backwards onto the floor, an official surprisingly called him for a foul.

"Brad Miller went over Jeff's back for a rebound and Jeff came down with the rebound, the whistle blew, and the Purdue guys started walking back on defense because they assumed that they called over-the-back on Brad Miller," explains Grzesk. "It certainly seemed that way."

"He threw Jeff down," comments Westlake. "Going down the stretch when you need to have something go in your favor, those hurt man."

A timeout on the floor gave everyone an opportunity to collect them-

Jeff Nordgaard looks to pass around Purdue's Cuonzo Martin during the Phoenix's NCAA tournament game on March 17, 1995. (AP photo / David J. Phillip)

selves, but the extra time also gave the broadcast booth time to check the tape. And as Sims and Bonner informed television audience, the officials had botched it: "Now watch Miller, he's got his elbow in the neck of Nordgaard, looks from that angle like he throws Nordgaard to the ground. The foul is called on Nordgaard, and Dick Bennett says, 'How can you make that call?!'"

UWGB would get a break when Purdue missed on the ensuing possession, and after working the clock under two minutes, the Phoenix regained the lead. With six seconds left on the shot clock, Jackson took two dribbles to his right, pointed at Nordgaard to get position in the post, before quickly crossing over to his left and pulling up for a three-pointer. Jackson's shot was true, sending the crowd into a frenzy.

UWGB had a 48-47 lead with less than 1:50 to play.

Both teams traded empty possessions, and with one minute to play, the Boilermakers had the ball, down one. This was it – the penultimate defensive possession of the season.

UWGB was in man-to-man and Grzesk was in full deny mode, successfully keeping the ball out of Cuonzo Martin's hands for the first twenty seconds of the possession. With 0:40 left, Martin finally got free enough to take a handoff at the top of the key, Grzesk in his hip pocket.

Miller came out to set a screen on Martin's right, with Nordgaard offering help over the screen. Grzesk, sensing that Martin would fake toward the screen before turning left, and knowing he had Nordgaard's help behind Miller, set himself directly in Martin's path.

"You could see they were setting up a high ball screen, and we had a guy there showing and helping on the ball screen, so I knew he was going to reject the ball screen and come back to his left, and I was just basically sitting there waiting for it," states Grzesk. "I took one slide and cut him off, and he ran right in the middle of my chest."

It was a masterful moment of defense, highlighting the workmanship in Grzesk's game. He knew Martin's tendencies, saw the strength of his teammate's help, and simply outwitted Purdue's best player, drawing the whistle.

"When that whistle blew and there was what little time left and we had the lead, and we were going to get the ball back, I had this unbelievably euphoric feeling that comes over you at a certain point. And I actually had that," remembers Bennett. "I wasn't even saying, 'Oh jeez, I hope we get this call.' You knew. You saw it, right there."

But ... somehow ... the call was a block on Grzesk, not a charge on Martin. Chaos erupted – the Purdue bench in exhilaration, the crowd in frustration, and Grzesk in exasperation. It was a seminal, back-breaking moment. And one of the most gut-wrenching calls in Phoenix history seemed to get worse with every angle of replay, each view confirming what had been apparent – it was a blatant offensive charge.

"It was a terrible call. Terrible call," recalls Grzesk. "Even if you watch, after the play, after I fell over, he's off balance and kind of stumbles over his feet. So I think it was a pretty obvious charge."

"He was there – it was clear. There was great hesitation on the part of the referee, and of course when he made the call, the crowd voiced its disagreement," Bennett says. "There's nobody from Green Bay who even has a doubt that that was a charge."

Ever the leader, Grzesk circled his teammates and gave a few words of encouragement before heading to the bench, his season hanging in the balance by the worst call in his career. Martin stepped to the line, and with the weight of his team and the entire Big Ten on his shoulders, buried two enormous free throws. Credit where it's due, Martin needed to make the shots and he did, giving Purdue the lead back, 49-48, with 35 seconds to play.

Down but not out, UWGB would have a final shot at winning the game. Bennett called a timeout, and the team agreed to work the ball to Nordgaard on the right side, clearing everyone else out. It was a strategy that worked against Marquette in similar circumstances, and Nordgaard was confident he could deliver again.

This time, things didn't go according to plan.

Jackson dribbled the ball down to 12 seconds as Nordgaard worked to get free from Martin. But Nordgaard struggled to shake loose, and with nine seconds left, Jackson picked up his dribble at the foul line and forced a pass to Nordgaard. He gathered it and took a dribble to his right, but the ball ricocheted off his foot toward the sidelines.

It was a precarious scenario, but Nordgaard was able to regain the ball with four seconds left and passed it back to Jackson at the top of the key. There were no options left. Jackson took two dribbles to his left and elevated, releasing a shot that seemed to float in the air for an eternity. With one second left, the ball connected with the front top edge of the rim, just an inch short of a swish, and bounced upward, hitting the backboard, and past the rim into the hands of the waiting Boilermakers.

Jeff Nordgaard battles through traffic during UWGB's last-second loss to Purdue at the 1995 NCAA tournament. (AP photo / Cliff Schiappa)

"I felt like I'd just died. I was empty. There was nothing there," noted Jackson.

For the fourth time in five years, UWGB's season ended in devastating fashion. Final score, Purdue 49, UWGB 48.

"Jeff probably views that as his worst moment in college because we had the play set up for him to take the last shot, and he just kind of mishandled it," Grzesk says. "You want your best player taking that last shot, and Jeff was definitely our best player. With that being said, Eric still had a clean, good look at the basket, but I know Jeff would've wanted to take the last shot."

Indeed, the missed opportunity haunted Nordgaard.

"I was supposed to take the last shot of the game, and we got the play called for me, and I got it on kind of on the top and I took a dribble to the right, and I kind of lost control of the ball," he says. "That was the biggest disappointment."

His coach was hard on him as well.

"Coach Bennett got on me afterwards, after the game. 'I don't know if you're ever going to be a player if you don't work on your ball-handling,'" remembers Nordgaard. "It wasn't like I was a terrible ball-handler. I just mishandled it on that one."

Few could argue that the officiating down the stretch severely ham-

The UWGB bench takes in the final moments of the Phoenix's 49-48 loss to Purdue. (AP photo / Cliff Schiappa)

pered UWGB's chances of moving on.

"That big call against Gary (Grzesk), that was really the turning point in the game right there. We thought we were in control of the game," remarks Berlowski.

A jaded Bennett, commenting on the Grzesk block, told reporters, "It was a critical call. I disagree with it, and I will until the day I die."

Decades later, the call remains one of, if not *the* worst call Bennett has chosen to remember.

"You're always going to see it more one way than the other; that just goes with the territory. But when you see a criminal call, that stays with you forever."

Turning out the Lights

As most March dreams do, this one ended abruptly. There would be no lead story on ESPN about another shocking first-round upset by the defensive-minded Fighting Phoenix from Green Bay. Bennett would not field questions from national media pundits about how his team was handling its new-found fame, or preparing on short notice for their second-round foe. There would be no need for the team to stick around Austin, or to practice on Saturday in preparation for a date with Memphis.

The 1994-95 season was through for UWGB, and though it ended on a sour note, there could be no denying the team had achieved greatness.

"I think all of us kind of had that 'We have something to prove' mentality," Westlake says. "I think most of us came from winning basketball programs in high school, which was a key, because we all valued winning. If I'm a player that had to sacrifice something in order to win, then I would be willing to do that because we put winning above everything else."

The Purdue loss ended Westlake's Phoenix career. The team's lone senior and most prolific junior-college transfer had endured a rocky junior season to establish himself as one of the keys to the 1994-95 team.

"(Bennett) was pretty hard and pretty critical of Chris, and that's a tough adjustment coming in as a junior college transfer into a new system," Grzesk recalls. "But then his senior year, I think he knew he was going to play, and was given the freedom to play through some of those mistakes."

Westlake finished fifth in school history in three-point percentage (44.0%). But it wasn't until his senior year that the ultimate shooter found his stride, making 87 three-pointers (second in school history) at a remarkable 50% clip.

"When Chris was hot, there wasn't anyone better in the nation," stated assistant coach Mike Heideman.

"I was just happy that he was really the critical piece to that '95 team, because if he did not play like he was capable of, we really would have struggled," agrees Grzesk. "He was a great teammate and did not complain during his junior year when he wasn't playing a lot, and then took advantage of his opportunity as a senior. He was really the key to that team."

It was a tribute to Westlake's resilience that he was able to achieve such success, given the touchy relationship he had with his head coach.

"There were some guys that either didn't pay attention to some of the mind games that Dick played or were motivated by it, and then there were some guys that it took them a long time to get comfortable with it. Chris was one of the guys that it took him a long time," remarks LeDuc. "It took him until his last year to really get to that point where he didn't led Dick get into his head."

And yet, Bennett's words and actions did affect the course of Westlake's career and life in ways that were hugely impactful. Decades after suiting up for his final game under Bennett, Westlake reflected on the importance of Bennett in his life – a voice that, whether intentionally, by accident, or a product of divine design, awoke Westlake's spiritual side.

"One thing I'll say about Coach Bennett, and this is the most important thing from my personal life that I can say – is forget about the basketball stuff. It's that he was a bit of a preacher in the way that he related our style of play to the Bible. I didn't understand what he was talking about, but the fact of the matter is I saw someone take the scripture, which I had not had exposure to at that point, and apply it to life in a real-life fashion," Westlake shares. "A year later, after I had finished playing and I didn't know what I was going to do, I was kind of lost. I needed some help, and so when I was reading those words, some of the things that Coach Bennett was saying came back to me at that point and I understood what he was saying then.

"Our relationship served as, so to speak, to kind of plow the ground up of my heart. If I didn't have that happen in my life, man, I don't know where I would be. Because I was a mess inside. It was that tension, that grinding, that breaking up the ground, that whole agricultural symbolism ... he was planting seeds, and then a year later, the plant grew and bore fruit in my life to where understanding came. And the light – so to speak, the light switch came on. It really saved my life in the end."

Divine Intervention

In the hours after the loss, Green Bay took comfort in the fact that they had, for no less than the third time, narrowly avoided a much bigger loss to the program — the potential departure of their iconic coach and architect of their nationally recognized defense. Dick Bennett had made it clear to the city, the team, and the administration that he wasn't going anywhere.

No one was more certain of his intentions to remain the head coach of UWGB than Bennett himself. Prior to the Purdue game, Bennett had asked Otis Chambers to arrange for a press conference, set to take place immediately following the game in Austin.

"I had told Otis, our A.D., that I wanted to get this thing wrapped up as to what I was going to do, and we would have a press conference right after the game down in Austin, win or lose. And I had decided to stay."

But, as is often the case in the most monumental of moments, fate intervened.

In the locker room after the loss, Bennett was reviewing his notes in preparation for the press conference when Chambers handed him an airline ticket to Columbus, Ohio. , Chambers instructed Bennett to head to the airport and catch a flight out of Austin so he could watch his daughter, Kathi, coach UW-Oshkosh in the Division III Women's National Championship game the next day.

Bennett was caught off guard and asked Chambers about the press conference.

"He said, 'Well, we can do that next week, no problem. I know you should be out there with her,' " Bennett recalls.

Touched and eager to see his daughter's team play, he accepted. The next day, Dick and his wife, Anne, watched their daughter's team lose and finish its season 30-1. The UWGB press conference had been rescheduled to Wednesday, so the Bennetts chose to drive back to Green Bay on Sunday. That night, Dick Bennett received a surprising call from none other than Pat Richter, the Wisconsin athletic director.

Richter put the hard press on Bennett, but Dick wasn't budging and told Richter about the upcoming press conference. Richter would not be turned away so easily.

"He said, 'Well, I just would like to talk to you, and I'm going to actually fly into Green Bay tomorrow morning and I'm wondering if you could pick me up at the private airport. Nobody's going to know, and I'd like to visit with you at your home,' " recalls Bennett.

Monday morning, Bennett picked up Richter at the airport and the two talked about the Badgers vacancy at the Bennetts' home. Dick was adamant that he was staying at UWGB.

"I said no, but he would not take no for an answer," he says.

So, reluctantly and at the suggestion of Anne, Bennett agreed to think about the job for a few days.

The night before his Wednesday press conference, Bennett met with his players. In his mind, he had made the decision to stay and, ready to end the matter once and for all, he told the players what had transpired with Richter.

And then something surprising and unprecedented happened.

"Gary Grzesk stood up and said, 'Coach, we're happy, we definitely want you to stay, but we also know how much you want to coach in the Big Ten. You want a chance to turn that program around, and we do not want you to miss that opportunity,' " remembers Bennett. " 'We really think that you should think very seriously about taking that position.' So in essence, they released me. They gave me permission to make a decision."

"Gary (Grzesk) and Jeff (Nordgaard) kind of took the lead," explains Berlowski. "They said, 'Coach, we'll be okay without you. This is your dream, go for it. If this is what you want, it's basketball, man, we'll be fine. You taught us a lot, you gave us a lot while you were here, go fulfill your dream of wanting to go to Wisconsin.' And when Gary and Jeff kind of took the lead by saying that, it was a huge relief off his shoulders."

"To a person, we knew that it was his dream job, and we all gave him our blessing," confirms Grzesk. "He definitely earned that right."

Freedom in one sense carried with it the pressure of committing to the most difficult choice of his life. It rekindled his desire to coach at the highest level of college basketball, to try and turn around a struggling Big Ten team in his home state.

"I didn't know what to say. I went home and had – it was just a real difficult time deciding," Bennett remembers. "I went home, press conference was the next day, that morning is when I decided I would go down and listen to what Wisconsin had to say."

While the team had been in the loop, Bennett's announcement that he was looking at the Badgers job shocked the media and rocked the city. It was the opposite of what the coach had proclaimed, and created animosity with the Badgers' tactics.

The same day, Bennett reached out to Chambers to discuss his potential successor if he would leave the program.

"I remember talking to Otis, saying, 'Look, if I were to leave, I would like to make sure that Mike Heideman would get the job. Can you push for that?' And he said, 'I'm in total agreement with it,' " Bennett says.

Bennett called Heideman next. "Mike, I would like to have you come with me. The job is yours, you know how much I would love that. But I also know that you'd like to get back into head coaching and I have reason to believe (the UWGB) job would be yours."

Two days later, Bennett visited Madison and met with Richter, the chancellor, and the board of trustees, patiently answering questions from everyone. He formally accepted the position later that Friday and the hiring was announced at a press conference in Madison the following day. Dick Bennett's career at the University of Wisconsin-Green Bay had come to an end.

"I always felt the Lord was in charge of that whole affair, because he allowed me to enjoy a couple of great years in Green Bay, and when I went there, it was the right time" he says.

Some, like Grzesk, traced Bennett's decision back to the poor call at the end of the Purdue game.

"I think that call led Coach Bennett to go to Wisconsin," Grzesk comments. "I don't think he thought that the little guy, the mid-major, would get a call at a critical time, in a critical game in the NCAA tournament."

History supported that opinion, seeing it happen with the LeMoine technical against Nebraska in 1991, the Rondorf call at Wisconsin in 1992, and the Berlowski charge in 1994.

But whether or not the Grzesk call itself was the catalyst, the Purdue loss had unexpectedly set in motion the most unlikely chain of events that completely altered the course of Wisconsin basketball forever.

"Had we won that (Purdue) game, I wouldn't have been going anywhere," admits Bennett. "We'd have had practice and got ready for the next game. I was all set to announce publicly to all of the reporters that were there: 'I'm staying.' That's how touch and go it was. That is absolutely the way it came down."

Farewell to Thee

Bennett's ten-year career in Green Bay was nothing short of spectacular in nearly every way. He left UWGB with a 187-109 career record, twice taking home Mid-Continent Conference Coach of Year (1990, 1992) and NABC District 11 Coach of the Year (1992, 1994) honors.

Bennett adeptly molded the Phoenix from a low-level Division I team, struggling to win a handful of games, to a perennial postseason entrant, taking UWGB to three NCAA tournament appearances and two NIT appearances in his final five seasons. To put that in perspective, only thirteen other schools sitting outside of major conferences were able to make at least three NCAA tournaments and at least five postseason appearances between 1990 and 1995.

While fans were disappointed that the golden era of Green Bay basketball looked to be waning, their reactions spread across a spectrum of emotion. Some – those who took particular offense to the treatment of the UWGB program from the University of Wisconsin over the previous few years – were incensed. How could the deep-pocketed, silver-spooned Wisconsin Badgers – a team that Green Bay, and Bennett personally, had struggled to obtain any respect from –swoop in and steal their coach?

Others were less critical of the Badgers and, seeing a silver lining, believed the Phoenix's loss could still benefit state of Wisconsin, improving the Badger program. Still others took the teams out of the equation and applauded the move, understanding that it would benefit Bennett and his family. For these latter groups, the Badgers' magical 2000 Final Four run under Bennett a few years later provided retroactive validation.

One common thread among those reacting to the news was there was no bitterness toward Bennett. His years spent building the program, improving the community, and developing young men left a lasting impression still palpable decades later.

"Coach Bennett had a way of making you think and believe you were better than you were," observes Ben Johnson. "That's one of his greatest gifts, just the belief he could instill in a player to actually go out there and think, 'Hey, I can do this. I can compete against anybody. I can take on the world.' "

"Coach Bennett would be literally chasing guys around the gym. And when I say that, I mean that," Johnson continues. "He would say, 'MOVE,' and he would start chasing me down the court. That was Dick Bennett – that's young Dick Bennett at his finest."

Bennett's unique fire for the sport gave his players a lifetime of memories ranging from the silly to crazy and everything in between.

"(*Green Bay Press-Gazette* beat reporter) Pete Dougherty and I kind of hit it off and we'd talk before the games," recalls LeDuc. "And for whatever reason, he ended up using a quote (when I was red-shirting). It said something about, 'We could be a better rebounding team.' Something about how 'I hope that I can bring that to the team next year.' I walked into practice the next day and Coach Bennett is waiting for me, and he's like, 'Who the hell do you think you are talking to the – you're not even playing!' "

Dick Bennett set the standard for all UWGB men's basketball coaches to follow during his 10 years leading the Phoenix. (University of Wisconsin-Green Bay Archives)

"We had a bad practice at Brown County Arena and I remember Coach Bennett saying 'Nordgaard, we just can't win big games with you.' And this is in practice, my junior year, *after* we had beat Cal. I had whatever, 26 points and hit the game-winner, *and* we beat Marquette," Nordgaard says. "I tell people, 'Don't take what he says with a grain of salt, take it with a cube of salt.' "

"One season he bought all of these like swim vests or whatever, and we would take turns in the swimming pool," recalls Scott LeMoine. "There were a couple of guys on the team that couldn't swim very well, and they were scared for their life, you know, jumping into an 18-feet deep pool with nothing but a piece of Velcro holding you Another practice, he came out donned in University of Illinois gear, because we were getting ready to play Illinois and he wanted to get us fired up. He would do some quirky things like that."

Beyond the accolades, Bennett's lasting legacy was the impact he had in shaping the futures of his players. Through Vince Lombardi-esque threads of tough love and painstaking devotion to his craft, Bennett had a unique imprint on his players' lives.

It began with his willingness to challenge his toughest and highest-potential players, looking to draw out their best qualities. This proved particularly successful with ultra-competitive players like Ben Johnson.

"He was always challenging me, daily, constantly, with leadership-type things," Johnson relates. "Or he would just say, 'I wish we had some leadership,' and look right at me. 'I wish we had some guys that understood what it took.' Just little comments like that daily that pushed you to be more and give more and demand more."

Many learned that drawing the coach's fire was as much a sign of his high expectations as it was indicative of frustration.

"My (initial) mindset was the coach was tough because he didn't like me," Rondorf says. "I realized that when Coach Bennett yelled at me, he really wanted me to get better. 'When we stop yelling at you or we stop acting like we're coaching you is when we really don't care about you anymore. We love you as a family, we want you, but maybe basketball-wise, you know, maybe there's someone else.'"

Nordgaard learned the same.

"He became quite hard on me, and looking back now, I know that it was to push me and he had expectations for me," he says. "I tell my kid the same thing. He gets mad at me for yelling at him for doing the wrong thing, and I said, 'That's because I have expectations. I don't yell at Joey over there because I don't expect much from him.'"

As did Logan Vander Velden.

"I realized this afterwards – that he was hard on me because he saw the potential that I had. When you're in the moment, you don't realize that at times or see that. But I knew he was hard on me because he believed in me and he knew the ability that I had. Off the court, he was just a great person and a great mentor."

Bennett was also savvy enough to know that what worked with one player wouldn't necessarily work with another.

"I think he recognized people had different characteristics and different ways of reacting to his coaching," observes Grzesk. "As you progressed in the system, he would tailor that to everyone's strengths and weaknesses."

"You went through an evolution with him from where he taught you to where he talked to you to where he discussed things with you," explains Dean Vander Plas. "My whole senior year, I could actually talk to Coach and just say, 'Hey, I think this' or 'I think that.'"

He was fair, but did he treat everyone the same?

"Hell no, he didn't," Ben Johnson says. "He coached everyone with the same intensity, and had the same demands of everybody, but no, no, no, no! When you coach that intensely, are that demanding of every play of every possession, well, things are going to be said at times that, you know, it was a very intense environment. Which again, we all loved. It's made us all better people for it."

"I always tell people he was the most passionate person in any career that I've ever seen," says Jeremy Ludvigson. "He was Bobby Knight without the swearing and the getting personal and stuff. He was really tough on us. Most of the guys knew where he was coming from and bought into what he was trying to do."

"His humanity and his willingness to accept people for who they are, he allowed us to grow," recalls Mike Karisny. "I was a very emotional player and he was an emotional coach ... we'd challenge each other. I remember laughing with him, but I also remember crying with him. And that's the type of person he's taught me to be."

"Coach Bennett to me was kind of like a father figure slash coach," says John Martinez. "I just always looked up to him, and he kind of helped me along with that as well, just not only as a basketball player but off the court as well. What I liked about it is that he held everyone accountable to do what they're supposed to do. There was no favoritism."

For players like Gary Grzesk and Dean Vander Plas, those teachings helped them share the same lessons with players they went on to coach after their playing careers were over.

"A big reason I got into coaching was because of that coaching staff. Coach Bennett certainly, but also Coach Heideman, Coach Swan, Woody Wilson, my senior year Ben Johnson, Bob Semling," notes Grzesk. "They had a huge impact on me in my personal life and ultimately got me into the coaching profession."

"Coach saw something in me that nobody else saw. Not even me," states Vander Plas. "And that servant's heart that he preaches, that he absolutely won't detour from, has allowed a pretty average athlete from Oostburg, Wisconsin, to have an amazing life. We've been able to impact a lot of people. I spent twenty-three years on the sidelines trying to basically pay back Coach Bennett and Coach Moriarty for the eight years of investment they made in me."

"I would not trade my experience playing for him for anything in the world," Grzesk concludes. "I was pretty fortunate to play for a coach that understood my strengths, was able to give me an opportunity, and then I just kind of found my niche and my role in the team. I'm not sure there's another Division I coach or program at the time that I could've played for with some of my limitations on the offensive end."

Chapter 20

Transitioning Leadership
(1995-96 - Part 1)

The mid-major coaching ranks have always served as stepping stones to the higher-paying and more prestigious major-conference programs. Indeed, nearly all major conference head coaches ascended to their role from jobs as either major school assistants or mid-major head coaches.

The difference between one-hit wonders and schools that can sustain mid-major success is how they handle the inevitable transition. Some schools scour the junior college or lower-conference ranks for signs of success, others look for talent backing up successful coaches at major programs, while still others look to promote from within.

Regardless of the method, those who extend their team's success usually excel at maintaining the philosophical and ethical foundations on which the program was built.

Alpha or Omega
With Dick Bennett's departure, UWGB was at a crossroads. Uncertain if its story was just beginning, coming to a close, or somewhere in the middle, the school's next move would undoubtedly author the team's next, but hopefully not last, chapter in a success journey.

Recent history offered no perfect roadmap. Between 1985 and 1995, mid-majors were faced with replacing successful coaches – those who had led their teams to at least two postseason bids in the preceding five years – on sixty-six occasions. By a slight margin, programs seemed to favor promoting an internal candidate, doing so on twenty-five occasions as opposed to hiring a major school's assistant (twenty-one times) or hiring a head coach from another school (twenty times).

	Internal Promotions	Major Assistants	Other Head Coaches
	25	21	20
Successes (2 or more postseason bids)	6 *24%*	10 *48%*	7 *35%*
Modest Returns (1 postseason)	6 *24%*	3 *14%*	4 *20%*
Failures (0 postseasons)	13 *52%*	8 *38%*	9 *45%*

Internal promotions appeared to have the lowest odds of continued success, though no route was a surefire hit or miss. Case studies of a few gold standard programs were equally ambiguous.

Tulsa, for one, had enjoyed success in replacing coaches on multiple occasions, though rarely with their own internal candidate. The Golden Hurricanes first faced the challenge in replacing the legendary Nolan Richardson in 1985. Richardson had built the Tulsa program in the Missouri Valley Conference, going to three NCAA tournaments and two NITs in his five seasons, as well as winning the 1981 NIT championship.

Tulsa first went external, bringing in VCU's former head coach, J.D. Barnett, who brought the program to a pair of NCAA tournament appearances along with two NIT visits, winning more than 100 games before leaving in 1991.

Tulsa then hit the jackpot in replacing Barnett, hiring little-known Kentucky assistant Tubby Smith. Smith coached Tulsa for four years, bringing the club to the Sweet Sixteen in in 1994 and 1995 before leaving for Georgia.

Life after Tubby wasn't quite as magnificent, but hardly a failure. Tulsa hired Kansas assistant coach Steve Robinson, who went two-for-two in returning Tulsa to the NCAA tournament, even as the Golden Hurricanes switched to the Western Athletic Conference (WAC). After Robinson left for Florida State in 1997, Tulsa hired former Oral Roberts head coach, Bill Self, who brought the program to the NCAA tournament two more times in three years before taking the head job at Illinois.

Self was replaced by Appalachian State head coach Buzz Peterson, who coached just one season, winning the NIT championship in 2001. For the first time in six hires, Tulsa finally promoted an internal candidate, John Phillips, who continued the success, bringing Tulsa to the NCAA tournament in each of his first two seasons.

The Murray State Racers provided another example of success in handling transitions. Like Tulsa, Murray State tried both external assistant coaches and internal promotions to replace Steve Newton, who had brought the club to the postseason on four straight occasions from 1988-1991 before leaving for South Carolina and the SEC. Murray State poached Scott Edgar, an Arkansas assistant coach. Edgar was a success, and in his four seasons helped the Racers get to two more NCAA tournaments and one NIT.

When Edgar left for Duquesne in 1995, he was replaced by UCLA assistant Mark Gottfried. Gottfried would last only three years with Murray State, but continued the winning ways in bringing the Racers to two more NCAAs and an NIT. Gottfried was quickly pried away by Alabama, at which point Murray State promoted associate coach Tevester Anderson to the head job. Anderson would win 103 games over five seasons, getting Murray State back to two more NCAA tournaments.

And then there were the Xavier Musketeers. In 1985, Xavier replaced Bob Staak with former Notre Dame assistant Pete Gillen. Gillen took Xavier to the NCAA tournament the next six years, and the postseason eight of nine years, before leaving for Providence in 1994. In the meantime, Xavier had elevated its prestige, rising above the mid-major moniker as they became a member of the Atlantic-10.

Gillen was replaced by one of his former assistants, Skip Prosser, who picked up right where Gillen left off, taking Xavier to three NCAA tournaments and two NITs in six years before he, too, departed. Xavier then nabbed Thad Matta from its former MCC rival, Butler. Matta immediately brought Xavier to three more NCAA tournaments before he left for Ohio State.

Having had success with both major assistants and outside head coaches, Xavier hit the trifecta by then promoting from within. Sean Miller, an assistant under Matta, became the head coach and brought Xavier to four straight NCAA tournaments.

Ringing Endorsements

All of that was moot in Green Bay. There was no doubt who Dick Bennett wanted to replace him on the Phoenix bench.

"Mike (Heideman) wanted the job at Green Bay, and I wanted him to have it," recalls Bennett. "If they hadn't given it to him, he would have come with me."

Otis Chambers leveraged his strong ties with the team's senior foursome in making the final call. He had developed relationships with the players in his role as head athletic trainer prior to becoming athletic director.

"He taped my ankles when I was a freshman, and then he gets into this position," remembers Ben Berlowski. "Otis was awesome ... and he pretty much gave us the opportunity to hire who we wanted. That's how much clout he gave us, which was kind of cool."

For those four, the decision was easy.

"We talked to Otis and said that we wanted Coach Heideman," explains Jeff Nordgaard. "Gary (Grzesk) and I and Eric (Jackson) and Ben are like, 'If we have a say, it's probably best if there's the least change possible.' "

"I think there was a natural pipeline to promote Coach Heideman from within," notes Grzesk. "We certainly wanted to see Coach Heideman get an opportunity to become a head coach and run his own program."

Of course, Grzesk's vocal support for Heideman sparked some gentle ribbing from his younger teammates.

"Some of the younger guys, were like, 'Man, that's just because you wouldn't see the floor if it was any other coach, because you got a broke jump shot Gary,' " relates Berlowski. "He'd get so mad."

With the team largely aligned, Nordgaard took the proactive step of calling Coach Heideman on the team's behalf to let him know that the players endorsed him. Nordgaard also reached out to prospective recruits to let them know the program was in good hands, hoping to keep the talent the staff had already landed.

"We want to let people know just because we lost our head coach doesn't mean the program is going down the tubes. We see no reason why we can't be back in the NCAA tournament," notes Nordgaard.

His move proved effective, as key recruits Mike Nabena and Matt Hill both declared their intentions to honor their commitments one day later.

One day after Bennett held his final press conference in Green Bay, Chambers met with Heideman to discuss the position. The meeting went well, and Chambers left the decision with Heideman, telling him the position was his if he wanted it. Two days later, and with the role officially vacant for less than a week, Mike Heideman made up his mind, and the position was his.

The Mike Heideman Era Begins

"This is a very special day for me. It's a long time coming," said Heideman at his introductory press conference. "It's something I have dreamed about for a number of years and I'm terribly excited and honored that I'm the next head coach."

Addressing the challenges in replacing such a successful predecessor, Heideman noted, "The legend of Dick Bennett is always going to be here. I cannot be Dick Bennett. I have to be Mike Heideman. I have talents. I have gifts. When you people let (Dick) go, it will allow me to be the person I am."

Chambers was thrilled with hire. "We didn't get to the NCAA or NIT until Mike was here. He was an integral part. I think he felt about as strong as Dick did about leaving the program he had built."

Mike Heideman succeeded Dick Bennett as head coach in 1995. (University of Wisconsin-Green Bay Archives)

With an internal hire, Chambers ensured that the Phoenix style of play would remain consistent.

"You won't see dramatic changes," Heideman confirmed. "You'll see subtle changes with the style of play, with how I deal with young people, with how I deal with the media.

"It's been proven that if you're going to compete at this level with the types of athletes you'll get at Green Bay, we can't run up and down the floor. We'll run when we can," Heideman added. "But I think Dick has shown everybody that if you make every possession important, if you value the ball, if you value teamwork, if you value the idea that you don't have to have the best players, but you have to play good basketball – that's important."

As sophomore Kevin Olm noted, "Most of all, it adds stability to the program. We have a good team, and this gives us a good chance to do a lot next year."

In addition to pedigree, style, and internal support, Heideman also carried with him a vast amount of community respect.

"He's a man of utmost integrity," praised Al Negratti, the former athletic director at St. Norbert College, where Heideman had been head coach prior to joining Bennett's staff at UWGB. "He's most trustworthy. He's highly organized. (The players) liked him because he's a very sincere guy. There's no double-talk."

Family Gathering

Heideman inherited a loaded, veteran lineup. His four seniors – Gary Grzesk, the top defender; Eric Jackson, the point guard; Ben Berlowski, the feisty deep-threat; and Jeff Nordgaard, the top scoring threat and one of the two best players in Phoenix history – were destined to be remembered as one of the greatest classes in school history. Behind those four, sophomores Kevin Olm and Pete Wade had each logged primetime minutes as freshmen and seemed willing to support the seniors.

With the core of his team was intact, Heideman set to work on two major outstanding issues: his staff and his recruits.

Heideman fully intended to keep as much intact as possible, and immediately offered Steve Swan and Woody Wilson positions on his bench. Wilson accepted, while Swan declined and instead took a fundraising position with the university.

That left Heideman with two positions to fill. He trimmed the more than 100 applicants to a final eight by May.

"I'm amazed at the quality of people," remarked Heideman. "I have men who would take substantial pay cuts. There are a lot of people with collegiate experience."

In mid-May 1995, Heideman filled his first vacancy with Bob Semling, a former Wausau West High School head coach and UW-Stevens Point assistant coach very familiar with UWGB's style of play. Semling's expertise was in training and weight room exercises, and at Heideman's request, he created a plan intended to improve the Phoenix's strength. Semling's impact with the players was immediate.

"I worked my butt off between my junior and senior year," observes Berlowski. "Looking back, I lifted weights every day, I spent a ton of hours in the weight room. I remember Eric LeDuc was living in Appleton and he came up and we went on a boat, and he was like, 'Dude, are you going to play football next year, or are you going to play basketball?' "

Semling also went to work on 6-10 Matt Hill, one of UWGB's tallest recruits ever. Hill had spurned interest from other Division I schools including Evansville, Seton Hall, and Sienna to join the Phoenix, but he was a beanpole.

"I believe that strength for Matt Hill will be the determining factor in how good he becomes. I would like to see Matt at about 230 pounds," noted Heideman. "It has nothing to do with his heart. It's just a matter of strength and power."

To boost his size, Semling had Hill eating high-calorie foods like peanut butter sandwiches, cheeseburgers, pizza, donuts, tacos, and nachos. The freshman was able to gain over ten pounds in the first few weeks of the season, all while hitting the weight room hard.

Heideman was happy about the early returns. "Our players attack the weights in a much more systematic, energetic way. I know they are stronger and because they're stronger, they can do more things on the court."

Heideman did not fill the second vacancy so quickly, though the delay was intentional. He had held his final bench spot for a former Phoenix family member who was finishing his professional playing career in Australia.

On July 5, 1995, Heideman officially announced Ben Johnson, one of UWGB's favorite sons, as his final assistant coach. Like Semling, Heideman had an immediate task for Johnson – solidify the team's recruiting.

"In Ben Johnson, I believe we have found a quality young man who typifies the type of young person that we are trying to bring into this program," glowed Heideman. "Ben made himself into an outstanding Division I basketball player through hard work, dedication, and commitment. I believe he'll continue to carry these traits into his position as a Division I coach."

Heideman made a few other modifications to his program. For one, he intended to bring film study to the program, asking Woody Wilson to splice together ten-minute clips from each opponent for the players to view during team meals.

"We're just trying to be consistent, whether it's an NCAA tournament game, the (conference) tournament, or a game with UW-Milwaukee," noted Heideman. "The players know this is what we're going to do and you can count on it."

After a few games, even Nordgaard was convinced: "We have stopped a certain move or play in games because we have seen it before. I wouldn't want to do it (film study) extensively, but the way we do it is really helpful."

Though Heideman still preached the value of working the possession, he loosened the reigns on his shooters. "If they get a good shot, I want them to take it."

Top Heavy

The 1995-96 version of the Phoenix would, without question, be a senior-led team, and the program's success would begin with superstar forward Jeff Nordgaard.

"He's truly one of the better players that have been in this program over the years, (and) will be counted on to have a very fine year," commented Heideman. "What I like about Jeff is his completeness. He has the ability to shoot the three-pointer, play outside, to even use his dribble. Yet, if you guard him with a small person, he's very good in the low post."

Sharpshooting guard Ben Berlowski would also be counted on to help carry the scoring load. Meanwhile, Heideman was looking for guard Eric

Jackson to provide energy and leadership on the defensive side of the ball.

"(Eric's) going to have to be one of our leaders on the floor," noted Heideman, "I want Eric, through his actions, to get us pumped up to play defense. He has to be one of our best defensive players."

The fourth and final senior, Gary Grzesk, was a known commodity and the glue of the team.

"Gary is our heart and soul," beamed Heideman. "With this team, Gary must be on the floor for us to be at our best. He does all the intangibles and small things that help you win basketball games."

It was a special group of seniors, and Heideman treated them as such.

"We didn't have to be told much. We understood what we had to do, we knew when we f***ed up," notes Berlowski. "We knew when we weren't playing well. We knew when we had to get on each other or what we had to do."

"I think the one thing in common that group had is that we all hated to lose," adds Grzesk. "If we would go out to a bar, we were playing darts, and you thought it would've been game seven of the NBA Finals. Or we get on the bus and we're playing *Trivial Pursuit*, we're competing to the very end."

The question marks for the 1995-96 Phoenix cropped up rather quickly after the top four. The team would unquestionably rely on sophomore point guard Kevin Olm, who had started ten games and led the team in assists as a freshman.

"Kevin Olm was phenomenal," recalls Berlowski. "Kevin could really handle the basketball. Kevin played defense."

But Olm would likely come off the bench and share time with Jackson, Grzesk, and Berlowski. To fill his fifth starting spot, Heideman looked to his three taller sophomores, Pete Wade, Gabe Stevens, and Tom Anderson.

Wade had started three games as a freshman, and as a decent shooter, was the lead candidate to play a major role. Stevens had also played in more than twenty games as a freshman, including notching a start against Wisconsin. He had shown flashes, but likely would back up Wade. Meanwhile, Anderson was athletically gifted, but an unproven talent.

The rest of the Phoenix roster amounted to players in early development. Talented sophomore Ryan Borowicz was returning from a freshman season filled with injuries, and redshirt freshman James Daggs was still building strength. Borowicz, in particular, had immediate potential given his shooting ability, though it would likely be a year or two before he saw major minutes.

"Ryan could shoot the shit out of the ball. Ryan was one of the best shooters I've seen in a long time, and from any range," states Berlowski. "We'd have these drills where you'd have to have seven stops in a row before we could go on to the next drill or whatever. We'd be on stop six, and out of nowhere, Borowicz would hit a 30-foot bomb, like falling away out of nowhere."

Incoming freshmen Matt Hill and 6-8 Mike Nabena were great pieces for the future, but both needed time to develop. Meanwhile, little-used junior Sam Maddox transferred out, allowing Heideman to add one final freshman piece.

Heideman took advantage, and made an offer to a 6-1 guard from Geneseo, Illinois, named Luke Kiss. Kiss was a highly successful player at Darnall High School, winning at least twenty games in each of his three varsity season. Like Hill and Nabena, Kiss would be a key building block in years to come.

So Many Channels

Between 1988 and 1996, the rapid proliferation of cable television played an integral part in the evolution of college basketball. With nearly double the audience from a decade prior and new channels springing up like popcorn, programming opportunities were plentiful.

Big players like ESPN, which began in 1979, experienced huge growth, adding ESPN2 in 1993, ESPN Classic in 1995, and finally ESPN News in 1996. The first effectively doubled the sports leader's programming, while the latter two enabled 24/7 sports news, rebroadcasting of classic matchups, and overflow broadcast opportunities.

Following ESPN's lead, other major networks also began investing in sports-centered programming. FOX launched FOX Sports in 1994 and quickly gained rights to broadcast Pac-12 and Big 12 college games. NBC followed suit with the NBC Sports Network in 1995. Meanwhile, numerous regional outfits – networks like The Sports Channel and New England Sports Network – expanded their original telecast options, increasing television exposure of teams generating local interest.

None of this expansion was lost on the sports organizations themselves. Leagues, like the NFL (Sunday Ticket, 1994), NBA (League Pass, 1995), and MLB (Extra Innings, 1996), all began offering full lineup telecasts to service the growing public demand for content.

Predicting this expansion, CBS had locked up exclusivity on the NCAA's crown jewel, buying the broadcast rights to the NCAA tournament for seven years with a record-setting $1 billion contract executed in 1989. That would seem like a steal compared to the renewal ten years later, an 11-year extension worth a whopping $6 billion.

At its core, all of this meant way more visibility for mid-majors like UWGB. Whereas the 1991-92 UWGB team played just one nationally televised game, the 1993-94 and 1994-95 squads had played on national television four times apiece, along with a half-dozen regional appearances. And in the summer of 1995, the MCC and ESPN agreed to a six-year television deal, with ESPN agreeing to broadcast at least one regular-season game on ESPN and an additional three on ESPN2. As the cream of the crop in the conference, UWGB was scheduled for two of the four MCC games in 1995-96 (at Western Kentucky on December 23 on ESPN2, and at Wright State on February 3 on ESPN).

"That explosion of college basketball on ESPN, or maybe that's backwards, the explosion of *ESPN* took college basketball along with it for winter programming," notes Butler's Barry Collier. "They were doing football up and down, and you could watch Arkansas Wednesday night at 11 o'clock if you wanted to, so college basketball was the perfect content for them during the winter, and that had a big effect on the game."

Beyond the immediacy of broadcasted matchups, cable television was enlightening college basketball fans. This awakening worked to erode long-held myths about the disparity of programs throughout the country. Extremely talented and successful mid-major programs, which historically were handicapped in recruiting, scheduling, and selection bias due to a lack of notoriety, discovered themselves evening the playing field.

At UWGB, this most notably manifested itself in scheduling opportunities.

For years, the Phoenix was constantly turned down by high-major programs fearful of suffering a loss at the hands of an unknown. But the tides were turning, and in 1995-96, Woody Wilson compiled yet another scheduling lineup to be proud of, including games against tournament teams Oregon and Western Kentucky, as well as a return invite to the Bradley Center for the First Bank Classic.

Then, with the Phoenix looking to fill one final slot, a pair of once-in-a-generation opportunities presented themselves: a road game at either #1 Kentucky or #2 Kansas.

"I remember Coach Heideman asking what we wanted to do," recalls Grzesk. "We said, 'Well, if we can play Kentucky, let's go play in Rupp Arena. Let's test ourselves against the best out there and have a great experience.'"

"I said, 'I don't want to start my collegiate coaching career at Kansas,'" joked Heideman. "There's a certain limit to how much I'm going to do."

Sweet Sixteen or Bust

In the midst of the regime change, Nordgaard and Jackson played on a traveling select team made up of MCC players that traveled to Kuwait during the summer of 1995.

"At the time, I hadn't been outside of America," explains Nordgaard. "We went and we had practice in Butler, so Barry Collier was the head coach there at the time. And then we went over to Kuwait and played the Kuwaiti national team in like four exhibition games."

By the time the pair returned and the team gathered for the start of organized practices that fall, all of the major outlets had picked the Phoenix to win the conference. And everyone had either Nordgaard or Cleveland State's Vitaly Potapenko as the conference's likely player of the year.

Inside the Phoenix facilities, a conference championship was just the first of many goals for the senior class.

"(We) had four seniors in that class that had been to two straight NCAA tournaments. You had the coaching change with Coach Bennett going to Wisconsin. So there were a lot of motivating factors to finish your career out on a high note," remembers Grzesk.

"Coach Heideman loosened the leash a little bit," says Nordgaard. "We had a goal and we were going to make sure everybody was on the same path as us."

And that goal was?

"We really wanted to play in the Sweet Sixteen," notes Grzesk. "If we could take the program another step further to where it's never been for, that's what we wanted to do for our senior year."

"We'd already done getting to the NCAA tournament," Nordgaard states. We'd already done 'get to the NCAA tournament and win.' We needed to get to the Sweet Sixteen."

Dawn of a New Regime

Mike Heideman's coaching career in Green Bay officially began with a pair of exhibition games in November 1995. The first, and by far tougher matchup, was against a preseason regular, the Athletes in Action, while the second was a traveling team from the Republic of Georgia.

A mere one-point victory over AIA caused some immediate heartburn, but UWGB soothed the stomachache with a solid 15-point victory over the Republic of Georgia a week later. Some of the young Phoenix talent in Hill and Kiss were on display in the latter victory, offering a suggestion that UWGB may not have to rely entirely on its seniors. But that love-fest was short-lived.

On November 28, 1995, UWGB opened up its regular season against a Morgan State team picked to finish at the bottom of the MEAC and serving probation with the NCAA. Heideman's Phoenix easily disposed of its opponent, 76-54, but it had come abnormally. Somehow, the Phoenix had registered the victory with just three players making more than one shot, and no one on the entire roster registering a single made three-pointer.

Mirroring the previous season and foreshadowing the year to come, nearly all scoring went through Nordgaard (29 points) and Berlowski (16 points). And predictably, the seniors had logged big minutes.

"We're still searching a bit for our identity," remarked a bemused Heideman afterwards. "I think we need more people being involved in taking good shots, and that will come."

With an invite to the First Bank Classic looming, Heideman needed to find it quickly.

Two for the Price of One

As it had in 1993, Marquette put the Phoenix in the first game of its tournament, making a Phoenix matchup with the Golden Eagles contingent upon a victory. But unlike in 1993, Marquette had struggled mightily to find an opponent who would come to Milwaukee and agree to take on the Phoenix in the first round of their tournament. For a while, the prospects looked so bleak that Marquette had asked if UWGB might be willing to play a single game against Marquette instead.

But at the last minute, Marquette officials convinced the Texas A&M Aggies of the Southwest Conference to join the tournament and take on UWGB. Texas A&M's coach, Tony Barone, was very familiar with the mid-major world, having coached at Creighton for six seasons before being hired at College Station in 1991. And if the name's familiar, it's because Barone had been one of the four finalists for the UWGB job way back in 1985, along with Dick Bennett, to replace Dick Lien.

Having just come off a mediocre 14-16 season, Barone's program was rebuilding. The Aggies did feature five players averaging eight or more points per game, but lacked any scoring leader or superstar. Nevertheless, it was a major-conference opponent and good barometer for the team Heideman had inherited.

UWGB held a 23-22 lead at halftime as both teams struggled. The Phoenix had been unusually trigger-happy with early shots, and that uncharacteristic play bothered Heideman. The coach reminded his players at the break to play with patience and make the Aggies work a full 35 seconds on defense.

The players immediately responded, going on an 11-1 run to create more than enough separation against Barone's Aggies. And each time Texas A&M threatened to make a run, Nordgaard put the team on his back, scoring 26 points and making big baskets down the stretch to close out a relatively easy 60-49 victory.

"Nordgaard is a heck of a player. He is relentless in his work ethic. That's what makes him so good," remarked Barone. "I don't know how talented he is from strictly a talent standpoint, jumping and running. He seems to just get everything done."

Heideman was less glowing. "Nordgaard's carrying too much of the scoring. That's not realistic through the season. Our kids realize it. We need some of our kids to step up and take the shot."

It was UWGB's eighth win over a major-conference opponent (including Marquette) since 1990, and given the Aggies' struggles, this one almost seemed like old hat.

Mike Heideman shows his displeasure as assistant coach Steve Swan looks on. (University of Wisconsin-Green Bay Archives)

With Marquette easily disposing of Coppin State, the Phoenix's win set up a championship matchup with the hosts. UWGB would play Marquette at the Bradley Center for the fourth consecutive season, this time in front of over 15,000 fans.

The 1995-96 version of the Golden Eagles were a veteran bunch, returning six of their top seven scorers from the previous year's NIT team. And none had not forgotten the embarrassing home losses to the Phoenix each of the previous two years. Those bad memories fueled Marquette, and an uncharacteristic off night for UWGB led to one of the team's biggest blowouts in recent memory.

Mike Heideman and assistant coach Bob Semling discuss strategy with the Phoenix during a timeout in the 1995-96 season. (University of Wisconsin-Green Bay Archives)

As it had a year prior, Marquette did an excellent job locking down the Phoenix's role players, holding everyone not named Nordgaard or Berlowski to six points or less. With only two players able to score – one less than the previous year's three-scorer Phoenix win – Heideman's team simply was overmatched. The Phoenix shot a dismal 30% in the first half and, down fourteen points at the break, never recovered.

Marquette won, 64-44, giving UWGB its worst defeat since a 21-point loss at Xavier in February 1995.

"I don't know *how* that happened. I don't know *why* that happened. The year before, three guys score and we beat a team that's almost the same," noted Nordgaard afterwards. He and Berlowski had managed just 13 points each, hardly enough to move the needle.

"That's the first time you really noticed how small we were and how big they were," Grzesk recalls. "They had length and size and skill at every position, and really kind of outclassed us for the majority of the game."

A day after, Heideman reiterated his primary concern about the 1995-96 bunch. "We're not happy with what's happening. We're searching. We've got Jeff at 22 (points), Ben at 13. Then they drop way down. Whether it is Eric, Kevin, or Matt Hill, we've *got* to get some more scoring."

There was little hope for an immediate change in fortunes, as the Phoenix prepared for its upcoming signature nonconference matchup against Kentucky.

The World's Greatest

The 1995-96 Kentucky Wildcats were great by every standard. It was the greatest club, led by one of the game's greatest coaches, with many of the nation's greatest players. Stacked up against the all-time teams, this one would (and in a 2020 online poll, did) rank near, if not at, the top.

Rick Pitino, the coach who had once led little Providence College to a Final Four in 1986-87, had been building his program in Lexington since 1989. His program had already been to the Final Four in 1992-93, but his 1995-96 club looked to be the best he had ever assembled.

"If you put their roster up against almost any other college basketball roster in the last thirty years, it's hard to compare when you have seven or eight NBA players on it," noted Nordgaard. Nordgaard was being modest. Kentucky's squad boasted a ridiculous *nine* players who would play in the NBA.

It started with senior guard Tony Delk – arguably the most famous "00" in college basketball history – and his senior cohorts forward Walter McCarty and center Mark Pope. Also along the front line were sophomore Antoine Walker, junior Derek Anderson, and freshman Ron Mercer. With Delk in the backcourt were future NBA guards Jeff Sheppard and Wayne Turner. Oh, and freshman Nazr Mohammed also came off the bench for good measure. The team was so deep that some media outlets had predicted Kentucky's *second string* could win the SEC championship.

On top of it all, UWGB was Kentucky's first home game of the season. "Their first three games, it was like at UMass, at Maryland, and at Indiana, and then their first home game was UWGB," notes Berlowski.

The deck was stacked against UWGB, but it was a great opportunity to see how a sound mid-major could perform against the best of the best.

"People say, 'Well, you play good people in the NCAA tournament.' But this is different. Not only is it in their gym, but it's early in the year," remarked Heideman. "If you were to name one of the best basketball programs in the nation, they will get to see it and experience it first-hand."

Building on the enormity of the event, the team received the royal treatment from local authorities upon arrival.

"I remember getting a police escort from our hotel right up to the back service entrance of Rupp Arena," recalls Grzesk. "Even in the past NCAA tournaments, I don't remember that ever happening. That was pretty amazing."

The spectacle continued as the team did its walk-through.

"I remember walking in to the gym, we were kind of waiting to see what our court time was, (and) Tony Delk was in the gym playing one-on-one," says Berlowski. "He did not miss. Like he did not miss *a shot*, it was unbelievable. I think I saw him hit like twenty shots in a row, it was unreal."

As the fans began to enter the arena, the atmosphere took shape.

"Man, 25,000 fans, there was nothing like playing in Rupp Arena," adds Berlowski. "They love their basketball down there, and the resources that they have, and it's just unbelievable."

"If it's not the number one, the top three places to play in college basketball," states Nordgaard. "And we went there and we did alright."

There is a reason Pitino was a highly successful college coach. He had his teams well-prepared, focused, and simply refused to overlook opponents. Before their game, Pitino let everyone know the Phoenix could not be taken lightly.

"This basketball game is interesting because of the way they play. They are a ball-control motion team that averages twelve, thirteen, sometimes ten, turnovers a game," he said. "It's not just ball control, it's also great defense. They play outstanding man-to-man defense. They have four starters that are seniors. They are experienced at this style. They'll present as big of a problem as Indiana and Massachusetts because of their style of play and experience."

On the other side, one of many concerns for Heideman was Kentucky's press and defensive quickness. To prepare, the Phoenix actually practiced against extra bodies on the court, often simulating Kentucky's press with six or seven defenders. But, as Grzesk noted, that could only go so far. "You can try to simulate in practice, but until you get in the game, you really have no idea what to expect."

Right from the start, Kentucky's press proved highly effective, forcing a turnover on the third possession of the game.

"The first time it hit me is when I caught the ball on the inbounds, and they took away the reversal on the press, and my next read was a guy in the middle at half court and when I saw him, he was wide open. And I threw the ball, and it got intercepted before it even got to the guy in the middle and they came down and scored in transition," remembers Grzesk. "So that was a pretty rude awakening just to see that length and athleticism."

The press led to a whopping fifteen first-half Phoenix turnovers, all while Kentucky built a 32-12 lead. But the Phoenix kept fighting and put together an 11-3 run before the half to cut the deficit to 14 points. "We didn't want to give up. That's a sign of quitters and losers," Grzesk declared after the game.

The second half saw both teams go on runs and the Phoenix continue to grind and battle. And while the Phoenix ultimately fell to Kentucky, 74-62, those in attendance witnessed something rather unexpected. In one day, Jeff Nordgaard became an immediate, legitimate NBA prospect.

Against the vaunted Kentucky defense, Nordgaard was unstoppable, scoring 29 points on a staggering 12-for-17 shooting, as well as eight rebounds.

"Nordgaard was incredible," states assistant coach Ben Johnson. "You're talking about Walter McCarthy, and all those guys, Delk – they had *nobody* that could stop him. Nobody."

"I remember somebody asked me who guarded me in that game,'" recalls a smirking Nordgaard. "I go, 'Well, Derek Anderson *tried*, Antoine Walker *tried*, Walter McCarty *tried*.' It was one of those things where – 'Ron Mercer *tried*.' They put a bunch of different guys on me ... I felt good that game and yeah, had a good one."

All of which impressed Pitino, who called him a "terrific player," and noted, "He's all blood and guts ... If our people played with that, we'd be unstoppable."

"All Pitino could talk about after the game, every question was like, 'Who is that Nordgaard?' " recalls Johnson. "He goes, 'If that's not the best damn college player I've ever seen, then I don't know who is.' That's what he said."

And though they'd lost by double digits, there were no heads hanging low in the Phoenix locker room.

"I think we kind of outplayed them in the second half," Berlowski says, "which kind of gave us a little bit of confidence."

"We were their closest home loss in the regular season," adds Grzesk. "It was never a blowout where we subbed out of the game and they played their bench players. They had to play all the way through to the end."

Old Grudges, New Faces, and Dogfights

Just four games into the season, some of the Phoenix were beat up, struggling with bumps, bruises, and ailments that forced the starters to play through given the team's lack of depth. Nevertheless, the quality play in Lexington had elevated UWGB's outlook, and the players were eager to exact revenge in their next game against Idaho State.

The Bengals were coming off of a solid eighteen-win campaign the previous year, including the game against UWGB where six Phoenix players fouled out. This year, without a lopsided foul distribution, Idaho State was doomed.

Nordgaard finally got some scoring help from Grzesk (12 points) and Berlowski (15 points), and in a game that was never close, the Phoenix cruised to an easy 73-56. UWGB was 3-2 on the year, ready for its fourth game against a major conference foe.

Four days later, on December 13, 1995, UWGB headed to Eugene, Oregon, for the third in a four-game series against the Pac-10's Oregon Ducks. The first two games in the series had been lopsided, with each team securing a 20+ point victory on its home floor. This affair would be very different.

Five games into the season, the Ducks – a tournament team in 1995 – were 4-1 and coming off an eleven-day rest period. Oregon was averaging more than 100 points per game, and Jerry Green's team loved to press, run the floor, and shoot three-pointers.

Heideman's game plan remained simple: slow down the pace of the game, work the ball offensively for good shots, and limit second chances.

Early on, it looked like the Ducks would fly to another big win. Behind a slew of three-pointers, Oregon claimed a 15-8 lead in the first few minutes of the game.

But UWGB would not be so easily disposed. With contributions from each senior, the Phoenix tied the game by the 8:00 mark and blew the game open with three-pointers from Jackson and Berlowski, taking a 31-22 lead with 3:51 to play in the first half.

UWGB carried a five-point lead to the locker room, but the gap closed quickly in the second half, and with 2:21 to play, Oregon had charged to a 61-57 advantage. It was a turning point for this senior-led Phoenix team, and the veterans closed the gap in the final minutes.

It began with a Jackson block, giving the Phoenix back the ball. Nordgaard missed a three-pointer, Berlowski grabbed the offensive board, was fouled, and knocked down a pair of free throws. Half a minute later, Jackson grabbed a rebound after an Oregon miss, and with regulation coming to an end, Nordgaard buried a floater that found nothing but net. After forty minutes, the score was tied at 61-61.

Jackson continued to be the star in the extra period, hitting a big-time three-pointer from the left wing, and following it up with a slick assist on a one-handed pass to a cutting Nordgaard for an easy layup. A Nordgaard jumper on the next possession, and the game was effectively over. Final score, UWGB 81, Oregon 71.

In addition to Jackson's play, Nordgaard logged another marathon effort, leading the team with 23 points in a whopping 43 minutes of action. Berlowski also rose up big, going for 22 points including four three-pointers in 41 minutes of action, while Grzesk also had a solid performance, logging nine points and five assists.

And though he wasn't big down the stretch, freshman Matt Hill had been an unexpected surprise. He recorded a double-double with 10 points (on 5-for-5 shooting) and ten boards while disrupting the interior.

"A very big win for us," Heideman noted. "This is a difficult place to play. This was a Pac-10 team with some very fine athletes."

It was Heideman's second win over a major-conference opponent, confirming continuity from the Dick Bennett era.

Back to Kentucky

A scary trend was emerging for Heideman's team. His seniors were logging almost unimaginable minutes and, between Nordgaard and Berlowski, accounting for almost all of the team's offensive output. Out of necessity, Nordgaard was playing an astounding 40.2 minutes per game.

"I don't think that people can do it now. And they don't do it now. Part of it is the style of play that we had," explains Nordgaard. "I vividly remember walking up the court many times on offense. I vividly remember never running to the timeouts when the coach calls a timeout. I had to find my time to rest, because I recognized that we just weren't deep. We didn't have the depth. It was the kind of things I had to do to make sure I could give my all during the times that were the actual plays that were important."

Heideman hoped a December 16 date against Division II Michigan Tech would give his team a rest. The Huskies were a schedule filler to replace a vacated game with Illinois State. Originally, UWGB was set to play the Redbirds, but when Illinois State was offered a chance to play Cincinnati on ESPN, UWGB paid it forward and agreed to move the game to the following season.

But Heideman's wish never materialized. The Huskies, meanwhile, proved up to the task. They put a legitimate scare in the Phoenix, trailing by just three with seven minutes to play. That was when Berlowski, who led the Phoenix in scoring with 22 points on 10-for-12 shooting, hit big buckets in the waning minute to finish out a 60-52 win. UWGB was 5-2, but fatigue remained a real concern.

A week later and two days before Christmas, UWGB headed to Bowling Green, Kentucky, to play Western Kentucky in a game broadcast on ESPN2. The Hilltoppers had gained national notoriety just a season before, having racked up twenty-seven wins and beaten Michigan in the first round of the 1995 NCAA tournament before falling in a close game to the highly touted Kansas Jayhawks.

That 1995 team had lost four of its top six scorers to graduation, but the 1995-96 team still returned the Sun Belt's Player of the Year and NBA prospect, forward Chris Robinson. As a senior, Robinson was averaging north of 16 points and six rebounds per game. It would be yet another high-profile matchup on national television.

When it was full with six thousand screaming fans, WKU's Diddle Arena, identified by *Sports Illustrated* as one of the toughest arenas in America, could challenge the Brown County Arena in intensity. Nevertheless, UWGB took the crowd out of the affair in the first half, beating the Hilltoppers' full-court press and man-to-man defense, forcing them into a 1-3-1 zone and building a 30-16 advantage. The Hilltoppers returned to a man-to-man defense in the second half, but the pace remained the same and UWGB still had an 11-point lead with seven minutes to play. Then, Chris Robinson took over. Robinson, who scored 18 of his 20 points in the second half, put together a 12-3 run that closed the gap, and Western Kentucky eventually forced overtime.

In the extra period, Heideman's surprise fifth starter, Pete Wade, finally came alive. He had been held scoreless through regulation, but came alive in overtime, first by grabbing an offensive rebound off a Berlowski miss and connecting on a put-back for the start of an old-fashioned three-point play. Two minutes later, with the lead expanded to 56-53, Wade again came up huge, securing a contested rebound where he was fouled, and calmly hitting two more free throws. The freebies put UWGB up five with just 45 seconds to play and it held on from there, notching a big 59-56 win on national television.

Maintaining their status quo, Nordgaard and Berlowski led the Phoenix with 21 points each, but Wade's play down the stretch gave the team some hope for the future. The win was UWGB's fourth in a row, and gave the Phoenix a solid 6-2 record.

Tournament of Champions

The Phoenix returned to action at the Brown County Arena on December 29, 1995, for its own two-day holiday tournament. The Pepsi-Bingo Classic was entering its third year, and in addition to becoming a fan favorite event, this year's version featured the best lineup yet.

The 1995 installment featured a first-round Phoenix matchup with the reigning three-time MEAC champions, Coppin State, led by four-time MEAC coach of the year Ron "Fang" Mitchell. The other first-round matchup was even more enticing, pitting the Ivy League's best, the Princeton Tigers, against an Ohio Bobcats team that had won twenty-four games the year before. It was a scheduling slate that could hold its own against any other mid-major tournament around.

There would be no gimmes, as evidenced by UWGB's first-round opponent. In 1994-95, Coppin State had won the MEAC, but lost in the conference championship and was forced to settle for an NIT bid. The Eagles made the most of it, beating St. Joseph's in overtime on the road before ultimately falling in the second round.

Though the Eagles had graduated their five leading scorers, the 1995-96 team that headed to Green Bay was still the class of the MEAC. Leading the way was 6-8 center Terquin Mott, a junior transfer from LaSalle who was averaging 19 points and seven rebounds a game.

Mott helped the Eagles played an up-tempo, run-and-gun style, averaging more than 84 points per game throughout the year, but Coppin State had yet to win a game where it scored less than 80 points. Heideman's version of Bennett's old pack defense typically fed on teams like that.

"I don't think anybody gets the pace they want against Wisconsin-Green Bay," remarked Fang Mitchell afterwards. "No matter how much you want to get and go, you just can't get and go unless you get the ball."

Even though the Eagles actually shot a higher percentage than the Phoenix, Coppin State's fatal 57-point showing would be its second-lowest output of the regular season. The lone bright spot for Coppin State was Mott, who dropped in 27 points and ten rebounds.

Heideman, who had deployed numerous strategies to try and slow down Mott, said, "I thought that kid inside – Mott – he's as good as we've played against. We had a difficult time defending him. He was so strong he went over, two, or three kids sometimes. And if he missed, he went over and got the rebound."

But Mott alone was not enough to down the Phoenix, who pulled out a 66-57 victory, again behind strong play from Berlowski. Coppin State was unable to find a defense that could stop the senior, switching between a 2-3 zone, man-to-man, and a matchup zone, all without effect. Berlowski notched a career-high 25 points with six three-pointers, marking his fourth consecutive 20-point performance.

Meanwhile, Pete Wade rode the momentum from his Western Kentucky overtime, delivering a surprisingly sound double-double performance.

With the win, the Phoenix was set for its third straight holiday tournament championship game, this time against the like-minded Princeton Tigers, who had rallied from a 16-point first-half deficit to sneak out a five-point win over Ohio. The tournament championship was shaping up as an epic mid-major showdown between two of the most fundamentally sound programs in college basketball.

Pete Carril, the mastermind behind the "Princeton Offense," was a Hall of Famer and legend in the sport. Carril began his career at Lehigh University before assuming the role as Princeton's head coach in 1967. In twenty-eight years with the Tigers, Carril's teams won twelve Ivy League titles and the NIT championship in 1975. Princeton's most lasting achievement came in 1989, when the 16-seeded Tigers nearly took down John Thompson's top-seeded Georgetown Hoyas in the NCAA tournament. The 1995-96 version of the Tigers looked to be one of Carril's best, off to a 7-2 start

Senior guard Eric Jackson and Mike Heideman watch the action during UWGB's re-sounding 55-35 victory over Princeton on December 30, 1995. (University of Wisconsin-Green Bay Archives)

and yet again favored to win the Ivy League.

Like UWGB, Carril's teams were patient offensively, worked the shot clock, moved without the ball, and patented the back-door cuts that, when performed by others, were labeled as "Princeton basketball." His teams were equally effective on defense, playing stifling man-to-man in low-scoring affairs.

"They were a similar mid-major that took pride in playing competitive in the postseason. And I think they play the right way as well – they play as a team, play good defense, move the basketball," recalls Grzesk. "That was a matchup that we really wanted to get in the championship game."

It was a game that many outsiders would bypass as boring, and figured to be a "first-to-40-points-wins" affair. But for Green Bay fans, it was the ultimate test of execution, and a whopping 5,861 fans showed up at the Brown County Arena to watch both teams scratch and claw for defensive supremacy. The Phoenix, unlike many of Princeton's other opponents, were not lured into a false sense of superiority.

"The reason Princeton has success is because teams think they're more athletic than Princeton so they deny deny deny, and being out in the gaps and all that, and then they get back-cut," noted Nordgaard. "We don't do that – we're in the gaps. You go out to catch the ball in the wing, that's fine. Go out and catch the ball on the wing, you just don't catch the ball down here (in the lane)."

Though the first twenty minutes was every bit the battle of wills everyone expected, the first ten minutes of the second half saw UWGB's defense clamp down on Carril's Tigers. Over that stretch, Princeton was able to make even one basket, and after an 8-0 run by the Phoenix, the game was effectively out of reach at 45-29 with 6:03 to play. Amazingly, UWGB would go on to hold Princeton to just *four* made baskets and 12 points in the entire second half, all while committing only three turnovers all game.

The result was resounding 55-35 Phoenix win in a game where UWGB simply out-Princetoned Princeton.

"In the second half, we played outstanding defense. They just played great as far as I'm concerned," remarked Heideman. "That's as good as we can play for a half of basketball."

"It's two teams together that are supposed to combine for about 30 (points), and so we beat them by 20. That's like beating a normal team by 40!" claims Nordgaard. "That was a big win because (Princeton) ended up winning an NCAA tournament game that year."

For his part, Nordgaard scored 28 points in the championship game, earning tournament MVP honors. Berlowski, who added 14 points, also was named to the all-tournament team.

After the game, Carril tipped his cap to the Phoenix: "They play great defense. They're well-coached. I wouldn't want to play them every day. I told my team this will be the best team we play all year."

Heideman reciprocated that respect.

"After the game, Coach Heideman went down to thank Pete Carril in the basement of Brown (County Arena), where the visitor's locker room was," Grzesk recalls. "Pete Carril was on the bench with his legs crossed and he had a stogie in his mouth, and Coach Heideman thanked him for coming to Brown County and playing us."

It was an amazing cap to an 8-2 nonconference season that included wins against major-conference teams Texas A&M and Oregon, an ESPN2 thriller at Western Kentucky, a solid showing at Kentucky, and another holiday championship. Riding a six-game winning streak, the Phoenix remained the favorite to win a weakened MCC.

Chapter 21

Closers
(1995-96 - Part 2)

Every attribute discussed in this book is a building block toward the construction of a stable, strong, unflappable program. Individually, none are enough. Together, they interlock to create a formidable institution.

We end with one of the most important attributes of successful programs – a concept that goes hand in hand with experience, skill, and talent. It is often mislabeled as "the will to win," which improperly implies that there are some who do not care to succeed and that the intangible is a skill inherent in an individual and cannot be learned. Both are incorrect.

Rather, here we are talking about precisely the honed skill of being a closer. Doubling as the team's star is not a de facto requirement, but when the game is on the line, closers are called upon to stay level-headed, rise to the occasion, and finish off their opponent.

Riding the Wave
With the conference season looming, the rising concerns Heideman had seen over the past month had not diminished. The team had grown much too reliant on its seniors, primarily Jeff Nordgaard and secondarily Ben Berlowski. Nordgaard was playing more than 39 minutes per game while averaging 22.6 points, while Berlowski had stepped up as a secondary threat, averaging 16.7 ppg.

With no one else scoring more than five points per game, the team's two-dimensional approach was certain to be challenged, both by double-teams and trick defenses. Heideman knew it simply wasn't possible for the Phoenix to continue to ride those two players offensively and maintain the same level of success they'd achieved through the first two months of the season.

Except, as the Phoenix began working their way through the conference schedule, that's inexplicably exactly what transpired.

First, the Phoenix thumped one of the MCC's upper-echelon teams in Wright State, 78-52 in its conference opener. Sitting at the top of the scoring list was Nordgaard with 25 points on 10-for-14 shooting in 37 minutes, while Berlowski seconded the effort with 12 points.

Two days later, on January 6, 1996, UWGB pulled off a 14-point win against Cleveland State. This time, Nordgaard poured in 28 points and seven rebounds in a full 40-minute effort. Berlowski, again Robin to Nordgaard's Batman, added 17 points. No one else scored more than six points. The following week, the Phoenix roll continued, with Nordgaard's 17 points in 40 minutes, and Berlowski's 14 points helping the Phoenix dispose of Loyola and improve to 11-2.

It wasn't as though Nordgaard and Berlowski were entirely alone in their offensive efforts. Eric Jackson, already a defensive sentinel, rode an incredible four-game stretch of 25 assists to just three turnovers, and sophomore Pete Wade had chipped in a career-high 14 points in the win over Loyola. Even the defensive glove, Gary Grzesk, chipped in 14 points in the last two contests.

But the season's story was becoming clear, and it started with Nordgaard. "I don't know what to tell you about Nordgaard. He's just an exceptional player. He's one that comes along very few times," remarked Heideman.

Dogfight

The Phoenix took its nine-game winning streak on the road to Hinkle Fieldhouse to play a strong 10-3 Butler team that was undefeated in conference play. The Bulldogs had been the one program that had consistently found ways to neutralize Nordgaard. In his past 50 games, Nordgaard had scored in double figures in all but two outings – both were against Butler. Barry Collier's strategy? Use all five players to shut down Nordgaard, Berlowski, and the year before, Westlake.

"That (1994-95) year we got a rivalry with Butler," remembers Nordgaard. "They made a game plan to stop me and that was probably the right way to do it. Put this young freshman thoroughbred Jon Neuhauser – he ended up being all-conference later, and then put big Rolf (van Rijn) right in the middle. I don't know if he face-guarded me or if he just defended me normally, but he made me work, and clearly it worked."

Collier's strategy worked like a charm in the past, but this senior version of Nordgaard was a different animal altogether, and nothing Collier could do seemed to slow him down. Nordgaard got his buckets inside and outside, delivering a 20-point, four-assist performance. He got plenty of help in this game, with Berlowski dropping in 16 points, and Jackson and Wade, starting his seventh straight game, each adding eight points.

And yet it almost was not enough. As the clocked ticked under one minute to play, it took a pair of Berlowski free throws, and then three more from Wade in the final few seconds to secure a 64-61 victory. Nevertheless, it was a big conference win for the Phoenix, and a major step toward capturing the conference crown.

The Phoenix took the court at the Brown County Arena two days later to play another conference stalwart, the 10-3 Detroit Mercy Titans. As with Butler, Perry Watson's Titans were a strong defensive team, ranking third in the conference in scoring defense. And like the Butler game, the match-up came right down to the end, this one going into overtime.

And the extra period belonged to – who else? UWGB's top closer. Nordgaard scored 30 points in regulation and added eight more in overtime to net a career-high 38 points, all while playing the entire 45 minutes.

"That was one of the best basketball performances I've seen, comparable to some of the nights of Tony Bennett," Heideman said afterwards. "If some people haven't seen him play, they're missing a real special player. He literally took this game on his shoulders and said, 'Just ride with me.'"

With a 71-69 overtime win, UWGB improved to 13-2 on the year and even garnered five votes in the AP's Top 25 the following week, all while showcasing the league's premier talent. Nordgaard ranked thirteenth in the NCAA in scoring, all while playing a ridiculous 40 minutes per game.

Professional Efforts

UWGB won its twelfth straight game on January 18, 1996, beating in-state rival UW-Milwaukee 67-54. Seven NBA scouts had requested credentials to the game, and they were treated to not just one, but a pair of career-high performances in scoring ... though neither came from the team's most likely candidate.

With UW-Milwaukee sagging everyone to help on Nordgaard, UWGB's defensive star, finding himself unguarded, picked up the slack. Grzesk went 9-for-12 from the free throw line and also grabbed five rebounds, leading the team in scoring with a career-high 13 points. Joining Grzesk in nabbing a career high was Jackson, who hit a pair of three-pointers as part of a strong 11-point effort.

"When you can hold (Nordgaard) to 12 points and Berlowski to eight, you did a pretty good job defensively," noted Ric Cobb, UW-Milwaukee's coach. "If Grzesk and Eric (Jackson) score those kind of points, it will be tough to beat Green Bay."

Cobb also praised the Phoenix squad as a whole, noting, "They've got to be the best team (in the conference). They're undefeated, they're the best team because those young men have played together for four years now."

The good times continued to roll two days later, when the Phoenix defeated UIC 73-67 in front of a packed Brown County Arena. This game was close early, with the Flames actually leading at the half. But UWGB held UIC scoreless for more than six minutes to start the second half, going on a 13-0 run that put the game away.

Wade, responding to recent discipline from his coach, came off the bench and scored a career-high 18 points and grabbed eight rebounds in 31 minutes. And yet, the Phoenix continued to rely on Nordgaard, who led all Phoenix scorers with 29 points and eight rebounds, and Berlowski, who added 22 points in 35 minutes.

"You know what these guys are going to do," UIC coach Bob Hallberg noted after the game. "You watch them on tape 10,000 times and you know Nordgaard is going to take all the shots and Berlowski is going to be right behind him. (But) knowing what they're going to do and stopping them are two different things."

With the win, the Phoenix were entering some uncharted territory. Its 13-game winning streak was the fourth-longest active streak in Division I, behind just UMass (17), UConn (16), and Kentucky (15). And with it, a spot in the Top 25 was creeping into view. Indeed, UWGB gained 10 votes in the AP's Top 25 poll and 12 in the *USA Today* Top 25 poll.

"I don't think the streak is as important as we just can't lose," noted Nordgaard. Recalling the devastation from 1992, he added, "If we let down, our dream season has the possibility of getting shattered."

In the last week of January 1996, UWGB played just one game – a snowy January 25 matchup at home against a very good Northern Illinois. The Huskies were a strong 12-4 team that, at 5-1 in conference, appeared to be UWGB's top competition for the regular-season crown. But Northern Illinois was also depleted, with two of its best players, Jamal Robinson, a preseason first team all-conference pick, and Donte Parker, having been ruled academically ineligible midway through the year.

The tough Wisconsin weather had flared up before the game, and was so bad that just two officials had made it to the arena in time for the tip. The match itself was closer than anticipated, but UWGB continued to make plays down the stretch of games and pulled out its fourteenth straight victory, 61-53.

Nordgaard again led the way with 31 points and four assists, while Berlowski added 21 points. Nordgaard's legs may have been tired, but his face was bright under the NBA spotlight. Multiple NBA scouts had sought credentials to attend each of his recent games, and he was not disappointing them.

"The bottom line is he really plays hard. Has a good feel for the game," Lee Rose, the VP-Player Personnel for the Milwaukee Bucks, was quoted saying. "Size-wise, he might be considered a (small forward). To be a (small forward), he has to develop his ball-handling skills, face-up shooting, passing."

Knocking on the Door

What UWGB was doing through the first part of 1996 was incredible. Like a finely tuned piece of machinery, all of the cogs and wheels appeared perfectly attuned to each other, leading to ideal performance. For the moment, the Phoenix was willing to ride its senior engine as far as his floppy hair and soft touch would take it.

So far, it was working. Heideman's club had strung together a winning streak the program had never seen, injecting itself in the middle of the national media discussion. As the team opened play in February, UWGB found itself unofficially slotted at No. 35 in the *USA Today* poll.

The team celebrated its ascension on February 1, 1996, with a 26-point whipping of an outmatched Cleveland State squad. The struggling Vikings were dominated in every facet, shooting just 33% against UWGB's defense while allowing the Phoenix to connect on 61% of its field goals. It was the first of four straight road games for Heideman's squad, and proved to be

Ben Berlowski shoots a free throw toward the Wright State faithful during the team's nationally televised meeting on Feb. 3, 1996. (Courtesy of Special Collections and Archives, Wright State University)

the easiest.

Two days later, the Phoenix headed to the Nutter Center for an ESPN matchup against Wright State. The worldwide leader in sports had sent a B-squad to the game, with John Walls and Terry Holland calling the matchup between preseason MCC favorites. And while the game did feature the two best players in the conference in Nordgaard and the "Ukraine Train" Vitaly Potapenko, the Raiders had fallen flat throughout the year, middling at 10-9 with a paltry 4-5 conference record.

That didn't stop 8,481 fans and six NBA scouts from packing the gym for the Saturday afternoon game, and the two stars did not disappoint. Potapenko opened it up by abusing the young Pete Wade on both of Wright State's first two possessions to give the Raiders a quick 5-0 lead and kick-starting his own 21-point performance.

Meanwhile, Nordgaard played another complete game, this time going for 24 points on 10-for-19 shooting as he recorded his thirtieth straight game in double figures. In the end, the Phoenix won the ESPN showdown, closing out the Raiders 60-53 to grab the school's sixteenth straight win.

The solid, two-win week with a national television appearance continued to bolster UWGB's national cred. The following week, the 18-2 Phoenix netted 77 votes in the AP Top 25, more than the blueblood Duke Blue Devils and Indiana Hoosiers combined, and the team scooted up to the No. 29 spot. All the while, Heideman was reaping well-deserved praise, particularly from his peers.

"I don't know if (UWGB) skipped a beat," remarked Butler's Barry Collier. "I think Dick Bennett is the best college basketball coach in the coun-

Wright State's Vitaly Potapenko muscles between UWGB's Matt Hill and Gary Grzesk during the Phoenix's 60-53 victory. (Courtesy of Special Collections and Archives, Wright State University)

try, bar none. Mike Heideman has a better record than Dick Bennett did. What else needs to be said?"

"Green Bay is Green Bay. There is no difference between Mike and Dick," added UIC's Bob Hallberg. "(UWGB) executes their tails off and you have to chase them through those screens."

Dick Bennett agreed with all of it. "I knew how good he was," Bennett said of Heideman. "I made a lot of mistakes ... Mike saw that. He's smart. He learned from it."

Just Keep Winning

If the Phoenix wanted a shot to crack the Top 25, they'd have to conquer a pair of difficult road challenges, first against a 14-6 Northern Illinois team, then two days later at 14-7 Detroit.

The first matchup on February 10, in front of the largest Huskies crowd in five years, was a defensive clinic. Grzesk, Jackson, and the rest of the Phoenix were unforgiving, holding the Huskies to a woeful 30% shooting. And the offense continued to roll, building an 11-point lead in the game's first 12 minutes and extending to a 15-point lead early in the second half before settling in for a comfortable 57-51 win. Unsurprisingly, Nordgaard dropped in a game-high 28 points to lead all scorers.

February 12, 1996, was almost the day that an opponent broke the Phoenix's seventeen-game winning streak. Perry Watson, Detroit's coach, hadn't forgotten his club's overtime loss a month earlier and was ready to even the score.

"It was a humdinger of a game up there," Watson said. "Nordgaard was in a zone the last time. You can't say that you're going to stop him, but you try to challenge every shot and hope he doesn't get in that zone against you again."

The first half barely saw the combined team scores top Nordgaard's previous 38-point performance. In a dogfight of a game, UWGB was able to muster an important 13-0 run midway through the first half, but with both teams playing blanketed man-to-man defense, points were hard to come by. By halftime, UWGB held a slim 23-21 lead as the Titans had held Nordgaard to just eight first-half points.

The second half was more the same, with UWGB clinging to a two-point lead in the last minute. Detroit had three possessions in the final sixty seconds to tie or take the lead, but squandered each as the Phoenix pulled out a squeaker, 46-44.

"A game of intense defense," summarized Heideman afterwards. "They're very athletic. They're well-coached. They use it to their advantage."

By besting Watson's Titans, UWGB collected its eighteenth straight win, improving to 20-2 overall.

Postseason Visions

"The excitement was continuing to build as the season went along. And you didn't want to drop a game and lose that momentum," Grzesk recalls. "There was some talk that if we continued to win at that high level, we could possibly get an at-large bid."

Bob Frederick, the NCAA Selection Committee chair, was quoted saying: "In the last two or three years, we have made an effort not to forget about teams that win their conference championship and may not win their conference tournament."

An additional factor in UWGB's favor was the boom in metrics being tabulated, analyzed, and disseminated. It had only been a matter of four years, but the level of sophistication interjected into the discussion had exponentially increased.

"Right now, UW-Green Bay would get an at-large bid because they're so high in the Sagarin and RPI rankings," noted Marquette coach Mike Deane. "But there's no more effective method than to just keep winning."

RPI had been a measurement tool the committee had used for years, but in recent seasons, the Sagarin ratings had taken a stronger foothold. Created by Jeff Sagarin, a statistician with a degree in mathematics from MIT, the Sagarin ratings took into account a variety of predictive measures, including margin of victory, strength of opponents, and home court advantage, proposing a fuller view of a team's true capabilities and success. The NCAA Selection Committee had used the Sagarin ratings during its evaluations going back as far as 1984, but they were increasingly viewed as mainstream metrics throughout the early 1990s.

Sagarin offered his own insight into UWGB's outlook, saying: "The way I have them in the paper, (UWGB is) 37th. But I did some other stuff involving wins and losses, only winning and losing. Scores don't matter. On that basis, Wisconsin-Green Bay would be ninth in the country. I know the NCAA is heavily involved in wins and losses. I think (the Phoenix) deserve it."

Of course, as Mike Deane noted, the easiest way to a bid was to win out. With just four conference games left, the Phoenix became dead-set on doing just that. Should they accomplish that goal, they would finish with an unthinkable 16-0 conference record and certainly crack the elusive Top 25.

Top 25

First up, UWGB gave Loyola a quick tour of the Brown County Arena before kicking the Ramblers back to Chicago with a 56-39 drubbing. The Phoenix defense was impenetrable, holding Loyola to 17 second-half points on 32% shooting.

"They're not the Chicago Bulls, but they're pretty good," noted Loyola coach Ken Burmeister. "We won three of four, but we weren't ready for this."

Perhaps the single memorable moment from the game was a made three-pointer by an unlikely character. Grzesk hadn't hit a triple since his sophomore year, having only attempted one in his last fifty-two games. But none of that quashed the itch Grzesk was feeling to try his luck.

"He was talking about it all week, 'I'm going to get a three,' " remembers Nordgaard.

With the lead ballooning against Loyola, Grzesk felt the time was right and he asked Heideman for permission to launch. The coach promptly denied the request, telling Gary "no, it's not over, keep playing." A few moments later, Grzesk asked again and received the same response. Sensing the moment was slipping, Grzesk took matters into his own hands.

"Maybe it was being a little greedy for once in my career, but it's winding down here," he says. "I thought the shot clock was winding down, maybe. I got open and I just had to let it fly."

When the ball splashed through the net, the crowd exploded. It proved to be the climactic moment for a team that had just clinched a share of the MCC regular-season title with three full games to play.

The win also put Heideman in rare company. At 20-2, he was enjoying the fifth-greatest start to a college coaching career *ever*, and best of any newcomer since 1979, when Bill Hodges coached Larry Bird's Sycamores to a 33-1 season and title game appearance.

The following Monday, February 19, marked a red-letter day in the history of the Phoenix program. A day earlier, UWGB had found itself sitting at No. 26 in the *USA Today* polls, but early Monday, the program received news that it was the final entry in the AP's Top 25 poll. The program had achieved a milestone that eluded them for Dick Bennett's entire tenure.

"The level of Division I where we're at, we don't get a lot of respect as far as nationwide press," states Nordgaard. "But as the wins started coming this year and we started rolling, we said, 'Hey, we can get in the Top 25 and that would be a real special way to end our careers here.' "

Heideman was thrilled with the news.

"Cracking the Top 25 from where we are, the University of Wisconsin-Green Bay, is amazing," he said. "When we started the year, we didn't say, 'Let's play great basketball and try to crack the Top 25.' That wasn't in our farthest dream. It is the result of them focusing one game at a time and every game trying to be a little better."

The Phoenix celebrated its notoriety in front of a rambunctious 5,906 home fans that evening. The game was almost an afterthought, as UWGB smashed in-state rival UW-Milwaukee 81-66 to improve to 21-2 overall and 14-0 in the conference.

"(The fans) were a major part of this victory. They came and they were a part of us," said Heideman. "They took some ownership of this program. That is super. They helped us win."

The seniors led the way, with Nordgaard posting a double-double 26-point, 11-rebound effort, Grzesk nearly doing the same with eight points and nine assists, and Berlowski booking a solid 15-point, five-assist night. But this was a complete win, with everyone getting in on the action including Tom Anderson, who scored a career-high 15 points, and sophomore Kevin Olm.

Nordgaard was happy to help provide the motivation, yelling at Olm during the game to shoot the ball. Olm responded with his own career-high of 15 points as well as his standard four assists.

"By far (my best game). This is the most solid I've ever felt," Olm admitted. "It just happened to be my night."

Like Wade, Olm was developing into a solid contributor and a potential leader of the program. Nordgaard's assessment was clear: "Very good defender, good passer, not much of a scorer, but good team player. He kind of came into Gary Grzesk's mold. More of a point guard clearly, but one of those guys that was going to do the role of defending, being unselfish, setting screens."

The victory extended the win streak to twenty games and brought the program within two games of completing a perfect conference season. As for the postseason, the question was no longer *if* UWGB would make the NCAA tournament, but rather *how high* it would be seeded.

Giddy

Three days later, UWGB went to Chicago and put a whooping on UIC with a 34-point victory, 90-56. It was the program's most lopsided victory since 1994, with Heideman's club tallying 30 assists versus just six turnovers.

"Green Bay kicked our butt, that's the reason they're ranked 25th," said Bob Hallberg, UIC's coach.

Nordgaard, ever the iron man, logged an entirely unnecessary 37 minutes, putting on a show as he scored 37 points and grabbed nine rebounds. Nordgaard entered the game ranked eleventh in the country in scoring and was virtually unguardable, hitting nearly everything he attempted.

"I don't think there is anything I can say I haven't tried to do (to stop Nordgaard). The only thing we didn't try was to have six guys out there," remarked Hallberg. "Anytime you can make 15 of 22, some guys can't do that playing H.O.R.S.E."

Nordgaard's draft hopes continued to rise, with his latest projection to be a late-second round pick.

"(He's) the best mid-range jump shooter I've seen in a long time," stated Vancouver Grizzlies scout Dave Predergraft, "He has a skill. He is an exceptional jump shooter. Exceptional. He can flat out shoot the basketball. Can he play? Maybe. Only a fool would say no."

Being in the top 25 also meant Nordgaard's highlights would make ESPN's SportsCenter.

"We played UIC and we were in the Top 25, it was a highlight on ESPN because we were in the Top 25," remembers Nordgaard. "And it was funny because I got a nickname from that. Craig Kilborn was one of the anchors at the time, and he did the highlights for that game, and I was – I don't know, I had 30-something against UIC, and a bunch of them were just mid-range jump shots coming off of stagger screens or whatever else. And he goes 'Nordgaard, *giddy*!' Like because I was on fire, he's like, 'Nordgaard, with another jumper, Nordgaard, *giddy*!' And so I got the nickname Giddy. You ask Gary Grzesk what he'll call me as a nickname, he'll say 'Giddy,' because of Craig Kilborn."

Seeking Perfection

Doubling as senior night, UWGB's final regular-season game was set for Saturday afternoon, February 24, against the Butler Bulldogs. It seemed fitting that for UWGB to complete the perfect season, it would have to play the one team that had been relatively effective over the years at slowing Nordgaard.

It would be a bittersweet day for the Phoenix players and fans, 6,000 of which smashed into the Brown County Arena to watch the greatest senior class the Phoenix had ever seen. With UWGB seemingly solidly in the tournament field, this was the last chance to witness Berlowski, Jackson, Grzesk, and Nordgaard.

"It was our senior night as well, which always brings in a whole different mix of emotions because it's your last home game of your career. So I remember that being pretty emotional, but a great electric crowd there for senior night," Grzesk remembers. "We were ranked and undefeated, and this would have closed out the regular season the way we wanted it to go."

Collier's club deployed the same strategy the Phoenix had seen over the past year and a half from Butler – a smothering man-to-man defense with significant and repeated help offered on Nordgaard and Berlowski, at the unabashed expense of defending Jackson and Grzesk. The result was a mad scramble of dark jerseys over-pursuing and swarming whenever Nordgaard or Berlowski touched the ball, with huge cushions offered to Jackson and Grzesk, daring the latter two to shoot.

As it had in the past, Butler's strategy succeeded in keeping Nordgaard (13 points) and Berlowski (16 points) in check. Nevertheless, UWGB built an 11-point lead five minutes into the second half. But Butler trimmed the deficit to six points with just four minutes to play, and the Phoenix turned to ice. With UWGB's offense sitting in the snow, Butler chipped away, first with a three-pointer, then a fortunate bank shot runner, and finally with a free throw. Worse yet, after a Phoenix miss, Butler had the ball back with under 20 seconds left, looking to win the game.

With a perfect season on the line, it was sophomore Kevin Olm who made the play of the season. Taking a risk, Olm reached in and poked the ball away from Butler's Jeff Rodgers as he was squaring for a three, forcing a turnover.

"Now, I look at it, it was kind of dumb," Olm said afterwards. "Risking it on a three-pointer. Instincts took over. He put the ball there."

For the fourth and final time in 1995-96, UWGB was headed to overtime; this time, with perfection on the line. All four Phoenix seniors logged at least 40 minutes of action, with Grzesk and Nordgaard playing the entire 45 minutes. But in the end, the hero of the extra period was Eric Jackson, whose decisive three-pointer with 2:12 to play put UWGB on top and helped seal the club's perfect conference season with a 73-66 win.

Jackson went 7-for-9 from the floor including a whopping 6-for-8 from three-point range, netting him his first and only 20-point game of his career.

"Eric Jackson had probably his career game," Nordgaard noted. "We won because of his performance."

Powered by Jackson's big day, UWGB had done it. The Phoenix had finished the regular season a flawless 16-0 in conference play, tallying a stellar 24-2 record that included a 22-game winning streak.

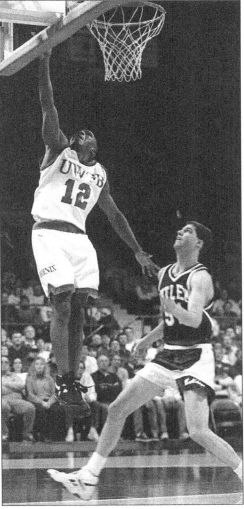

UWGB's Eric Jackson puts in a layup during the Phoenix's 73-66 overtime victory over Butler on senior night, February 24, 1996. (University of Wisconsin-Green Bay Archives)

In a new tradition, Heideman gave his seniors an opportunity to address the crowd after the game, and each took a few minutes to give a heartfelt thank you to a crowd that remained in their seats for nearly a half hour after the final buzzer.

Nordgaard capped the theater with a poignant reminder that, in spite of the undefeated regular season, the team's work was far from over.

"Our career has been real special. I think this year, though, we want it to be very *Sweet*, if you know what I mean," he said to a cheering crowd.

No one wanted to say goodbye to the greatest senior class in school history, so most simply continued the celebration on through Green Bay the rest of the afternoon and evening, even inviting the opposition to join.

"I had 100-plus people from Dawson, Minnesota, came out for the last game, huge caravans coming out," recalls Nordgaard. "The Butler guys came and hung out with us, and I had fifty of my high school buddies there and then parents and all that. It was a fun night."

Money Talks

For all the Phoenix success over the past half-decade – multiple tournament appearances, wins over major teams, conference championships, and even a No. 2 ranking in the AP poll – the financial realities of a small state school remained. It was a financial predicament the school had grown to live with, going all the way back to the early Dick Bennett days.

"We were a Division II, Division III school playing against Division I people. And I'm not even talking about the athletes now, I'm talking about how GB was run," says Nordgaard. "We weren't getting ten jogging suits, we got one ugly one each year, and it was not how Michigan was doing things, or North Carolina."

"Our pre-game meal was always like Country Kitchen, and we'd always have little a bowl of soup, you know chicken noodle soup, and half of a sandwich. And I don't mean to sound like, 'Oh, woe is me,' but that's just what we ate," notes former player Ben Johnson. "We were satisfied and thankful, and if you weren't, you know, tough luck."

And for additional culinary support? "We had a (protein) shake that we had to make ourselves, and one vitamin pill," adds Berlowski.

The entire athletic department was a floundering business, having lost $70,000 in 1994-95, and tracking to lose more than $100,000 in 1995-96. Every cent earned was vital to the lifeblood of the sports programs.

"Winning a (NCAA tournament) game is important for the financial aspect," explained athletic director Otis Chambers. "Last year, everybody said, 'Oh, Eric Jackson missed a shot.' I said, 'Yes, but that shot was worth $25,000.' I'm probably the only one who looks at it that way, but that's the truth."

As the conference's top program, UWGB easily topped the MCC in ticket revenue in 1995-96. And yet, the Phoenix remained dead last in total athletic department revenue, largely as a result of minimal state support and student fees. So as 1995-96 wound down, UWGB was faced with a difficult decision.

With demand for the Phoenix product as high as it would ever be, local television outlets were chomping at the bit to broadcast Phoenix games. But so much of UWGB's revenue stream was tied to ticket sales, the administration found itself in the precarious position of denying local television offers to protect ticket income and a paying fan base. The same fan considerations limited UWGB's ability to bid on future conference championships, because the school refused to guarantee 150 seats in the locations needed to meet the MCC's requirements. As Chambers noted, "It's a great thing to host the conference tournament, but the last thing you want to do is make a season ticket holder mad."

Foreshadowed Frustrations

None of the financial challenges dampened the excitement in Green Bay upon hearing that Mike Heideman was named MCC Coach of the Year.

"Because we were a veteran group, I think Coach Heideman really let us enjoy each and every win, and really kind of celebrated that, and knew how hard it was to win games," Grzesk remembers. "It was refreshing and energizing as a senior to be able to enjoy some of the games and enjoy the process a little bit."

Heideman, ever the class act, credited those around him.

"I look at (coach of the year) as an award for the staff and the players," Heideman noted upon hearing the news. "It belongs to everybody. I don't win that without the players playing like they did and the staff coaching like it did."

Equally exciting and expected, Nordgaard earned the MCC Player of the Year Award. Nordgaard was in the top fifteen in the country in scoring with 23.6 ppg while shooting 56% from the field, all while playing an incredible 39.7 minutes per game. He was the ironman of all ironmen.

To the team's pleasant surprise, each of the other three Phoenix seniors were also recognized. Jackson and Grzesk were named to the MCC's All-Defensive Team, while Berlowski joined Nordgaard as a First Team All-Conference player, having averaged just over 15 points per game.

"I'm happy and surprised. I didn't think I'd make it," said Berlowski. "I owe a lot to my teammates. They're the ones who helped me achieve it."

Decorated with new hardware, UWGB headed down to the E.J. Nutter Center on the campus of Wright State, home of the MCC conference tournament for a second consecutive year. On paper, the top-seeded Phoenix were preparing for a game against eighth-seeded Loyola, and Heideman wanted his team to focus on the challenge at hand.

"In general, we ask (the players) not to talk about the NCAA. I want them to just worry about what is in front of us," he stated before the game.

But with the Big Dance just a week and a half away, it was hard not to look ahead.

"We make the Top 25, that means if you do the math, if we get to be 22nd that means we're a 6 seed or whatever," recalls Nordgaard. "This is what we felt – we're not going to be a 12 or a 14 seed, we're going to be a 5 or a 6."

The Phoenix took the court against the Ramblers, and as they were expected to, jumped out to a quick 10-2 lead in the first five minutes. But Ken Burmeister switched his club to a matchup 2-3 zone that proved very effective at slowing UWGB.

Whether it was the defense or fatigue, Nordgaard struggled with his shot and at times looked a step slow. Berlowski stepped up early, scoring 11 first-half points, but when he was whistled for his fourth foul just three minutes into the second half, Loyola mounted a comeback.

Without Berlowski, the Phoenix shot a horrific 25% in the second half, and with 3:47 left in the game and UWGB holding a tenuous 47-45 lead, it looked like Loyola was on the precipice of a major upset. Candidly, a better team would've defeated the Phoenix, but Loyola was overmatched. Behind a pair of critical rebounds and free throws by Kevin Olm in the final minutes, UWGB snuck away with a 58-48 win.

While the team did continue the nation's second-longest winning streak at twenty-three games and moved on the semifinals, the real story, and potential concern, was Nordgaard. The senior had played the full forty minutes, but had been held to just nine points and looked sluggish. He downplayed the issue afterwards.

"Whenever an eighth seed finds success against a number 1 seed, you gain confidence," he said. "At the end, we put the clamps on defense and said we're not going to let this happen."

Heideman was cautious with his postgame remarks and may have been trying to light a fire under his players.

"We may struggle," he said. "I don't know if the will to win will be good enough to win this tournament."

Tired Legs

UWGB took the floor the next day to play the Detroit Titans. Perry Watson's club had finished the year 8-8 in conference play, 17-10 overall, and had beaten the fourth-seeded Wright State Raiders in the first round.

Everyone knew Detroit was dangerous. The Titans had given the Phoenix two of its toughest challenges of the year, with UWGB sneaking out a two-point overtime win at home in January, and a two-point road win at Detroit in February. Watson's club was athletic, playing a stretched man-to-man defense that contested every shot, no matter how far out.

For thirty-four minutes, the Phoenix looked every bit the best team in the conference, building a solid 48-40 lead and looking in complete control.

"We felt we had the game in hand," noted Nordgaard. "We were playing the way we needed to play to win."

But Detroit's Iapo Montgomery took over in the final six minutes, hitting three-pointers on three straight possessions as Detroit closed out a 16-2 run to pull off the major upset, 56-50. The Phoenix win streak ended and UWGB was left without an automatic NCAA tournament bid.

"I don't think we played poorly, but I think Detroit just played really well," recalls Grzesk. "Where we had always made the timely plays, the big shot, or got the stop when we needed to, Detroit did that to us in that conference tournament game."

Losing was something the players weren't used to.

"I don't even think I can describe my feeling. It's just empty," said Berlowski afterwards. "We haven't lost in so long it's hard to describe. We thought we had the game under control."

Most concerning, for the second straight game, Nordgaard played a full forty minutes and was held in check, scoring just 11 points.

"I remember crying in the press conference because I remember saying that at Green Bay, we talk about roles," recalls Nordgaard. "My role was to score and I didn't get it done. I let my guys down by not performing my role."

What few wanted to consider was the potential impact the massive minutes Nordgaard played may have been having on his game down the stretch.

"I talked to Jeff after the Detroit game. I asked him, 'Have we worn you out?'," Heideman explained. "He said, 'No.' He was excited to play. He felt good. He is getting a lot of sleep. It just didn't happen. I'm going to take Jeff at his word. He has always been straight with me."

Aside from Heideman, one of the only players to talk candidly about fatigue was sophomore Pete Wade.

"The season has been going on for a long time. A lot of people's legs are getting tired. The pressure, from the winning streak, the rankings, the NCAA tournament talk, it all adds up."

Anticipation

Like UWGB's early exit in 1992, the loss to Detroit left the Phoenix with some degree of uncertainty. And, unfortunately, the two teams had certain similarities. Both had exceptional regular-season records (24-3 in 1991-92, 24-2 in 1995-96). Both were led by prolific senior classes, each of which had made the NCAA tournament the year before. Both had logged wins against major conference teams (Purdue in 1991-92, Oregon and Texas A&M in 1995-96) and ESPN-televised mid-major battles (Butler in 1991-92, Western Kentucky in 1995-96). Both had made serious runs at the Top 25 in February. And disappointedly, both had flamed out of their conference tournament in the semifinals.

Could the committee do the unthinkable and somehow keep UWGB out of the tournament? Whether naïve or supremely confident, some on the 1995-96 Phoenix team remained certain they were in.

"I think we're in," said Nordgaard. "If someone can tell us we're out after the season we've had, then it's just terrible."

Heideman felt the same way. "They deserve to be in the tournament. It's not in our hands. But they deserve to be in the tournament."

Grzesk was more of a skeptic. "We don't know for sure if we're in. "We're going to put it in the hands of the committee. Hopefully, they'll look at the whole season, not just this last game, and realize we deserve to be in."

The polls indicated the team's chances were better than 1992. No eligible team in the 1990s had ever been left out of the tournament when finishing in the top 25, and with UWGB dropping just one spot to No. 23, that was a comfort. And unlike in 1992, the national media seemed to be favoring the Phoenix.

"I think they're probably on pins and needles. They're in. Tell them," noted ESPN's Dick Vitale. "I think they're a shoo-in to get a bid."

Determined not to repeat the public relations disaster from 1992, Heideman and the players watched the selection show privately at Heideman's home. This time, they did not have to wait long to see their name appear.

Just three minutes into the show, UWGB found out it had indeed received the school's first ever at-large bid, and it was a doozy. The Phoenix

The 1995-96 UWGB coaching staff included (from left) assistant Bob Semling, head coach Mike Heideman, and assistants Woody Wilson, and Ben Johnson. (University of Wisconsin-Green Bay Archives)

were an 8-seed, and as the higher-ranked team, would wear the program's home white jerseys.

But the committee had done UWGB no favors – their 9-seed opponent, Virginia Tech, was vastly underseeded. At one time ranked in the top 10 in the country, the Hokies were ranked No. 15 in the season's final poll and were coming off an Atlantic 10 regular season championship with a strong 22-5 record.

Like the Phoenix, the Bill Foster's Hokies had bowed out of their conference tournament early, losing to Rhode Island, but this veteran team was battle-tested, having won the 1995 NIT championship.

"You might as well be playing (UMass) – Virginia Tech can beat UMass," noted Wright State's Ralph Underhill upon hearing the matchup. "Don't even think about taking this ball club lightly. They only won the NIT, *and* got everyone back, *and* three more besides."

Worse yet for UWGB, if it were able to get past Virginia Tech, the #1 seed staring them in the face was Kentucky. Any road to the Sweet Sixteen now seemed almost impossible.

"You try not to look past the first game, but you can't help but notice that Kentucky would be the potential next game," Grzesk admits. "In some ways, you're better off being seeded worse or higher so if you do upset that first game, you'd have a better chance to win that second game."

"We were doubly mad because even if we win that first game, we had Kentucky in the next game," remembers Nordgaard. "And then Virginia Tech got kind of screwed on a seed, too. They shouldn't have been a 9, they should've probably been a 6 or 7. But we played ourselves into the seed we got unfortunately."

"We're like, 'What the f***!' " Berlowski said in the moment. "Because not only did we have to match up against – we looked at Kentucky looking forward – but Virginia Tech, we already knew. Like, dude, that's a tough matchup for us. I mean, we're not surprising anybody there."

In a twist of fate, UWGB would be matching up against two of Berlowski's high school teammates – Jim and Dave Jackson – both of whom had reunited in Blacksburg midway through their college careers.

No Good

Nordgaard, shaken from his tournament letdown, spent the week working on his shot.

"It's been cold the last several games, but it feels good now. I think it will be there for the rest of the games," he said. "It's got to be there for us to win, I think."

Heideman also focused his team's practices on scoring.

"I think our defense is very good. We'll work real hard on offense," he said. "We won't practice long. Try to keep them upbeat. I'm not going to change things, just try and get better."

"They were built similar to us as far as a good half-court defense, good solid offense, and they were very balanced," recalls Grzesk. "Even though Ace Custis was their marquee guy, you look at their scoring, they were very balanced, which kind of made us a little nervous."

Indeed, like UWGB, the Hokies were small, with no starter taller than 6-8. But Virginia Tech was experienced, with four senior starters, and extremely talented, led by Custis, a first-team all-Atlantic 10 forward. Custis was a versatile player, able to step out and hit the long-range shot while also scoring on the interior. Behind Custis, forward Shawn Smith and guard Shawn Good were both capable scorers.

On game day, Heideman threw a wrinkle into the lineup, alerting freshman Mike Nabena that he would get first career start just minutes before tip-off. Nabena took the floor with the team's four seniors as Mike Gorman and George Raveling began the call for CBS.

Raveling gushed about Nordgaard as the teams shook hands, pointing to a conversation he had with Rick Pitino earlier in the week.

"(Pitino) said, 'George, Jeff Nordgaard is one of the best-kept secrets in America. This kid can flat out play!' He had 29 points, 12 rebounds against Kentucky, that's unbelievable!"

True to form, Nordgaard knocked down the game's first basket, a long-range two pointer that found nothing but the bottom of the net. And with turnovers on each of Virginia Tech's first three possessions and a pair of Eric Jackson free throws, UWGB looked like it had settled right into their old ways. But the Hokies' experience helped them persevere, and being down a few to a mid-major did not intimidate them.

The teams traded buckets for the first ten minutes, but at the 13:00 minute mark of the first half, UWGB turned to ice. Missed shots, careless ball handling, and unforced turnovers littered the next few minutes. The Hokies methodically built a 15-8 lead and maintained that margin the rest of the first half, taking a solid 27-19 lead in to the locker room. The Hokies' stars, Custis and Good, were carrying the load, combining for 22 of the team's 27 points.

Coming out of the break, the Phoenix knew it had business to take care of and quickly went to work. Nabena scored on the team's first possession, and Berlowski knocked down a triple on the next possession. Suddenly, it was a four-point game just moments into the second half. UWGB continued to score, hitting its first six shots.

But on the defensive end, the Phoenix were uncharacteristically awful, committing needless fouls and putting the Hokies in the bonus with more than 13 minutes to play. A Nordgaard jumper with 12:33 to play narrowed the deficit to 34-32, but that was the closest UWGB would come to realizing their Sweet Sixteen dream.

Ironically, as the Phoenix was flailing, the CBS coverage switched to an Eastern Michigan vs. Duke matchup that saw the MAC's mid-major underdog pull a monumental upset over Mike Krzyzewski's Blue Devils, largely on the back of little Earl Boykins.

By the time the coverage returned, Virginia Tech had opened up a 44-34 advantage. That lead grew to 12 points when Shawn Good, who had taken over in the second half, hit another three-pointer, adding to his career-high 25 points. When it was all over, Virginia Tech had earned a 61-48 victory.

"They always had us kind of at arm's length and were always leading by five, seven, nine points," Grzesk notes. "They never really got outside of their personality, and just kind of kept us at arm's length where we were competing and fighting and scrapping, but we could never close in on them."

The Phoenix's dream season had come to a close, as had the careers of its greatest senior class. Nordgaard led the way with 22 points, but the team just didn't have enough against the Hokies.

"We need somebody to step up if we're going to win a ballgame against Virginia Tech, other than Ben Berlowski and Jeff Nordgaard," noted Heideman afterwards.

Decades after the dream-crushing loss, Nordgaard continues to blame himself.

"I again did not have a great game. I ended up with 20 or something like that, but I went for probably a stretch of twelve minutes without scoring, and that was enough," he said. "I didn't have an MVP-type performance, and we needed it against a team like that."

Tell Me Why

This wasn't how that senior class, the most successful in school history, was supposed to go out.

"We thought we had one of the best teams we've ever had at Green Bay and we thought we could do some damage in the NCAA tournament," remarked Nordgaard. "I think we have the desire to win and to make our dreams come true. Somehow, it didn't work out that way."

"I just think we lost our hunger to win," added Berlowski. "I don't know where it went. But it just seems as the season progressed, we started to go downhill."

Perhaps part of the issue was the improbability facing the team's ultimate goal of a second-weekend trip, with Kentucky staring them in the face.

"I was definitely less angry, upset, sad after that game than I was after the Detroit game ... if we (beat) Virginia Tech we would've lost to Kentucky anyway," recalled Nordgaard. "We never think that, but that was a team we weren't going to beat that year, Kentucky."

In any event, fatigue unquestionably had crept in, particularly for Berlowski, Grzesk, and Nordgaard, all of whom averaged more than 33 minutes per game.

"We played a lot of minutes that year ... we were worn out a little bit," recalls Berlowski. "I think fatigue kind of caught up with us, and they were just a little bit better than we were at every position, and it was just a tough end of the year for us."

Nordgaard agreed. "I think we were at our best with five games left in the regular season. I think a lot of it had to do with fatigue, and we just didn't have enough horses." Speaking about his own body, Nordgaard added: "I did get worn out my senior year. I clearly did. I didn't realize it, but my last few games I was not the player I was leading up to it."

Nordgaard had completed one of the most strenuous seasons in NCAA history, having played an astounding 39.8 minutes per game – a mad figure then and now. Indeed, when comparing to the first ten years that the NCAA started officially tracking the statistic (from 2009-2020), Nordgaard's 1995-96 season would have ranked second, trailing only Bryce Cotton from Providence in 2013-2014 with 39.94 minutes per game.

"That'll never be touched," states Ben Johnson. "We ran him into the ground, because we – we weren't really deep that year."

"I never ever once asked to come out ever. I found time to get extra rest and even sometimes I would kick the ball away, they'd have to go get it, and I'd just (breathe)," Nordgaard recalled. "I never asked to come out ever. I don't remember him saying, 'Tell me when you're tired.' I just think that the expectation was if we want to win, you got to be in there. I think that's just how it was."

Stacking Up

"In time, when we look back, people will realize we really had a special year," Grzesk said after the game. And indeed, decades later, the loss in the 1996 NCAA tournament to Virginia Tech has done little to dampen the senior's memories.

"If you would've told me that we would end up playing in three NCAA tournaments and pulling off a major upset against California, I would never have guessed that could've been possible," Grzesk recalls fondly. "Growing up in grade school and high school, I dreamt of going to Wisconsin or Marquette. I would not have traded my experience at Green Bay for anything. And we ended up having more overall success and postseason success than either of those programs."

"The things that stand out the most are that group of seniors of that '94 team, and then our group of four that '96 team. Just the comradery that we had, and the things we did on and off the court that brought us close while we were all striving for the same goal," explains Nordgaard. "The games and stuff is what you guys see, but that other stuff is the memories that make college athletics so unique."

Grzesk agreed. "It's the relationships with those guys. We all continue to stay in touch with each other, probably not as much as we'd like to or used to, but we always have those friendships and memories."

As a group, the 1995-96 version of the Phoenix had a fair claim of being one of the school's best.

"Green Bay had its greatest season," notes Dick Bennett. "That was really a good team. I'm glad we (Wisconsin) didn't have to play them that year. They would've beaten Wisconsin for sure."

"The '96 team had more success (than the '94 team), meaning we beat everybody," Nordgaard says. "In our conference, we beat everybody. We lost at Kentucky, the best college basketball team ever, and we lost to Marquette. And we just didn't make it happen in the postseason. But that '94 team was a better team. We were deeper, and five seniors, and lots of role players."

John Martinez had his thoughts, adding the 1991-92 Phoenix to the mix as well.

"I want to say '92 (was the best team) because I was healthy and we were 25-3 or whatever it was. There's a reason we got further in the '94 team, so maybe I think as a team, that team was better because we were more balanced. And hey, we were able to win a game even with the point guard having two ACL injuries. You're splitting hairs at that point, you know. All things considered, if everybody was healthy, it would've been two great years in the NCAA tournament."

Life after College

"The group that followed us, Jeff Nordgaard, Gary Grzesk, Eric Jackson, Ben Berlowski, those guys took winning and took it to a whole nother level," recollects a prideful Ben Johnson. "Going to three straight NCAA tournaments as a mid-major, low-major, whatever the heck you'd call us, which at that time was unheard of. But it shows you how great Coach Bennett is, and again, the whole idea of synergy, the parts, the chemistry."

Ben Berlowski finished his playing career fourth in three-point percentage and second in school history in three-pointers made, trailing only the legendary Tony Bennett. He chose to travel with the remaining Phoenix members on the program's trip to France in the summer of 1996, and briefly extend his playing career, joining the newly formed Wisconsin Blast as both a player and as a sales director in 1997 before eventually transitioned away from basketball.

Eric Jackson immediately moved from player to coach, taking the teachings from Bennett and Heideman, and applying them to the next generation of collegiate players. Jackson got his start as an assistant at St. Norbert College in 1996, and continued as an assistant coach at various institutions for decades.

Gary Grzesk finished his career third in school history in assists and fourth in steals. Like Jackson, Grzesk also got the coaching bug, beginning his career with Youngstown State as an assistant for six years, then returning to UWGB as an assistant before eventually landing the head coaching job at St. Norbert College in 2006. Grzesk continues to enjoy tremendous success, building a traditional winner on the same principles his former coaches imparted on him, all while compiling more than 275 career wins with the Division III Green Knights.

And then there is Jeff Nordgaard, one of the two greatest players in school history. As a scorer, Nordgaard was nearly unmatched, able to use his unique combination of size, ball handling, and shooting touch to take advantage of matchups against smaller and larger defenders alike.

Statistically, Nordgaard was incredible. Over his career, he averaged 15.9 ppg and 5.8 rpg (numbers which jump to 18.8 PPG and 6.7 RPG when his freshman year is excluded), and finished his career ranked second all-time for the Phoenix in career Division I points, second in scoring average at the D-1 level, and second in field goals made, all behind only Tony Bennett. Not just a scorer, Nordgaard also grabbed more than 700 rebounds in his career, good for fourth in Phoenix D-1 history, and chipped in 104 steals and 48 blocks, placing him in the top fifteen on both of the respective Phoenix lists.

Nordgaard and Bennett were the only two players in Phoenix history to be named first team all-conference three times, and were the only two players to be named Conference Player of the Year along with Keifer Sykes in 2013-14. To put that in perspective, UWGB only had six other players named first team all-conference even once. On top of that, those two and Sykes were the only honorable mention all-Americans to ever play for UWGB.

As a postscript to his Phoenix career, Nordgaard's dream of playing professional basketball became a reality. As it had with Tony Bennett, Nordgaard's journey started with pre-draft camps, his in Portsmouth, Virginia.

"I made the all-tournament team and had a nice Portsmouth tournament," Nordgaard remembers, "and then I also went for a workout with the Sixers, and that was it. I didn't go to another pre-draft, I didn't go work out for anybody else."

A number of NBA scouts and talent evaluators were high on his potential, but unsure how his lack of size would transfer to the next level. One who was already convinced was Celtics legend Kevin McHale, who noted, "He'll have an opportunity to make the next level, which is all you can really ask for. I really like the way he plays. He really works hard out there all the time. He's a very good shooter."

On draft night, Nordgaard went over Chris Westlake's apartment and watched the selections with a few friends.

"The Sixers, who I worked out for, had three second-round picks. So I thought, 'Ah, maybe,' but then they went with Ryan Minor with one of their picks. He was essentially the same position as me, at least at the next level. So I thought, 'Eh, it's not going to happen.' "

Nordgaard had nearly fallen asleep on the couch when he finally saw his name appear on the screen. Out of nowhere, the Milwaukee Bucks – a mere 100 miles down the road – had taken a flyer on him.

"They did not call me, it just happened on TV," Nordgaard recalls. "I don't think you really get a call from somebody in the second round, (other than) I got a call from my agent congratulating me. And I think I went then to like a little press conference at Gipper's (Sports Bar & Grill in Green Bay)."

Nordgaard played in the summer league for the Bucks in 1996-97, but he was in a difficult situation as the Bucks had no open roster spots. It wasn't until 1997-98 that Nordgaard would finally get his chance, and it started with a breakout performance at his old stomping ground.

"I had a good preseason, and actually, probably the one that ensured that I got the spot was at Brown County Arena," he says. "The Bucks played against the Celtics. Rick Pitino was the (Celtics') coach, I played against Rick at Kentucky. And we played the Celtics at Brown County Arena, thousands of fans there, many of them to see me, which is pretty cool. I made my first six shots, ended up with 13 points, bunch of rebounds, and some steals. Had a great, great day, so that was probably what did it."

That season, Nordgaard would play for the Bucks over two different stints, logging time in thirteen games. Short as his stint was, Nordgaard brought the Green Bay Way with him to Milwaukee. And amazingly, his work ethic and demeanor had a memorable impact on his teammates.

Twenty years after Nordgaard's brief run with the Bucks, Ray Allen still had fond memories of his time as a teammate with him. Speaking on the *Dan Patrick Show* in 2018, when asked about how he became such a great shooter, the Hall of Famer pontificated that success boiled down to hard work.

"It's not talent," Allen said. "A lot of people don't know this, but I credit a player in Milwaukee by the name of Jeff Nordgaard. Early in my career, I played with him, and Jeff and I used to always have a free throw game, and he was an incredible free throw shooter. And early on, he gave me somebody to challenge, somebody to compete against. And he was always swishes. Always swishes. And so I constantly was out there doing that with him. And so for the rest of my career, that's what I did."

Epilogue
Ashes (1997-2020)

Though the Phoenix sputtered out at the end and didn't achieve its goal of making the Sweet Sixteen, the program appeared to have found Dick Bennett's heir, and Mike Heideman seemed poised to keep the program humming.

"They have sustained it," noted Northern Illinois coach Brian Hammel. "The changing of the guard from Bennett to Heideman hasn't missed a beat."

"You can watch college basketball all day long on ESPN and not find a team in America that plays basketball the way Green Bay does," said UIC's Bob Hallberg. "You'll see some of the elements, but no one is like them. They play an organized system, the ultimate team in America, a team of role players. All their guys are willing to sacrifice ego for the good of the team. I think they can keep that system going because they recruit the kind of players that can blend in."

Butler's Barry Collier agreed. "I think their recruiting – as much as some will have you think these kids aren't top drawer – is outstanding."

"What a great year for Coach Heideman to take that team that – obviously a great team that was built for him, but you still got to coach them," comments Ben Johnson. "I thought Mike did a great job with that team that year."

"Mike (Heideman) was just salt of the earth," Dick Bennett says fondly of his friend, who passed away in 2018. "He just knew the game, he loved, great teacher. He would always start the day with the same statement: 'It's a great day to play basketball.' Mike and Steve (Swan) never got enough credit, but I want you to know they were invaluable in any success that we had. They were just good in what they did, and on top of that, they were just really good people."

And yet, there were warning signs. On paper, the double-digit Virginia Tech loss marked the most lopsided season-ending game since 1987-88, the year before Tony Bennett arrived on campus. And with just three returning players who played more than ten minutes per game, none of whom averaged even five points, 1996-97 was going to be a tough rebuilding year. Furthermore, the fire, the intensity, the commonality of goals, the singular focus – none were quite replicated going forward.

"I say this in the best possible way, but there was a point where that team just didn't have anybody who was kind of an asshole," recalls Eric LeDuc. "When Jeff (Nordgaard) and Gary (Grzesk) and Eric Jackson and that group left, they struggled. They struggled to find that person who was going to be, or people who were going to be the dominant personalities. There didn't seem to be the sense of comradery, the sense of that little bit of a chip on their shoulder attitude. You saw success become more and more fleeting. And then I think the program kind of lost its identity."

From 1988-1996, UWGB was one of the most prolific and dominant mid-major programs in the country. Major conference foes feared it while mid-major peers respected it. The Phoenix had success on the biggest stages with teams that bought into Dick Bennett's core principles. It was the ultimate underdog tale.

"Our story was a little more – you know, we're Green Bay, a little more remote, smaller ... but we were just good," states Tony Bennett. "And I think, before the Gonzagas and all those got going, our situation was pretty special because it was ours of course, and maybe not as well publicized."

"You look back to the beginning of Gonzaga – now obviously they've built themselves into a power program, but at that point, when they first started going to those tournaments, I don't think they had any better teams than Green Bay had or any of the other mid-majors you saw make deep runs, whether Sweet Sixteen or Elite Eight runs," adds LeDuc.

"There are so many things in terms of what a true mid-major has to be," explains Dean Vander Plas. "It has to captivate a lot of different things. It has to captivate a community, it's got to captivate a college, but it's got to captivate a group of people that believe there is more in them together than they individually have, and you've got to have a person at the helm that just every day believes that relentlessly. It's the ability to captivate and grab."

The blueprint for their success was not a mystery. Coaches such as Jim Larranaga and Barry Collier saw it, built from it, and found grand success. Green Bay has the building blocks for a stable foundation, and if anything, the eight years of greatness it achieved gives the program one huge advantage – a built-in legacy and support network to show the next generation how to win.

After the 1995-96 season, Heideman's next four teams finished in the middle of the pack and missed postseason play, the first three of which were knocked out of the MCC tournament in successive years by the Butler Bulldogs. By 2000-01, Heideman's program had fallen to seventh in the conference, and after another year at the bottom of the heap, it was time for the program to hit the reset button.

UWGB replaced Heideman in 2002 with Tod Kowalczyk. Like Bennett and Heideman before him, Kowalczyk was a Wisconsinite (De Pere native) who could rally the community. But unlike his predecessors, Kowalczyk promoted an up-tempo offense. Though he was unable to break through with an NCAA or NIT bid, Kowalczyk's refreshing brand of basketball helped return the Phoenix to the top half of the rebranded Horizon League a remarkable seven consecutive seasons before he departed for Toledo.

Kowalczyk's replacement, former Marquette player Brian Wardle, finally succeeded in returning the Phoenix to the NIT. Under his guidance, UWGB earned a bid to the second-tier tournament in 2014 and 2015 before Wardle, too, left Green Bay for another head coaching job, this one at Bradley.

Using Wardle's roster as a foundation, his replacement, Linc Darner, took the program to the NCAA tournament in his first season. The unexpected trip in 2016 was a boost for the school, but proved to be a one-hit wonder. Darner, a former Purdue player under Gene Keady who'd witnessed UWGB's win in the Boilermaker Invitational in 1991, eventually flamed out, and

Mike King attempts a tip-in during UWGB's 59-54 victory over Drexel in the opening round of the Oneida Bingo & Casino Classic at the Brown County Arena on December 29, 1999. (University of Wisconsin-Green Bay Archives)

by 2020, UWGB was starting over again.

Stated simply, though each had successes of their own, Bennett's replacements have yet to find and maintain the same magic that his teams enjoyed from 1988-96.

"You had those eight years at Green Bay where it was like everyone was on the same page. (Dick Bennett) recruited those guys and got everybody to buy into that same common goal," remarks Scott LeMoine. "To me, there was absolutely no surprise that they were as good as they were."

Coaching changes brought different schemes and varying commitments from the school and community. The once-formidable home court advantage provided by the outdated Brown County Arena has been supplanted by the state-of-the-art Resch Center, which offers all the amenities and twice the capacity, but too often in front of less than half the fans. For years after Bennett's departure, the roster featured fewer in-state players, and alumni involvement and program continuity waned. The combination dropped UWGB into mid-major purgatory.

"We were just kind of disappointed that it hasn't continued a little bit," adds Berlowski. "We want someone who wants to be there, who wants to build a program and kind of get us involved. I want to be part of a university like a Butler or a Gonzaga and proud to represent Green Bay basketball, what we did there, and what other guys have done there."

And yet, there's reason for optimism as of this writing. In 2020, UWGB hired former Wisconsin coach Bo Ryan's son, Will, to take over. Like the Bennetts, the Ryans have long ties and deep roots to the state, and Will himself shares a long history with Tony Bennett.

"I had the pleasure of building a strong relationship with Tony Bennett while he was coaching on my dad's staff at UW and the years that have followed," Will Ryan says. "He is the consummate professional and someone I've always looked up to not only as a player and a coach, but as a person. Tony has been nothing but kind and supportive toward my family and me for the past twenty-plus years. Hopefully we can make him a proud alum as he cheers on his nephew, Lucas Stieber, and the rest of his Green Bay Phoenix teammates."

Tony Bennett's coaching accomplishments have exceeded even those of his father by winning the national championship in 2019 with the University of Virginia. (University of Wisconsin-Green Bay Archives)

It's no surprise, then, that Ryan's principles and philosophies sound very familiar. Ryan's thoughts on building his team?

"We strive to recruit not only talented and athletic players, but also high-character, motivated, hungry and humble student-athletes. A healthy program is one where the student-athletes embrace their role, get better in their role, and sacrifice stats and accolades for the good of the team."

His view on Wisconsin athletes?

"Being a Wisconsinite through and through, and knowing what a tremendous job the high school coaches in this state do to help prepare their players for the next level, I firmly believe we can recruit Wisconsin and the Midwest for players who embody the tough-nosed, blue-collar 'Green Bay Way' mentality."

How about a dedication to the basics?

"Fundamentals are an absolute, non-negotiable pillar of Green Bay basketball. Regardless of size and athleticism, if you have players who pass and catch well, maintain proper footwork, play on balance, utilize shot fakes and ball fakes, and don't beat themselves with silly mistakes, you will always give yourself a chance to win."

And where does defense fit in?

"Solid, tough-nosed, man-to-man defense where all five players are working together as one is also another non-negotiable of Green Bay basketball. In order to get playing time in this program, one must first be able to defend on and off the ball. It's imperative that all five guys are locked in every possession. Our goal is to make every possession a grind on the opponent while defending without fouling. If we are disciplined, on the same page, and playing as one, we will get teams to squirm a little bit and ultimately make mistakes. Every possession is a battle."

The city is ready and willing. Perhaps the time is right for Ryan to lead the Phoenix from the ashes to greatness once more.

Legacy

Barry Collier

Butler University Basketball Coach
1989 - 2000

My first college head coaching job came at Butler University in 1989. The team I inherited had seen its share of struggles, having posted just two winning seasons in the previous eleven years. Meanwhile, Dick Bennett's teams at UW-Green Bay were just taking off and winning twenty-five games a year.

As a young coach and product of the Don Monson and Jud Heathcote coaching tree, I was always studying the game and searching for more. I knew about Dick's success at UW-Stevens Point, and I'd heard that he'd put out some coaching tapes, so naturally, I studied them closely.

My first coaching interaction with Dick came a few years later in 1992, and as fond as I was of Dick Bennett, the game left me with a sad memory of a loss. That was a game created by and for ESPN between our two conferences, and it was a

Barry Collier brought Butler University's men's basketball program to national prominence. He currently serves as the university's vice president / director of athletics. (Butler Athletics)

great game at Hinkle Fieldhouse. Dick's son, Tony, cranked one in from what felt like about 90 feet away to win the game. That ball felt like it was in the air forever, and Tony nailed it.

UWGB joined our conference a few years later, and we got to compete against his impressive teams twice a year. In 1995, after he had accepted the head coaching job at UW-Madison, I reached out to Dick and asked if I could pick his brain for a couple of days. He agreed, and Jim Larrinaga from Bowling Green came with me.

I have good memories of many who have helped me in coaching, but those two days with Dick were an epiphany for me, and I think Jim would say the same thing. I found a man who connected my life with my coaching job. He has a very strong faith and it spoke to me, highlighting universal truths that have been around forever. It struck me that as fierce a competitor as he was, he was also willing to share. As great as he was as a coach – and his numbers are ridiculously good as far as I'm concerned – he's even a better human being. I think that had a lot to do with his having success everywhere he's been.

We took his teachings and adopted the five principles at Butler. We were probably amateurs compared to what he was doing, but nonetheless, he deserves all that credit. It was really the start of the Butler Way, and the returns were immediate. Those next five years at Butler were the best teams that we had, and I would credit Dick as a significant spark to all of that.

A lot of things go into building a successful mid-major program, but topping the list is a philosophy or culture that breeds success and builds on itself. You need a coaching staff that establishes culture. You need a team that is grounded in values that allow you to reach your potential, or at least touch it from time to time. You need a program that has student-athletes that model, and then train their younger teammates. And I think it's really important to recruit the right kind of players – those who embrace your philosophy.

It's not anything magical, and it can be replicated. But it's a longer road than some people recognize, and it takes persistence and patience. Dick Bennett set a great example for coaches everywhere.

Acknowledgements

I've been a UW-Green Bay Phoenix fan virtually my entire life. My dad took me to my first game in 1989 – an exhibition against the Soviet Spartak team – and I was hooked.

My childhood memories are inextricably linked to UWGB's history. The DePaul game in 1990? Christmas party at our house in the basement, the game on the radio while my parents entertained friends. The conference tournament run in 1991? Stationed in our courtside seats, screaming like crazy with my dad, Don, and Tim. Purdue in 1995? A sleepover at the Schoenebecks' house and an upset stomach from the loss.

Fast forward twenty years and my nostalgia became an outlet. It took five years of nights and weekends, watching old tapes and reading newspaper clips, researching and interviewing, scouring archival photos, writing and editing to the see the project to completion, and I could not have done it without the immense support of so many.

For starters, I want to thank the many players and coaches I interviewed for their time, enthusiasm, and patience. Never having done anything like this before, I anticipated hurdles and skepticism, but what I found over and over again was openness, forthright storytelling, and laughter.

There's an anxiousness that accompanies meeting people you've held in high regard from afar; a fear of being let down balanced delicately with a hope of validation. The interviews I conducted did nothing but solidify my passion for the program, highlight the class of those associated with it, and enhance my most treasured childhood memories.

No one was more invested in supporting my efforts than Coach Dick Bennett. Dick and I spent many evenings time traveling to decades past, discussing long-forgotten games and events. What began for me as a dream interview expanded into a winding exploration of Phoenix and basketball history, and culminated, quite surprisingly, in something of a long-distance friendship. Thanks for everything, Coach.

I want to thank UWGB and the many great people there for their unbridled enthusiasm and encouragement. I want to especially thank Deb

Aaron A. Mitchell

Anderson with UWGB Archives, who in some regards was the catalyst to this whole journey. Deb, I'll always be indebted to you for offering me a most valuable window into the precious past.

To Mike Dauplaise, my editor and designer. I thank you for all of your wisdom, and particularly your patience, as you educated me throughout this publication process.

I want to thank my good friends the Donarskis, Don, Kathy, Matt, Tim, Ken, E. You've all been an integral part of this story (and my life), and I consider myself so fortunate to have had such wonderful friends with whom to share these experiences.

I also want to thank my mother, Betsy Mitchell, both for her direct support with this project and for the incredible wisdom and opportunity she has afforded me over my life. My mom's most impactful and lasting piece of advice – *Life is all about relationships* – is something I thought of often during this journey, and has never rang truer than it does today. Thanks for everything you've given me and for always being there, Mom.

To my sister, Emily. Thanks for so many things over the years. As kids, you were gracious enough to relent when I begged to go to the games you'd been promised. As collegiates, you were a sounding board for my early writing. As adults and parents, you've helped us all stay close and been an awesome aunt to the kids. You certainly paint with all the colors of the wind.

To my children, Amelia, Bella, and Lincoln. Thank you for your humor, your love, and your youthfulness. I find inspiration in each of you every day, and I'm eternally grateful to have a window into my own childhood every time we play, read, or tell stories.

To my loving wife, Amy. Thank you for everything. And I mean, everything. I remember your indoctrination into the Phoenix Way, beginning with our first trip to a Horizon League tournament at Valparaiso a decade back and continuing to this day. Throughout this project, your commentary and big-picture vision have made this a far more rewarding project than if I'd ever tried this alone. You are the rock that keeps us grounded, the glue that keeps us together. You're the best around, and nothing's going to ever keep you down. Thank you and I love you!

Finally, I want to thank my dad, Peter Mitchell, for igniting my sports passion and being the best father any kid could ask for.

About the Author

Aaron A. Mitchell was born and raised in Green Bay, Wisconsin, where he grew up an avid fan of the state's sports teams. Today, he lives in southeast Wisconsin with his wife, Amy, and three children.

Additional Photo Citations

Purdue University Archives and Special Collections
Page	Full Citation
i	UA 62, Box 70 Folder 15. Purdue University Marketing and Media collection.
179	UA 62, Box 29 Folder 1. Purdue University Marketing and Media collection.
180	UA 62, Box 29 Folder 1. Purdue University Marketing and Media collection.
323	UA 62, Box 28 Folder 8. Purdue University Marketing and Media collection.

University of Colorado Boulder Libraries
Page	Full Citation
112	University of Colorado Boulder Publicity Offices collection, COU: 3331, Box 168, Folder, Item 113238, Frame 5, Rare and Distinctive Collections.

University of Wisconsin-Green Bay Archives
Page	Full Citation
Cover	Negative Collection. Accession 2002.9, Box 10, CN/ATH 165 #2.
Cover	Negative Collection. Accession 2002.9, Box 6, ATH 1351 #23.
1	University Archives Print Photo Collection. Album 11, #P1136B.
4	Negative Collection. Accession 2002.9, Box 1, ATH 232 #4.
5	1977-1978 Men's Basketball Team Photo. Chuck Aslakson Collection. Accession 2018.8, Box 2.
7	University Archives Print Photo Collection, Album 8 #P841.
8	University Archives Print Photo Collection, Album 9 #P1034.
12	Negative Collection. Accession 2002.9, Box 21.
18	Negative Collection. Accession 2002.9, Box 7, CN/ATH 4 #16.
21	Negative Collection. Accession 2002.9, Box 7, CN/ATH 74 #6.
24	Negative Collection. Accession 2002.9, Box 7, CN/ATH 74 #13.
29	Negative Collection. Accession 2002.9, Box 7, CN/ATH 93 #2.
30	Negative Collection. Accession 2002.9, Box 6, ATH/PGS/BM 134.
35	University Archives Print Photo Collection, Album 6 #P633.
36	Negative Collection. Accession 2002.9, Box 6, ATH/PGS/BM 135.
39	University Archives Print Photo Collection, Album 7 #P791.
45	Negative Collection. Accession 2002.9, Box 7, CN/ATH 88 #11.
48	Negative Collection. Accession 2002.9, Box 7, CN/ATH 95 #3.
57	Negative Collection. Accession 2002.9, Box 6, ATH/PGS/BM 161.
59	Negative Collection. Accession 2002.9, Box 9, ATH 1510 #13.
60	Negative Collection. Accession 2002.9, Box 6, ATH 1351 #29.
63	Negative Collection. Accession 2002.9, Box 7, ATH 109 #34.
64	Negative Collection. Accession 2002.9, Box 7, ATH 112 #14.
66	Negative Collection. Accession 2002.9, Box 6, ATH 1375 #8.
67	University Archives Digital Photo Collection.
68	Negative Collection. Accession 2002.9, Box 6, ATH 1371 #31.
72	Negative Collection. Accession 2002.9, Box 6, ATH 1373 #6A.
73	Negative Collection. Accession 2002.9, Box 6, ATH 1382 #4.
74	Negative Collection. Accession 2002.9, Box 7, ATH CN/ATH 120 #2.
75	Negative Collection. Accession 2002.9, Box 6, ATH 1399 #20.
77	Negative Collection. Accession 2002.9, Box 6, ATH 1407 #15A.
93	Negative Collection. Accession 2002.9, Box 6, ATH 1438 #8.
95	Negative Collection. Accession 2002.9, Box 6, ATH 1438 #10.
96	Negative Collection. Accession 2002.9, Box 6, ATH 1438 #32A.
98	Negative Collection. Accession 2002.9, Box 6, ATH 1438 #12A.
101	Negative Collection. Accession 2002.9, Box 6, ATH 1438 #5.
102	Negative Collection. Accession 2002.9, Box 6, ATH 1440 #25.

108	Negative Collection. Accession 2002.9, Box 6, ATH 183 #2.
111	Negative Collection. Accession 2002.9, Box 6, ATH 1487 #15.
117	University Archives Digital Photo Collection.
120	Negative Collection. Accession 2002.9, Box 6, ATH 1501 #36A.
127	Negative Collection. Accession 2002.9, Box 6, ATH 1554 #15.
129	Negative Collection. Accession 2002.9, Box 7, CN/ATH 156 #1.
132	Negative Collection. Accession 2002.9, Box 10, CN/ATH 164 #34A.
140	Negative Collection. Accession 2002.9, Box 6, ATH 1566 #20.
141	Negative Collection. Accession 2002.9, Box 6, ATH 1565 #15.
143	Negative Collection. Accession 2002.9, Box 10, CN/ATH 165 #2.
144	Negative Collection. Accession 2002.9, Box 6, ATH 1568 #11.
146	Negative Collection. Accession 2002.9, Box 10, CN/ATH 165.
150	Negative Collection. Accession 2002.9, Box 7, ATH 162.
160	Negative Collection. Accession 2002.9, Box 10, CN/ATH 166 #2.
170	Negative Collection. Accession 2002.9, Box 6, ATH/PGS/BM 208 #15.
173	Negative Collection. Accession 2002.9, Box 10, CN/ATH 197 #10.
175	University Archives Publications, Intercollegiate Athletics, Box 1 Folder 7 1991-1992 Media Guide.
176	Negative Collection. Accession 2002.9, Box 10, CN/ATH 186 #17.
184	Negative Collection. Accession 2002.9, Box 6, ATH 1625 #24A.
187	Negative Collection. Accession 2002.9, Box 6, ATH 1629 #10.
192	Negative Collection. Accession 2002.9, Box 6, ATH 1657 #6.
198	Negative Collection. Accession 2002.9, Box 6, ATH 1656 #3.
214	Negative Collection. Accession 2002.9, Box 6, ATH 1715 #19.
222	Negative Collection. Accession 2002.9, Box 6, ATH 1740 #22.
225	Negative Collection. Accession 2002.9, Box 6, ATH 1751 #23.
230	Negative Collection. Accession 2002.9, Box 6, ATH/PGS/BM 248 #7.
232	Negative Collection. Accession 2002.9, Box 6, ATH/PGS/BM 241 #2.
246	Negative Collection. Accession 2002.9, Box 6, ATH 1804 #10.
249	Negative Collection. Accession 2002.9, Box 10, CN/ATH 311 #2.
252	Negative Collection. Accession 2002.9, Box 10, CN/ATH 312 #9.
259	Negative Collection. Accession 2002.9, Box 6, ATH 1823 #9.
287	Negative Collection. Accession 2002.9, Box 10, CN/ATH 263 #12.
291	Negative Collection. Accession 2002.9, Box 6, ATH 1830 #26.
294	University Archives Digital Photo Collection.
312	University Archives Print Photo Collection. Album 27 #P3727-3729.
312	University Archives Print Photo Collection. Album 27 #P3727-3729.
334	Negative Collection. Accession 2002.9, Box 6, ATH 1656 #6.
340	Negative Collection. Accession 2002.8, Box 13, F 23.
347	Negative Collection. Accession 2002.9, Box 6, ATH 1830 #8.
348	Negative Collection. Accession 2002.9, Box 6, ATH 1830 #8.
355	University Archives Print Photo Collection. Album 27 #P3723-P3725.
367	Negative Collection. Accession 2002.9, Box 6, ATH 1829 #27.
372	University Archives Print Photo Collection. Loose Folder, B1F12 Folder.
381	University Archives Print Photo Collection. Album 27 #P3726.
382	University Archives Digital Photo Collection. April 2008- April 25 star alumni folder.

Made in the USA
Monee, IL
13 November 2021